A History of Hygiene in Modern France

A History of Hygiene in Modern France

The Threshold of Disgust

Steven Zdatny

BLOOMSBURY ACADEMIC
LONDON • NEW YORK • OXFORD • NEW DELHI • SYDNEY

BLOOMSBURY ACADEMIC

Bloomsbury Publishing Plc, 50 Bedford Square, London, WC1B 3DP, UK
Bloomsbury Publishing Inc, 1359 Broadway, New York, NY 10018, USA
Bloomsbury Publishing Ireland, 29 Earlsfort Terrace, Dublin 2, D02 AY28, Ireland

BLOOMSBURY, BLOOMSBURY ACADEMIC and the Diana logo are trademarks of Bloomsbury Publishing Plc

First published in Great Britain 2024
This paperback edition published 2025

Copyright © Steven Zdatny, 2024

Steven Zdatny has asserted his right under the Copyright, Designs and Patents Act, 1988, to be identified as Author of this work.

Cover image: Boilly La Toilette intime ou la Rose effeuillée. (c) Rapp Halour / Alamy

All rights reserved. No part of this publication may be: i) reproduced or transmitted in any form, electronic or mechanical, including photocopying, recording or by means of any information storage or retrieval system without prior permission in writing from the publishers; or ii) used or reproduced in any way for the training, development or operation of artificial intelligence (AI) technologies, including generative AI technologies. The rights holders expressly reserve this publication from the text and data mining exception as per Article 4(3) of the Digital Single Market Directive (EU) 2019/790.

Bloomsbury Publishing Plc does not have any control over, or responsibility for, any third-party websites referred to or in this book. All internet addresses given in this book were correct at the time of going to press. The author and publisher regret any inconvenience caused if addresses have changed or sites have ceased to exist, but can accept no responsibility for any such changes.

Every effort has been made to trace the copyright holders and obtain permission to reproduce the copyright material. Please do get in touch with any enquiries or any information relating to such material or the rights holder. We would be pleased to rectify any omissions in subsequent editions of this publication should they be drawn to our attention.

A catalogue record for this book is available from the British Library.

A catalog record for this book is available from the Library of Congress.

ISBN: HB: 978-1-3504-2869-0
PB: 978-1-3504-2868-3
ePDF: 978-1-3504-2870-6
eBook: 978-1-3504-2871-3

Typeset by Deanta Global Publishing Services, Chennai, India

For product safety related questions contact productsafety@bloomsbury.com.

To find out more about our authors and books visit www.bloomsbury.com and sign up for our newsletters.

To Isabelle and Sam

Contents

List of Illustrations	viii
Introduction	1
1 The Old Regime of Hygiene	9
2 Peasant Bodies, Peasant Homes	31
3 The Smell of the City	53
4 The Republic of Hygiene I—Dirt and Defense	85
5 The Republic of Hygiene II—In the Schools	111
6 Water in, Water Out	131
7 The Lived Environment of the *Fin-de-Siècle*	159
8 How Clean Was the Belle Epoque?	185
9 "A Decent Place to Live"	211
10 Hygiene between the Wars	233
11 The Hygiene Revolution	257
Conclusion	295
Index	299

Illustrations

Figures

1.1	André Bouys (1656–1740). *La jeune femme au bain*	15
2.1	*A Peasant Interior. The Opening; Martin and Jouan with two oxen, being fed fodder mixed with bran* (~1900)	38
2.2	*Farm Courtyard with Dung Heap.* Tigny-Noyelle, Pas-de-Calais, France (1916)	44
3.1	*Central Paris before Haussmann. Rue Basses-des-Ursins* (1865)	66
4.1	*Hygiene in the Trenches. A Soldier Being Shaved* (1916)	102
5.1	*Washing the Students: "In the Carl Hansson's system, students are immersed in vats containing 90–100 liters of water"*	122
6.1	*It is hot in Paris. A little girl takes some water at a standpipe during a hot summer day in Paris (France) in 1921*	136
7.1	*Garnis: 15, rue Liancourt* (~1910)	164
7.2	*"Vespasienne" with three stalls made of slate, with a street lamp. Avenue du Maine, Paris* (1865)	177
8.1	*Paving the road by hand*	186
8.2	*A working-class home, rue de Romainville, 20th arrondissement, Paris* (1910)	189
9.1	*Slum of the Poulettes Quarter, Villeurbaine, Lyon* (1930)	213
9.2	*Îlot insalubre number 1: Rue de Venise* (1931)	219
10.1	*Privies at the Boussevillers school before Paul-Edouard Glath*	245
10.2	*Sewer worker with his security mask, Lyon* (~1935)	247
11.1	*Working-class housing, Villette quarter, Lyon* (1964)	265
11.2	*"75% of Parisians can have hot running water tomorrow!"*	284

Maps

4.1	Geographical distribution of military heights in France	90
4.2	Geographical distribution of exemptions for insufficient height	91
9.1	Deaths per 100,000 inhabitants, 1932–4	220
9.2	Index of overcrowding in Paris by arrondissement	221

Tables

4.1	The Number of Military Exemptions for Insufficient Height out of 10,000 Men Examined, 1830–61	89
4.2	Typhoid Fever: Morbidity and Mortality, 1888–1903	105
6.1	Infant Mortality Rates in Diverse Industrial Countries, 1906–10 (per 1,000 Live Births)	132
6.2	Apartments without Private Bathrooms by Floor, Paris 1871	149
7.1	Foreigners in *Garnis* (Boarding Houses) in Paris, 1876–1936	165
8.1	Mortality in France, 1902	195
8.2	Comparative Infant Mortality, 1909	204
9.1	Percentage of Income Devoted to Rent in 1940	215
9.2	Percentage of Family Budgets Devoted to Rent	215
9.3	Number of Housing Units Built, 1918–39	225
9.4	Public Subsidies for New Housing, 1918–39	225
10.1	Infant Mortality Rates (p. 1000) in Various Industrial Countries, 1937–9	234
11.1	Infant Mortality Rate in France, 1938–46	258
11.2	Distribution of Amenities among the Population of Paris, 1944	260
11.3	Destruction of French Housing, 1939–45	263
11.4	Percentage of Income Devoted to Rent, 1940–8	266
11.5	*Conforts* in French Households, 1946 and 1954	268
11.6	Housing and Satisfaction among Urban Wage Earners, 1955	273
11.7	Soap Consumption by Country, 1954	279
11.8	Infant Mortality Rates in Europe, 1901–48	280
11.9	*Conforts* in French Homes, 1962–75	281
11.10	Level of *Équipement* of Household (as a Percentage of Households in the Category)	283
11.11	Index of Household Consumption for Hygiene and Health, 1950–9	285

Introduction

In a country where everyone is barefoot, does the man who wears shoes live in luxury?[1]

Historians reflecting on the trajectory of urban, industrial societies usually think of factories and railroads, schools and shops, trade unions, women's rights, and the extension of the franchise. But any of us dropped into the daily life of fin-de-siècle France would be struck before anything else by the stink—of streets littered with horseshit, reeking *pissotières*, crowded apartments without ventilation or water, outhouses unconnected to sewers and shared by dozens of families; of clothes never changed, feet never washed, and teeth that had never met a toothbrush.

The reek of the past was no mere offense against twenty-first-century delicacy, however. Even before germ theory, people understood perfectly well how the itch of lice, the stench of leaking cesspits, or contaminated wells debased their lives. Escape from these troubles was another matter. To be sure, in the nineteenth century, the array of evils that accompanied industrialization and urbanization added to the litany of human misery. But pollution and overcrowding predated the factory system, and conditions were almost always worse in the countryside, where backbreaking work, animals, and piles of manure were the unavoidable features of everyday life.

Cleanliness is not part of the natural order, and it has no ideal level. If it is true, as the anthropologist Mary Douglas posits, that "dirt is essentially disorder ... there is no such thing as absolute dirt: it exists in the eye of the beholder," then "proper" hygiene is a historical and cultural artifact, and "modern" is a description of change rather than a teleology.[2] Indeed, notions of what is proper have differed markedly across time, geography, and social condition. They were not the same in Ancient Rome as at the Palace of Versailles, in England as in China, in the towns as on the farms, between the upper and lower classes—or even, more recently, between contiguous generations. Everywhere in premodern Europe the dirtiness of life was endemic. And where this changed at all, it changed only slightly and very slowly. The Middle Ages have a reputation for extreme dirtiness, and the Age of Enlightenment for a certain *délicatesse*. In neither case, however, did people wash with any regularity, wear clean underclothes, or understand the link between dirt and disease. To borrow the language of the *Annales* school, the history of hygiene was more *longue durée* than *événementielle*—at least before the twentieth century.

The novelty of the history of French hygiene, then, lies in the inflection of age-old traditions and constraints throughout the last 200 years. Public works projects of record scale and cost, employing the newest technologies, built networks to distribute fresh water and laid sewer pipes where none had existed. Factories produced washable cotton clothes and affordable packaged soap, and these became the foundation of a modern commerce of cleanliness. This added up to a veritable renovation of the human condition, propelled by an unprecedented accumulation of wealth that allowed societies and individuals to pay the huge cost of keeping clean.

In a reciprocal process of cause and effect, advances in the material history of hygiene translated into changes in the way people thought about and treated their bodies and their environment. Together, the material progress and the evolution of sensibilities constituted an essential element of what sociologist Norbert Elias, in his celebrated study of the history of manners, called "the civilizing process." This was more than a simple question of esthetics, though. The modernization of hygiene helped to triple life expectancy in France.

It is therefore curious that, despite the epic nature of this revolution and its consequences for people's lives—to say nothing of their deaths—the topic has attracted comparatively little interest among researchers and left a gap in our understanding of what happens to individuals as traditional societies become modern ones. Apart from a specialty literature on the history of toilets, bathtubs, and bidets (objects of enduring fascination, it seems), information on the history of cleanliness tends to be scattered among studies aimed at other targets. Historians Georges Vigarello, Fabienne Chevallier, Alain Corbin, Stéphane Frioux, Julia Csergo, and Jean-Pierre Goubert examine the history of water and its place in popular culture and practice. Folklorists like Françoise Loux collect old nuggets of vernacular wisdom relating to washing, health, and fortune. Anthropologists Laurence Wylie and Jakez Hélias, among others, provide insights into the habits of *propreté* (cleanliness) in rural France, while scholars of consumerism from Dominique Veillon to Rebecca Pulju trace the particular role of women in extending commodity culture and directing family economies. Business histories, such as Geoffrey Jones's studies of Unilever and global beauty culture, and Michèle Ruffat's monograph on Synthélabo,[3] France's pharmaceutical and healthcare behemoth, document the developing French market for toiletries, cosmetics, and household cleaning products. Surveys of successive French Republics by Jean Fourastié and Jean-Pierre Rioux treat the matter in passing, as an incidental aspect of the housing crisis or of postwar progress. Eugen Weber's epic work on the "frenchification" of the peasantry—in its scope and specificity, its long view of the historical process, and its insistence on telling stories about the past—serves as both model and inspiration for this study. Yet no book-length study exists of the passage from the noisome world of the past to today's more fastidious routines.

If historians and social scientists have passed by the history of hygiene without noticing, however, it is not for a lack of evidence. Archives and libraries are full of material related to its many aspects. Teachers' memoires recall the primitive conditions they encountered on assignment. Government surveys and censuses counted spigots and bathtubs and indoor toilets. Urban reformers and doctors of public health described in ghastly detail the particulars of slum housing and the rude poverty of rural life. Dozens of local hygiene councils met to consider sewer projects, infected wells, poisonous latrines, and the construction of public baths. Experts at international conferences gathered to discuss ways to clean up water supplies and get rid of sewage.

In the 1950s, women's magazines began obsessing about clean bodies and clean homes, while offering advertisements on every page promoting products to help readers achieve this perfection. In a sense, information about hygiene is everywhere.

However, we might find and measure it, the history of hygiene follows the same trajectory as so many other markers of modernization—the classic "hockey stick" graph of GDP, life expectancy, calories consumed, and so on. Two hundred years ago most lives in France were deformed, to one degree or another, by filth. Infant mortality rates were high, as was the incidence of epidemic disease. It is true that individual behavior and public policy were guided to some extent by an intuitive sense that dirt and disease were linked, even before anyone knew what a germ was. Miasmatic theories of disease made this explicit: filth caused stench, stench caused sickness.[4] And, even though the logic behind them was specious, efforts to clean up the muck and the rubbish often had an impact on morbidity and mortality. The point is that hygiene, even incompletely understood, was recognized as a social good. The problem was that it remained largely out of reach.

Over the last 200 years this became increasingly less true, a story that this book will reconstruct from the ground up, looking at specific practices of keeping clean and setting those practices in the concrete circumstances of home, work, field, and street. The narrative moves along two tracks. First, it proceeds chronologically, from the Restoration into the Fifth Republic. Every one of these regimes recognized the importance of hygiene to national strength and political stability. Each had a social conscience, to one degree or another, and each attacked the challenge of sanitizing the lives of French men and women with the resources, both financial and technological, at its disposal. Naturally, some were more successful than others. Democracy facilitated this process by giving the public a voice and making the state more responsive to popular needs. Meanwhile, industrial development provided the tools, and the arc of history began to bend toward *salubrité*.

The second narrative track is thematic, as each chapter looks at recurring issues across these two centuries: What kinds of homes do people inhabit? How much water do they have? Is it clean? Do they wash? Which bits? Do they change their clothes? How often? What do they do with their garbage and human and animal waste? What are governments of the day doing to ameliorate the awful conditions that are so clearly visible? How does the war against dirtiness move along differently in the cities and in the countryside? And how can we assess any progress that is being made?

The book begins with a simple idea about all this, that better hygiene constituted a fundamental element in the transformation of societies we often call modernization. To simplify somewhat, the process had two mutually enforcing aspects. The first was material. It consisted of pipes and pumps and filtration systems, of factories that produced cheap and comfortable clothes, precut soap, enameled bathroom fixtures, water heaters, washing machines, cotton knickers, and the rest of the arsenal of contemporary sanitariness. All these changes depended on an economy that produced levels of affluence unique in human history. We will repeatedly make the rather obvious point that hygiene is expensive, whereas filth is the child of poverty.

This is not to say that the rich were always clean. From the court of Louis XIV—a dense collection of the richest people in the richest country on earth, but devoid of even the most rudimentary plumbing and as foul-smelling as the vilest slum—to eighteenth-century *hôtels particuliers* and the bourgeois townhouses of the Proustian age, it is clear that money and privilege did not always translate into punctilious habits. In 1900, even the fashionable classes, who could certainly afford to do so, seldom bathed or washed their hair. Meanwhile, among the masses, few people had access to anything more commodious than a basin and a hole in the ground. Before the 1960s, virtually no one in France had a shower, which explains why the census did not bother to count them. Yet between the Battle of Waterloo and the end of the *trentes glorieuses*, dirtiness beat a steady retreat.

Sometimes that retreat was slowed down by the huge expenses required for the delivery and evacuation of water or the construction of new housing. Sometimes it was impeded by culture and tradition. Consider, for example, the deep discomfort with nakedness that ran through French society from rich to poor and religious to secular, and which seriously constrained the way people washed—and, in particular, *where* they washed. For the religiously inclined, the more intimate routines brushed up uncomfortably close to sin. For others, less worried about their eternal souls, taking off their clothes and washing their *parties sexuelles* merely seemed indecent. As Lynn Payer has demonstrated for medical culture, societies with comparable levels of technology can have significantly different ideas about what is "appropriate."[5] The mere presence of a bathtub will not tell you how often people are likely to use it.

Culture, however, is not static, and the threshold of disgust is not fixed.[6] In the history of hygiene, opportunity and practice moved together hand in hand, and water, unpolluted and in ample supply, was the most basic component in its advancement. Precious and expensive at the beginning of this period, it became cheaper and more convenient by the end. In one staggering statistic, economists Jean and Françoise Fourastié estimated that the cubic meter of water that had cost a manual laborer 20 wage-hours in 1840, by 1973 cost him only 6 minutes.[7] Moreover, instead of having to lug heavy buckets from the neighborhood or village fountain, a person needed only to turn the tap. The washing of clothes and bed linen, a semiannual event that lasted two or three days in the nineteenth century, became quick and routine with the arrival of the automatic washing machine in the 1950s.

Quite apart from the new labor-saving appliances, the consumer revolution of the second half of the twentieth century altered the landscape of hygiene. Cotton clothes and underwear did not cost much and could be washed without falling apart, which meant they could be changed every day. An entirely new industry of health and beauty aids multiplied the means of keeping homes neat and bodies clean. The first bar of soap, *Cadum*, hit the French market in 1912. Deodorant and shampoo did not exist when the Eiffel Tower was erected. By the end of the 1950s, they had begun to populate entire aisles of the supermarkets—which, for that matter, also did not exist in 1889. Cheap water, cheap detergent, and cheap cotton were the ingredients in the cleanliness revolution that washed over the country after 1945.

Of course, revolutions do not just happen; they need revolutionaries. If material progress and wealth were a precondition, they were turned into infrastructure and habit by government policy. The Third Republic stands out for its efforts to modernize the French population. In the wake of the humiliation of defeat and occupation in

1870–1, Republican authorities came to believe that a cleaner, healthier citizenry was key to securing a strong nation and a functioning democracy. Thus, as they built systems of universal primary education and universal conscription, they put lessons on hygiene in school textbooks and in training manuals for military recruits. More than that, municipal governments began to install the water and sewer pipes, and to institute the regular trash collection, that facilitated both collective and individual sanitation. These efforts advanced piecemeal and unevenly, depending on the available technology, the state of public finances and the voters' willingness to pay taxes. They accelerated considerably after 1945, as France became a much richer country. But the campaign had been gathering steam for a century before that.

Together, plumbing and education buried most of the old folk notions about the dangers of too much cleanliness. Nineteenth-century peasants had found strong, earthy smells "sexy" and thought of dirt as a sort of carapace that protected vulnerable bodies against penetration by harmful elements. This was a natural complement to the plain truths of country existence: where hard physical labor was the main fact of life, where daily chores involved intimate contact with animals and mud, and where washing was difficult (and in the long view rather pointless), standards of *propreté* remained different from what they were in the towns.

Nevertheless, the village schools also taught children about germs and the blessings of regular washing, and when country folk gained access to wool and cotton, they did not reach back for hemp shirts and canvas trousers. Meanwhile, rising incomes allowed farmers to replace earthen floors with stone and thatch roofs with slate—materials less hospitable to vermin. As the living distance between man and beast expanded, the dirt and smell of livestock became less inevitable and less sexy. Running water arrived late, but it made a crucial difference to practice. Fifth Republic farmers still worked with soil and manure, but with easier access to soap and hot water, they washed it off more often.

The point is that all practices and sensibilities are infused with cultural notions of what is dirty and what is clean and hemmed in by what is possible. Habits and smells that would have passed for perfectly proper in 1830, and regarded as negligent in 1900, would today be considered downright sociopathic. There is an exemplary moment in the New Wave film classic, *Breathless*, released in 1960. In one scene, Jean-Paul Belmondo, a small-time hood, is in the *chambre de bonne* of an American exchange student, Jean Seberg, trying to talk her into having sex with him. All of a sudden, Belmondo changes the subject: "Can I pee in your sink?" he asks. Seberg says okay. Belmondo clearly did not think the question would hurt his cause; today it surely would. Proprieties change with the plumbing.

Of course, expectations vary substantially from one person and one place to another. Yet these persistent disparities should not obscure the fact that the narrative presented in the chapters that follow bears steadily, if not consistently, in the direction of greater hygiene. The threshold of disgust may not be immovable, but it seems only to rise. This leaves us with two paradoxical truths: where everyone smells bad, no one smells bad; and yet, given the chance to be cleaner, most people seized it—not because they were hoodwinked by advertisers or bullied by government but because history had finally given them options. That is to say, in the end, the modernization of hygiene was not some sort of predetermined march toward a shinier future. It was an emergent reality, the sum of millions of personal choices and collective efforts by individuals who decided it was better to be comfortable than lousy, better to be healthy than sick, better to smell like rose petals than manure, and better to live a long life than a short one.

* * *

Every book is in some sense a collective enterprise, and so I naturally have many people and institutions to thank for their help and support. First of all, I want to acknowledge the efforts of my student research assistants: Megan Barnes, Nick Thompson, Kirstin Tiffany, and especially Samantha Sullivan. Several colleagues have made various contributions to the project: Sarah Fishman, Vicki Caron, Ludovic Cailluet, Hélène Gorge, Kolleen Guy, Stephen Harp, and Sophie Kurkdjian. Nancy Green and Marie Chessel graciously invited me to work with their research groups at the École des hautes études en sciences sociales. Anonymous readers for the *Journal of Modern History*, *Rural History*, and Bloomsbury Press made useful comments on parts of the manuscript. The rounding up of images and permissions to use them required the assistance of several archivists, librarians, and colleagues. Eva Lorenzini, at the Fragonard Museum of Perfume in Grasse, gave me permission to use the wonderful painting that hangs in that museum. Vincent Touchais at the Paris Archives; Anne Marie Delattre at the Archives Municipales, Lyon; and Alice Leblanc and Sylvie Lefebvre at the Archives Départementales du Pas-de-Calais helped me find what I was looking for. Bernard Cloup helped me discover his marvelous photo archives. Jacques Lucan and Philippe Dufieux likewise gave me kind and key advice. Jean-David Sichel, who inherited the right from his mother, Colette Sichel, granted me permission to use a photograph from his grandfather's book.

Chrystel Dozias Bonfils made my two research stays at the Résidences Récollets congenial and enriching. I finished the manuscript under the most auspicious circumstances, as an academic visitor at the Oxford Centre for European History at the University of Oxford. I am grateful to Henry Woudhuysen, rector of Lincoln College, Oxford, for his invitation to spend six months living in that wonderful place and getting to know a brilliant and welcoming group of colleagues. Thanks to the History students at Lincoln and Merton College, along with Alys Berton and Cassie Watson of Oxford Brookes University, and the folks at the nineteenth-century French seminar—Will Clement, Ksenia Butuzova, and Peter George—for inviting me to try out some of my ideas on them. I would be remiss if I did not acknowledge the unfailing help I received from Ewelina Jaworska, in the Domestic Bursary at Lincoln College.

The Fulbright Senior Scholar program and the University of Vermont provided me with the time and the funds for research and writing. My editor at Bloomsbury, Rhodri Mogford, answered all my questions promptly and made this whole process as frictionless and pleasant as it can be.

Special thanks always go to Edward Mcnally for forty-plus years of friendship and unfailing hospitality; to my wife Sophie, who took such wonderful care of things while I was away; and to my children, Isabelle and Sam, who helped out . . . most of the time. This book is dedicated to them.

Notes

1 Voltaire, "Luxury," in *A Philosophical Dictionary*, vol. IV (London: John and Henry L. Hunt, 1824), 381.
2 Mary Douglas, *Collected Works: Purity and Danger: An Analysis of Concepts of Pollution and Taboo* (New York: Routledge, 1996), 2.
3 Michèle Ruffat, *175 ans de l'industrie pharmaceutique française: Histoire de Synthélabo* (Paris: La Découverte, 1996).
4 For a brilliant elucidation of this, see Steven Johnson, *The Ghost Map: The Story of London's Most Terrifying Epidemic—and How it Changed Science, Cities, and the Modern World* (New York: Riverhead Books, 2006).
5 Lynn Payer, *Medicine and Culture: Varieties of Treatment in the United States, England, West Germany and France* (New York: Henry Holt, 1988), 62, 67.
6 On the matter of disgust, see Susan B. Miller, *Disgust: The Gatekeeper Emotion* (Hillsdale and London: The Analytic Press, 2004), 2, 28, and *passim*.
7 Jean et Françoise Fourastié, *Histoire du confort* (Paris: Presses Universitaires de France, 1973), 65.

1

The Old Regime of Hygiene

The Old Regime of Hygiene

On the eve of the French Revolution, the state of man in France remained what it had always been: solitary, nasty, brutish, short, and filthy. What Jacques Léonard, a historian of medicine, calls the "old regime of hygiene" persisted as a world of poisoned wells, verminous clothes, unwashed bodies, polluted public spaces, and "pestilential odors." "We must be surprised," he adds,

> by the sheer physical resistance of our ancestors, their capacity to endure bad weather and fatigue, to make do with frugal and monotonous diets, their tightly controlled gestures and instincts; surprised by the slowness of their rhythms, the pestilence of their odors, the rudeness of their habits, the character of the sounds and images that struck their senses every day.[1]

Far removed from the great issues of the time—from Crown debt, mercantile wars, the Enlightenment, the collapse of the guild system, and so on—for most people living in eighteenth-century France, it was the gritty struggle against this dirt and disorder that defined their lives and often, their deaths.

The history of hygiene proceeded quite apart from the more familiar narratives that frame the transition from traditional to modern France. The political upheaval that saw off the Old Regime left virtually no mark on the day-to-day life of the countryside. The National Convention could wage war and bring politics to the "little people." The Directory could conquer much of Europe and Bonaparte build an empire. None of these regimes, however, could do much to change the age-old structures and conventions that ruled the world of *salubrité*. They could not put "citizens" in fresh clothes or decent housing. They could not deliver ample supplies of unpolluted water, flush the streets, remove the garbage and the sewage, or drive down the infant mortality rate. The priests may have gone underground for a few years, but the lice and bedbugs never did. In short, when it came to matters of hygiene, the Revolution bequeathed to the nineteenth century almost exactly what it had inherited from the Old Regime.

* * *

It does not take much searching to find pungent descriptions of life in Paris. In the Middle Ages, "filth spread like a leper in homes and on streets." And for 700 years before that, according to Louis-Narcisse Girard, inspector general of public works, "the city did not have level streets, and puddles habitually stagnated everywhere. The ground, without any runoff, was perpetually soggy and muddy. The inhabitants, who knew nothing of cesspits, accumulated rubble and refuse, picked at incessantly by the ubiquitous domestic animals—rabbits, ducks, pigs, etc." Private latrines were rare, and people relieved themselves more or less anywhere, "inside towers and casemates or in the porches of private houses in the less frequented streets."[2] In 1185, according to Girard, King Philippe Auguste ordered the paving of the Cité. Despite the "mud tax" of 1506 that was supposed to pay for street cleaning, the spreading city remained a soup of mud, trash, and shit. Parisians commonly dumped their litter in front of their neighbor's door or in some other public spot. Historian Ned Rival paints a grim picture of the medieval urban landscape: "narrow alleys, cesspools fed by pigs and other beasts, streets running with urine, excrement, and rubbish tossed from windows after a perfunctory 'Heads up!' piles of garbage and old bones." The "city of mud," as Rousseau called it, had street cleaners that by the end of the Old Regime were removing a quarter of a million tons of "mud"—to be more precise, a viscous mix of earth and manure—a year and bringing it to dumps scattered throughout the city. Everyone who could ride instead of walk did so, and all attempts to introduce some order into this chaos ran into apathy and anarchy.[3]

The epic filth of public spaces reflected the simple fact that cities had not figured out a way to get rid of all the garbage and sewage produced by their dense populations. Architect and historian Witold Rybczynski describes the sixteenth-century sanitation system in the French capital:

[A] Parisian city ordinance required that all houses be equipped with a privy emptying into a cesspool built beneath the courtyard. A common privy was located on the ground floor, and sometimes on an upper level, off the staircase. Considering that thirty or forty persons were living in the building, two or three toilet seats were hardly a luxury. Chamber pots were popular. As there were no sewers and no wastewater pipes, their contents, like all dirty water, were disposed of in a haphazard fashion, which on the upper floors meant directly out of a window and into the street.[4]

Two centuries later, urban hygiene had not much improved. Swept along, perhaps, by Enlightenment dreams of a better world and by the scientific logic that equated unpleasant smells with miasmas and miasmas with disease, public authorities made an effort to clear Paris of the rotting corpses by digging up old cemeteries, removing the bones to catacombs and the graveyards to the edges of town; the Père Lachaise cemetery, for example, opened for business in 1804, just beyond the old walls in the city's northeast. But visitors to Paris in the Age of Enlightenment still condemned it as a huge garbage dump and sewer. The cesspits that served as the repository for the capital's enormous store of fecal matter remained typically leaky and badly evacuated, while most people continued to empty their chamber pots out of their windows. The sewer system consisted of 24 kilometers of mostly open gutters running down the streets. They overflowed when it rained and left pools of water and rotting garbage when it stopped.

The *Philosophes* were particularly critical of the muck and muddle, which they considered the antithesis of Reason. Voltaire decried the "narrow streets displaying dirtiness, spreading infection and causing public disorders." Visitors and tourists, he added, continued to be scandalized "by the practices of throwing urine and feces out of windows and on to the heads of passers-by." Rousseau's *Confessions* leave us with an image of the faubourg Saint-Marcel, later a Jacobin stronghold, filled with "small, dirty and stinking streets, ugly black houses [and] an air of filth."[5] Louis-Sebastien Mercier, the peripatetic chronicler of everyday Paris, noted that signs warning "No dumping of garbage," and threatening miscreants with corporal punishment, seemed to serve as an invitation for people to do precisely the opposite. His description of one working-class flat in the faubourg Saint-Marcel, a neighborhood renowned for its griminess, leaves an indelible impression: an entire family in one small room, "four grubby walls enclosing curtainless *grabats* (flea-bag beds) and kitchen utensils mixing with *vases de nuits* (chamber pots)." Sadly, even this slum was too expensive for many working-class families, who had to move every three months, not because of the disgusting conditions, but because "they can never pay their rent."[6]

When asked how anyone could live amid the repellent mix of "butchers' shops, cemeteries, hospitals, drains, streams of urine, heaps of excrement, dyers', tanners', curriers' stalls [and the] continual smoke from the unbelievable quantity of wood and the vapor of all that coal," Mercier replied that "familiarity accustoms the Parisians to humid fogs, maleficent vapors, and foul-smelling ooze."[7] He illustrated his point with this tableau: "an amphitheater of latrines" perched one on top of the other, placed next to the staircases of an eighteenth-century tenement, just outside the doors, right next to the kitchens, and *exhaling* everywhere the most fetid odors. The pipes (of these outhouses) are too narrow and easily get stopped up; nobody unblocks them; the fecal matter piles up in a column, climbing toward the toilet seat (*siège d'aisance*); the overstuffed pipe breaks; the house is inundated; infection spreads, but no one leaves; Parisian noses are used to it.[8]

But were they "used to it?" In his excellent essay on "the actual smellscape of the past," historian Mark Jenner calls into question the notion that our sensibilities have been, in the words of Roy Porter, "deodorized" and that odors the modern world would consider intolerable "were once unavoidable and ubiquitous." Jenner suggests instead that people in the past did not experience the "good old smells" as good at all, alluding to evidence in the science of olfaction that being repulsed by the smell of excrement and putrefaction is not historically conditioned but wired into our brains. This is the sensory intuition that led to miasmatic theories of disease; that is, to the idea that bad smells are not merely unpleasant but are dangerous.[9]

A cheap, ample supply of water would have helped alleviate some of these conditions, but eighteenth-century Paris had no such supply. Water was inconvenient. It required fetching, often from a distance, and then hauling, often up several flights of stairs. And it was expensive. According to historian Daniel Roche, at the end of the Old Regime a cubic meter of water (1,000 liters) cost the equivalent of three to four days of wage labor.[10] And, weighing a 1,000 kilograms (2,200 pounds), it was a lot to lug around. Understandably, then, most people used very little of it. There were fountains in some neighborhoods, fed by old and unevenly maintained aqueducts, but most of the water came from the Seine and was distributed throughout the city by tens of thousands of water carriers. As to the quality, Seine water was muddy, although it was better "than water from the wells on the Left Bank, which were never protected from the terrible infiltrations and from which the bakers made their bread." At any rate, remarked Mercier, "One drank [the] water without really bothering about it."[11]

The poor in this "old regime of hygiene" suffered the most sordid conditions, of course. Yet decent hygiene was not a simple question of means. The early modern era had a different sense of propriety, shared by the elites, and even those who lived in luxury enjoyed little in the way of comfort and fresh air. The offensiveness of the court at Versailles, for example, is legendary, even if some of the more gruesome details are likely metaphorical. At the palace, since privies were considered "plebian," the most privileged people did not "go to the loo," the loo came to them—usually in the form of a "close stool"; that is, a box with a padded lid which servants brought into the room as necessity dictated. They were not left for long, though, because, as one nineteenth century wit (reminded us), this was a *meuble odorant* (a smelly piece of furniture) and best admired at a distance.

These primitive amenities were normally deployed in what to modern sensibilities seems an uncomfortably public manner and, in any case, there were not enough of them to satisfy the needs of all the palace residents. An inventory drawn up for Louis XIV listed a total of 264 *chaises percées* (mobile toilets). Consequently, urination at court usually occurred in a more casual and haphazard way—both indoors and out. "There is one dirty thing at court I shall never get used to," the Duchess of Orléans wrote in her diary, "the people stationed in the galleries in front of our rooms who piss into all the corners."[12]

Traditional bodily hygiene was scarcely more punctilious. The most "audacious" doctors in the Age of Enlightenment prescribed frequent hand washing. But most medical opinion held that "one should never wash the head, rarely the feet, and often the hands." Ablutions were especially dangerous for children. According to the proverbial wisdom: "To wash them at night with water leads to bad teeth and catarrhs, deforms the face, and brings on cold and hailstorms in summer." Best just to wipe the young with a dry, clean linen.[13]

"It is difficult to imagine," wrote the doctor and medical historian Augustin Cabanès in his 1908 survey of history's intimate customs, that "in those boudoirs, those love nests . . . where lords and beautiful ladies had their trysts . . . these rich jewels and sumptuous clothes disguised the most repugnant dirtiness."[14] Although, according to Lawrence Wright, every important suite at the palace had its own bathroom (i.e., a room for bathing)—a hundred in all, and often in marble and gilding—Louis XIV, with a reputation for having "a holy horror of water," tended to build bathrooms with more avidity than he used them.

Indeed, the sanitary habits of the French court seem to trace very neatly the curious evolution of what sociologist Norbert Elias called "the civilizing process," particularly as it reflected thinking about what was dirty and what was clean. Elias referred specifically to a "rising threshold of disgust" from the medieval period into the modern era.[15] As historian and sociologist Georges Vigarello, building on Elias's insight, explains, early modern France experienced no steady and inexorable climb toward more rigorously scrubbed bodies. Medieval culture had an ambiguous relationship with water and baths. Jules Arnould offered perhaps the dimmest view of medieval practice, where "cleanliness was a vice and bathing indecent." Although, in fact, as historian Peter Ward remarks, "we know almost nothing about how many people bathed in medieval society, how often they washed, and what parts of their bodies they cleaned when they did."[16] We do know that the monastic tradition condemned bathing as it condemned any concern for the sensual body. Sainte-Agnès, for example, died martyred but unwashed at the age of thirteen. As Holly Brubach put it, "Christians, it seems, [were] unique among religious zealots in their disregard for cleanliness."[17]

Yet other historians believe the Middle Ages were cleaner in many respects than the centuries that followed. Wright, for example, alludes to an English monastery with a routine that called for warm water and soap for baths four times a year, with provisions for head shaving every three weeks and a footbath on Saturday. Cold baths could serve for penance, warmer baths for medical treatments. Beyond the monastery wall, the countryside was streaked with streams and creeks, perfect for bathing in summer. In the towns and cities, while few people enjoyed the means to bathe at home, public baths dotted the local riversides and offered people a rich choice of bathing options at affordable prices—even the option of tubs large enough to allow two people to bathe together, at a lower cost to each. Naturally, the possibility of such intimacy "tended to quickly transform respectable establishments into brothels, where bathers could eat and drink together"—alongside more carnal activities.[18]

For Vigarello, it was not that the Middle Ages lacked a notion of hygiene, only that the notion itself was fluid and its content changed considerably in the centuries that followed. More archaic practices, for example, involved washing the *visible* parts of the body, especially the hands, mouth, eyes, and face. Foot washing was sometimes recommended as a way of avoiding corns and eliminating unpleasant smells. The rest of the body was ignored or out of bounds. Indeed, religious considerations prevented even a discussion of these "private" areas.[19] In other words, society took cleanliness for a moral, not a sanitary quality, and viewed proper washing as a question of good manners, not good health.

Where propriety was an aspect of social performance, cleanliness attached to the clothes, rather than to the bodies beneath them. A man who sweated changed his shirt; he did not wash. Vigarello offers the exemplary story of a poor fifteenth-century scholar who wanted to get rid of the vermin infesting his clothes. He washed his shirt in the river, then threw the lice he had picked off into a hole, filled it in, and planted a cross on top. It never occurred to him to use the river water on his body. The logic of this "aesthetic of surfaces" eventually dictated that even clean shirts, hidden as they were beneath other clothing, were beside the point. If the visible parts of the shirt, collars and cuffs, were suitably white, then decorum was served. Between clean cuffs and dirty torsos, perfume made up the difference. Among the masses, on the contrary, there was neither linen nor perfume, and little chance of being "clean."

Such practices helped make the seventeenth century "the grimiest in history," in the view of historian Geneviève Cerisier-Millet.[20] Whereas Paris at the end of the thirteenth century had twenty-six public bathing establishments, only two remained four centuries later, "where elegant men and women, deployed a profusion of scents to hide the pong caused by their dirtiness." The Counter-Reformation cracked down on the sins of the flesh, in particular as they had long been practiced in those notorious dens of iniquity, public baths: the privileged site of "debauchery, homosexuality, prostitution—outrages to morality and modesty." The elites took their example from the Sun King himself, who reportedly took but one bath in his life. History recorded the year: 1665.[21]

If, even among the elites, the age of the Sun King saw a decline in bathing, in the Age of Enlightenment many recovered the habit of doing so. People with money could bear the cost of private baths. Soaking behind closed doors, these bathers posed no threat to public order. The greater public, however, mostly had to go without. According to contemporary chronicler Nicolas Restif de la Bretonne, hardly anyone in pre-Revolutionary Paris took baths, "and those who did confined them to once or twice [per year]."[22] This made for a stark contrast, notes Fernand Braudel, with the contemporaneous situation in Muslim cities—or recently Muslim cities like Buda—which all had public baths that "had admitted everyone, without charge, since the time of the Ottoman domination."[23]

Vigarello hazards two explanations for the early modern retreat from washing. First, as baths had more to do with "festive sociability" than with propriety or health, their absence produced no negative social effects: where nobody bathes, nobody needs to bathe—or at least no one stands out for not having done so. Second, Vigarello—whose idea, cited over and over in the literature, has become a touchstone—proposes that people increasingly avoided baths because they came to consider water a dangerous medium. For example, sixteenth-century doctor and journalist Théophraste Renaudot warned that,

> Apart from its medicinal function, baths are not merely useless but downright dangerous. They kill the fruit in a mother's stomach [and] threaten serious harm to people with scabs, erysipelas, people who are fat or plump, and all those unaccustomed to the experience, because it relaxes the ligaments, irritates the nerves, stirs up the humors, and fills the head with vapors.[24]

In effect, the popular imagination worried about the "mechanical effects of water" on the body—"a precarious shell . . . agitated and shaken by a water which was alien to it," and which was assumed to penetrate the body, weaken the organs, and leave behind "fragile pores." Babies' bodies were considered "completely porous." In a world without germ theory, water was dangerous not because it carried vectors of disease, like cholera bacilli, directly through the skin and into the body; the effect was less biologically specific, although it was no less threatening for that. Understandably, the sense that immersion was fraught with danger did not encourage the practice. Even in the middle of the nineteenth century, according to sociologist Julia Csergo, there were experts, such Dr. Beaugrand, who held on to the eighteenth-century theory that the skin absorbed the liquid that surrounded it, which explained why, after a bath, people ordinarily needed to urinate.[25]

Csergo also reminds her readers that the prevailing miasmatic theory of disease attributed the properties of health to air rather than to water. Doctors always prescribed fresh air for their sick patients. One of the critical changes in thinking about hygiene between the ages of Louis XIV and Dreyfus, she concludes, was precisely the elevation of water as the critical element and the relative depreciation of the role of air.²⁶

Both Csergo and Vigarello offer complex accounts of the history of water and of cleanliness, which were never a simple question of health and good manners but remained always and organically linked to notions about the body, disease, strength, and social tact; that is, the fear of water was more than just a practical concern with drafts and chills. Rousseau was virtually alone in recommending washing and baths for a healthy body.²⁷ It was a deeply conceptual, even magical, matter and only began to lose its power with the demystification of the natural world in the century of Enlightenment. As a matter of historical method, the accounts of Vigarello and Csergo contain a strong speculative element, since documentary sources on the conceptualization and use of water in the early modern period are thin.

They are nevertheless consistent with the considerable evidence indicating the resurrection of bathing in the eighteenth century (Figure 1.1). In the age of Louis XV, baths became part of daily life at Versailles, while architects included functional bathrooms in the new urban mansions being built at the height of the Old Regime. The most modern of these added a kind of rudimentary plumbing to the premises. According to Lawrence Wright, the first advertisement for a house in Paris with a bathroom appeared in 1765, but the fixture became more common in the great townhouses as the century moved on. By the eve of the Revolution, the bathroom had gone from "the last private room on clients' lists to being an indispensable space."²⁸

Figure 1.1 André Bouys (1656–1740). *La jeune femme au bain.* Courtesy of the Collection du Musée de Parfum, Fragonard parfumeur, Grasse.

And two new objects had begun to appear in that space. The first were the primitive versions of flush toilets, invented by Sir John Harrington in 1596 and "one of the technological innovations of which modern architects were most proud." It should be noted, however, that until the invention of the U-bend, introduced by Thomas Crapper in 1880, even where these gadgets existed in the eighteenth century, "the house still needed to be cleared of pestilential odors."[29] The second was the bidet. The history of the bidet is cloaked almost entirely in anecdote and mystification, but the stories suggest that this innovative little device was invented around 1720 and became common in the *cabinets de toilette* of the aristocracy around the middle of the century. In 1740, only 7.5 percent of households had one—and still only 10 percent when Louis XVI came to the throne—almost all of them in Paris.[30] It remained an exceptional piece of furniture among the bourgeoisie until the eve of the Revolution and was completely unknown to the lower classes, save for those individuals in contact with the elites, especially servants. Given their novelty, and the fact that they sat mostly in aristocratic homes, it is no surprise that the era's bidets tended to be fancy, rather than merely functional. Joan Dejean writes that the one Madame de Pompadour had delivered to the king had "gilt bronze mounts and was veneered in rosewood," along with a padded backrest, hand rest, and a removable cushion that concealed a porcelain bowl for washing. Although the nineteenth century came to believe that bidets could be useful for contraception, their initial appeal was as a convenience for washing *les parties génitales* in a culture where bathing remained both infrequent and partial.[31]

It is easy to exaggerate the renaissance of bathing culture in the eighteenth century. Economist and demographer Louis-François Benoiston de Chateauneuf reckoned that Paris had 150 bathtubs at the time of the Estates General, which number had grown to around 500 by 1816. The city also offered a choice among twenty or twenty-five bathhouses, in addition to four bathing ships on the river. He estimated that, on average, each provided twenty-five baths a day, which added up to 22,500 baths monthly and 270,000 a year for a population of more than 700,000 people.[32]

Moreover, the renewed interest in baths did not signal any revolutionary commitment to modern standards of hygiene. Chateaubriand, for example, remarked in his memoirs that his weekly bath in the river "has nothing to do with washing; it's just a sort of entertainment, a bi-weekly day out."[33] On the other hand, even a bath whose principal object is amusement can make you cleaner. For their part, the popular classes remained untouched by the new bathing culture, since a tub full of hot water, and even the public baths, remained well beyond their means. A session at Poitevin, a new sort of hot bathhouse built on the Seine in 1761, for example, cost three livres per visit, at a time when a craftsman's daily wage was half a *livre* and a day laborer's a quarter-*livre*. The poor just swam in the Seine and the Ourcq—although not very often.

Quite apart from the cost of a bath, the body's interaction with water remained in the popular mind a more complex affair than the simple removal of dirt from the surface of the skin. And insofar as popular minds worried about the permeability of skin, the dangers inherent in bathing made the water temperature all the more crucial, because of the different effects that cold and hot water could have on a body. The *Encyclopedia* dispensed the standard advice: different sorts of baths were appropriate to different conditions and purposes. A warm bath would serve to soften the nerves and relax the tissues. Conversely, a bracingly cold bath promised to tighten up a body gone too slack. In other words, baths had a moral, not a strictly hygienic function.[34] Cold baths built up vigorous good health and moral fiber; they did not cleanse the body so much as they strengthened it. In contrast, warm baths represented "ostentatious luxury." They were sensual, indolent, erotic. Once again, Vigarello points out that contemporaries emphasized the effect of a bath on a person's *inside*: "The hot bath soothed because it made the humours circulate, and that was its chief virtue."[35]

It was therefore with caution that writer Élise Voiart imparted the beauty secrets she had learned in service to the Princesse W*** in the 1740s. Mme. Voiart prescribed washing as an essential part of any beauty regime. The light scrubbing and delicate rinsing of face, neck, and chest practiced, for example, by the "celebrated beauty" Princess Amélie aimed to whiten her skin; it had little to do with cleanliness. The same was true of the baths she took. They served not to dissolve grime but to impart energy, beauty, and fortitude. At the same time, Mme. Voiart understood that the ambiguous qualities of water dictated prudence. These suspicions led some women to substitute milk as the foundation of their toilette. Milk served the same cosmetic purposes as water, with less potential for damage. Voiart's advice to her young princess was thus embedded in a whole eighteenth-century science of baths, whose details were adapted to the particular needs of each woman but always in the interests of beauty rather than of *propreté*.[36]

Cold or warm, taken for vigor or pleasure, baths nonetheless remained infrequent, even among those who could afford them—the striving bourgeoisie and the languorous aristocracy. Peter Ward, for instance, repeats the popular notion that cleanliness became "a defining characteristic of bourgeois life, one of the cultural pillars of bourgeois self-awareness." But this fact is not reflected in the ascertainable numbers of baths and bathtubs.[37] Marie Antoinette was said to have bathed every day and Napoleon to have started his mornings with a hot bath. Perhaps they did, although such stories are probably apocryphal. In any case, the experience of Mme. de Maraise, an enlightened bourgeoise of the eighteenth century, probably sits closer to the average. Madame bathed for the first time in her life in the Seine in 1780, after which she might take "two or three baths a year there, though still sometimes abstaining for several seasons."[38]

All the same, something was beginning to change in the Age of Enlightenment. A timeless fatalism in matters of hygiene began to give way to an increased urge for and sense of control over the lived environment. A scientific understanding of the link between filth and disease still lay a century in the future, but public authorities and health experts, continuing to work through the old categories of dampness, fogs, rotting flesh, and poisonous miasmas, tried to clean up the towns. The first Chair in Hygiene at the Paris Faculty of Medicine was named in 1793. To the degree that technology and resources made it possible, they attacked piles of rubbish, stagnant water, decomposing corpses, and the other disgusting, dangerous elements of overcrowding and decay. Even a wrong theory of disease, it turned out, could produce some effective prophylactic response. Meanwhile, a limited consumer revolution that touched even the working population of the cities meant that people had more clothes and were likely to change them more regularly.[39]

Success did not always crown these efforts, nor did they always meet with public approval. Dr. Cabanès, for example, tells the story of the King's Director General of Public Works, who almost produced a riot when he tried to tear down an alley of yew trees in the Tuileries Gardens—that had long served as a "discreet retreat for strollers tormented by their pressing needs"—because the authorities had put up "latrines payantes"; that is, pay toilets.[40]

The central element in the state's sanitary project was water, forever in high demand and forever in low supply—although estimates of exactly how much there was and how much people used vary considerably. In the sixteenth century two aqueducts brought enough water into Paris from the Pré-Saint-Gervais and Belleville to provide each Parisian with 1 or 2 liters of water per day. Under the new Bourbon dynasty, however, much of that flow was diverted to the Louvre and Tuileries palaces. In 1750, writes Ned Rival, Paris had sixty public fountains. But they were unequally distributed across the city, and even the most favored Parisians used no more than 3 liters of well water a day, on average. Historian Jean-Pierre Goubert cites a source that put the figure at about 5 liters per person in 1802, two liters short of what was considered an acceptable minimum.[41]

According to other sources, fed principally with water taken from the Seine, and carted about by an army of servants and professional water carriers—Mercier counted 20,000 of the latter, moving around Paris, selling their precious liquid out of big barrels sitting on horse-drawn carts—daily consumption almost tripled between the reigns of Louis XIV and Louis XVI, from 8 to 20 liters per person. Even this, however, was not very much by later standards, and it still left the authorities unable to keep up with the rising demand. Water usage in the capital rose steadily through the second half of the century, and the Revolution only made the situation worse, given the general breakdown of public order.

That was certainly the opinion of Pierre Chauvet, whose *Essai sur la propreté de Paris, par un citoyen français* (Essay on the Cleanliness of Paris, by a French Citizen), written in 1797, portrayed the capital as an immense assortment of private and public stinks:

> Everywhere one goes to charm the senses—the Palais de Justice, the Louvre, the Tuileries . . . he is pursued by the stench of outhouses, worse than the ubiquitous smell of cheap, burning oil. In the so-called Palais "Royal" in the summer, there is no hiding from the odor of urine on the trees perpetually thus "watered," and the merchants who occupy this place of commerce are so inured to the filth, that there is no surprise in seeing one of them put his stall right next to one of the public "toilets" one finds there.[42]

Chauvet believed that dirtiness grew out of ignorance, whether it was a question of savages in America, "who satisfied their needs without modesty or restraint," or the Catholic population of Spain, "who spent half their time and their fortunes praying while being devoured by vermin," or "the Jewish people, who have unquestionably been among the most ignorant people on earth and are today still one of the dirtiest." The practical impossibility of keeping such a huge, crowded city clean only compounded the problem. How, Chauvet asked, was it possible that all those trades that produced liquid filth—butchers, tanners, and so on—could get rid of it, other than sending it from their homes and shops into the street? And then how to keep the streets clean—especially since to require all these people to sweep and clean the city streets would amount to an urban version of the *corvées* that angered the peasants and helped bring on the Revolution?

Chauvet nevertheless dreamed of a different Paris, where paved streets covered a system of canals and sewers; where a small army of workers emptied the city of garbage every day and citizens enjoyed a sort of outhouse utopia, where they could do their business, men and women separately, in clean, free public toilets "conforming to the laws of sanitation and decency." In other words, he dreamed of the twentieth century.

Peasant Bodies in the Nineteenth Century

This picture of early modern hygiene drawn above, offensive as today's sensibilities might find it, nevertheless overstates the progress of the civilizing process. Few eighteenth-century Français lived in palaces or townhouses, and only a small minority in towns and cities. Beyond the city walls, in *la France* profonde, the world inhabited by the overwhelming majority of the population, any sort of plumbing was beyond the imagination, and the sanitary problems created by overcrowding, depicted by Mercier and Chauvet, an irrelevancy.

A few words of caution: the story that follows about life on the land is a grim one, and because I have not spared the disagreeable details it is easy to imagine that the story is grimmer than it should be—a function, perhaps, of bias in the sources; a surrender to "history from above"; or a reflection of the prejudices of a twenty-first-century American.

It is true that information about peasant hygiene almost never comes from the peasants themselves. Overwhelmingly, the descriptions that follow are filtered through the "gaze" of others—principally government agents and professional reformers, usually urban and obviously literate, who arrived in the villages with aim of "improving" things. Condescension was not a bug but a feature of this process, as it inevitably is when one group of people sets out to bring "progress" to another. Nineteenth-century French peasants would not have seen themselves as "primitive and dirty," as the improvers did. They simply lived as people on the land had more or less always lived.

In their descriptions, the reformers, as missionaries predictably do, no doubt exaggerated for effect or because what they saw in the countryside so offended their sensibilities. The historian's judgment may require some discounting for the horrified tone of some of their accounts, but the reformers did not invent the danger and discomfort of rural existence. The essential elements of their depictions are so ubiquitous, and the absence of any countervailing evidence so complete, that it seems reasonable to take them for a decently accurate picture of daily life and prevailing standards. Of course, we are not allowed to judge what we see as the missionaries did. Still, in the end, either peasants changed their clothes or did not, lived with their livestock or did not, piled their manure next to their wells or did not.

That said, the behavior of people in the countryside throughout the nineteenth century suggests that, while they conceived the matter differently, when they found the wherewithal to follow the reformers' advice, they often did so. More and more households covered their dirt floors with stone, replaced thatch with slate, constructed outbuildings for their animals, and exchanged rough wool shirts for cotton. This is not a story of irredeemable backwardness. The peasants had agency and, as the century wore on, they increasingly used it to improve their own lives.

* * *

Historian Ronald Hubscher depicted the grim reality of rural life at the beginning of the nineteenth century: "the insecurity of tomorrow was permanent, penury threatened at every moment; life was hunger punctuated by famine."[43] And, he might have added, by a dirtiness that imposed itself on life even before a child's first breath. "We can be almost sure," writes historian Pierre Goubert,

> that the mother gave birth sitting down, with her clothes on, and strongly supported, and that the midwife worked in unimaginable conditions, with unwashed hands, fingers, and fingernails, preparing dressings which were the reverse of sterile, containing spider's webs, pounded leaves, and insects and dried dung.[44]

Medical crusader Dr. Louis-August Maréschal believed he had discovered the zero degree of hygiene in early-nineteenth-century Brittany.[45] The filth and neglect he found began at birth in a process presided over by "inept matrons, hungry for their fees, with reputations established by one or two 'cures' that owed nothing to their 'knowledge' and that could not make up for the greater damage they did, for which their ignorance was truly guilty."

Martin Nadaud, the militant worker and future politician, remembered "Old Fouésonne," the only midwife in his native village of La Martinèche (Creuse):

> She was the only doctor who had ever practiced in our village. Accustomed to never being contradicted, she would affirm with imperturbable self-assurance that Tom, Dick, or Harry, who had been dead for several years, had come to visit his former neighbors and told them the names of others from the village who had gone either to heaven or to hell. She would also tell us the names of those known to be werewolves as well as those who had exerted themselves to vanquish them.[46]

Such was the state of obstetric expertise in 1815.

Brittany was not exceptional for its primitive birthing routines or its lethal outcomes. In the Brenne region (Indre), according to anthropologist Jacqueline Tardivon, 50 percent of babies were stillborn at the turn of the nineteenth century, a figure that had everything to do with the deplorable hygiene of childbirth, with deliveries occurring in all sorts of unfortunate circumstances, supervised by accomplices who were little more than the agents of infant mortality and puerperal fever—closer in their methods to witches than to nurses.[47] As for postpartum care, in lower Brittany, new mothers received a day of bed rest and a glass of "hot wine to repair their strength." It was not rare to see the midwives sending new mothers back to their arduous chores "the day after giving birth."

Because a woman who managed to dodge the many perils of childbirth returned quickly to her labors, it made sense that folk wisdom prescribed swaddling the little creature, even in the face of doctors' reproof. Maréschal, one of those engaged in a "holy crusade" against the practice, described it:

> Seated on a large stone, our Breton mother laid out a jersey of thick cloth destined to imprison the poor child more tightly than before his birth. The height and tightness of the wrap form a draft collar around the neck, keeping the head fixed and straight. In this prison of linen and bandages [the baby] looks rather like a mummy.

Parents in villages across France wrapped up their infants like sausages. In the Burgundian hamlet of Minot, newborns were tightly bound from head to toe in feather duffles, topped with a bonnet, and placed lying down until they were ready to walk. In the Pyrénées, they were merely strapped into their cradles and placed near enough to the fire that they would keep warm, but not so close that they would burn, and left, in Pierre Goubert's evocative expression, to "marinate" throughout the day.[48]

The tragedies that often resulted from the lack of supervision left Maréschal aghast. "The habit of leaving the swine to come and go freely through all parts of the house," he wrote,

> has been the cause of quite a different set of misfortunes. We have seen the pigs devour hands, faces, and even the entire heads of newborns without these horrible accidents leading to closer surveillance or to closing off the entrance of the house against these animals of such a "dangerous voracity."

The care that infants did receive was frequently more dangerous than the neglect.[49] Henri Blanc, the twentieth-century hygienist whose own work leaned so heavily on Maréschal's, pointed particularly to the custom of feeding newborns solid food, sometimes leading to "death by indigestion." Medical authorities complained that Breton parents gave their infants cow's milk instead of breastfeeding them. Quite apart from the newborns' inability to digest raw cow's milk, the milk itself came from filthy udders, and the unwashed hands of those who handled the milk naturally contaminated it further. Moreover, it could not have helped the youngest Bretons that their parents often added a few drops of alcohol to the milk, believing "this detestable practice to be a source of good health and vigor." Or that the parents, certain that the ability to eat grown-up food was a sign of an infant's strength, fed them such things as lard and salted sardines. "When they say of a baby, 'He eats like us,' [parents] are expressing the greatest possible admiration," wrote the prefect of the Finistère department.[50] No wonder infant mortality in the province could run to double the national average.

Similar practices elsewhere meant that a "monstrously high" number of French children died before their first birthday. Infant mortality rates were especially elevated in places like the Morvan, where the wet-nursing business for abandoned children was well established. But even where bottle feeding was expanding among mothers, the consequences for infant health were very bad, "since poor quality milk was often used and the [unsterilized] bottles acted a breeding ground for microbes."[51]

Even older babies in the Basse-Bretagne were left in what the doctor called a virtual state of nature: awakened in the morning, put to bed at night, and fed in between. Past that, young children were largely ignored, neither hugged for being good nor beaten for being bad—at least until they were older. Maréschal concluded that, "At an age when all the lessons about what is good and what is bad engrave themselves easily on young souls, [young Bretons] easily preserve the habits of dirtiness and savage ignorance in which they are steeped."[52]

To modern eyes this might look like child abuse, but adults hardly treated their children's bodies with less care than they treated their own. Indeed, the ignorance and "extreme dirtiness" of the Bretons were axiomatic to contemporaries.[53] "Let us add," wrote Jacques de Cambry in his book *Voyage dans le Finistère* (1794),

> [a word about] the almost hereditary scabies among fathers and children, the filthiness of individuals who neither bathe nor wash, climbing out of the pits, the ponds, the cesspits whence their drunkenness had tossed them; observe the long, slimy hair, the thick beard, the faces laced with grimy crevices, and you will have an idea of the Breton peasant.

"Poor Brittany," added Victor Hugo, "land that has kept everything, its monuments and its inhabitants, its poetry and its filth, its old color and its old grubbiness underneath. Wash the buildings, they are superb; but as for the Bretons themselves, I defy you to wash them."[54] Indeed, with what would they have washed? Household inventories for the Ille-et-Vilaine in the first part of the century reveal the total lack of any sort of *objets de toilette*: "Basins and water bowls were completely absent from these one-room dwellings . . . toothbrushes and nail files seem perfectly unknown."[55] In Jules Renard's lapidary observation: "[The peasants] fight dirt only with sweat."[56]

The effects of crude material conditions and lack of knowledge were compounded, in the words of the great reformer Louis-René Villermé, by "the fatalism [and] ignorance of those who endured them." At mid-century, before the era of universal primary education, some 80 percent of those condemned in the assize courts of Brittany could neither read nor write; the province counted four of the ten departments in the country where this was true.[57] And the peninsula was continually placed among those areas of the country whose army recruits were rejected for being too short and too sickly—physical stature serving as a good proxy for general health and health for the general level of hygiene.[58]

Both contemporaries and historians have wondered if this insouciance about salubriousness was linked to the deeply Catholic culture of the Breton peasantry and to the conviction that the body was "the instrument of sin [and] vessel of evil." A worldview that understood the concern for cleanliness as a temptation for "luxury and voluptuousness" would explain the derisory place hygiene occupied in Christian education and serve as testimony to an aversion to washing and nudity that survived well into the twentieth century and that helped the Bretons earn their reputation for good morals and bad sanitation.[59]

On the other hand, if peasants in the backwaters of the far northwest stood out for their deficiency of *propreté*, it was only a matter of degree. "Nothing," remembered Ramonde Anna Rey, "was more miserable than the condition of peasants in the Lozère."[60] And the same relentless inattention to hygiene, reflected in the misshapen bodies and poor health of so many inhabitants, characterized almost every corner of the French countryside. The imperial prefect of the Eure-et-Loir complained in 1806 about the "scrawny bodies, the skinny thighs, the spindly legs, and the feet deformed through the habitual use of big, heavy *sabots* [simple, wooden shoes]" that he saw in the poorer parts of his department. No wonder so many conscripts in the Beauce were rejected by the Grande Armée for being too short or for "faiblesse de constitution."[61]

By the middle of the century, draft boards had long remarked on "the extraordinary filth in which countrymen wallowed," which they saw every year when a substantial portion of the nation's twenty-year-olds presented themselves for induction. Historian Eugen Weber called the draft "a sad tale of rural ills: deafness and sore eyes, tapeworm and hernia, goiter and scrofula, stuntedness, twisted limbs, weakness of constitution, and 'diverse maladies.'" In Rozier, a rural commune not far from Clermont-Ferrand, near the end of the Napoleonic Wars, the army rejected fully 57 percent of recruits for a "lack of height" or other physical deformities. In particular, it commented on the "lack of care for their bodies that accounted for the early mortality and revealed the fragile health" of these young men. "These conscripts," the army explained, "are often weak, with delicate constitutions and some grave disability"; that is, completely unsuited to the military profession.[62]

Likewise, it was not only in Brittany that parents killed their infants with inappropriate diets. In the Nivernais, wrote Heulhard d'Arcy, one has only to see "the horrible, thick concoctions, yellow and fibrous, to be struck dumb." It is enough, he wrote,

> to have tasted them to understand the revolt of young stomachs against the milk, corrupted by these things; and to the disgust inspired by their appearance must be added the fermentation, during the summer and even the winter, of milk left out in a warm and densely occupied room.[63]

Of course, parents could only poison children who survived their first meal, and plenty of them did not. All across the country, infected bottles and indigestible food killed French babies in huge numbers: 100,000 every year, estimated Dr. E. Boell. Infant mortality reached 50 percent among babies raised on *biberons* (baby bottles), he added, whereas the rate for breastfed infants was only 10 percent.[64] We may question the precision of Boell's numbers, while accepting that tainted milk left a significant mark on infant mortality rates. These rates reached 24 percent in the Beauce countryside at mid-century, and only a little less for children between one and four years old.[65]

On the other end of childbirth, becoming a mother remained a dangerous business. By the mid-nineteenth century, writes ethnographer Maurice Robert, women in the

Limousin no longer had their babies standing up, as in the old days. But the death of mothers from puerperal infection remained common, since no one involved in delivering the new baby washed her hands (or the baby), at least, not very often or very well.[66] "The dirtier the babies, the healthier they are," it was said in the Limousin. And the same was apparently true in the Nivernais, where it was considered a dangerous error to change infants' swaddling clothes at night—leaving them, in the words of Heulhard d'Arcy, to steep (*macérer*) for eight or ten hours in their urine and feces. The mothers and nurses, with "a veritable horror of water [and] using neither water nor sponge," would then wipe the baby off in the morning with a bit of spittle on an unsoiled corner of the swaddling cloth.

Filth, thought Heulhard, was only one form of neglect, and he recalled with horror a scene reminiscent of Breton infants gnawed by pigs: a hysterical mother who arrived at the local clinic in 1828 with her baby who had been left alone for the day with the domestic animals and had the fingers eaten off both hands by the cat.[67] Add to these the various sins of *commission*, such as the practice of head-swaddling, condemned by Dr. J.-P. Des Vaulx as "a true barbarity, [this practice of] squeezing the heads of these poor little children with bands in order to give them a certain shape [and] one of the main causes of epilepsy and insanity, which were, after all, questions of life and death."[68]

A Philosophy of Hygiene

Heulhard, like Maréschal and other frustrated crusaders for hygiene, attributed the primitive practices he found in the countryside to a combination of ignorance, custom, and superstition, reinforced by religion—a convergence of factors reflected in folk wisdom and local proverbs. In fact, a brief survey of these casual elements of "mentalité" in the countryside, although it does not establish the precise means of exchange among culture, circumstance, and practice, can elucidate the way that peasants commonly thought about matters that were, after all, questions of life and death.

Peasant culture was rich in homespun aphorisms, providing a predigested understanding that casts a fascinating light on the rural thinking about sickness, sanitation, and the prudent disposition of scarce resources. There existed, in effect, a genealogy of dirt. Rules on washing often had some connection to the religious calendar. In the Nivernais, for example, it was deemed bad luck to wash children's clothes on August 15 (the Assumption of Mary) or at the end of Holy Week, or to change bed sheets in May, a month devoted to the adoration of the Madonna. "To cut your nails on Sunday," warned one Breton saying, "is to give blessed bread to the Devil"; likewise, in the Guyenne, where "To cut your nails on Friday brings Evil." Other superstitions had nothing to do with saints' days and other religious moments, like the popular belief in the Forez that cutting hair under a new moon makes it longer whereas cutting it under a full moon makes it thicker, or the proscription against clipping the fingernails of children under age seven, "to avoid their becoming thieves."[69]

Other proverbs were more practical and tightly prescriptive.[70] Insofar as they addressed issues of hygiene, they sometimes celebrated dirt and other times pointed to its dangers. "Clean body, clean soul," went one piece of customary advice. In Gascony it was said that "a clean face is always pleasing," and in the Anjou that "to wash your hands makes for good health." Some proverbs hedged: "Wash your hands often, your feet rarely, and your head never." Still others warned peasants about the cost of too much cleanliness: "Neither cheese nor soap ever make a house's fortune," cautioned one. "Filthy hair is healthy hair," observed another. Several maxims extolled the value of parasites: "There is neither man nor woman without vermin," peasants told one another, adding that "He who loses lice gets fleas" and that "lice protect health."[71]

Clothes, like bodies, were washed according to the guidelines provided by these ancient proverbs—at least insofar as proverbs organized real life. Some washdays were luckier than others, and some were fraught with hazard, the schedule of prohibitions once again following the religious calendar in some cases. In the most pious regions, Good Friday was particularly taboo—a malediction extended in Brittany to every Friday: "Whoever boils the laundry on Friday, cooks the blood of our Savior." Elsewhere it was said that to do the laundry on those days dedicated to the Holy Virgin would torment souls in Purgatory, or that clothes washed on Saint-Sylvester's Day (New Year's Eve) would be gnawed by rats. Exchanging religious injunctions for mere magic, peasants in the Vosges believed that washing clothes in the house of a pregnant woman could kill the baby—hence the advice to keep the laundry vat as far as possible from the mother.[72]

All in all, the counsel that country folk gave themselves in the form of proverbs and other bits of folk wisdom did not depart very far from everyday practice and the possibilities of life on the land. Where dirt and sweat were the companions of hard work, where water was cold and inconvenient, homes unheated, and linen sparse, standards of personal hygiene naturally remained lax. These hard realities persisted, largely resistant to the instruction of reformers. The more optimistic among nineteenth-century disciples of hygiene, like Dr. Monin, believed that cleanliness was "instinctive," and that men had always seen it as the "keystone of good health," since dirt was "one of the great agents of death."[73] Indeed, the Third Republic was to adopt this optimism as social policy, using its schools and its army to stimulate and instruct this "instinct" for hygiene. For the moment, however, across the French countryside at mid-century, prescriptions for cleaner bodies and homes typically went unfilled. Dirt, discomfort, and disease remained the familiar partners of country life.

Notes

1 Jacques Léonard, *Archives du corps. La santé au XIXe siècle* (Rennes: Ouest France, 1986), 9.
2 Georges Vigarello, *Concepts of Cleanliness: Changing Attitudes in France since the Middle Ages* (Cambridge: Cambridge University Press, 1988), 56–7.
3 On the state of hygiene in the Middle Ages, see Louis-Narcisse Girard, *Le nettoiement de Paris. Conférence faite aux ingénieurs des travaux publics de la Ville de Paris, le 6 janvier 1923* (Paris: Librairie de l'Enseignement Technique, 1923), 7–11; Ernest

Monin, *La propreté de l'individu et la maison* (Paris: Au Bureau de la Société Française d'Hygiène, 1886), 13; Donald Reid, *Paris Sewers and Sewermen: Realities and Representations* (Cambridge, MA: Harvard University Press, 1991), 11; and Ned Rival, *Histoire anécdotique du lavage et des soins corporels* (Paris: Jacques Grancher, 1986), 34.

4 Witold Rybczynski, *Home: A Short History of an Idea* (New York: Viking, 1986), 37.

5 The Voltaire quote, from *Les embellissements de Paris* is cited in Colin Jones, *Paris: Biography of a City* (New York: Viking, 2004), 208; the Rousseau citation comes from David P. Jordan, *Transforming Paris: The Life and Labors of Baron Haussmann* (Chicago: University of Chicago Press, 1995), 13.

6 Quoted in Elsi Canfora-Argandona and Roger-Henri Guerrand, *La répartition de la population: les conditions de logement des classes ouvrières à Paris au XIXe siècle* (Paris: Centre de Sociologie Urbaine, 1976), 11.

7 Constance Classen, David Howes, and Anthony Synott, *Aroma: The Cultural History of Smell* (London and New York: Routledge, 1994), 56, citing the quotation in Alain Corbin, *The Foul and the Fragrant: Odor and the French Social Imagination* (Cambridge, MA: Harvard University Press, 1986), 34.

8 Louis-Sebastien Mercier, *Tableau de la vie parisienne en 1789*, vol. XI, cited in Dr. Augustin Cabanès, *Moeurs intimes du passé. Premier volume* (Paris: Albin Michel, 1908), 257–8.

9 These citations come from Mark S. R. Jenner, "Follow Your Nose? Smell, Smelling and their Histories," *American Historical Review* 116, no. 2 (April 2011): 338–40; also see Susan B. Miller, *Disgust: The Gatekeeper Emotion* (Hillsdale and London: The Analytic Press, 2004), 2 and 28.

10 Daniel Roche, *A History of Everyday Things: The Birth of Consumption in France, 1600–1800* (Cambridge: Cambridge University Press, 2000), 157.

11 Even rich cities like Venice suffered from the same lack of usable water. In normal times supply did not meet demand, and if there was no rain for a couple of weeks, wrote Braudel, the cisterns that fed the city went dry. If there was too much rain, they were tainted with salt water. This was also true "in all the towns of Holland": Fernand Braudel, *Civilization and Capitalism, 15th–18th Century, vol. 2: The Structures of Everyday Life: The Limits of the Possible* (New York: Harper & Row, 1982), 228–30.

12 Cited in Rybczynski, *Home*, 41–2. Also see Lawrence Wright, *Clean and Decent: The Fascinating History of the Bathroom and the Water Closet and of Sundry Habits, Fashions & Accessories of the Toilet principally in Great Britain, France, & America* (New York: Viking, 1960), 100.

13 Rival, *Histoire anécdotique*, 120–1.

14 Cabanès, *Moeurs intimes*, ix.

15 Norbert Elias, *The History of Manners. The Civilizing Process*, vol. I (New York: Pantheon, 1978).

16 Arnould, *Nouveaux éléments d'hygiène* (Paris: J.-B. Ballière et fils), cited in Monin, *Propreté*, 13 and Peter Ward, *The Clean Body: A Modern History* (Montreal and Kingston: McGill-Queens University Press, 2019), 39.

17 Holly Brubach, "Soap Dish: All the Dirt on the History of Hygiene," *New York Times Magazine*, October 21, 2007, 644.

18 Wright, *Clean and Decent*, 24–6; also Rival, *Histoire anécdotique*, 36–7.

19 Séverine Parayre, *L'hygiène à l'école: Une alliance de la santé et de l'éducation, XVIIIe-XIXe siècles* (Saint-Étienne: Université de Saint-Étienne, 2011), 69 and Armand-

Pierre Jacquin, *De la santé, ouvrage utile à tout le monde* (Paris: G. Desprez, 1771), 289.

20 Geneviève Cerisier-Millet, *Un siècle de bains et lavoirs: Châtellerault, 1830–1930* (Châtellerault: Cerisier-Millet, 2003), 14.

21 On the evolution of bathing habits in the Old Regime, see Archives de Paris (hereafter cited as AP) série DM 5 0017, "Contrôle des bains douches," letter from the Syndicat général des propriétaires des bains to the Paris City council, March 25, 1914; also Julia Csergo, *Liberté, égalité, propreté: La morale de l'hygiène au XIXe siècle* (Paris: Albin Michel, 1988), 201; and Augustin Cabanès, *Moeurs intimes du passé. 2e série: La vie aux bains* (Paris: Albin Michel, 1954), 159.

22 Cited in Jacques Pinset and Yvonne Deslandres, *Histoire des soins de beauté* (Paris: Presses Universitaires de France, 1960), 64.

23 Braudel, *Civilization and Capitalism*, vol. 1, 286.

24 Cited in Rival, *Histoire anécdotique*, 120.

25 Csergo, *Liberté, égalité, propreté*, 76. Vigarello, *Concepts of Cleanliness*, 3–9, 15–16, and 95–8. For a similar analysis, see Sara F. Matthews Grieco, "The Body, Appearance, and Sexuality," in Natalie Z. Davis and Arlette Farge (eds.), *A History of Women in the West, Renaissance and Enlightenment Paradoxes*, vol. 3 (Cambridge: Belknap Press, 1993), 46–8.

26 Csergo, *Liberté, égalité, propreté*, 24. On the struggle to establish water as the carrier of disease, see Steven Johnson, *The Ghost Map: The Story of London's Most Terrifying Epidemic—and How It Changed Science, Cities, and the Modern World* (New York: Riverhead, 2007).

27 Séverine Parayre, "The Cleanliness of the Child between Social Standards and Care Concerns (16th-20th Centuries, France)," *Italian Journal of the History of Education* 9, no.3 (2017): 26.

28 Cited in Joan Dejean, *The Age of Comfort: When Paris Discovered Casual—and the Modern Home Began* (New York, Berlin, and London: Bloomsbury, 2009), 72. Sadly, Dejean's popular histories are under-researched and often contradicted by more knowledgeable sources; see, for example, her assertion that, "In seventeenth-century Paris, when one absolutely had to bathe ... ," Dejean, *The Essence of Style: How the French Invented High Fashion, Fine Food, Chic Cafés, Style, Sophistication, and Glamor* (New York: Free Press, 2005), 255.

29 Dejean, *Age of Comfort*, 53 and Braudel, *Civilization and Capitalism*, 310. For a popular history of toilets, see Susan Goldman Ruben, *Toilets, Toasters & Telephones: The How and Why of Everyday Objects* (New York: Scholastic, 1998), 3–6.

30 Fanny Beaupré and Roger-Henri Guerrand, *Le confident des dames. Le bidet du XVIIIe au XXe siècle. Histoire d'une intimité* (Paris: La Découverte, 1997), 82.

31 On the bidet, see Cabanès, *Moeurs intimes*, 229–31; Dejean, *Age of Comfort*, 4; Vigarello, *Concepts of Cleanliness*, 162; and Wright, *Clean and Decent*, 115.

32 Louis-François Benoiston de Chateauneuf, *Recherche sur la consummation de tout genre de la Ville de Paris en 1817 comparées à celles qu'elles étaient en 1789*, pt. II (Paris: Chez Marinet, 1821), 141–2.

33 Parayre, *L'hygiène à l'école*, 69.

34 See "Hygiene (Medicine)," in *ARTFL Encyclopédie Project*, Robery Morissey, general editor (http://artflsrv02.uchicago.edu/cgi-bin/philologic/getobject.pl?c.7.1408.encyclopedia0513.3933557), 8:335.

35 Vigarello, *Concepts of Cleanliness*, 104.

36 Mme. Élise Voiart, *Lettres sur la toilette des dames* (Paris: Audot, 1822), 62, 68, 129–31.
37 Ward, *The Clean Body*, 24.
38 Vigarello, *Concepts of Cleanliness*, 121–2.
39 See, for example, Daniel Roche, *The People of Paris: An Essay in Popular Culture in the Eighteenth Century* (Berkeley: University of California Press, 1987), chapter 6: "Popular Dress," 160–94.
40 Cabanès, *Moeurs intimes*, x.
41 On the water situation in eighteenth-century Paris, see Rival, *Histoire anécdotique*, 79–97 and Jean-Pierre Goubert, *La conquête de l'eau: l'avènement de la santé à l'âge industriel* (Paris: R. Laffont,1987), 51.
42 Pierre Chauvet, *Essai sur la propreté de Paris, par un citoyen français* (Paris: Imprimerie de Cordier, 1797), quotations on 5–8, 14–15, 17–18fn, and 22.
43 Ronald Hubscher, "L'identité de la terre," in Yves Lequin (dir.), *Histoire des Français, XIXe-XXe siècles—la société. Livre III: Les villes et l'industrie: l'émergence d'une autre France* (Paris: Armand Colin, 1983), 18–19.
44 Pierre Goubert, *The French Peasantry in the Seventeenth Century* (Cambridge: Cambridge University Press, 1986), 47–8.
45 Maréschal's work is cited in Henri Blanc, "L'hygiène infantile en Basse-Bretagne au commencement du XIXe siècle" (thèse pour le doctorat en medicine, Faculté de Médicine de Paris, 1937), subsequent citations from 23, 29, 33, 38, 41, and 43.
46 Martin Nadaud, "Memoirs of a Former Mason's Assistant," in Mark Traugott (ed.), *The French Worker: Autobiographies from the Early Industrial Era* (Berkeley: University of California Press, 1993), 184.
47 Jacqueline Tardivon, *Usages et coutumes en Brenne* (Paris: Royer, 1991), 83; also see Pierre Pageot, *La santé des Limousins et des Périgourdins au XIXe siècle: malades, maladies, soignants* (Paris: Harmattan, 2011), 63; and Maurice Robert, *Mémoire et identité: traverses éthnohistoriques en Limousin* (Limoges: Maison Limousine des Sciences de l'Homme, 1991), 255.
48 Tina Jolas, Marie-Claude Pingaud, Yvonne Verdier, and Françoise Zonabend, *Une champagne voisine: Minot, un village bourguignon* (Paris: Éd. de la Maison des sciences de l'homme, 1990), 284; also Georges Augustins and Rolande Bonnain, "Maisons, mode de vie, société," in Isaac Chiva and Joseph Goy, *Les baronies des Pyrénées: Anthropologie et histoire, permanences et changements*, tome I (Paris: École des hautes études en sciences sociales, 1981), 45. For the situation in nineteenth-century Languedoc, see Daniel Fabre and Jacques Lacrois, *La vie quotidienne des paysans du Languedoc au XIXe siècle* (Paris: Hachette, 1973), 94.
49 Gustave Tarlé, "À propos de l'hygiène du paysan en Bretagne" (thèse présentée et publiquement soutenue à la Faculté de Médecine de Montpellier, 1911), 72.
50 Louis Dujardin, "Basse-Bretagne et bas-bretons: étude d'hygiène" (thèse pour obtenir le grade de docteur en médecine, Université de Montpellier, 1912), 56, 60.
51 Marie-France Morel, review of Catherine Rollet-Échalier, *La politique à l'égard de la petite enfance sous la IIIe République* and of Alain Norvez, *De la naissance à l'école: Santé, modes de garde et préscolarité dans la France contemporaine*, in *Population Studies* 47, no. 2 (July 1993): 373.
52 Blanc, "L'hygiène infantile," 55–6.
53 François-Xavier Merrien, *La bataille des eaux: l'hygiène à Rennes au XIXe siècle* (Rennes: Presses Universitaires de Rennes, 1994), citing a Dr Redon, 65. Also Jacques de Cambry, *Voyage dans le Finistère ou État de ce département en 1794 et 1795*

(Rennes: Presses Universitaires de Rennes, 1986 [1795 original]), 116; Hugo quoted in Léonard, *Archives du corps*, 117.
54 Quoted in David S. Barnes, *The Great Stink of Paris and the Nineteenth-Century Struggle Against Filth and Germs* (Baltimore: Johns Hopkins University Press, 2006), 88.
55 Léonard, *Archives du corps*, quoting de Cambry, then his own words, 116.
56 Jules Renard, *Le Journal de Jules Renard* (Paris: Lafont, 1990), entry for August 1, 1903.
57 Henri Baudrillart, *Les populations agricoles de la France. 1ère série: Normandie et Bretagne, passé et présent* (Paris: Librairie Guillaumin, 1885), 432.
58 Georges Morache, médecin-majeur de première classe, *Traité d'hygiène militaire* (Paris: Librairie J.-B. Ballière et fils, 1874), 96–7. On the matter of the height of army recruits generally, see Hector Bertrand, *Études statistiques sur le recrutement dans le départment de l'Indre de 1838 à 1864* (no publisher, 1865); Dr. Devor, "Essai statistique médicale sur les principals causes d'exemptions du service militaire et recherches dans la fréquence et leur distribution géographique en France" (thèse, Faculté de Médecine, Université de Paris, 1885); Antoine-Hudet d'Hargenvilliers, *Recherches et considérations sur la formation et le recrutement de l'armée en France* (Paris: Didot, 1817); and Louis-René Villermé, *Mémoire sur la taille de l'homme en France* (Paris: Gabon, 1829), 551.
59 The first quote is from Pierre Levêque, "Avant-Propos," in *Éducation et hygiène du corps à travers l'histoire. Actes du colloque de l'Association interuniversitaire de l'Est (26–27 septembre 1989)* (Dijon: Éditions Universitaires de Dijon, 1991), i. The second comes from Csergo, *Liberté, égalité, propreté*, 32.
60 Raymonde Anna Rey, *Augustine Rouvière, Cévenole* (Paris: Laffont, 1989), 65.
61 Jean-Claude Farcy, *Les paysans beaucerons au XIXe siècle* (Chartres: Société archéologique d'Eure-et-Loir, 1989), 360–1.
62 On the physical condition of recruits to the French army, see, for example, Gérard Berber, *Le pays de Saint-Bonnet-le-Chateau (Haut-Forez) de 1775 à 1975: flux et reflux d'une société* (Saint-Étienne: Presses de l'Université de Saint-Étienne, 1985), 395; Jean-Christian-Marc Boudin, *Études ethnologiques sur la taille et le poids de l'homme chez divers peuples et sur l'accroissement de la taille et de l'aptitude militaire en France: deuxième mémoire* (Paris: V. Rozier, 1863), 1–3; Paul Broca, *Mémoires d'anthropologie* (Paris: C. Reinwald, 1871), 17; Théodore Garnier-Léteurrie, *De l'enseignement de l'hygiène dans les corps de troupe: Pour compléter l'instruction réglementaire du soldat* (Paris: Rignoux, 1845), 25; Alphonse Laveran, *Traité d'hygiène militaire* (Paris: G. Masson, 1896), 2; and Eugen Weber, *Peasants into Frenchmen: The Modernization of Rural France, 1870–1914* (Stanford: Stanford University Press, 1976), 151.
63 M. Heulhard d'Arcy, *Lettre sur le rétablissement des tours et l'allaitement artificiel* (Paris: Delahaye, 1879), 43.
64 Dr. E. Boell [Officier d'Académie Chevalier du Mérite agricole], *L'hygiène du paysan: traité populaire d'hygiène rurale* (Angers: Imprimerie, Gaton Pare, 1896), 2.
65 Farcy, *Les paysans beaucerons*, 354.
66 Ignaz Semmelweis published his work on puerperal fever, recommending that doctors wash their hands in a chlorinated lime solution before leaving their corpses to deliver babies, only in 1847. Because it conflicted with contemporary medical orthodoxy, it was completely ignored for the next thirty years. See Kay Codell Carter and Barbara R. Carter, *Childbed Fever: A Scientific Biography of Ignaz Semmelweis* (New Brunswick: Transaction Publishers, 1994); Sherwin B. Nuland, *The Doctors' Plague: Germs, Childbed Fever, and the Strange Story of Ignaz Semmelweis* (New York: Norton,

2003); and Theodore G. Obenchain, *Genius Belabored: Childbed Fever and the Tragic Life of Ignaz Semmelweis* (Tuscaloosa: University of Alabama Press, 2016).
67 Heulhard d'Arcy, *Lettres*, 49.
68 Dr. Jean-Pierre Des Vaulx, *L'hygiène au village* (Lille et Paris: J. Lefort, 1873), 44.
69 Guy Thuillier, *Pour une histoire du quotidien au XIXe siècle en Nivernais* (Paris: Éditions de l'EHESS, 1977), 52, 132; Françoise Loux and Philippe Richard, *Sagesses du corps: La santé et la maladie dans les proverbs français* (Paris: G.-P. Masonneuve et Larose 1978), 124; also Robert Bouiller and Louis Challet, "Ethnographie," in Bruno-Jean Martin (ed.), *Forez: De la Madeleine au Pilat* (Paris: Christine Bonneton, 1987), 100–4. On objects that are good to think with, see Françoise Loux, *Pratiques et savoirs populaires: Le corps dans la société traditionnelle* (Paris: Berger-Levrault, 1979), 91.
70 All the following proverbs are taken from Loux and Richard, *Sagesses du corps*, 115–21. Where Loux includes the regional source of these proverbs, I have included that information.
71 Kathryn Ashenburg, *The Dirt on Clean: An Unsantized History* (New York: North Point Press, 2007), 194.
72 Rival, *Histoire anécdotique*, 69–71.
73 Monin, *Propreté*, 10.

2

Peasant Bodies, Peasant Homes

Country Grime

Théodore Chalmel knew the peasants well. Born in the village of Noyal-sous-Bazouges (Ille-et-Vilaine), not far from Saint-Malo, in 1867, he spent his entire career, from 1895 to 1918, teaching in the local school. Attached as he was to his native *pays*, however, he was unsparing in his description of the local hygiene: "Throughout the centuries," he wrote,

> No one paid attention to hygiene in the villages. The habits of personal cleanliness were unknown. Filth reigned everywhere [and] . . . a profound ignorance favored misery. . . . The manure pile sat at the front door, with the new constantly slung on top of the old. Instead of stones, the streets were paved with straw, reeds, ferns—spongy material that quickly turned into stinking cesspools. The church itself was a den of infection, full of the poorly buried bodies of ecclesiastics and other notables. The feet [of the worshippers] stirred up the dirt [while] the faithful breathed the mephitic dust, to which they added in their turn their own deadly germs . . . malnourished, exhausted by their crushing labors, their bodies offered fertile ground for these deadly seeds. After that, it's easy to understand the grip of dirtiness on individuals, homes, food, air, and water.[1]

At the age of fourteen in 1830, Martin Nadaud, the aspiring mason who went on to become a leading member of the Chamber of Deputies, brought that dirtiness with him, walking to Paris with his father from his native Creuse. When the two men arrived in the capital weeks later, having apparently not washed along the entire journey, they immediately headed to the Seine in front of the Hôtel de Ville, a popular spot for cleaning up "the vermin that were devouring [us]" and that he had probably acquired at one of the inns along the way: "Not beds," he wrote of the furnishings in these way-stations, but "grain husks and straw that had been broken up by previous use and that was naturally full of vermin. When you opened the sheets, you saw they were black as soot and bore, in addition, various signs of uncleanliness." The other "guests" advised father and son not to undress for bed but assured them that, "You'll even find that exhaustion makes your sleep pleasant and deep even though you're being roused by fleas and bedbugs."[2]

But peasants did not need to cross the country to get dirty; dirt was an ineradicable part of life on the land. "The negligence of the peasant for his body is well known," wrote the novelist and playwright Gustave Drouineau, "and everyone who has lived in the country is unanimous on this point."[3] These "muddy asses," as Munaret, the country doctor, called them, washed only when they *fell* into water.[4] "We wash our dogs and our horses from head to toe," complained nineteenth-century archaeologist Jacques Boucher de Perthes, "but [never] our children and ourselves." It is true that the prospect of Sunday, or some other holiday, might prompt a quick rinse in the *cuvette* (a shallow wash basin) and a change of clothes, but this habit looked to appearance, not to cleanliness.[5] And it did not apply to the rest of the week. In the countryside, wrote one teacher in the Morvan, the peasant "washes his face a little when he gets shaved, but the rest of his body hasn't felt a drop of water since he was born."[6]

Nineteenth-century physician, Dr. Ernest Monin, likewise did not hide his scorn for the locals. "Covered in a thick and irremovable grime," he wrote:

> [the peasant] bathes only when it rains. . . . Filthy in his linen and his clothes, he offers in his enduring dirtiness, the most favorable terrain for parasites: larvae, flies, fleas, ringworm, scabies, etc.—all attach themselves early to children less cared for than pigs, and whose foulness stands hereditary and respected.[7]

"Many peasants never washed at all, even after the labors of a summer's day," writes historian Gillian Tindall, in *Célestine*, her study of a nineteenth-century village. "A good sweat was held to be cleansing in itself." This was not a simple consequence of poverty or lack of opportunity. Even those villagers who had servants to fetch their water "did not indulge in much cleanliness beyond cosmetic attention to face, neck, and hands."[8] In what Dr. Paul Chavigny later described as a national culture of dirt, there was "an almost total absence of hygiene."[9] Grime built up on peasants' bodies, and sweat soaked their clothes, "agglutinating and attaching itself to hair and beards," producing such a "nauseating, penetrating odor" that Dr. Munaret grumbled about having to "air out [his] office after only a fifteen-minute consultation" with one of them. Country people, he wrote, spent their lives covered in a "patina of filth."[10]

Munaret's contemptuous remarks suggest that he saw peasant practices, not simply as ignorance and cultural inertia, but as a moral failing—just as historian Alain Corbin in his study of mob violence and murder in the Dordogne in 1870 remarked on the particular dirtiness of the inhabitants in this part of the so-called Chestnut Belt, whose bodies, he wrote, quoting a contemporary observer, "were encrusted with 'something like scales.'" The implication was clear: incivility was of a piece, and the primitive peasant was as filthy as he was vicious.[11]

Dirt clung to the bodies of women and children as to their husbands and fathers. Alexandre Layet, professor of Social Medicine in Bordeaux, referred with palpable disgust to the "repugnant spectacle of young brats, spotty children with rheumy eyes, whose nostrils and eyelids are filled with the flies that buzz around them."[12] The hard life of the country aged women with a particular vengeance. "When you marry," the proverb told young men: "Look for a woman who's thin and clean; she'll get fat and dirty soon enough."[13]

Dirtier in some body parts than in others, however, since washing was not only impractical and morally suspect, it was invariably *partial*, which meant that some areas got washed more often, others less. At the top of peasant heads, stuffed under a cap or a bonnet and "ceaselessly accumulating sweaty, sebaceous secretions and dandruff," hair received less care than most other parts of the body. Any inclination peasants might have had to wash their hair was defeated by the bother of it and a fear of "cerebral overheating," which popular wisdom warned might cause fainting, or even a stroke.[14]

More critically, given widely shared principles of modesty, some parts never got washed. As Dr. Lucien Gretelly noted in an 1867 report to the labor minister, Victor Duruy, "Because of a ridiculously exaggerated sense of 'decency,' there are certain regions [of the body] that are considered shameful and with which people are careful to avoid."[15] Predictably, these taboos weighed more heavily on women, who were often warned that washing itself was an indolent and dangerously sensual practice.[16] Religious authorities discouraged the violation of any of the strict rules of modesty. Emile Erckmann, for example, told the story of a young boy, his trousers rolled up, swimming in a stream under the eye of his little girl friend when a passing priest saw them and "exploded with anger": "You're not ashamed to look at a naked boy in the water? A ten-year old girl, you're not ashamed? Both of you," he scolded, "are in a state of mortal sin!"[17]

As a practical matter, taboos around washing weighed most heavily of all on the old women who, in their "incomparable foolishness," were proud of being "virgins of any ablution in these places."[18] Julia Csergo tells the story of one old woman in the Aveyron, who fought off the doctors in the hospital shouting: "I am over sixty-eight, and never have I washed *there*!" Yet these inhibitions also applied to younger and married women. As one popular song of the nineteenth century testified, "Married women never wash their c . . . s."[19] Dr. Layet deplored the inevitable effects of this systematic neglect: "[pervasive] irritations of the vulva in women and herpes of the foreskin in men."[20]

Rural society was accordingly used to strong body odors. It is difficult to say exactly how strong was too strong, and what a doctor of public hygiene found intolerable might not have struck fellow peasants with the same wallop. Men and women used to working on the land, in almost constant and promiscuous contact with animals, often prized a piquant personal bouquet as a sign of vigor and virility in men and sexiness in women. The writer Charles-Augustin Saint-Beuve confided that, "Filth [on women] doesn't bother me, I love filth."[21]

A member of the Académie Française, and thus no rustic, Saint-Beuve was probably expressing a personal eccentricity, rather than reflecting the general feeling among "les Immortels." But things were different on the farm. Ethnologist Yvonne Verdier underlines the powerful erotic effect of "pungent and nauseating" odors like sweat and excrement. "The smellier the billy-goat," went the old peasant saying, "the more the nanny-goat loves him."[22] The reverse was also believed to be true. "The abuse of cleanliness," in men, moralist Joseph Virey wrote in his *Dictionnaire des sciences médicales* (1820), "leads to their *effemination*."[23]

Love it or not, most country people had to get used to filth, since they had very limited options for avoiding it. Material conditions and culture worked together to repress whatever urge peasants had to bathe. A "progressive" like Charles Collas, writing in 1850, might consider two baths per month an "indispensable" regime, but in the Limousin, according to one regional guidebook, they "hardly even knew the word." In the Morvan it was said that, if a doctor told a peasant he had to give his child a bath, his advice would be met with "stupefaction": "Excuse me, doctor," the mother would say, "but my child is too weak. He would *die* in the bath."[24]

Such fears aside, across the French countryside, the hovels that most country people called home had none of the *conforts*—water, privacy, tubs, heating—that would have made indoor bathing feasible. True, nature provided rural folks with opportunities the cities lacked, in the creeks and streams that ran through the countryside. The evidence suggests, however, that peasants took infrequent advantage of these resources. For one thing, it was possible only in the summer. For another, the discretion that kept peasants from washing their "private parts" militated even more strongly against taking off their clothes and plunging into the water. Besides, open-air bathing was full of dangers, both real and imagined. Even reformers who touted the virtues of a good summer's soaking urged caution in doing so, since the majority of peasants, who could not swim very well, risked drowning in a deep and fast-moving river or catching a fatal chill when they came out.

Lingering suspicions about the effect of water on the human body were reflected in the very strict rules experts prescribed for safe bathing. Dr. Des Vaulx dispensed the standard advice to his readers to avoid bathing "unless their stomachs were perfectly empty," normally 3 hours after eating, or when the body was moist; and to stay out of water containing "corrupt and putrefied matter"—a stagnant pond, for instance.[25] Ernestine Wirth, headmistress at a girls' *collège* in the Aisne department, prudently counseled her pupils not to bathe when the sun was too strong or to climb into a fierce current during a storm. And while Dr. Boell urged people to take baths—cold river baths in summer and *bains tièdes* in winter—he also warned them not to do so when they were sweaty or less than 4 hours after having eaten.[26]

A Clash of Cultures

When the apostles of hygiene arrived in the countryside, therefore, they discovered not just ignorance but a fundamentally different set of attitudes and practices. Peasants appreciated strong smells, equating sweat and stench with robustness and fertility: "the product of a disposition inclined to procreation," in the words of Dr. Théophile de Bordeu.[27] They believed in the curative power of dung and the prophylactic effect of a layer of dirt. They accepted that lice cleansed the blood of "bad humors" and that one should never wash an infant's head, since grime helped protect the fontanel (the soft, membranous gaps in its young skull).[28]

A serious disagreement about how to understand this native culture runs through the social science literature. Many reformers reacted with disgust and condescension, in the manner of economist Michel Augé-Laribé (1879–1954), who wrote that the nineteenth-century peasant simply had "not acquired the desire to be clean and therefore accustomed himself to being dirty."[29] Ethnographers and folklorists have tended to be more sympathetic to the exotic customs of nineteenth-century French rustics they describe. Thus, what Augé-Laribé, trained in law and dedicated to the modernization of French agriculture, considered mere poverty and ignorance, anthropologist Françoise Loux sees as a different sensibility. In her view, washing is not so much an instrumental practice as it is a ritual. That is to say, peasant dirtiness did not represent the imperfect application of an incontestable principle: personal hygiene. It existed rather as "a complex system where protection of the body and magical power are profoundly mixed together"—for example, the young girls in the Brenne region who washed themselves in rose water at sunrise on May Day, in order to guarantee fresh and clear skin throughout the year. They were not practicing hygiene in a way the twentieth century would recognize; nonetheless, their behavior was valid and coherent on its own terms. "We cannot speak of the absence of hygiene in traditional rural society," she wrote, "but only of different norms."[30] There is no reconciling these two perspectives: the one critical, the other comprehending. They would agree on one thing, however: that people living rough on the land had little incentive to spend precious energy and resources on washing their bodies, since there was little prospect of keeping them very clean for very long.

Dirty Clothes

"It is beneath the countrified clothes of a farmer and not beneath the gilt of a courtier that strength and vigor of body will be found," wrote Jean-Jacques Rousseau in his *Discourse on the Sciences and the Arts*.[31] Whatever the vigorous quality of farmers' bodies, Rousseau was right about the agrestic quality of their clothes. "A French peasant," wrote Jean-Baptiste Moheau in 1778,

> is badly dressed, and the rags which cover his nudity are poor protection against the harshness of the seasons; however, it appears that his state, in respect of clothing, is less deplorable than in the past.... Coarse linen, the clothing of many peasants, does not protect them adequately [from the cold] ... but for some years ... a very much larger number of peasants have [begun] wearing woolen clothes.

Well into the nineteenth century, peasants even in the relatively prosperous regions of the Chalonnais and the Bresse were still wearing "coarse cloth dyed black, with the aid of oak bark."[32]

At the most intimate and immediate level, peasants dressed for work—and they worked almost all the time—in simple, durable, rough, and uncomfortable garments, produced at home or handed down from previous generations or the better-off classes. Clothes needed two essential qualities. First, they had to shield the body from the elements and "brusque changes in temperature." Second, they had to hold up forever against the rigors of a hard life. That is why "the fabrics and the shapes do not vary," as Théodore Chalmel explained, and a "piece of clothing lasts a lifetime."[33]

A typical man's outfit consisted of a jacket, worn over a vest, on top of a shirt, and fashioned of "rude" materials: trousers of hemp or canvas, shirts of wool or, less commonly, linen. "Coarse, but sturdy," was Pierre Lévêque's description of the standard outfit of agricultural workers in mid-century Burgundy.[34] Peasants favored wool, irritating as it must have been against the skin, for its insulating effect and its ability to draw off moisture without getting so wet that it threatened to bring on a chill. The future belonged to cotton, of course, but until the end of the nineteenth century that gentle fabric was reserved mostly for handkerchiefs, scarfs, and women's headdresses. Trousers were sometimes held up by suspenders, more often with a belt made of wool and wrapped around the torso several times, in order both "to hold the pants and protect the abdomen [and the kidneys] against the cold."

"Saturated in sweat" and covered in the local dirt, these garments were never washed, although they might be brushed off from time to time, and they were changed "as rarely as possible." Many of those who worked on the land had nothing to replace them; besides, what sense did it make to soil a second set of clothes? Only on Sunday, or some other occasion that did not involve labor were working people in the country inclined to put on their "better" clothes. Then again, while "Sunday" suits did not get dirty in the same way as work clothes, they were not much likelier to get washed. Shoes were a small luxury.[35]

Underwear in the modern sense simply did not exist—at least not out in the country and not in the middle of the nineteenth century. The first *caleçons* (men's underpants) arrived in the Limousin canton of Eymoutiers only in 1885, with returning army recruits.[36] Instead, peasant men wore leggings of fustian or wool. Like the rough blouses that covered the torso, these would absorb a certain amount of "the impurities excreted through the skin," but at the price of ceaseless chafing and itching. Jules Renard noted with disdain that these clothes produced women "who walked comfortably only when their thighs were rubbing together."[37] Wool socks that "made their own contribution to excessive and incommodious" sweatiness completed the daily ensemble of the average rural laborer.

Women wore skirts instead of trousers, of course, but their clothes were made out of the same materials: shirts and skirts of thick, rough cloth; aprons of even thicker, rougher fabric, wool stockings, and clogs.[38] Dr. Des Vaulx, writing in 1873, noted the "revolution" in clothing that was on its way, based on the expanding use in the countryside of softer fabrics like linen and cotton. In areas with a lot of out-migration habits changed faster, as seasonal workers returned home with clothes they had bought—or been given—in the city for themselves and their wives. However, most *paysannes* at mid-century would still have dressed like their mothers and grandmothers.

Two separate features of a countrywoman's wardrobe stand out. First, like their menfolk, peasant women did not wear proper underwear, but rather an "accumulation of skirts supporting the waist and forming a heavy and disgraceful bumper (*bourrelet*) at the base of the thorax." Without any sort of bloomers or other protection, both cold and heat easily penetrated the "lower regions," leading, doctors warned, to "infections and frequent menstrual problems."

If the *paysanne*'s legs were bare, however, her torso was doubly reinforced by a corset. Naturally, this did not resemble the whale-boned, waist-pinching corset of the urban bourgeoisie. It offered suppler support for a working woman's upper body, keeping her internal organs warm and in place while helping her breathing. The rural corset, like the rest of a countrywoman's ensemble, had nothing to do with coquetry and everything to do with the practicalities of toil.

Dirty Surroundings

Standards of cleanliness applied to skin and clothes were simply the most intimate part of the larger economy of hygiene that characterized life in the countryside, where dirty bodies lived in dirty houses set in dirty villages. Waves of reformers recoiled at hamlets "wrapped in suffocating stinks," with roads full of stagnant water, polluted by runoff from adjacent dung heaps (*fumiers*) and littered with the excreta of animals and even humans.[39] In the Breton commune of Saint-Père Marc-en-Poulet (Ille-et-Vilaine), for example, rain turned streets—"paved" with straw, reeds, and ferns—into "nauseating cesspools."[40] It would be easy to multiply such descriptions.

Manure is a ubiquitous and essential piece of the agricultural ecology, so there is no surprise in the general tolerance for it or the widespread belief in its benefits, even aside from its fertilizing qualities. "This filth," wrote Agricole Perdiguier, "this muck, so despised in cities, is a treasure to which we owe the most precious and beneficial things, and those most pleasant to the senses of smell and taste." "On the judgment day," it was said, "shit will be worth more than money."[41]

The safest and most productive *fumiers* would be found at a distance from people's homes, and in particular, from their water supply, and there would be some means to control the liquid runoff—the *purin*—that contained most of the nutrients in the manure and that most easily penetrated through the soil and into the ground water or flowed into the streets and ponds. Yet what hygienists found when they visited the peasantry was a depressing and dangerous casualness: dung heaps piled higgledy-piggledy in courtyards—or, even worse, right outside doors and below windows, where one might expect to see flowerbeds—filling peasants' houses with "disagreeable and harmful odors"[42] (Figure 2.1). Louis-René Villermé, the renowned economist and social reformer, was horrified to find in the "typical" Breton village of Saint-Sulpice-des-Landes, that every house kept a manure pile on its doorstep. But in this respect conditions in Brittany were hardly worse than anywhere else, and it is difficult to find a contemporary depiction of a French village that did not condemn the state of the *fumiers*.

As disagreeable as city-dwelling reformers found the smell of manure, they were more concerned by the pollution of the water supply, since this posed the greater threat to public health. Peasants were remarkably insouciant when it came to mingling their dung and their water. The village of Les Andelys (Eure), for instance, had three ponds where villagers washed their clothes and whose water reputedly made the best cider in the region: each one had a manure pile sitting beside it.[43] Even near the end of the century, Henri Baudrillart described Angevin villages with "stacks of *fumiers* [without pits to collect the *purin*] leaking on every side into the ponds where the cattle drank."[44]

Figure 2.1 *A Peasant Interior. The Opening; Martin and Jouan with two oxen, being fed fodder mixed with bran* (~1900). (Louis Pachedeuy). F. Bernède, photographer, Arjuzanx-Morcenx (Landes).

And not only the cattle. Even if peasants did not take their water directly out of fetid, polluted ponds and puddles, as their animals did, they sometimes dug wells next to dung heaps and stables, from which urine and *purin* seeped into their own drinking water.[45] The effect of dirty water on morbidity and mortality in the countryside was multiplied by what agronomist Max Le Couppay de la Forest called the peasants' "almost criminal" indifference to the quality of what they drank. Eugen Weber set the scene: "Sources befouled with worms and putrid matter, the absence of ducts and sewers, and the lack of clean water were a leitmotif of rural documentation—when observers thought to mention it, that is."[46]

The peasants did not seem to share the reformers' sense of urgency. Rather, they did the calculations. Remembering his boyhood home in the Touraine, Leopold Mabilleau spoke of one neighbor who had a dung pit in his courtyard that leached into his well, sickening his animals and even his family. Concerned, the peasant consulted an architect, who announced it would cost 3,000 francs to seal off the well from the pit. The peasant recoiled at the enormity of the expense. He resigned himself to losing an animal or two a year to bad water and to spending "a serious sum" to care for the members of his family who might get sick. But he did not fix the well.[47]

Consequently, whole populations consumed nothing but dirty water. Peasants used cisterns and reservoirs to try to collect whatever rainwater fell, without thereby being able to satisfy their own needs or those of their livestock. In the small village of Merilheu in Languedoc, recalled Pierre Manse, there was plenty of rain. But it quickly ran off the clay soil into the rivers and streams, leaving only shallow, stagnant ponds behind, and hot summers left peasants without reliable supplies of water for months. In the Nivernais, the *corvée d'eau*, the daily slog to fetch water, could force people to travel up to a kilometer, back and forth.⁴⁸ In those hard times, as in a scene out of a Marcel Pagnol novel, the peasants often loaded up their carts and took their barrels to be filled in the public fountain in the nearby town of Bagnères, where on Sunday the *curé* led a prayer for rain. What water they had was mostly saved for drinking and cooking; there was little left over for washing.⁴⁹

Dirty Homes

The houses that surrounded these dry puddles and leaky piles of manure did not provide much respite from the dirt. "Insalubrity reigns everywhere," wrote Roger Merlin, along with ignorance "of the most elementary rules of hygiene."⁵⁰ Sources describe a substantial range of peasant abodes, varying by region, local building materials, and the economic circumstances of the inhabitants. Jeanne Deneboude-Soulet remembered the house in the Aveyron where she was born, built in 1879, as "rather bourgeois." It had a main floor with two storage rooms, a dining area, and a kitchen opening on to a garden and laundry; on the second floor, five rooms and an attic above.⁵¹ But this must count as an exception. The quarters where most country people grew up remained cramped, dark, smoky, humid, and foul. "Every child I knew," remembered Eugène Kammerer, who spent his childhood on the Île de Ré, off the West Coast of France, near La Rochelle,

> lived in a house with cracked walls covered in soot, with holes so big the sparrows could come and go as they pleased. A cross in the wall covered in oil paper was wide enough to be able to look out on the duck who played in the muck or to smell the stink of the pond where rainwater mixed with the runoff from the dung heaps piled up in the streets.⁵²

Traveling the French countryside at the end of the Old Regime and comparing what he saw there to conditions in his native England, Arthur Young had written disparagingly of the low quality of the dwellings. Things were much the same a half-century later. Some corners of the Auvergne found peasants living in structures that "were not even shacks but mere sheds so steeped in misery that the inhabitants burned straw to warm themselves."⁵³ In the Jura and the Basses-Alpes, the hills were dotted with wood *cabanas* covered in grass, with only a small hole in the ceiling for the smoke to escape, like "eskimo huts." Poor chimneys—or no chimneys at all—remained a particular hazard in many peasant dwellings, helping to kill the youngest inhabitants and blind the older ones.

Without the means to cart heavy building materials across any great distance, peasants built their homes from local resources. In the Touraine some people lived in carved-out rocks—primitive in one respect, but more solid and drier than much of the rural housing stock. In the high villages of the Auzat, in the Ariège, the houses were all built of slate, from floor to roof.⁵⁴ The worst abodes were virtually prehistoric, like the circular huts of the Auvergne and the Velay. The best ones, as in the Ardennes, had thick stone walls and slate roofs. In the Pyrénées, thatched roofs were most common. Ironically, the most solid structures often proved to be the dirtiest, as they also tended to be the oldest. Before 1870 in the Limousin, one house in three was more than a century old.[55] Ethnologist Albert Goursaud compares the houses there to sheepfolds—dark and dank, revoltingly dirty—with the children, the dog, the goat, and the fowl "lying about pell-mell."[56]

A simple but reliable rule of thumb emerges from the many descriptions of nineteenth-century peasant housing: its quality deteriorated from east to west and from north to south; from the plains to the mountains, and from peasant proprietors to common laborers. "What a contrast," wrote historian and ethnologist Albert Babeau, "between the heavy brick houses and slate roofs of the Ardennes, somber but spotlessly clean, and the structures of the Midi, with their white stone walls and their flat, tile roofs." But virtually the whole of the Midi and the West lived "amid filth and stench."[57]

The real menace to hygiene and health, however, lay within these unprepossessing exteriors. Robert Louis Stevenson, traveling through the Cévennes in 1876, left this portrait of an *auberge* in the village of Bouchet-Saint-Nicolas: "a one-story cottage, with the kitchen attached to the stable, sparse, simple furniture, and a dirt floor. There was a single room for travelers, whose sole amenity are the beds. The family sleeps all together in the kitchen," and whoever wants to wash "is obliged to do so in public at the common table."[58]

With houses often erected on impermeable soil in low-lying areas, if not beside actual swamps, walls dripped with moisture, bathing the interiors in a "pernicious humidity." Stone walls and slate roofs provided a tighter barrier against the elements and a less welcome habitat for vermin than wood, daub, and thatch. But that only sealed in the humidity more effectively. Damp and cold in the winter, damp and hot in the summer, peasant homes were in desperate need of air and light. The reek of these "mausoleums" must have been suffocating—the air "acrid and fetid, combining the smell of smoke, of rancid butter, moldy bread, worm-eaten wood, dirty clothes, and sweat."[59]

An era that still believed in the miasmic origins of disease had a particular sensitivity to smell, and so virtually all of those who turned their attention to the conditions of peasant life fixed on the toxicity of the atmosphere in these dwellings as the most serious threat to the health of inhabitants.[60] While it was easy to tell peasants they needed to brighten and aerate their homes, however, a sizeable majority of these structures lacked the *ouvertures*—the windows and doors—that would make such relief feasible. "More or less everywhere," writes Jacques Léonard,

> the rural home invites the same reproach: doors and ceilings that are too low; windows that are narrow, often closed, and sometimes obscured by a board, a grill, or a sheet of cardboard or wax paper; incommodious rooms, filled with smoke from blocked chimneys or from *les mauvais résins*, bad candles, or some sort of cheap oil; the smells accumulated by souring milk, dirty dishes, straw pallets, and rags—the hygiene of living space as neglected as the hygiene of the bodies that lived there.[61]

The scarcity and tiny size of doors and windows was no construction necessity but a response to the tax the state levied on them. "Rich or poor," wrote economist

Alfred de Foville, "the peasant seeks to avoid paying the taxman."[62] And the effects of this perverse incentive made themselves felt everywhere, from the "ridiculously small" windows in heavy Breton farmhouses to dwellings in the Haute-Marne having only a single window composed of four tiny, dirty panes of glass. One study of the Charente at the turn of the nineteenth century found that 80 percent of houses had but one window and one door; 3 percent had no windows at all.[63] And at night or in the winter even these were tightly shut—which might not have been so bad, remarks Alain Corbin, "in view of the fetid odors that surrounded the habitation."[64]

An inquiry on the state of rural housing—from 1912, but the situation could hardly have been better a half-century earlier—in several regional prefectures produced some grim statistics. In the countryside surrounding Limoges, Nîmes, and Besançon, few houses had more than four *ouvertures*. Many had only two, and a substantial number had only one opening for light and air to enter. Around Laon, in the Aisne department northeast of Paris, things were only slightly better.[65] A similar survey published by the Société d'hygiène publique de Bordeaux (1881) calculated the extent of the problem and its cost in mortality. Across France, the average number of doors and windows per capita was 1.49. Fifty-three departments, almost all in agricultural regions, had a lower figure, thirty-two a higher one. The survey collated these figures with health statistics and found unsurprisingly that mortality and morbidity were highest where *ouvertures* were fewest. The two prominent reformers who cited this study, Henry Napias and Alexandre Layet, drew the obvious conclusions: the government should eliminate the tax; in the meantime, peasants should ignore the law.[66]

Sunlight shining through windows and doors, while it might have had some benign effect on the occupants of these lodgings, would have illuminated a gloomy interior scene. The typical peasant home consistent of one or two rooms: low, messy, crowded, and dirty. Layet offered this picture of a house in the Vosges, where,

> the whole family lives, eats, sleeps almost pell-mell, without distinction of age or sex, inside walls smeared by smoke and filled with animal secretions. The furniture, in harmony with everything around it, consists for a big family of one or two sleeping pallets stuck in some dark, airless corner or under the stairs: a buffet or an armoire; a couple of chairs or wooden benches. The rest of the place dominated by a cast-iron stove, red hot and ready for cooking. Dirty house-rags, hanging on cords, occupy the rest of the space between the ceiling and the floor.[67]

Small proprietors lived a bit better, with more space and more furniture. Agricultural laborers made do with less. Ragotte, the eponymous character in the Jules Renard novel, notes that at sixty years old she slept on a mattress for the first time; she had always had to make do with a thin feather quilt (*couette*).[68] Even slightly better homes offered little in the way of comfort or propriety. Inhabitants got by with a minimum of furniture: "no armoire for storing linen, no comfortable bed, [only] a table, a couple of benches, and a trunk" for most people; richer homes might add a sideboard on a dresser, a breadbox, and a stool for grandpa.[69] Without easy access to water, inhabitants used it "parsimoniously," rinsing off plates and other cooking utensils in a shallow basin, or perhaps a hollow scraped into a stone sink, in whatever passed for a kitchen, then pouring the dirty water out into a "marshy and malodorous" corner of a nearby field while saving the greasiest water for the pigs. The same shallow basin, with a pail of cold water nearby and a handy hole in the exterior wall for pouring out the dirty water, also served for simple ablutions after a day in the fields or at some other sweaty occupation.[70]

In the virtually waterless world of the peasant home, observed Eugène Bougeâtre, "one would search in vain for a toilet; there were none. Nighttime needs were satisfied in a chamber pot that was emptied in the morning onto the dung heap. During the day, men urinated against the nearest wall, while women relieved themselves in a corner of the yard. Otherwise, everyone simply used the stable or the shed."[71] In spite of the countryside's obvious familiarity with effluence and tolerance for strong smells, it made sense to keep the *fosse d'aisance*, the outhouse, at a polite distance from the living quarters. In fact, "outhouse" is something of a misnomer, in so far as it implies a permanent, even if jerry-built, structure. To the end of the century, according to Guy Thuillier, outhouses remained rare in the countryside. The sources suggest that most peasants had something more primitive, if they had anything at all. Albert Goursaud, the ethnologist, describes peasants who had neither outhouses nor chamber pots, but who had to go outside in the middle of the night, "barefoot and in nightshirt, whatever wind might be blowing," to answer nature's nocturnal call. In his tour of the pays d'Othe (Aube), Foville wrote of "certain kiosks summarily built outside the house, at the end of the garden," and the Fourastiés of wooden planks erected carelessly over a rudimentary wooden seat, hovering over a shallow hole. Many homes did not have even this. In lower Brittany, according to Gustave Tarlé, "fecal matter" was hardly ever buried and was usually scattered a bit here and there. In the Limousin it ended up in the spaces next to the house that served for piles of garbage and animal carcasses. In the Dombes, it was thrown to the swine and the cows. Other folks simply tossed it on the dung heap.[72]

Back inside the house, dirt began with the floor. Some of the better homes had flagstones, or cement, or wooden planks ideally set a few inches above the earth. In the great majority of rural dwellings, however, bare feet trod on bare earth. Families used to these conditions might not have found them vexing. Pierre-Jakez Hélias had rather pleasant memories of the mud floor of his Breton youth: "Of course," he wrote,

> it's cold when you sit on it with a bare behind, but it's so easy to keep in good shape, it's so easy to live with! No need to clean your *sabots* before coming in. The wet mud on your soles doesn't dirty anything at all. Either it blends in with the rest or, once it's dry, it is swept out with a branch of broom. You never feel uneasy about throwing bones on the floor or even scraps to the dog. One basin of water is enough to wash the whole thing down, and the mud floor feels all the better for it.[73]

This was not exactly what Tarlé found in the Ille-et-Vilaine, where he described uneven dirt floors, scarred by little ravines filled with dirty water—the disorder made worse by the fact that nineteenth-century farmhouses did not always distinguish between human space and animal space.[74] In winter especially, propriety was often sacrificed to the need to keep warm. Public health doctor Louis Dujardin wrote of Hélias's native province that a wall commonly separated homes from stables. But this is not the testimony from other sources, which describe "men, women, children, and quadrupeds" living in "deplorable promiscuity" under the same roof, with pigs grunting and cows ruminating behind a low partition, livestock tainting the atmosphere and filling the air with flies—not just in Brittany but across the country. In the Roussillon, according to Albert Babeau, the ethnologist, villagers not only piled manure outside their doors, but lived with their pigs. In the Périgord, they shared their houses with the goats and chickens. In the Auvergne, living space was divided in three: to the right, the stable; to the left, the barn; in the middle, connected directly to both, the peasant lodgings. In the Haute-Marne, remembered Joseph Cressot, pigs were not only *allowed* in the house but were considered "worthy" of the privilege.[75] In the Creuse, recollected Nadaud:

> People alike would come in through [the front door]. The animals would turn left, where a simple partition separated them from the room that served as both bedroom and kitchen to the family that slept pell-mell on wretched litters of straw. . . . But that was not its greatest drawback. The animals' fodder was brought into the loft above and spread out to dry on a floor of un-joined planks that separated it from the room in which we lived. As a result, hay seeds and bits of straw were constantly falling onto the table where we ate our meals.[76]

Moreover, as we have seen above in the case of voracious pigs, even where the henhouse, the rabbit warren, and the pigsty did not open immediately onto the peasants' living quarters, the animals often came and went with casual ease.[77] Albin Mazon, the journalist-turned-historian who wrote his celebrated "Voyages" series under the pen name Docteur Francus, left us the most pithy description of relations between the species in the isolated farmhouses of the Haute-Loire: "They consist of only one room," he wrote "[where] men and beasts live fraternally; the former eat the latter"[78] (Figure 2.2).

The proximity of livestock was not the only troubling promiscuity in the typical peasant home. Sleeping conditions in these crowded and undifferentiated spaces excited quite as much concern among reformers as the mixing of peasant and livestock. This centered, first of all, on the sheer lack of hygiene in the habits and material culture of sleep. Gilbert Garrier writes of young shepherds in the 1870s sleeping on the straw alongside their lambs. Joseph Cressot's father Philippe had to sleep on a straw pallet, waking up in the morning only to find that the sheep had eaten his "bed." In the Brie, Pierre-Edouard Vialhe's laborers slept on the floor of the damp old stable, each one "wallowing in his own muck."[79] One observer described with some disgust what he saw in the home of a Limousin family:

> in the same space four beds for eleven people. And what beds! Above one there sat a roost for the chickens, above another a jumbled mess of assorted objects, a rabbit hutch under the third; in the corner a pit to feed the dog and allow the chickens and ducks to splash around.[80]

It is difficult to imagine what counted for comfort and rest in these dank, verminous hovels, where the day's smoke filled the lungs at night. No wonder public-health

Figure 2.2 *Farm Courtyard with Dung Heap.* Tigny-Noyelle, Pas-de-Calais, France (1916). Médiathèque de l'architecture et du patrimoine.

authorities considered them the perfect breeding grounds for tuberculosis. The distance between houses meant the disease was unlikely to spread from family to family, as it did in the crowded towns, but within the country *foyer* maladies of the lungs could not have found a more propitious setting.

A typical arrangement would have one big bed for the parents, whose privacy, such as it was, came from the heavy curtains that hung around it. The Bretons were particularly renowned for their "lits clos"—virtually rooms of their own—widely condemned for providing a welcoming home to the tiny creatures that proliferated inside most homes and for preventing the penetration of air and light that might have had some sanitizing effect. "The individuals who slept there," wrote Maréschal,

> often several together, rarely change their linen and never bathe, even after they climb out of some muddy ditch where they've been working—or into which they've fallen when drunk. To complete this picture, let us add that the duvet and the pillows are made from rolled up oats, the sheets, always too short, from the coarsest fabric, and the cover from raw wool.[81]

"Every bed has fleas," noted the Corsican proverb, and this could not have been far from the literal truth.[82]

Scattered around the main bed on the floor would be three or four—up to ten, according to one study of the Morvan—miserable *paillasses*; that is, pallets with a thin mattress on top. The parish archives of Le Vigen in the Limousin described one house with four beds for eleven people. The mattresses themselves, universally described as appalling and uncomfortable, were ordinarily handmade affairs, with some rough sacking stuffed with various materials—feathers, straw, hay, distaff, horsehair—replenished every few months and rotting in the meantime. Babeau reckoned that feather mattresses dominated in the northeast, while Bretons slept on hemp or horsehair sacks stuffed with tillage, for the poorest among them.[83] The older generation, if any survived, would find themselves exiled to a *paillasse* in some corner or alcove, which, if it were near the fireplace, would at least be warm.

On top of the beds, the bedding. More prosperous peasant households might contain an armoire filled with extra sheets and blankets. Indeed, extra linen was often the mark and pride of a well-to-do peasant family. Poorer families, the majority in most regions, slept on sheets and under blankets that were rarely changed and seldom washed more than once or twice a year. Consider that bedding was in daily contact with bodies and clothes that themselves were generally caked in dirt and sweat, and it is easy to imagine the deplorable state of hygiene in which country folk took their rest from hard and unceasing labor. Most people slept in the same clothes they had worn during the day. Some of those at the bottom of the social ladder, agricultural laborers, commonly went to bed "tout habillés"—that is, wearing all their clothes—on straw in the barn. But even the majority, who spent their nights in some sort of bed, "knew nothing" about nightshirts and "were hardly less dressed at night than during the day."[84]

Neither was dirt accumulated during the day mitigated by any sort of bedtime toilette. In a domestic world where water was scarce and *objets de toilette* "perfectly unknown," a splash of cold water on hands and face was the standard end-of-day lavation. Household inventories for the Ille-et-Vilaine in the first part of the century reveal the lack of virtually any material culture of hygiene: Jacques de Cambry, the Breton writer and expert in Celtic France remarked on the absence of virtually any objects in these one-room hovels that would serve the cause of personal hygiene.[85]

Public-health reformers had begun to preach the virtues of oral hygiene in the countryside, but these efforts usually knocked up against the peasants' "utter indifference" to any such routine and the total deficiency of brushes and dentifrice. The consequences of this inattention to clean teeth did not escape the notice of contemporaries. Dr. Jean-Baptiste Fonssagrives, for example, deplored the "greenish fungal vegetation" that grew around peasant teeth. Army doctor Théodore Garnier-Léteurrie described the scurvy, gangrene, and cancer he found in the mouths of many recruits. The tooth-pullers who were a fixture of country fairs, and the folk wisdom surrounding bad teeth likewise spoke to the grim state of dental care in the countryside.[86]

Finally, as the agents of rural improvement peered in on sleeping families, they found more to worry about than bedbugs and tuberculosis. The lack of privacy in these crowded dwellings—which necessarily meant that when the parents had sex, everyone knew about it—and the need to share beds, which often led to young brothers and sisters sleeping side by side, posed an ongoing threat to innocence and morality. Capitaine Levainville assured his readers that, at least in the Morvan, despite the close cohabitation of whole families, "there does not seem to be any harm to morals." He added to this observation an anecdote cribbed from Albert Foville, who told a story about attending a wedding in a village far from any railroad station and found, to his surprise, that there were three beds in the *chambre nuptiale*—including one for the niece and the sister of the bride, another for the sick grandmother. "The individuals involved," Foville remarked, "seemed to find this completely natural," adding that these were utterly honest people, "of strict conscience and pure morals."[87] But not everyone was convinced. In the warm weather, some of the family might sleep outdoors. While this might spare the more delicate sensibilities, however, it exposed them to colds and other respiratory ailments that might kill them.[88]

The Beginning of the End of the Old Regime of Hygiene

What can we conclude from this snapshot of rural life? The look and the feel and the odor of peasant existence were rooted in old practices and cultural understandings of hygiene. Nineteenth-century French farmers did not, of course, experience the dirt and the stink as some sort of horrible anomaly, as we would, if we were suddenly deprived of clean clothes, indoor toilets, and a good supply of fresh water. Accommodations with the inevitable were built into the culture. Peasants lived with a different economy of the body; they were, in some sense, used to the smell and the itch—to the sheer discomfort of life. It is easy to guess that they did not enjoy having lice in their shirts and fleas in their beds, but also that they must have thought about it as they thought about capriciousness of the weather or the chances of early death or the endless days of hard labor: both unfortunate and unavoidable.

It did not seem unavoidable, however, to the missionaries of health and hygiene who set off to convert the peasantry to modern ideas and practices. Sometimes, they wrote books that aimed to break through the fatalism that stood in the way of progress. "Modify domestic habits," advised Hippolyte Meunier, "change practices regarding clothes and food, according to the seasons; show some responsibility for one's actions; never accept sickness as the work of Providence but seek to prevent it through proper conduct: this is the task for which women are best suited." Meunier set up her didactic drama as a series of dialogues among "the Doctor" and the peasant couple "Claude and Rosalie," and their friend "Jacques." In one exemplary episode, the doctor visits the couple, whose child is suffering convulsions. Rosalie worries that he will die. In the exchange that follows, the doctor tries to turn her from the path of "Ignorance, Tradition, and Christianity" onto that of modern science:

- Doctor: "You have good intentions. You love your son. But you treat him badly! Why don't you clean him up? Why do you allow him to be so filthy? Why not bathe him? The water costs nothing. There's a stream at the bottom of your garden."
- Rosalie: "But I never thought about putting a little baby in the water. That would kill him!"
- Doctor: "To put a new-born in the stream would be absurd and would kill the poor creature soon enough. But you need to wash him with great care every day, because cleanliness promotes health."

- *Rosalie:* "Oh, my. I don't dare. I am too afraid he'll catch cold. He needs to be kept warm, don't you think? I wrap him up tight, and it feels like I never have enough blankets!"
- *Doctor:* "Quite simply, it is in treating him this way that you make him sick. You child needs air, my dear. He needs water; the state of irritation in which you keep him is precisely what is causing the convulsions."
- *Rosalie:* "[But he's so well fed. I nurse him.]"
- *Doctor:* "Which is precisely why it would be a sin to let him die."
- *Rosalie:* "If the Holy Virgin accepts him into Heaven, I could not hope for better."
- *Doctor:* "You must do one more thing for him, which appears less difficult but is more useful. You have to use your <u>reason</u>! God gave you reason to guide you in your life, to help you find the best way. You need to use it, my dear, and understand what I'm telling you."
   - *[He then tells her about pores and why they need to be kept open so that the body can breathe.]*
- *Rosalie:* "Then it is so the air can penetrate under the skin that you want me to wash my son?" *[And she notes how much her own cow Nanette loves to be washed]*
- *Doctor:* "Is it not inhuman to wash our children less carefully than we wash our animals? They need washing just as much. You have seen, my dear Rosalie: it's an easy thing, and every attentive mother needs to give her child a* bain complet *every morning [using a sponge and a bit of lightly soapy water]."*
   - *[In response to Rosalie's view that maybe it's better just to leave the little ones alone]* "I beg you, my dear, not to give in to your doubts. I know it is more convenient to let the dirt build up on children, rather than to wash it off. But a woman like you, intelligent and kind, must listen to your reason and see that, if it is a good thing to wash the cow, it cannot be a bad thing to wash the children!"
   - "Little children are like flowers [the doctor concludes]: God has meant them to have water and sun. Thus, it is necessary that mothers, like gardeners know how to use these heavenly gifts. I hope, my dear, that you will no longer be afraid to give the little one a warm bath."

The doctor then explains to Rosalie and her husband Claude, who is renovating it, how to make the inside of their home cleaner and healthier. In the end, thanks to the doctor's counsel, Rosalie and Claude have charming, elegant home, full of light and air and even with bookshelves, where they keep the books they borrow from the commune's library, along with the occasional volume they buy for themselves. In short, it is an optimistic fairy tale of reform.[89]

* * *

While there is no denying the hard realities of agrarian life, it is worth wondering to what extent the picture of peasant ignorance and dirt drawn by so many reformers cited above was colored by the condescension, if not the outright contempt, of educated city people observing rough country people. Recall Maréschal's remarks about "the dirtiness and savage ignorance" of the Bretons or the insulting depictions left by doctors Chavigny and Munaret, among others. The peasants, if they could speak directly for themselves, would surely use different words to describe their circumstances.

All the same, and patronizing language aside, the images passed on by nineteenth-century hygienists seem broadly accurate, and even sympathetic observers describe the same dire conditions. Indeed, in those few cases when people who actually grew up on the land left us their memories of the experience, those memories convey the same impressions of the cold, dirt, and discomfort of everyday life on the land.

That said, if we insist too much on the common misery of rural life, as it came to the nineteenth century from the long and unhappy past, we risk missing the fact that the very presence of crusading doctors and amateur hygienists points to cracks in the wall of fatalism and inertia. In the short term, their efforts to "improve" the peasants seldom met with immediate success. As we shall see, however, despite their grumbles about the immovability of the peasantry, the peasantry was beginning to move.

Notes

1 Théodore Chalmel, *Une commune rurale à travers les siècles: Saint-Père-Marc-en-Poulet (Ille-et-Vilaine)* (Rennes: Imprimerie Brevetée Francis Simon, 1931), 231–2.
2 Martin Nadaud, "Chapter 4: Memoirs of a Former Mason's Assistant," in Mark Traugott (ed. and trans.), *The French Worker: Autobiographies from the Early Industrial Era* (Berkeley: University of California Press, 1993), 193–4.
3 Gustave Drouineau, "Hygiène rurale," in Jules Rochard et al., *Encyclopédie d'hygiène et de médecin publique*, tome IV (Paris: Veuve Babé et Cie., 1892), 667; also see Michel Augé-Laribé, *La révolution agricole* (Paris: Albin Michel, 1955), 181.
4 Jean-Marie-Placide Munaret, *Le médecin des villes et des campagnes* (Paris: Ballière, 1862), 78.
5 Jacques Boucher de Perthes, *Petit glossaire, traductions de quelques mots financiers, esquisses de moeurs administratives* (Paris: Treutter et Werth, 1835), 44; also see Monique Eleb and Anne Debarre, *L'invention de l'habitation moderne: Paris, 1880–1914: Architectures de la vie privée, suite* (Paris: Éditions Hazan et Archives d'Architecture Moderne, 1995), 247.
6 Jean Simon, *Statistique de la commune de Frétoy* (La Rochelle: Imprimerie Astoul, 1883), 180.
7 Dr. Ernst Monin, *La propreté de l'individu et de la maison* (Paris: Au Bureau de la Société, 1886), 32.
8 Gillian Tindall, *Célestine: Voices from a French Village* (London: Minerva, 1996), 96.
9 Dr. Paul M. V. Chavigny, *La psychologie de l'hygiène* (Paris: E. Flammarion, 1921), 81.
10 The phrase is Munaret's, cited in Monin, *Propreté*, 16; also Julia Csergo, "Propreté et enfance au XIXe siècle," in Didier Nourrisson, dir., *Éducation et santé, XIXe-XXe siècle* (Rennes: Editions ENSP, 2002), 43.
11 Georges Marbeck, *Cent documents autour du drame de Hautefaye* (Périgeux: Pierre Fanlac, 1983), 10, cited in Corbin, *The Village of Cannibals: Rage and Murder in France, 1870* (Cambridge, MA: Harvard University Press, 1990), 56.

12 Alexandre Layet, *Hygiène et maladies des paysans: Étude sur la vie materielle des campagnards en Europe* (Paris: G. Masson, 1882), 312.
13 Françoise Loux, *Pratiques et savoirs populaires: Le corps dans la société traditionnelle* (Paris: Berger-Levrault, 1979), 121.
14 Théodore Garnier-Léteurrie, *De l'enseignement de l'hygiène dans les corps de troupe. Pour compléter l'instruction réglementaire du soldat* (Paris: Rignoux, Imprimeur de la Faculté de Médecine, 1845), 25.
15 Dr. Lucien Gretelly, *De quelques progrès de l'hygiène à réaliser dans les pensionnats* (Macon: Protat Frères, 1897), 65.
16 See the comments of Julien-Joseph Virey, *Dictionnaire des sciences médicales* (Paris: C. L. F. Panckoucke, 1820), n.p.
17 Emile Erckmann-Chatrian, *Contes vosgiens. Annette et Jean-Claude. Le récit du Père Jérôme. Le trompette des hussards bleus. Le vieux tailleurs* (Paris: J. Hetzel, 1877), 28.
18 Eugen Weber, *Peasants into Frenchmen: The Modernization of Rural France, 1870–1914* (Stanford: Stanford University Press, 1976), 148. The previous quote comes from Dr. Gallipe, cited in Drouineau, "Hygiène rurale," 675.
19 Cited in Julia Csergo, *Liberté, égalité, propreté: La morale de l'hygiène au XIXe siècle* (Paris: Albin Michel, 1988), 242.
20 Layet, *Hygiène et maladies*, 311.
21 Cited in Edmond et Jules de Goncourt, *Journal des Goncourts. Deuxième volume, 1862–1865* (Paris: G. Charpentier, 1888), entry for February 14, 1863.
22 Yvonne Verdier, *Façons de dire, façons de faire* (Paris: Gallimard, 1979), 329; the second quote is from Françoise Loux, *Sagesses du corps* (Paris: G.P. Maisonneuve et Larose, 1978), 121.
23 Cited in Jacques Léonard, *Archives du corps. La santé au XIXe siècle* (Rennes: Ouest France, 1986), 115.
24 Charles Collas, *Le médecin des villes et des campagnes: répertoire de médecine pratique à l'usage de tout le monde* (Paris: Chez C. Collas, 1850), iv; and Haute-Vienne, *Limoges et le Limousin historique, administratif... Guide de l'étranger* (Limoges: Ardant frères, 1865), n.p.; also Anne-Marie Sohn, *Chrysalides: Femmes dans la vie privée (XIXe-XXe siècles)*, vol. 1 (Paris: Publications de la Sorbonne, 1996), 115.
25 Dr. Jean-Pierre Des Vaulx, *L'hygiène au village* (Lille et Paris: J. Lefort, 1873), 56.
26 Dr. E. Boell [Officier d'Académie Chevalier du Mérite agricole], *L'hygiène du paysan: traité populaire d'hygiène rurale* (Angers: Imprimerie, Gaton Pare, 1896), 151. Also see Mlle. Ernestine Wirth, *La future ménagère. Lectures et leçons sur l'économie domestique, la science du ménage, l'hygiène, les qualités et les connaissances nécessaires à une maîtresse de maison. À l'usage des écoles et des pensionnats de demoiselles* (Paris: Hachette, 1882), 391.
27 Théophile de Bordeu, *Oeuvres,* vol. 1 (Paris: Caille et Ravier, 1818), 959.
28 On the positive effect of dirt and vermin, see Augé-Laribé, *La révolution agricole*, 24; Loux, *Pratiques et savoirs populaires*, 91; François-Xavier Merrien, *La bataille des eaux: l'hygiène à Rennes au XIXe siècle* (Rennes: Presses Universitaires de Rennes, 1994), 72; and André Rauch, *Histoire de la santé* (Paris: Presses Universitaires de France), 71.
29 Augé-Laribé, *La révolution agricole*, 181.
30 Loux, *Pratiques et savoirs populaires*, 92, 129.
31 Jean-Jacques Rousseau, *The Social Contract and Discourses* (London: Penguin, 1968 [1761]), 132.
32 Jean-Baptiste Moheau, *Recherches et considérations sur la population de France* (Paris: Presses Universitaires de France, 1994 [1778]), 261–2; also see Pierre de Saint-Jacob,

Les paysans de la Bourgogne du Nord au dernier siècle de l'Ancien Régime (Paris: Société des Belles Lettres, 1960), 542.
33 On the peasant wardrobe, see Chalmel, *Une commune rurale*, 622–5; Des Vaulx, *L'hygiène au village*, 35–9; Drouineau, "Hygiène rurale," 677–84; Layet, *Hygiène et maladies*, 299–307; Ronald Hubscher, "L'identité de la terre," in Yves Lequin (ed.), *Histoire des Français XIXe–XXe siècles: la société* (Paris: Armand Colin, 1983), 23.
34 Pierre Lévêque, "Les salairés agricoles en Bourgogne au milieu du XIXe siècle," in Ronald Hubscher and Jean-Claude Farcy (eds.), *La moisson des autres: les salariés agricoles aux XIXe et XXe siècles* (Bar-le-Duc: Créaphis, 1996), 94.
35 Max Chaleil, *La mémoire du village* (Montpellier: Presses du Languedoc, 1989), 43.
36 Alain Corbin, *Archaïsme et modernité en Limousin au XIXe siècle, 1845–1880. La rigidité des structures économiques, sociales et mentales* (Paris: Éditions Marcel Rivière et Cie., 1975), 81.
37 Jules Renard, *Nos frères farouches: Ragotte* (Paris: Fayard, 1908), 16.
38 On the ubiquitous *sabots*, see Robert Bouiller et Louis Challet, "Ethnographie," in Bruno-Jean Martin (dir.), *Forez: De la Madeleine au Pilat* (Paris: Christine Bonneton, 1987), 120.
39 Georges Grau, "L'habitation isolée et des agglomerations agricoles," in Alliance d'hygiène Sociale, *L'hygiène sociale par l'enseignement et l'éducation: Congrès de Paris, 14–15 mai 1913* (Agen: Imprimerie Moderne, 1913), 191.
40 Chalmel, *Une commune rurale*, 231–2; also M. Théron de Montaugé, *L'agriculture et les classes rurales dans le pays toulousain depuis le milieu du dix-huitième siècle* (Paris: Librairie Agricole de la Maison Rustique, 1869), 453.
41 Agricole Perdiguier, "Memoirs of a Compagnon," in Traugott (ed. and trans.), *The French Worker*, 120–1.
42 Louis Fortoul, *Les veillées de la ferme: notions élémentaires d'agriculture et d'hygiène rurale* (Paris: Librairie Classique de Paul Dupont, 1868), 91.
43 Cited in David S. Barnes, *The Great Stink of Paris and the Nineteenth-Century Struggle Against Filth and Germs* (Baltimore: Johns Hopkins University Press, 2006), 204.
44 Henri Baudrillart, *Les populations agricoles de la France. 2e série: Maine, Anjou, Touraine, Poitou, Flandre, Artois, Picardie, Île-de-France passé et présent* (Paris: Librairie Guillaumin et Cie., 1888), 81, 204.
45 The sources speak unanimously on this point: see, for example, Boell, *L'hygiène du paysan*, 72; also Baudrillart, *Les populations agricoles*, 1ère série, 313; Max Couppey de la Forest, *Alimentation en eau potable dans les compagnes* (Paris: Imprimerie et Librairie A. Munier, 1904), 5; and Alfred de Foville, *Enquête sur les conditions de l'habitation. Les maisons-types, tome II, avec une étude historique de M. Jacques Flach* (Frionne: Gerard Monfort, 1980 [1894]), 200.
46 Eugène Bougeâtre and Marcel Lachiver, *La vie rurale dans le Mantois et le Vexin au XIXe siècle* (Meules: Éditions du Valhermeil, 1996 [1971]), 120; Forest, *Alimentation en eau potable*, 4; and Weber, *Peasants into Frenchmen*, 147.
47 Alliance d'hygiène sociale, *L'hygiène sociale*, 75–6.
48 Guy Thuillier, *Pour une histoire du quotidien au XIXe siècle en Nivernais* (Paris: Éditions de l'EHESS, 1977), 11–12.
49 Pierre Manse, *Merilheu de mon enfance* (Pau: Éditions Marrimpouey Jeune, 1988), 26; also see Bougeâtre and Lachiver, *La vie rurale dans le Mantois*, 119.
50 Roger Merlin, *La crise du logement et les habitations à bon marché* (Paris: Commission d'Action Sociale, n.d. [but probably 1913]), 24. "All, or almost all peasant houses, and especially in the central plateau and in Brittany, are low-lying, humid, airless, poorly

constructed, cold in winter and hot in summer": Dr. Louis Cruveilhier, "Le taudis dans les agglomerations rurales," in Alliance d'Hygiène Sociale, *L'hygiène sociale*, Congrès de Paris, 14-15 Mai 1913, "Nécessité de l'uniformisation des statistiques en matière de mortalité infantile," 51.

51 Jeanne Deneboude-Soulet, *Je suis née à Mur-de-Barrez (Aveyron) le 13 mars 1908 . . . Album de famille d'une enfant du Carladès* (La Téoulare [Hautes-Pyrénées]: Imprimerie Bihet, 1987), 21.
52 Eugène Kammerer, *Histoire de l'île de Ré, L'insula Rhea* (Marseille: Lafitte, 1984 facs.), 307.
53 André Gueslin, *Gens pauvres, pauvres gens dans la France du XIXe siècle* (Paris: Aubier, 1998), 61.
54 Max et Denise Dejean, *L'Ariège d'autrefois* (Le Coteau: Horvath, 1988), 102.
55 Maurice Robert, *Mémoire et identité: travers ethnohistoriques en Limousin* (Limoges: Maison Limousine des Sciences de l'Homme), 136.
56 Albert Goursaud, *La société rurale traditionnelle en Limousin. Ethnographie et folklore du Haut-Limousin et de la Basse-Marche*, tome I (Paris: G.-P. Maisonneuve & Larose, 1976), 70–1.
57 Albert Babeau, *La vie rurale dans l'ancienne France* (Paris: Didier et Cie., 1883), 3 and Augé-Laribé, *La révolution agricole*, 182.
58 Robert Louis Stevenson, *Journal de Route en Cévennes. Édition critique à partir du manuscrit intégral* (Toulouse: Éditions Privat/Club Cévenol, 1978 [1876]), 40.
59 Léonard, *Archives du corps*, 59–60, quoting from *La Science Illustrée*, October 18, 1875.
60 Antoine Chapelle, *Traité d'hygiène publique* (Paris: V. Masson, 1850), made some very precise calculations of the volume of air necessary to avoid these problems, 30–6.
61 Léonard, *Archives du corps*, 59.
62 Foville, *Enquête II*, 154.
63 Drouineau, "Hygiène rurale," 474 and François Julien-Labruyère, *Paysans charentais: histoire des campagnes d'Aunis, Saintonge et bas Angoumois: tome 1: économie rurale* (La Rochelle: Rupell, 1982), 237.
64 Corbin, *Archaïsme et modernité*, 76.
65 Cruveilhier, "Le taudis," 53–5.
66 Henri Napias and A.-J. Martin, *L'étude et le progrès de l'hygiène en France de 1878 à 1882* (Paris: G. Masson, 1883), 248 and Layet, *Hygiène et maladies*, 82–4.
67 Drouineau, "Hygiène rurale," 472–3; also see Jean Guibal, *Bourbonnais, Nivernais: L'architecture rurale française, corpus des genres, des types et des variants* (Paris: Berger-Levrault, 1962), 29.
68 Renard, *Nos frères farrouches*, 38.
69 Corbin, *Archaïsme et modernité*, 77; on the Savoie, see Sohn, *Chrysalides*, 115.
70 Manse, *Merilheu de mon enfance*, 24; Jacqueline Tardivon, *Usages et coutumes en Brenne* (Paris: Royer, 1991), 97.
71 Bougeâtre and Lachiver, *La vie rurale dans le Mantois*, 120.
72 Foville, *Enquête sur les conditions de l'habitation, tome I: les maisons-types* (Paris: Ernest Leroux, 1894), xxxi and *tome II*, 192; also see Desforges, *La vie dans un coin de Morvan*, 31; Jean Fourastié et Françoise Fourastié, *Histoire du confort* (Paris: Presses Universitaires de France, 1973), 73; Gustave Tarlé, *À propos de l'hygiène du paysan en Bretagne* (Montpellier: Imprimerie Grollier, 1911), 71; and Thuillier, *Pour une histoire du quotidien*, 61, n. 42.
73 Pierre-Jakez Hélias, *The Horse of Pride: Life in a Breton Village* (New Haven and London: Yale University Press, 1978), 48–9.

74 Tarlé, *À propos de l'hygiène*, 68.
75 Joseph Cressot, *Le pain au lièvre* (Paris: Stock, 1943), 57.
76 Nadaud, "Memoirs of a Former Mason's Assistant," 185.
77 For example, see Babeau, *La vie rurale*, 12–13; Drouineau, "Hygiène rurale," 476–8; Foville, *Enquête I*, xxxii–xxxiii; Monin, *Propreté*, 30; Henri Napias, *L'assistance publique dans le département de Sambre-et-Loire* (Paris: L. Battaille et Cie., 1893), 35–6; and Tarlé, *À propos de l'hygiène*, 67.
78 Albin Mazon [Docteur Francus], *Voyage fantaisiste et sérieux à travers l'Ardèche et la Haute-Loire*, vol. 2 (Le Puy: A. Pradès-Freydier, 1895), 40.
79 Gilbert Garrier, "L'apport des récits de vie et des romans 'paysans,'" in Hubscher and Farcy (eds.), *La moisson des autres*, 22.
80 Cited in Robert, *Mémoire et identité*, 145.
81 Cited in Henri Blanc, "l'hygiène infantile en Basse-Bretagne au commencement du XIXe siècle" (thèse pour le doctorat en médecine, Faculté de Médecine de Paris, 1937), 39–40.
82 Quoted in Léonard, *Archives du corps*, 60–1.
83 Babeau, *La vie rurale*, 34.
84 Foville, *Enquête I*, xxxvi; also see Thuillier, *Pour une histoire du quotidien*, 51 and 267–8, n. 3.
85 Jacques De Cambry, *Voyage dans le Finistère* (Paris: Imprimerie du cercle social, an VII [1799]), 116.
86 Csergo, *Liberté, égalité, propreté*, cites Dr. Fonssagrives, 63; Garnier-Léteurrie, *De l'enseignement de l'hygiène*, 37. Also see Lise Bésème-Pia, *Folklore des dents en Champagne-Ardennes, à l'usage des dentists, des patients et des petits enfants* (Langes: Éditions Dominique Guéniot, 2010), 41–3 and F. Fabret, *Soignons nos dents. Livre III: L'hygiène dentaire à l'école* (Nice: Imprimerie Spéciale du 'Petit Niçois,' 1910), 23.
87 Capitaine J. Levainville, *Le Morvan, étude de géographie humaine* (Paris: A. Colin, 1909), 229.
88 Desforges, *La vie dans un coin de Morvan*, 32.
89 Hippolyte Meunier, *Le docteur au village: entretiens familiers sur l'hygiène* (Paris: Hachette, 1877), 8 and 71–83.

3

The Smell of the City

City Grime

If the countryside, dirty and uncomfortable, was an excellent place to leave, the ambitious and desperate peasants who abandoned their sordid villages for the excitement and opportunity of the city would soon have found that conditions within the town walls were no more salubrious. In many ways they were worse. The philosopher Victor Considérant called the city "an immense workshop of putrefaction, where misery, plague and sickness work in concert."[1] New arrivals brought with them "the same habit of treating streets like dumping grounds, of urinating and defecating in the open, the same stench of manure, the same plague of flies [and the] aerial assault" from emptying chamber pots—whose noxious effects were multiplied by sheer human density.[2]

The concentration of garbage and sewage, on top of the need to house all these people and meet the ever-accelerating demand for clean water, posed an existential challenge to the new industrial cities of the nineteenth century—literally so for their inhabitants, as endemic diseases like tuberculosis and murderous epidemics of cholera and typhoid fever combined to make urban existence precarious.

The challenge increased along with the flood of migrants, both seasonal and permanent, to work in the early factories or to service the growing population: domestics, construction workers, water carriers, prostitutes, and the rest. The half-century between 1831 and 1881 marked the moment of most rapid increase, but the process had begun earlier.[3] Bordeaux, an administrative more than an industrial center, expanded its population from just over 100,000 at the end of the Old Regime to 130,000 at the fall of the Second Republic. Lyon, by French standards an industrial powerhouse, grew from 100,000 inhabitants in 1789 to almost 300,000 by 1860. Even Rennes, a provincial capital of a relatively backward province (Brittany) with 25,000 inhabitants at the start of the Revolution, needed room and provisions for 40,000 by the middle of the next century—a period of "black misery" for the Breton peasantry.[4]

Naturally, the monster of urban growth was Paris, whose population of 630,000 when the Bastille was taken swelled to 700,000 at the Bourbon Restoration and to over a million by mid-century. Parisians, as we saw in the observations of Louis-Sébastien Mercier, had always lived in a "dirty and stinking" city; the *cahiers de doléances* were full of complaints on that score. But the influx of people from the countryside made old problems of crowding and pollution much worse. In a capital that remained fundamentally "medieval, malodorous, and unsanitary," the battle against sickness, mortality, and social disorder became more and more difficult.[5]

The capital offered a prime example of the demographic cycle that defined nineteenth-century urbanization. Cities had long been net killers. Statistics suggest that well into the 1800s, one Parisian child in three or four died before his first birthday. Thousands of babies were abandoned annually, and 10 percent of them would not see out their first year. Add these numbers to the toll of epidemic disease—cholera, tuberculosis, typhoid fever, diphtheria, and so on—and it is clear that cities required large numbers of immigrants to survive and grow. Typically, these immigrants crowded into the poorer faubourgs, where they found "existing networks of their fellow countrymen": building workers from the Limousin, water carriers from the Savoie, stone cutters from the Lyonnais, and so on. Construction, however, could not keep up with the steady flow of new residents. Under Napoleon, Paris contained 24,000 houses; by the end of the July Monarchy it had 31,000. But a 30 percent increase in houses fell far behind the doubling of population: "[The city]," wrote writer and photographer Maxime du Camp, was on the point of becoming uninhabitable. "Its population [was] suffocating in the tiny, narrow, putrid, and tangled streets in which it had been dumped. As a result of this state of affairs, everything suffered: hygiene, security, speed of communications and public morality."[6] It was a wretchedly housed population that sent Louis Philippe into exile and manned the barricades during the June Days of 1848.

Other factors added to the repellent urban cocktail. Animals remained a familiar sight in the new industrial city and added their effluence to the general fund. Moreover, industrial cities retained a significant population of artisans—tanners, cobblers, parchment makers, and others—whose labor also helped pollute the local environment, and even as "unhealthy, disagreeable industries were expelled from city and town and settled on the outskirts . . . outside, out of sight, smell, and mind for urban elites."[7] Even after early-nineteenth-century reforms, like the 1810 regulations on abattoirs, pushed much of this activity to the edge of the city and into the *banlieues*, the problem remained. Slaughterhouses and other animal-based industries that "had not yet learned to use the whole of the animals they dismembered" produced a disproportionate part of the pollution and spread an "insufferable stench" across the towns.[8]

No one who lived in a city could be ignorant of the appalling scene around him. It is what inspired the efforts of the new group of pioneering social reformers of the July Monarchy—among them Louis-René Villermé, Adolphe Blanqui, and Alexandre Jean-Baptiste Parent-Duchâtelet—whose investigations tell us much of what we know about life at the bottom of urban society in the 1830s and 1840s. Villermé's 1840 report on the Parisian working class underlined "how the ignorance of any notion of wholesomeness and morality" compromised their health. More than this, "these dens of incest, as well as disease, where brothers and sisters, parents and children, lie together in filthy intimacy, and where women piss in the streets," also undermined public order. The social effect of this, according to Blanqui, was compounded by the habit of the dirtiest of the poor tending to cram together in the worst slums: "these burrows that hardly deserve the name dwellings," he wrote, "where this species of humanity breathe poisoned air that attacks babies at their mothers' breast and plunges them into early decrepitude by way of the saddest of diseases—scrofula, rheumatism, and consumption."[9]

In 1851, the brand new *commission des logements insalubres* (commission for insalubrious housing: hereafter, the Housing Commission), focusing for the moment on the grim neighborhoods around the Jardin des Plantes on the eastern edge of the Left Bank, described the pervasive humidity of the ground that seeped into the buildings and disappeared only in the hottest parts of the summer, along with its unfortunate inhabitants—poor "workers" from lowest trades—who made conditions worse through their "ignorance of any principles of hygiene and cleanliness." The newspaper *L'Ère Nouvelle* described the nearby streets extending from the Montagne Sainte-Geneviève to the Gobelins, "narrow and tortuous, where the sun never penetrates,"

> [but where] on either side of foul gutter rise buildings five stories in height, with some squashing together up to fifty families. Low-slung rooms, humid and vile are rented for 1,50 francs per week, when they have a chimney, and 1,25 francs when they don't. No wallpaper, and often not a stick of furniture, hides the nakedness of their sad walls.[10]

One account of the 1832 cholera epidemic reported finding dwellings with inhabitants "as squalid as their surroundings." Deprived of regular work and sufficient income, most of them spent the day "sorting through the product of their nighttime rounds, crouched around their dirty swag; stuff is piled everywhere, even under the bunks: bones, old soiled linen from which fetid miasmas spread across these awful garrets, where entire families lived in less than ten square meters."[11] Even the financial paper, the *Édile de Paris*, hardly a friend of the poor, regretted these "ghastly and cadaverous [people], pushed like pariahs into the vilest hovels, which some dare to call houses." The streets, remarked the Comte de Rambuteau, Louis Philippe's prefect of the Seine, smelled of rotten cabbage, "by which any native Parisian returning from a trip could recognize his city."[12]

Naturally, Paris was not alone. Historian Olivier Le Goff refers to the "triumphant squalor" of any new industrial city—engorged, sordid, putrid, smoky, and reeking of "proletarian sweat." Working-class housing in Limoges was notoriously backward, but it was hardly worse than elsewhere in the Limousin, where "dwellings are generally stuffy, their walls bare and stained by smoke or covered in some old paper that has become a refuge for fleas [and where] one finds chamber pots still full of urine and even fecal matter." In Lyon, Jean-Baptiste Monfalcon found in 1846 "filthy, stifling, sad, and narrow" streets of that served for nothing so much as to furnish patients for the local *Hôtel-Dieu* (a combination of hospital and poorhouse).[13]

Conditions were not much better in Lille, where "dark, humid, narrow alleys piled up with refuse" and poisoned the unfortunate inhabitants. "Come with me," Victor Derode invited readers of his *Histoire populaire de Lille* (1848). "Follow this narrow alley, where the putrid mud infects the very air; look at these basement windows, these doors exhaling miasmas, groans, and curses." Humidity made poor housing worse, as noted in one report that described a street in the working-class section of Moulins-Lille, where "Each house had a hole dug in front for the wastewater [and where] the rain seeped down the gutter-less roofs to soak the rotting walls." They were scarcely more habitable than they were stable, but they were better than the worst Lillois districts, where people were still living in caves.[14]

In Rennes, as the new textile factories killed *industrie à domicile* in the countryside, the surge of displaced rural workers stretched the city's resources, bringing it one of the highest rates of indigence in the country and causing a spike in mortality, especially among the poor. Its mortality rate of 44.7 per 1,000, in 1845, was almost twice the French average of 24 per 1,000. This was no anomaly. Poverty and death slept together under the same blanket. Villermé calculated for the eastern industrial city of Mulhouse in 1830 that 96 percent of twenty-year-old laborers would die before their sixtieth birthday; for the privileged classes of high-level functionaries and businessmen, the figure was 22 percent. In Grenoble, 90 percent of immigrants found lodging in places "that had already been slums under the Old Regime."[15]

The worst housed among the poor often ended up in *garnis*, "where landlords often speculate shamelessly on misery." In those wretched furnished rooms, many little bigger than closets, recent arrivals with few prospects and fewer resources spent their first days in the city, and older workers, used up and still without resources, spent their last days. "It was a peculiar dwelling that I was going to inhabit," remembered the journeyman mason Martin Nadaud of the flat that he shared with his fellow construction workers:

> It was located on a sort of mezzanine between the ground floor and the first floor and had such a low ceiling that you could hardly stand up straight.... I should add that it was barely ventilated at all and that half the floor tiles were missing. Now [1890s] that there are laws about unsanitary dwellings, the police would not fail to prohibit this sort of slum. But [in the days of Louis Philippe], our room was hardly different from the sort that workers lived in everywhere else.[16]

Sometimes the *garnis* served as lodgings for entire families with no option for anything better, while the authorities counted them as sources of both social disorder and contagion: "I am aware," wrote the prefect of the Seine in 1825, "that the pox is rampaging through the population of the *maisons garnies*, where workers, both infected and not, are squashed together in small rooms—the ideal conditions for an epidemic."[17] The *garnis* naturally attracted enhanced police surveillance. The police were more interested in sedition than in hygiene, but there was in any case little they could have done to improve the existing state of affairs.

Honoré de Balzac painted a graphic picture of Paris in 1819, in his depiction of the Maison Vauquer, the down-at-the-heels boarding house that served as the setting for his novel *Old Goriot*: a sad, three-story structure, with small, smeared, glass-painted windows. As for the grim interior, "Although actual filth may be absent, everything is dirty and stained; there are no rags and tatters, but everything is falling to pieces in decay." Behind the house sat a 20-foot square yard, "inhabited by a happy family of pigs, hens, and rabbits," along with the meat-safe, where "the greasy water from the sink flows below it." At the front, "The cook sweeps all the refuse of the house into the [street] through a little door in the yard and uses floods of water to clean it up for fear of an epidemic." The neighborhood around it was "a valley of crumbling stucco and gutters black with mud." Indeed, the whole city was a sea of mud; only the poor walked from place to place.[18]

Old Goriot was fiction, but Balzac could easily have cribbed his description of the Saint-Marcel quarter from an 1852 report by the Paris Housing Commission: dark between the tall shanties; lined with steep, muddy streets; and a suffocating humidity in all seasons. Those with the courage to enter these slums find the inhabitants enclosed in light- and airless rooms, often overlooking narrow courtyards where garbage, wastewater, and the overflow from unflushed latrines produce the most fetid miasmas. "The quarter remains more or less what it was in the Middle Ages," the commission concluded.[19]

An 1856 report described a similarly appalling scene on the rue Courmont, in Lille:

> [The latrines] were set up in the basements, at the entrances to the courtyards, or in the hallways and stairwells of the buildings; the smallness of the wooden pits was extreme, and they were only emptied once every week or ten days; in fact, they overflowed regularly, producing a nauseating spectacle.... Must we add that, toilet paper being unknown and newsprint rare, people used straw instead—with what disgusting consequences is easy to guess.[20]

This combination of degradation and crowding inevitably pushed urban mortality rates above what pertained beyond the city walls. "The urban environment," wrote historians Robert Woods and John Woodward,

> was generally more unhealthy than the countryside. Infectious diseases were more likely to be endemic; epidemics developed more frequently and were easily maintained; poor sanitary conditions meant that food, milk, and water supply were liable to be contaminated; whilst overcrowding provided both a source of psychological tension and an aid to the easy communication of disease.[21]

Governments, both municipal and national, were not unconcerned with these evils, although different authorities were concerned to different degrees—and not all out of a selfless interest in the lives of the unfortunate. But what weapons did they possess in this battle?

The July Monarchy (1830–48) has earned a reputation for ignoring the plight of what Adolphe Thiers later called the "vile multitude," aside from the threat they posed to social and political stability. Its repeated repression of worker uprisings in Paris and Lyon made the point more violently. However, while it is true that the governments of Louis Philippe were afraid of the poor and solicitous of the better-off, this one-dimensional view of the so-called bourgeois monarchy ignores the extent to which even leaders like Thiers and François Guizot, its most emblematic politicians, thought about ameliorating the conditions of poverty—if only out of crass self-interest.

In fact, two of the most impressive studies of hygiene of the first half of the nineteenth century, by the eminent doctors of hygiene, Jean-Baptiste Monfalcon and Auguste-Pierre de Polinière, were published during the July Monarchy. Their idea was a simple one and common to most experts of the era: cleaning up the deplorable slums was the best way to improve public health, reduce mortality, and lift the pressure on dispensaries and hospitals.[22]

Expert consensus was produced by the obvious fact that any strategy of social improvement had to attack the filthiness of everyday life in the nineteenth-century city, where to be poor was perforce to be dirty.[23] It is easy to understand why. Even apart from the wretched housing, notes historian Jacques Léonard, "the majority of manual trades were messy; soap was expensive; water was a bother, and to heat it for washing was a waste of wood . . . and most dwellings offered little in the way of privacy for personal *toilettes*."[24]

The documents leave us surprisingly little direct evidence about the toilettes of ordinary people; that is, about the way that the dirtiness of the environment imprinted itself on early-nineteenth-century bodies. Hygienists spared no details in their depiction of life in those urban slums. We can almost smell the humid, rotting walls and the soiled linen in their lurid descriptions of tenement apartments or the muddy streets full of sewage and garbage the inhabitants faced on the other side of the front door. The poor themselves are inevitably presented as repulsive, unwashed, and wrapped in the most miserable sorts of clothing. But the details of personal hygiene are mostly lacking.

It is nonetheless a simple matter to reconstruct plausible practices from the abundant circumstantial evidence. We have no reason to believe, for example, that most people went to the heroic lengths that would have been necessary to stay clean amid the general *insalubrité* of everyday life. The cramped and dusty spaces in which most folks lived in the city—just as dirty and probably smaller than peasant houses—offered little reward for the effort involved. Where water was scarce and costly, exhausting to get and difficult to get rid of, people did not wash extensively or regularly, especially since heating water required even more effort and more expense. Soap was dear and there was not much of it around—which partly explains the paucity of demand. In the 1840s, France produced about half as much soap as England.[25]

In his study of mid-century Lille, Pierre Pierrard painted a picture of street kids in the summer, bathing "in the hollows of the city fortifications, in animal troughs, under the bridges—despite the fact that this spot was formally reserved for the only swimming school in Lille; they preferred this to the stinking, sulfurous baths administered by the welfare bureau (*bureau de bienfaisance*)." But most working-class families had neither the water, the time, nor the space for regular washing.[26] The summer dips in the local stream that might rinse the sweat off peasant life were impractical in the city, and most towns contained little in the way of public bathing facilities. Geneviève Cerisier-Millet writes, for example, that Paris had nine public baths in 1773—mostly boats on the Seine with *cabinets* for bathing—and that entrepreneurs had added dozens more by the middle of the next century. She cites the soldier, essayist, and monarchist politician Abel Hugo, who estimated that Parisians took three baths a year in 1835. This might have been true for Hugo's privileged friends in the faubourg Saint-Germain, but it certainly was not true for the huge majority of Parisians. Dr. Jean-Baptiste Fonssagrives estimated an average of one bath per Parisian per year in 1851, which is undoubtedly closer to reality. Meanwhile, the Poitou town of Châtellerault, which is the focus of Cerisier-Millet's study, had not a single public bath in 1800 and only one such establishment along the Vienne river by mid-century.[27]

John Merriman finds the same standards of personal tenue in Restoration Limoges, where even those who could afford to do so rarely took baths, perhaps because the houses of the rich had the same "inadequate means of providing water" as those of the poor. The young, he adds, might have bathed in the Vienne, "under the gaze of the laundresses and river workers." The most fastidious citizens took themselves to one of the three public baths operating in the city. The most elegant of these, the Chinese baths on the fashionable rue Banc-Léger, charged up to four francs for a "luxurious Russian bath"—prices that went far beyond the wages of most workers.[28]

Two notable exceptions punctuate this general picture of inaction and failure. The first was an expensive bust, the second a one-off success. In 1853, work began on a publicly funded laundry facility in the Parisian working-class district of the Marais, after the new Emperor, Saint-Simonian that he was, agreed to pay for it. But the cost of the project—200,000 francs at a time when laundresses earned one franc a day—was high enough and the operational problems numerous enough that the underused and bankrupt Temple washhouse and public bath shut its doors in 1864, leaving the wives and mothers of the Marais to do their laundry at home and to hang the damp clothes to dry in their already dank apartments.[29]

The second, more successful, venture also came in the 1850s, when a group of philanthropic factory owners in the town of Mulhouse pooled their resources to build housing for their workers in the city's textile, tools, and chemicals factories. Company housing in itself was not unique, but in this case the *patrons* included inexpensive baths and laundries for the working-class residents; and that was.[30] However, for reasons that are not clear, the example was not copied elsewhere.

The pragmatic response to these constraints, in the city as in the countryside, was *lavage partiel*—partial washing. Katherine Ashenburg cites the response of a Lancashire collier to questions from the Commission on the Sanitary Condition of the Labouring Population of Great Britain: "I never wash my body; I let my shirt rub the dirt off; my shirt will show that. I wash my neck and ears, and face, of course." The same practices would describe the toilette of the ordinary working-class Frenchman: wash the parts that show. The *lavage entier* (washing the whole body) remained the preserve of an "aristocratic elite."[31]

Did these practices make the inhabitants of French cities dirtier than their neighbors in England, Germany, or Switzerland, for example? It is difficult to know for sure. When historian Hippolyte Taine visited England in the 1860s, he found the houses plain and lacking in taste. But he was astonished at the "comfort and service" they offered, with water jugs, toothbrush holders, zinc basins, and thick dry towels—evidence, he thought, of the Anglo-Saxons' penchant for excessive cleanliness. Cultural historian Augustin Cabanès relates a very different story, which he borrowed from the well-known British psychiatrist George Fielding Blandford. "In the middle of the nineteenth century," wrote Dr. Blandford,

> there was but one bathing establishment in all of London, and the two occasions on which a working man bathed were the day he was born and the day he died.

The upper classes were scarcely cleaner, though. A great English dame, Lady Mary Montagu, who was both a professional beauty and a spirited woman, recalled that she responded one day to someone who noticed her soiled hands: "You call that dirty? You should see my feet!"[32]

Such practices were neither unreasonable nor unconscionable. Taking the trouble to wash made little sense for people whose bodies were inevitably draped in dirty clothes and put to bed in dirty sheets—which was certainly the case for the great majority of urban *Français*, as it was for their country cousins.[33] Add to this the matter of discretion and modesty. Working people who lived in cramped apartments had few options for privacy. Peter Ward writes that parents "generally took great pains to conceal their nakedness from their children" and that of their opposite-sex children from one another.[34] These considerations made comprehensive washing at home virtually impossible.

In a sense, water for washing clothes and linen was more accessible than water for washing bodies, even in the cities. Most towns had rivers and rocks down by the flowing cold water where the family laundry could be beaten and rinsed. According to Cerisier-Millet, the first *bâteaux lavoirs* [laundry boats] in Paris had been launched in the time of Henri IV, off the Île-Saint-Louis and the Île de la Cité—although, since the Seine was full of human waste, washing clothes in it "presented some dangers for public health." Napoleon had aimed to make Paris an important port and so pushed many of the boats off the river, creating instead land-locked public *lavoirs*, of which there were twenty by 1830 and seventy-one in 1848.[35] Meanwhile, the laundry boats relocated to the Canal Saint-Martin—the Ourcq river as it flowed through Paris before emptying into the Seine at the Bassin de l'Arsenal—where legions of laundresses could usually be found, occupying themselves with the dirty garments of the better-off classes. An ambitious law of 1851 sought to organize, alongside public baths, the construction of modern public *lavoirs*, complete with *chaudières*—boilers for drying clothes.[36] But little was done to make it happen.

By the 1830s, therefore, and thanks largely to the work of the pioneering hygienists like Villermé, Blanqui, and Parent-Duchâtelet, the link between dirt and poverty had been firmly forged in the public mind. "I have studied with a religious solicitude," wrote Blanqui, "the private lives of a group of workers, and I can assuredly say that the insalubrity of their dwellings is the basis of all the misery, all the vices, and all the calamities of their social condition."[37] The lurid descriptions of Blanqui and his colleagues bear out the remarks of historian David S. Barnes about the vocabulary and grammar of disgust that run through the moralizing agenda of these would-be reformers, who were especially concerned by the way crowding, dirt, and moral decay captured in the scenes of promiscuity they often found on their visits to the slums: "in most of the beds . . . individuals of the two sexes and of very different ages, lying together without *chemises* and in repulsive filth," as one crusader described the scene.[38] As the poor became distinguished by their dirt, to clean up the "dangerous classes" was to make them less dangerous.[39]

In the end, however, dirt's link to disease counted for more than its link to depravity. And it is no coincidence that the work of the hygienists accelerated following the arrival of cholera in France. While a comprehension of the true etiology of disease remained decades in the future, the notion that smell and disease were organically related was an old one. English reformer Edwin Chadwick put the matter plainly: "All smell is, if it be intense, immediate acute disease."[40] When scientists and laity alike believed that miasmas emitted disease—which many doctors and most people did at least to the end of the century—the leap from stink to epidemic made perfect sense. Dr. Antoine Chapelle, writing in 1850, offered his professional opinion that it was precisely the toxicity of bad air—*le méphitisme*—that made unhygienic homes so dangerous to health, as exhalations of "carbonic acid" combined with "emanations from the lungs and skin" produced by all living things in the space. Piles of garbage or the presence of "a great number of wounded men," along with "artificial light" and "bad chimneys," could likewise produce miasmas. Working from wrong assumptions, hygienists thus "convinced local politicians and bourgeois elites that . . . urban filth was not an ineluctable and merely disagreeable aesthetic fact . . . but a mortal enemy to the population."[41]

Indeed, as the first wave of cholera passed over Paris in 1831–2, carrying off 18,000 of its inhabitants, it showed a particular preference for those who lived in the most crowded and insalubrious conditions. It seemed almost scientific, therefore, that working-class families be reproached for their lazy and slovenly ways. They brought cholera upon themselves. Worse, they endangered everyone else.

Cholera did not invent the association of dirt and disease. But it did help anchor the idea that *logements insalubres* were a public menace—not only to the unfortunate inhabitants but also to their better-off neighbors. It did not matter that the authorities misunderstood the nature of cholera and its means of transmission. Since statistics gathered in the 1830s revealed higher mortality rates in the most "miserable and crowded" corners of the city, the authorities naturally concluded that it was "the conditions themselves, including housing conditions, *and not bad habits* that promote mortality from cholera" (my emphasis).[42] The point is that even a regime without much sympathy for the poor could recognize the wisdom of state action to clean up the cities, and even a mistaken theory of disease could lead to policies that worked with some effectiveness to contain it.

The Water Question

A society several decades from accepting the waterborne causes of cholera could nevertheless recognize clean water as the "fundamental ingredient in the battle for healthier cities."[43] This had been true even before water was identified as the medium for epidemics in the 1850s and 1860s, since one way to battle the miasmas that people thought caused disease was to get rid of the dirt and garbage that created them. Moreover, even if people did not equate water and mortality, they still needed to drink. In other words, the problem of bringing sufficient quantities of water into the cities was a long-standing one, and as the nineteenth century reconnected water to cleanliness and cleanliness to health, the problem multiplied in importance.

The "Old Regime of water," as Guy Thuillier calls it, was pretty dry. Estimates of the volume of water available to Parisians vary considerably, but all of them speak to the same problems of insufficiency, expense, and underuse. At the turn of the nineteenth century, Parisians made due with 8,000 cubic meters of water a day, feeding eighty-three *bournes-fontaines* (a sort of fire hydrant) and forty-five private water dealers. This marked a substantial improvement in both volume and availability since the days of the Sun King, but it remained insufficient to meet demand, which in the early 1830s still depended on the 25,000 wells scattered throughout the city.[44]

In the middle of the eighteenth century, no Parisians had running water in their homes. Even at Versailles, while copper pipes fed the fountains beginning in 1761, the palace itself had no plumbing at all. It was only in the 1770s, when the Périer brothers, masters of pumping technology, founded the Compagnie des Eaux, bringing water into the city's reservoirs and even into some of its most privileged residences by subscription, that the modern system of pipes and pumps and spigots was launched. There is a story about Napoleon I, who asked his Interior Minister Jean-Antoine Chaptal how he intended to capture the favor of the people of Paris: "Give them water," he responded. Not a man to refuse good advice, the First Consul duly began work on the new Ourcq canal in 1802, aimed at bringing water into the city from the north. A second project, the aqueduct de ceinture, was launched in 1808.[45] Several regimes later Louis Philippe's prefect of the Seine, Claude-Philibert, the Count de Rambuteau, who described his chief job as providing Parisians with "air, water, and shade," endowed the city with more than 1,500 fountains.[46] Yet it was not enough, and every year supply fell further behind demand.

Tight supplies, of course, meant high prices. For most Parisians the cost of water remained prohibitive: 20 wage-hours per cubic meter for a common laborer in 1840. People could take themselves to the neighborhood fountain, if there was one, for free. But then they had to lug it home themselves. Those who could afford it might hire water carriers, who could buy water at one centime per 10 liters and sell it for five or ten centimes for a 20-liter bucket. According to Julia Csergo, better-off Parisians bought their water by subscription: 2f50 per month for 20 liters a day or three francs for 30 liters. There also existed an illicit trade of porters who peddled unfiltered water—"greyish, sandy, and unappetizing to drink"—drawn from the Ourcq but costing just as much as Seine water.[47]

Given the expense and inconvenience of water, it is not surprising that most people did not use very much of the stuff. According to economist Jean Fourastié, 20 or 30 liters of water sufficed to wash a family of six.[48] As for drinking, the quality of the water lagged behind the quantity. In the view of one American visitor, "the water from the Ourcq canal [was] very hard and unwholesome, whilst that of the Seine has been, without doubt, very impure and still receives some part of the sewage of the metropolis." "Unwholesome" hardly begins to describe the state of affairs in Saint-Etienne, where,

> The Furan [river] was barely more than a filthy stream into which butchers and tanners casually tossed animal parts, and into which other industries, and residents as well, emptied their waste. Mercifully, it had already been covered over in places,

but it was particularly noxious during the summer, when little water flowed to keep the muck moving.[49]

In cities less favored by government attention than Paris, people continued to depend on wells for their water—especially for their drinking water. But this system had its own problems, as we have seen in the countryside. Émile Duclaux, the famed microbiologist, painted a lurid picture of insufficiently deep wells, with only a thin water table: "uncovered, muddied by rain, dry in summer, contaminated by dung heaps, furnishing only a diluted sort of urine."[50] Wells dug into ground "infected by leaky sewers, contaminated sumps, and permeable cesspits" became permanent sources of cholera and typhoid fever. Such polluted wells provided much of the water supply for the city of Lille. Rouen continued to be fed through fountains filled with water taken from the Seine—a system that remained largely unchanged from what it had been in the sixteenth century. Nevers, having installed a steam pump to get water from the Loire, was able to give each of its citizens 28 liters of water a day by mid-century. (Then again, that system remained essentially unchanged until after the First World War.) Historian John Merriman writes of Limoges—which, aside from the "poor, stagnant" city of Rennes, remained one of the most notoriously filthy towns in France—that well past mid-century it had *no* adequate source of water. Only three of what had once been thirty-five large public fountains still served a water-deprived population alongside nine reservoirs of questionable purity.[51]

These figures suggest that the French suffered a significant deficit of water, compared to industrial cities in other countries, especially in Germany and England. In London, for example, one source estimated the average household use at 160 gallons a day in 1850. According to historian Judith Flanders, by mid-century, most urban middle-class English homes had a connection to a water company's pipes. But it was expensive—nearly 10 percent the cost of rent—and sometimes deadly. Similarly, in Hamburg in 1850, a city waterworks fed from the Elbe river above the city had connections to 4,000 out of some 11,500 houses. Although, of course, that supply was periodically contaminated with cholera.[52]

The expense and inconvenience of water in French cities had a profound effect on the *salubrité* of everyday life. As Mrs. Trollope, the dour and judgmental English observer, wrote in 1835, "Almost all Parisian households make due with only two pails of water for their daily needs . . . the French don't wash."[53] This was not the result of some conceptual quirk, of the sort Vigarello attributes to the seventeenth century, with its waterless standards of cleanliness. It reflected the plain fact that the majority of inhabitants had neither the money nor the strength to acquire the quantity of water necessary to decent hygiene. The average Parisian used a mere 5 liters of water a day in 1830, according to the *Annales des Ponts et Chaussées*; although that had already increased to 30 liters by 1850.[54]

To be sure, practical limits accounted for only part of the distance separating early-nineteenth-century hygiene from later practices. As the century progressed, experts more and more asserted the "natural-ness" of washing—"one of those instinctive needs commanded by nature," in the words of Augustin Cabanès, the great doctor and historian of the fin-de-siècle.[55] Perhaps, but in a world with such limited access to water, people had a different relationship to the wet stuff, and even the "techniques and gestures [of washing] did not look like ours [today]."[56] Indeed, as we saw in the case of rural folk wisdom, even if people were not exactly dirty by choice, the link between *salubrité* and good health ran up against ancient popular ideas that considered dirt protective and hygiene a "feminine indulgence" that would weaken the body.[57] Certainly, people needed more water than they had. Whether that in itself would revolutionize popular habits remained to be seen.

The Sewer Question

In the meantime, even the slow increase in the amount of water available to urban residents, added to the increase in their numbers, posed a second question: Where would this water go when people were done with it? The streets often served as gutters, into which city inhabitants would simply empty their liquid waste, and these would flow principally, when they flowed at all, into local streams or rivers. Thus, Alain Corbin writes of mid-century Limoges that "it would be difficult to find another large city as badly constructed or as dirty [where] garbage of all sorts is thrown out of windows into the street and into the spillways that run down the gutters"—adding that the city had not a single public latrine before 1877 and that public plazas were transformed into rubbish heaps, which also functioned as open-air urinals. He adds frighteningly that conditions were even worse in the smaller provincial towns of the Limousin.[58]

Sewers could provide a place for water to go and to flush some of the filth off the streets. Limoges did not begin to build its system until 1875, but other French cities had them even before the fall of the July Monarchy. The best known, of course, were the Paris sewers, through which Javert famously chased Jean Valjean in Victor Hugo's novel *Les Misérables*. However, these old sewers were not very extensive. The Paris system extended a mere 24 kilometers in 1806, extended to 37 kilometers in 1824, and to 130 before Louis Napoleon's ascension to power. They were technically primitive: "poorly sealed, without much slope, often clogged, sometimes cleared out by heavy rain, and open to the sky."[59] Moreover, these sluices, intended to clear rainwater off city streets and ideally to wash dirt and debris away with it, were not built to deal with what the nineteenth century called *eaux vannes* [blackwater]; that is, with urine and feces. In the countryside, night soil easily became manure. In mid-nineteenth-century cities it served primarily to pollute the water supply and as the medium for epidemics.[60]

The problem of what to do with accumulating human waste did not suddenly appear in the growing cities of the industrial age. It had existed as long as there had been towns, and city leaders had always struggled to address it successfully. For example, a royal decree of 1530 had aimed to clean up Paris by requiring that all buildings install *fosses d'aisances*—cesspools for collecting the feces produced by the inhabitants. The primitive cesspits in Rennes consisted of simple holes, dug under buildings, often lined with stone or brick. Other cities took more care to dig deeper or seal their *fosses* more tightly, but none succeeded entirely.[61]

These *fosses* were then periodically emptied by so-called *vidangeurs*—"small businessmen who before eight o'clock in the morning pulled their carts carrying their copper barrels full of night soil from house to house, crying 'Four sous a load!'" Standards of hygiene were lax. Sometimes the *vidangeurs* carried vegetables on the cart alongside the barrels, and they inevitably spilled a trail of shit behind them. Across the country, when the *vidangeurs* had collected and hauled off the garbage and fecal matter, they often piled it up by their own homes in the suburbs or the near countryside—a practice that commonly attracted complaints from their neighbors—before selling it as fertilizer to local famers. In Paris, the *vidangeurs* took their nightly swag to the pits at Montfaucon, the huge dumping ground for trash and animal carcasses north of the city that Napoleon III's chief landscape architect Jean-Charles Alphand later turned into the Parc des Buttes-Chaumont. Here it began the process of turning into *poudrette*, a dry fertilizer. In Lille there were no public latrines, and the private *fosses* were emptied by *bernatiers* or *berneuses*, "small traders who crisscrossed the city before 8am pulling their carts loaded with copper barrels," going house to house and buying the sewage that they would then go off and sell to local farmers for fertilizer.[62] Such was the waste management system of the early industrial city.

Through the eighteenth century and the Revolution, regulations concerning the *fosses d'aisances* were tightened and extended.[63] By the 1830s, however, the *fosses* themselves, which were often poorly sealed and frequently overflowed, had become a serious source of pollution. Many hygienists believed that the best ones, copious and impermeable, represented substantial progress. Yet *fosses* that did not leak favored the fluidity of their contents, which meant they needed to be emptied more frequently. This was costly for landlords, who often put it off for as long as possible. It likewise made the whole operation more disgusting: "As for the emptying itself," wrote historian Elsbeth Kalff,

> It remained a painful ordeal for the inhabitants of the house as for the whole neighborhood, such was the insupportable stench. And it made the work of the *vidangeuers* more dangerous. Imagine these fetid cesspools, with the fumes released by the decaying feces and by the ammonia it produced, often over-filled, spilling over, viscous, where you had to sink your arm in to fill up the pails of shit, then tossed into the dumper.[64]

Jules Rochard considered the system of *fosses fixes* to be a great improvement over the old habits of *tout au ruisseau*—throwing "everything into the gutter." At the same time, they served to poison the ground and the atmosphere around them, while their excavation led to the creation of "filthy reservoirs of fecal matter" that began to pile up on the edge of towns. In other words, the old system of *fosses* provided an inadequate answer to the essential question: How to get rid of excrement "in a manner that is both salubrious and economical?"[65]

The Housing Question

It is probably a stretch to say that the general filthiness of French life in itself killed the July Monarchy and resurrected the Republic. But even the Conservative Party recognized "bad housing" as one of the principal causes of the "savage revolts" that brought political revolution and social civil war in 1848. "The slum is not only a cause of early death for its inhabitants," wrote the Breton landlord and legislator Anatole de Melun, "it is the germ of all these fearsome maladies that, giving birth to a population that is sickly, weak, and degenerate, are the starting point of every vice and all the ills of the social order." This was the reasoning and sentiment that closed the circle linking housing, social pathology, and state action and that led to the new law of April 1850, "concerning the appalling state of housing occupied by the working class in France's industrial cities"[66] (Figure 3.1).

The law provided for the establishment of local housing commissions, under the authority of the prefects, to identify the most egregiously dirty buildings and apartments and to force their landlords to clean them up.[67] The system was simple enough in conception: the prefect appointed the members of the commissions; the commissions solicited complaints and conducted investigations. When they found sufficiently insalubrious conditions, they asked landlords to repair them within a reasonable time frame. If landlords complied, the matter ended there. If not, it was passed along, in Paris, to either the prefecture of the Seine or the prefecture of Police. The law contained provisions for fining uncooperative landlords and even for condemning their properties. A subsequent police ordinance of September 1853, issued

Figure 3.1 *Central Paris before Haussmann. Rue Basses-des-Ursins* (1865). Charles Marville, photographer. State Library of Victoria, Melbourne, Australia.

by authorities who now answered to the Second Empire and no longer to the Republic, tightened the regulations with specific standards for outhouses [*cabinets d'aisances*] and rules for the upkeep of interior courtyards, cesspits, and exterior walls—"in order to prevent these dwellings from killing so many people."[68]

In the early years, complaints to the commissions tended to focus on "the fetid odors emitted by the *lieux d'aisances*," the outhouses in every courtyard of every building, where residents had to perform their natural functions in what were often the most revolting conditions. For example, a group of renters in a building in Montmartre complained to the local commission of "pernicious vapors escaping from the outhouses in the courtyard [that] in the absence of proper maintenance have become a source of contamination—all the more so, as we pass through a period of warm temperatures." Yet another outhouse, even though it was regularly mucked out, still produced ammonia gas "that rendered even a brief visit painful."[69]

The omnipresent problems of *cabinets d'aisances*, and the commission's efforts to ameliorate them, punctuate the annual reports on its activities. In 1862, for example, it recommended seats for all toilets and a system that would seal outhouses off from the resurgence of offensive smells. "We do not hope," it added, "to immediately effect a change in the bad habits of maintenance that so often leave these latrines *in a state of the most hideous filth*. We believe, however, that the most effective way of correcting bad habits is to fight them with a tireless perseverance and to give people the experience of clean and comfortable *cabinets*" (my emphasis). To move toward this goal the commission recommended installing seats in all the lavatories, as well as siphons that would keep the stench of the *fosses* from backing up into the *cabinets*.[70]

Yet whatever the good intentions of the authorities, the technology of the period—in particular, the absence of modern plumbing—meant that it was all but impossible to eliminate the noxious evidence of collective outhouses. Kalff and Lemaître see in these complaints about "fetid emanations" evidence that the new sensibility to hygiene passed "primarily through the nose." Whether this is true or not, it is interesting to note the way these poor inhabitants ranked their misfortunes—with the stench proving the most objectionable element of existence in *logements insalubres*, rather than, say, the dankness of apartments, the crowding, or the discomforts of heat and cold.[71]

At the same time, the hygiene commission found, much to its satisfaction, that landlords cooperated more often than not. Typically, of the almost 14,000 cases where it intervened between 1862 and 1865, the commission sent only 1,600 up to the *conseil municipal*. The prefecture of police had to intervene on only eighty occasions (5 percent). But, of course, even a cooperative landlord could do little about the state of the plumbing or the habits of the occupants. Moreover, while cooperative owners faced serious expenses with little prospect of a return, recalcitrant landlords did not have much incentive to do as the housing commissions instructed. At worst they suffered modest fines that were applied unevenly—and then only after a long, uncertain process. Besides, the authorities' respect for the sanctity of private property limited the commissions' ability to coerce landlords who dragged their feet. And the laws on salubrious housing did not even apply to the interior of *logements* occupied solely by their owners.

A report published in 1852 summarized the work of the commissions and emphasized the obstacles they faced.[72] What do the commissions look at, the report asked? At the "insalubrity wherever bad smells poison the air of apartments, wherever humidity, filth reign and are and light are absent," it responded. On the exterior of buildings, it focused on the garbage that piled up in courtyards, at the pools of stagnant water that gathered in the absence of any sort of pavement; at the defective pipes and channels that failed to get rid of wastewater; at the stink of outhouses; at polluted wells, dilapidated walls, grimy staircases and hallways. Inside these run-down dwellings it cast a reforming eye on the damp, the lack of space, light, ventilation, and *propreté*.

It makes perfect sense, of course, that a society holding on to miasmatic theories of contagion should be so susceptible to offensive odors. But Kalff and Lemaître also see it as a political fact; that is, as proof that the lower classes were gradually being assimilated into the more refined sensibilities of the higher classes, and as the triumph of "bourgeois" standards over more tolerant "popular" traditions. This is a highly speculative and tendentious assertion, which likely overstates the extent to which middle-class sensibilities had become refined by the middle of the century. Moreover, there is little evidence that the elites before 1850 had put much effort into "civilizing" the sensibilities of the lower classes, as they were to do with gusto under the Third Republic. More likely, all those complaints about putrid outhouses reflected something more elemental about the sensibility of smell: however much the boundaries of what is tolerable and what is disgusting are set by historical and social context—recall the acceptance of strong earthy smells in the countryside—some stenches remain insufferable even when they are ubiquitous.[73]

In one respect, these horrid conditions were all of a piece, and they were largely the consequence of overcrowding. But the housing commission admitted it could do little to remedy this basic problem, since, when they fell afoul of the commission it made sense economic for landlords simply to evict their poorest and most crowded tenants—or not to rent to them at all—rather than to clean up the apartments they let. And this would likely push the family into even worse lodgings. What is more, landlords regularly contended that the inhabitants themselves were the source of the dirtiness.

In fact, the commission did not entirely disagree, noting that their own good advice to tenants often came up against the "inveterate habits and the insouciance of people who do not understand the value of this advice and for whom the word *dirtiness* has no meaning at all." Hygienists working for the hygiene commission in Rennes, less energetic and perhaps more cynical than their colleagues in Paris, never ceased to bemoan the "deplorable and unsanitary habits of the locals." Squalor, they concluded, was not the consequence of overcrowding or the lack of government action "but simply of the ill will of the poor".[74] To make the job of the commissions more difficult, the inhabitants of these wretched slums tended to avoid them, partly because they did not trust the police and partly because "they were often enough up to something (like keeping animals illegally) that they did not want the authorities to know about."[75]

In spite of the obstacles and the frustrations, agents of the housing commission continued to circulate through Paris, acting largely on the basis of complaints addressed to the commission itself or to the prefecture, using their powers of persuasion and coercion to force landlords to clean up the worst instances of urban blight. The number of recorded cases investigated by the Paris Housing Commission rose from 160 in 1851 to 1,656 in 1860, to a high of 3,611 in 1866. By 1882, the commission des logements insalubres had dealt with some 63,000 *affaires* and had no doubt made some contribution to improving the lives of the worst-housed inhabitants in the city.[76]

Unlike the housing commission in Rennes, that in Lille proved to be one of the most "dynamic" in France, although energy often proved no match for dirt. It did make some progress in getting the most unfortunate Lillois out of their caves. As in Paris, however, the whole process of forcible hygiene ran into the dilemma that landlords who spent money to improve their property then wanted to charge higher rents, which the old tenants could not pay. The problem was even sharper where new buildings replaced old tenements.[77]

Despite a good number of individual triumphs, therefore, it became obvious that neither individual landlords nor any group of motivated and energetic hygienists had the resources to address the problems of pestilential housing and the other structures of urban depravity. Even the housing commission recognized that "it is only by big public works [*grands travaux*] that we will be able to change a reality to which all these small improvements can offer but an insufficient remedy." Any substantial progress in the battle against the entrenched seediness of city life would require, not a well-intentioned law and a dollop of social services, but a massive and enormously expensive effort by the state.

Hygiene and the Second Empire

The Second Republic might have imagined such an endeavor, but it did not have the solidity or organizational power to carry it out successfully or the time. It lasted a mere three years before Louis Napoleon replaced it with his peculiar version of dictatorship. France's new leader, who had made himself president-for-life in late 1851 and emperor a year later, is one of history's most singular political figures. His detractors have dismissed him as a cheap imitation of his imperial uncle and vilified the Second Empire as history's first fascist regime. To be sure, the ignominious end of his reign at Sedan in 1870 at the hands of Bismarck and Von Moltke hardly contributed to his reputation as a great leader. Yet Louis Napoleon's political vision extended beyond personal ambition and vainglory. The new emperor came to power with a genuine desire to improve the lives of his countrymen, even the poorer ones. In an age when most lives remained wrapped in darkness and filth, that meant above all a commitment to better hygiene. "He worked," as the writer Victor Fournel put it, "simultaneously against plague and against revolutions."[78]

Wandering around Paris in the winter of 1865, the American doctor Frederick Simms recognized the progress that had been made in a generation. He found the place in a very different state to what it had been in Mrs. Trollope's time, thirty years earlier, when streets full of mud and garbage "were a far more frequent occurrence than they are at present." To be sure, the government's efforts to clean up the urban environment were "to a great extent defeated by the bad, unwholesome practices of individuals."

"I feel sure," he wrote, "that a great part of [the city's] unhealthiness in the autumn months, when it smells abominably, must be laid to the door of the people, and not to the state." Yet in Simms's professional medical opinion, "by the removal of narrow streets and lanes, and by the creation of large boulevards and numerous open spaces in various quarters, [the authorities] have done an immense deal since the year 1848 towards lowering the death rate of this city, and with great success."[79]

Simms might have been too enamored of state action or too critical of the people's contribution to the foulness of their lives. But his sense of a regime that had worked hard to clean up Paris and had achieved some success is roughly accurate. The Second Empire had almost immediately reinforced the efforts of the Republic with respect to the activities of the housing commissions and the parallel bodies, the public health commissions (commissions d'hygiène publique). A police ordinance of September 1853, for example, laid out these rather stringent guidelines:

> Houses must be kept, on the outside as well as the inside, in a constant state of cleanliness. Outhouses will be situated and ventilated according to the appropriate rules of architecture; the floors must be impermeable and properly maintained. In order to prevent these habitations from killing people through the spread of lethal fermentations, sinks and interior courtyards must also be kept clean, along with a system of cesspits; the walls of cellars, kitchens, and courtyards whitewashed every year; and houses must be sited at a reasonable distance from any substances susceptible to decomposition.[80]

The housing commission continued to work diligently to enforce these high standards, and their reports, published every four years, describe a broad assault on the conditions that did so much to blight the lives of most Parisians: soliciting complaints and intervening between tenants and landlords, bringing the weight of the government to bear on behalf of the most miserable inhabitants.

The government did not restrict its efforts to the capital, and a circular of December 1858, sent to all prefects, urged them to facilitate the creation of housing commissions in every commune, because "Humanity does not allow any tolerance for housing that will compromise the health of its occupants."[81] Unsurprisingly, the campaign against substandard housing and the general lack of public hygiene was waged unevenly across the country. Not all prefects showed the same initiative in setting up commissions and not all commissions showed the same drive. In the provinces, the housing and hygiene commissions often took a long time to organize and had only begun to attack the problem before the regime collapsed—although they soon continued their work under a new set of political authorities. And certainly, no other cities received the support the government gave to Paris.[82]

The Paris commission report of 1860 summarized its annual activities for the preceding years. In 1857, it took up 492 *affaires*, of which 369 were settled amicably, 94 submitted to the city council, and 29 referred to the prefecture. In 1858, it considered 512 *affaires*, of which 355 were resolved and 157 referred up the chain of command. In 1859, it achieved an amicable settlement in 373 of 641 cases, sending the rest along for further adjudication and action. As the years passed, the number of *affaires* increased.

Predictably, the older and more squalid neighborhoods of the center of Paris, and the newly incorporated working-class arrondissements of the north-east, produced more complaints than the newer, airier districts in the western parts of the city. The commission congratulated itself in 1860 with having contributed to the "improvement of the lives of more than 70,000 souls, among whom are counted a great number of the elderly, a lot of children, and a crowd of unfortunate individuals who might have had better luck."[83]

In one initiative, the state attacked the problem of substandard housing directly, by building its own. In 1849, then-president Bonaparte had sponsored the construction of a Cité Napoléon—200 units of modern, salubrious apartments for working-class families on the rue Rochechouart in the 9th arrondissement. The president had been inspired by the workers housing he had seen in London, sponsored by the Society for Improving the Conditions of the Labouring Classes (1844) under the patronage of Prince Albert, and he wanted to pull French philanthropists along the same route, which was critical, given the severe restraints on public finances in France. Bonaparte, like the Prince Consort, donated his own money to get the project underway. The architects designed four buildings of four stories each, eighty-six units in all. They maximized the amount of air and light available to the residents by building apartments with plenty of windows around little courtyard gardens and put four water closets (W.C.) on every floor—located at the far ends of the hallways, so as to keep them as far as possible from the individual flats. They also included collective spaces for schools, workshops, and stores, along with a washroom, a drying room, and a bathhouse.[84]

Construction of the Cité Napoléon finished in November 1851. Despite its advantages, especially from a hygienic point of view, and the rent subsidies offered by the state, the project was not a success. It consisted mostly of small one- and two-bedroom apartments. It also contained some larger flats, but these proved too expensive for most working-class families from the neighborhood and often stayed empty, since the middle-class families that could afford them had no desire to lodge alongside working-class elements. Most off-putting to potential tenants, the Cité not only looked like a barracks, it operated like one, too. Workers understandably hesitated to move into an apartment complex with only one entrance that was closed every night at 10:00 p.m. And the police kept a close eye on what they worried would become a hotbed of workers' opposition to the regime. Ironically, although the Cité Napoléon was intended to be the first in a series of modern, subsidized housing developments for the capital's working class, it turned out to be the last. The working poor might have wanted a healthy place to live, but they wanted autonomy even more.

In any case, attempts to improve the quality of life in Paris, house by house and *fosse* by *fosse*, were soon dwarfed by the epochal reconstruction undertaken by the new prefect of the Seine, Baron Georges Haussmann. The emperor himself was concerned primarily with "the fluidity of traffic and the adaptation of the city to the new railroad lines being built."[85] He was not at all interested, at first, in subterranean Paris. However, Haussmann seized the opportunity to destroy medieval Paris, which he considered "an open sewer," and succeeded in convincing his master of the necessity of extending the reconstruction of the city below ground. Haussmann envisioned a revolutionary overhaul of the system for delivering clean water to the city and flushing dirty water out of it, and he believed that the street excavations provided the ideal occasion not only for constructing "an urban circulatory system free of blocked arteries and fouled orifices" but also for clearing out "the sluggish intestine left by the old *régime*."[86]

The Second Empire inherited a water system that was, as we have seen, woefully inadequate to what the capital required.[87] In the early 1850s, Parisians still depended on an army of water carriers to move water from source to consumer. It was estimated that only 3 percent of apartments had running water when Haussmann began his epic project. Even though the housing commission noted in 1857 that for a small sum—75 francs a year—a landlord could install a spigot in his building that all the inhabitants could use, the great majority of them neglected to do so. Paris had only 70 kilometers of water pipes, most of small diameter, delivering water that was always "cold in the winter, hot in the summer, suspect at all times, and of very mediocre quality." The commission regretted this situation, since it believed that an ample supply of clean water was the indispensable weapon in the war against social filth: "Without any pressure on our part," wrote the housing commission in 1860, "the easy availability of water means that even tiny apartments are kept with the *salubrité* of a bourgeois house."[88] The trouble was that "easy availability" was the rare exception.

Napoleon I had tried to integrate water from the Ourcq canal into the system. Forty years and four regimes later, though, the Seine remained the dominant source of water for drinking and other purposes. This was so despite the obvious problems, the most troubling of which was that the city continued to empty its sewers into the river. The dangers of contamination were widely suspected, if not yet scientifically explained. The authorities knew that water immediately downstream from sewer outlets at Asnières and Clichy, which poured literally hundreds of thousands of kilograms of sewage a year into the Seine, was undrinkable. Indeed, for 70 kilometers downstream, the water was "black."[89] Water sellers faced strict regulations as to where they could draw their water but generally felt free to ignore them with few consequences—at least to themselves.

Haussmann's great collaborator in "the engineering challenge of his generation; that is, bringing water to and from Paris" was Eugène Belgrand—"a geologist and hydrologist of the first order," who had come to Haussmann's attention when he was an engineer in the town of Avallon and later prefect of the Yonne department. Historian Fabienne Chevallier calls him a visionary, whose originality lay in his intention to bring water directly into every home, and in his distinction between water for public uses, like street cleaning, and water for such private needs as drinking and washing. In the end, Belgrand and Haussmann ended up building what amounted to two parallel systems, one for expensive potable water, brought into Paris from far away, and another for cheaper, undrinkable water for industrial use and street cleaning.

For a time this led to a very unequal economy of water in Paris, with the better districts having easy access to highly drinkable spring water, while the poorer and outlying neighborhoods continued to receive their "private" water from the Seine and the Ourcq.[90] In other words, the geography of water, in Haussmann's Paris, reinforced the general geography of "two cities": a privileged inner core, surrounded by "a veritable Siberia" of "disinherited" districts, largely untouched by the empire's accomplishments in urban hygiene, and riddled with disease, overcrowding, and social pathology. As the Second Empire was pushed off the historical stage, some 82 percent of homes in the affluent inner-city *arrondissements* were hooked up to the new water distribution network, compared to only 48 percent on the periphery.[91]

Notwithstanding the inequities, by 1869, Haussmann and Belgrand had built a system that "provided daily, for the private use of [Parisians], from 24,000 to 30,000 cubic meters of well water, admirably limpid, of perfect quality, at constant temperature"—compared to the 8,000 cubic meters of polluted water that had fed Paris at the beginning of the century.[92] The key to this achievement was the location of a source with both potable qualities and the height to allow the water to run down an aqueduct into the highest point of the city—70 meters, after the inclusion of the outlying arrondissements in 1860. They had found it in the spring-fed rivers of the Dhyus and the Vanne, a 100 miles to the east/northeast of Paris.

Not everyone was pleased. The "fanatics of Seine water," as historian David P. Jordan calls them, insisted that river water "had more character [and] more taste than other sources." Besides, it had served the city for centuries and required only some additional pumping capacity and stiffer regulations to make it adequate to the needs of mid-century Paris. Most of all, though, Haussmann's critics saw his "enormous expenditures" as unwarranted and representing only "another aspect of his penchant for destructiveness and desire for novelty." The American doctor Frederick Simms, meanwhile, was pleased with the ample quantity of water in Paris, which he compared favorably with the "niggardly one hour's daily supply [in London]." On the other hand, he wrote, the quality remained quite poor: hard, unwholesome, and impure—"one of the chief predisposing causes of cholera," in his medical opinion. But Simms lived in the wrong neighborhood and still received his drinking water from the Seine and the Ourcq.[93]

If getting clean water to Parisians was one half of Belgrand's engineering masterpiece, getting rid of the dirty water was the other. When Haussmann began tearing up the streets, Paris contained 107 kilometers of sewer line—which already counted a fourfold expansion under the Orléans monarchy—the largest of which was under 2 meters in height, with another 40 kilometers in the near suburbs. When he had finished, the city had over 500 kilometers of sewers, well over 2 meters high everywhere and up to 4 meters in some places.[94] The new system drained the city in two directions and included a clever system that allowed the sewers to be regularly flushed and cleaned: an animal carcass ran the length of the city in eighteen days, confetti in 6 hours.[95] So remarkable were these "underground boulevards" that tours of them became one of the main attractions of the 1867 International Exposition, and even Tsar Nicholas I made an official visit.

On the other hand, Haussmann's sewers remained a conduit almost entirely for "the drainage of storm waters" and for whatever liquid flowed through the city's gutters. Dr. Simms praised the new system:

> Nothing but the street water and the water from the urinals passes into these drains. . . . One result of cutting off all this [raw sewage] from the Seine must be to make the health of the Parisians better. . . . It is a notorious fact that the elements of urine and fecal matter introduced into drinking water, although they may not alter its appearance to any great degree, are among the most frequent exciting causes of

disease; and it may possibly have been due to past arrangements that typhoid fever has been constantly endemic in Paris, and diarrhea one of its most frequent visitors.[96]

Haussmann was reluctant to let feces into his system. He worried not only about typhoid fever and cholera but also that "the dilution of human waste in water would reduce its value as fertilizer and thereby disrupt the organic economy of the city"; he balked, moreover, at confronting the economic interests invested in the cesspits and their cleanup. Because so few buildings had direct connections between their *cabinets d'aisances* and the sewers in the 1860s, it was unavoidable that the army of night-soil collectors would continue to take care of the capital's solid waste.[97]

As remarkable as it was, therefore—and David Jordan calls the water and sewer systems "the only uniformly praised aspects of haussmannization"—the Baron's work remained incomplete. Even within the charmed inner circle of reconstructed Paris, not everyone was included. A regime that respected the rights of property owners would not compel all landlords to hook their buildings up to either system, water, or sewer. Connection to the city's water system involved an expensive subscription, and many proprietors decided against it. All new and substantially renovated buildings *were* obliged to tie into the sewer system, but only for wastewater, while older buildings escaped these requirements entirely.

The expansion of sewer and water lines, although they represented a great step forward in the modernization of public hygiene, nonetheless had some unexpected, even ironical, effects. For instance, when Haussmann and Belgrand built two separate systems, one for water-in and one for water-out, they allowed households to use considerably more water without necessarily giving them direct access to the sewers. As a result, a lot more water found its way into the *fosses d'aisances*, which made them even more dangerous for being more liquid—sloppier to empty and more likely to leak or overflow. For all its engineering wizardry, moreover, the sewer system still emptied through the *grand collecteur* directly into the Seine, without much in the way of treatment. True, Haussmann's sewers did not contain *much* feces, except what washed in off the streets, and it was no longer a matter of drains emptying helter-skelter into the river at various points along its course through Paris, as in the past. In the new system, sewage now met the Seine some 4 miles further along, at Asnières and Saint-Denis—whose own stretch of river now became "a cauldron of bacteria, infection, and disease."[98] This presumably reduced the incidence of cholera, typhoid fever, and diarrhea in Paris, but at the cost of passing it along to the unfortunate folks who lived further down river. The next step in the assault against urban filth—that is, doing something with the sewage besides giving it to someone else—was, in effect, handed off to the future.

A new underground world of sewers and water pipes was not Haussmann's only contributions to public hygiene. His urban renewal project also included turning ragged bits of the Parisian landscape into parks. At the northeast edge of the city, for example, he converted what in the late Middle Ages had been its busiest execution site—and what had become in the nineteenth century one of the city's "principal garbage dumps," the end of the line for "clapped-out horses," and a rag-pickers' bazaar—into the landscaped park of Buttes-Chaumont.

It was also under Haussmann and the municipal engineer Jean-Charles Alphand that the so-called *Vespasiennes* (after the first-century Roman emperor)—that is, public urinals—became a familiar part of the "street furniture" of modern Paris. The problem of public urination had long concerned police and hygienists. It was the prefect of the Seine Rambuteau who had first introduced these *pissotières* on to the streets of the capital in the 1830s. But Rambuteau had not built nearly enough of them. And to judge by the 1850 police ordinance that forbade public urination on all streets that had these *pissoirs*, even where they existed, their use was hardly universal. To its credit, the empire installed hundreds of additional *pissotières*, and they slowly began to change both practices and sensibilities.[99]

Elsewhere, in the provincial towns and cities that did not receive the huge amounts of Imperial attention and finance that Paris did, personal habits and public sanitation took longer to reform. Urged on by the Saint-Simonian regime in Paris, the city of Lyon paved roads and added sidewalks; motivated by the floods that had swept through in 1856, it began building a water and sewer system.[100] Energetic municipal authorities in Lille made similar efforts—with mixed results. An 1862 ordinance required the construction of sidewalks. But since it left the project to the energy and finances of the property owners, city sidewalks remained "irregular and impractical." Likewise, when an 1868 regulation ordered owners and renters to sweep the front of their houses, to pile up the mud, and to maintain a slope for the water to run down, it had the perverse effect of creating great swamps of mud at the bottom. "Observers," wrote historian Pierre Pierrard, "felt like they were back in the Middle Ages."[101]

In Brittany, wrote Jules Rochard, "where people drink a lot of cider and *eau de vie*, the cities are crossed by streams of urine," forcing pedestrians to jump over or find a way around them. Lille at mid-century had not a single public urinal. Municipal authorities during the Second Empire constructed some makeshift *vespasiennes* against building walls and around public monuments. As Pierre Pierrard notes, however, "exposed to the sun and without ever being rinsed off [these spots] gave off a disgusting odor." The Lillois, unaccustomed to these amenities, referred to their usage as *pisser à la mode de Paris*. Facilities, such as they were, also began to appear on some bridges, where they emptied directly into the canals and continued to offend the locals. In the especially grubby city of Limoges, according to the departmental hygiene commission, there were no public facilities at all, and the streets had become a series of garbage tips. It noted with particular chagrin that public urination had turned the beautiful eighteenth-century Place d'Orsay into "a disgusting cesspool, where no decent person would dare to venture. Employees from the local workshops [urinate] openly, without taking the least account of passers-by."[102]

Urban geographer Matthew Gandy offers another approach to the history of the Haussmann Revolution, mixing conventional assessment of its accomplishments with a more literary way of thinking about its impact—not only on the bodies of Parisians but also on their fantasies.[103] Beginning with his observation that sewers had a long history as "metaphors for the hidden worlds of crime, poverty, and political insurrection," and basing his analysis in large part on the evocative photographs of Félix Nadar (1820–1910), whose images helped fix the popular idea of this underground world he described as "a deformed tangle of filth and entrails beyond the imagination."

Gandy remarks—quite correctly, as we will see—that Haussmann did not effect a full modernization of the water and sewer systems of Paris. What he did instead was to craft "metaphors of progress and the application of scientific knowledge" that "became entangled" with the spirit of the modern age.

What does this mean? Well, first, that Haussmann and Belgrand created a modern economy of water that linked "bodily hygiene and the progressive application of new advances in science and technology." With more of it available, water began to lose much of its mystique—for example, its old associations with sensuality and sin—neither worshiped nor feared, but merely appreciated for its usefulness. At the same time, and several orders of magnitude of abstraction beyond this, Gandy writes that the improved infrastructure of water led to a new "holistic conception of the relationship between the body and the city, which drew on a series of organic analogies to compare the new city with a healthy human body." He links this to Alain Corbin's well-known ideas about the nineteenth century's "olfactory revolution," in which, led by a "bourgeoisie" increasingly detached from its five senses, people became more sensitive to and less tolerant of powerful bodily odors.[104]

Extending his metaphors, Gandy further argues that the "dichotomous olfactory universe of the 'foul' and the 'fragrant'" became increasingly gendered, with the urban and the technology associated with men and "the opposite world of nature and unreason" (and no plumbing) with women.[105] "In Second Empire Paris," he concludes, "the repression of bodily functions in bourgeois society became increasingly manifested in a fear of women and the poor."

Historian Donald Reid likewise untethers his search for meaning from the mere "realities" of Paris's sewer system. Building on insights he borrows from Marx, Freud, and the anthropologist Mary Douglas, Reid also examines the "representations" of urban reform—warning that "fixating on the hygienic and technological" aspects of this history risks missing the "imbricated representations of the aesthetic and the moral, of barbarism and civilization." His narrative thus tries to reach past efforts to battle waterborne diseases and to make Parisian's lives cleaner and safer, in order to see the hidden side of this process; that is, to capture sewers and sewermen within "the signifying systems that inscribe and describe them." With "the sewer," Reid concludes, "the antithesis of the sublime, became also the seat of sublimation." And he calls these workers a "model army" in the battle for the bourgeois desire to impose order on a disordered world—of which terrible sewers are the ultimate example.[106]

Evidence for the assertions of Gandy and Reid—insofar as they are susceptible of evidence—remains necessarily literary, intuitive, metaphorical, and occasionally misleading. For one thing, "bourgeois society" hardly needed differences over "bodily functions" to make them fear the poor. Besides, the notion of rapidly refining bourgeois sensibilities does not fit very well with what we actually know about people's lives and practices at the time. Bourgeois homes and bourgeois bodies of the Victorian age were hardly clean and odorless by our standards. Meanwhile, the slow spread and comparatively high cost of the "new economy of water" set off by the Haussmann Revolution still left the working classes unable to emulate the bourgeoisie, even had there been something to emulate and a manufactured desire for emulation. As Napoleon III surrendered his sword to Bismarck, *both* the elites and the masses remained pretty thoroughly unwashed. The Second Empire had inaugurated a new economy of water and the set of practices that would accompany it. It remained for the Third Republic, eschewing metaphor for industrial engineering and education, to take the next step in public health.

Notes

1 Victor Considérant, quoted in Nicholas Chaudun, *Haussmann au crible* (Paris: Éditions de Syrtes, 2000), 76. Quoted in Julia Csergo, *Liberté, égalité, propreté: La morale de l'hygiène au XIXe siècle* (Paris: Albin Michel, 1988), 12.
2 Jacques Léonard, *Archives du corps. La santé au XIXe siècle* (Rennes: Ouest France, 1986), 63.
3 David Weir, "Economic Welfare and Physical Well-Being in France, 1750–1990," in Richard H. Steckel and Roderick Floud (eds.), *Health and Welfare during Industrialization* (Chicago: University of Chicago Press, 1997), 166.
4 François-Xavier Merrien, *La bataille des eaux: l'hygiène à Rennes au XIXe siècle* (Rennes: Presses Universitaires de Rennes, 1994), 32.
5 Elsbeth Kalff and Lucie Lemaître, *Le logement insalubre et l'hygiénisation de la vie quotidienne. Paris (1830–1990)* (Paris: L'Harmattan, 2008), 13–15. Their study is based on a collection of some 3,000 *plaints pour l'insalubrité* in Paris between 1830 and 1990.
6 Maxime du Camp, *Paris, ses organes, ses fonctions et sa vie dans la seconde moitié du XIXe siècle*, vol. VI (Paris: Hachette, 1879), 333–4; also Colin Jones, *Paris: Biography of a City* (New York: Viking, 2004), 207, 285–6, 295, and 395.
7 Merrien, *La bataille des eaux*, 72. And John Merriman, *The Margins of City Life: Explorations of the French Urban Frontier, 1815–1851* (New York: Oxford University Press, 1991), 17.
8 Ambroise Tardieu, "Equarrissage," in *Dictionnaire d'hygiène publique et de salubrité, ou Répertoire de toutes les questions relatives à la santé publique . . . complété par le texte des lois . . . qui s'y rattachent* (Paris: J.-B. Ballière et fils, 1862), 64–5.
9 See the comment on the Villermé report in Kalff and Lemaître, *Le logement insalubre*, 32.
10 Roger-Henri Guerrand, "Aux origines du confort moderne," in Jacques Lucan (ed.), *Eau et gaz à tous les étages. Paris: 100 ans de logement* (Paris: Éditions du Pavillon de l'Arsenal, 1992), 17.
11 Département de la Seine. Ville de Paris, Commission des logements insalubres, *Rapport général des travaux de la commission, pendant l'année 1851* (Paris: Vinchon, Imprimeur de la Préfecture de la Seine, 1852), 11–12.
12 On the Jardin des Plantes neighborhood, see Commission des logements insalubres, *Rapport général des travaux de la commission* (1852), 10–11, in the Archives Nationales (hereafter cited as AN) F8 211, Police Sanitaire. On the Cité Doré, see Préfecture de Police. Conseil d'hygiène publique et de salubrité, *Rapport sur l'insalubrité de la Cité Doré et de la Cité des Kroumirs (13e arrondissement)* (Paris: Imprimerie Chaix, 1882), 6. Also see *L'Édile de Paris: Journal des propriétaires, ou Recueil d'observations, de faits, de renseignements, tendant à les éclairer sur leurs véritables intérêts, et à faciliter les opérations qui peuvent assainir et enrichir la ville* (February 5, 1833); Jacques Sellier, *Le choléra à Paris, essai de*

topographie biologique (thèse pour le docteur en medecine, Paris, Sorbonne, 1973), 40; and Comte de Rambuteau, *Mémoires du Comte Rambuteau publiés par son petit-fils (avec une introduction et des notes par Georges Lequin)* (Paris: Calmann-Levy, 1905), 375–6.

13 Olivier Le Goff, *L'invention du confort: naissance d'une forme sociale* (Lyon: Presses Universitaires de Lyon, 1994), 34. À propos of Limoges, see Alain Corbin, *Archaïsme et modernité en Limousin au XIXe siècle, 1845–1880: La rigidité des structures économiques, sociales et mentales* (Paris: Editions Marcel Rivière, 1975), 85–6. On Lyon, see Philippe Jean-Baptiste Malfacon and Auguste-Pierre de Polinière, *Traité de la salubrité dans des grandes villes* (Paris: Ballière, 1846), cited in Philippe Dufieux, "A propos de l'hygiène de Lyon (1800–1960)," in Conseil d'Architecture, d'Urbanisme et de l'Environnement du Rhône, *Le confort moderne dans l'habitat* (Lyon: CAUE, 2007), 11. Also, Yves Lequin, "Les espaces de la société citadine," in Lequin (dir.), *Histoire des Français XIXe-XXe siècles: la société. Livre III: Les villes et l'industrie: l'émergence d'une autre France* (Paris: Armand Colin, 1983), 361.

14 Victor Derode, *Histoire de Lille et de la Flandre wallonne* (Lille: Vanackere, 1848), quoted in Pierre Pierrard, *La vie ouvrière à Lille sous le Second Empire* (Paris: Bloud & Gay, 1965), 80 and 88; on people living in caves, see Alfred de Foville, *Enquête sur les conditions de l'habitation en France. Tome I: Les maisons-types* (Paris: Ernest Leroux, 1894), 33.

15 For Rennes, see Merrien, *La bataille des eaux*, 32–4; for Villermé's figures on mortality in Mulhouse, see Jean Fourastié, *Les trentes glorieuses, ou la Révolution invisible de 1946 à 1975* (Paris: Fayard, 1979), 63. For Grenoble, see Lequin, "Les espaces de la société citadine," 361.

16 Martin Nadaud, "Memoirs of a Former Mason's Assistant," in Mark Traugott (ed.), *The French Worker: Autobiographies from the Early Industrial Era* (Berkeley: University of California Press, 1993), 225.

17 Alain Faure and Claire Lévy-Vroelant, *Une chambre en ville: Hôtels meublés et garnis de Paris, 1860–1990* (Saint-Etienne: Créaphis, 2007), 125.

18 Honoré de Balzac, *Old Goriot* (New York: Penguin, 1951), 27–8.

19 Département de la Seine, *Rapport général des travaux de la commission* (1852), 9–10.

20 Pierrard, *La vie ouvrière à Lille*, 84–5.

21 R. Woods and J. Woodward, eds., *Urban Disease and Mortality in Nineteenth-Century England* (New York: St. Martin's, 1984), 20.

22 Jean-Baptiste Monfaucon, *Hygiène de la ville de Lyon ou opinions et rapports du conseil de salubrité du département du Rhône* (Paris: Ballière, 1845), 45.

23 André Gueslin, *Gens pauvres, pauvres gens dans la France du XIXe siècle* (Paris: Aubier, 1998), 64.

24 Léonard, *Archives du corps*, 115.

25 Geoffrey Jones, *Beauty Imagined: A History of the Global Beauty Industry* (New York: Oxford University Press, 2010), 71; Roger Leblanc, *Le savon de la préhistoire au XXIe siècle* (Montreuil l'Argille: Éditions Pierann, 2001), 274.

26 Pierrard, *La vie ouvrière à Lille*, 66.

27 Geneviève Cerisier-Millet, *Un siècle de bains et lavoirs: Châtelleraut, 1830–1930* (Châtelleraut: Cerisier-Millet, 2003), 15–24 and Jean-Baptiste Fonssagrives, *Dictionnaire de la santé, ou Répertoire d'hygiène pratique, à l'usage des familles et des écoles* (Paris: C. Delagrave, 1876), 50.

28 John M. Merriman, *The Red City: Limoges and the French Nineteenth Century* (New York: Oxford University Press, 1985), 38.

29 Adolphe Chauveau, "Bains et lavoirs du Temple," *Journal du droit administratif* 3 (1855): 271–4.
30 Achille Penot, *Les cités ouvrières de Mulhouse et du département du Haut-Rhin. Nouvelle édition, augmentée de la description des bains et lavoirs établis à Mulhouse* (Mulhouse: L.L. Bader, 1867), cited in Peter Ward, *The Clean Body: A Modern History* (Montreal and Kingston: McGill-Queens University Press, 2019), 54. Also see Will Clement, "The 'Unrealizable Chimera': Workers' Housing in Nineteenth-Century Mulhouse," *French History* 32, no. 1 (2018): 66–85.
31 Edwin Chadwick, *Report on the Sanitary Condition of the Labouring Population of Great Britain* (Edinburgh: Edinburgh University Press, 1965), 316 and Csergo, *Liberté, égalité, propreté*, 70.
32 Cited in Dr. Augustin Cabanès, *Moeurs intimes du passé, deuxième série: La vie aux bains* (Paris: Albin Michel, 1909), 368, n. 1; the Taine story comes from Katherine Ashenburg, *The Dirt on Clean: An Unsanitized History* (New York: North Point Press, 2007), 165–6.
33 Anne-Marie Sohn, *Chrysalides. Femmes dans la vie privé (XIXe-XXe siècles)*, vol. 1 (Paris: Publications de la Sorbonne, 1996), 120.
34 Ward, *The Clean Body*, 34.
35 According to J. Moisy, in 1849 there were altogether eighty-one *bateaux-lavoirs* on the Seine and the Canal Saint-Martin: Moisy, *Les lavoirs de Paris* (Paris: E. Sausset, 1884), 20–2.
36 Cerisier-Millet, *Un siècle de bains*, 120. On the 1851 law, see Léonard, *Archives du corps*, 137; and on the lack of washing facilities in Nantes, see M. Hertaux-Varavaux [Unions de la Paix Sociale—Groupe de Nantes], *Enquête sur la condition des petits logements dans la ville de Nantes* (Paris: Au Secrétariat de la Société d'Économie Sociale, 1888), 8.
37 Adolphe Blanqui, *Des classes ouvrières en France, pendant l'année 1848* (Paris: Pagnerre, 1849), 71.
38 Claude Lachaise, "Topographie médicale de Paris" (1832) cited in Elsie Canfora-Argandona et Roger-Henri Guerrand, *La répartition de la population: les conditions de logement des classes ouvrière à Paris au XIXe siècle* (Paris: Centre de Sociologie Urbaine, 1976), 21.
39 Cited by Martin Nadaud, the reporter for a proposition for the eponymous law aimed at reinforcing the power of the commissions and conseils d'hygiène, Chambre des Députés, session de 1883, in AN F8, Police Sanitaire, carton 212, "Logements insalubres, 1881–1896," 2. Also see David S. Barnes, *The Great Stink of Paris and the Nineteenth-Century Struggle against Filth and Germs* (Baltimore: Johns Hopkins University Press, 2006), 92–3 and Georges Vigarello, *Concepts of Cleanliness: Changing Attitudes in France Since the Middle Ages* (Cambridge: Cambridge University Press, 1988), 194.
40 Quoted in Mark S. R. Jenner, "Follow Your Nose? Smell, Smelling, and their Histories," *American Historical Review* 116, no. 2 (April 2011): 338.
41 Antoine Chapelle, *Traité d'hygiène* (Paris: Victor Masson, 1850), 28 and 33–5; also Merrien, *La bataille des eaux*, 63.
42 François Delaporte, *Le savoir et la maladie. Essai sur le choléra de 1832 à Paris* (Paris: Presses Universitaires de France, 1990), 61.
43 For hygienist Émile Cheysson, it was the "question primordiale." "Without water," he wrote, "no cleanliness, no hygiene, no health, no dignity, no virtue": Cheysson, *Le confort du logement populaire* (Paris: Imprimerie Chaix, 1905), 3.

44 Guy Thuillier, *Pour une histoire du quotidien au XIXe siècle en Nivernais* (Paris: École des hautes études en sciences sociales, 1977), 13; Ned Rival, *Histoire anécdotique du lavage et des soins corporels* (Paris: Jacques Grancher, 1986), 77–81; also Jean-Pierre Goubert, *La conquête de l'eau: l'avénément de la santé à l'âge industriel* (Paris: Éditions Robert Laffont, 1986), 7. According to Jules Rochard, the average Parisian enjoyed 13 liters of water a day on the eve of the Revolution, a figure well above the consensus: *Traité d'hygiène publique et privée* (Paris: Octave Doin, 1897), 261; Kalff and Lemaître, *Le logement insalubre*, 81–2.

45 On the Périer brothers, see Joan Dejean, *The Age of Comfort: When Paris Discovered Casual—and the Modern Home Began* (New York and London: Bloomsbury, 2009), 75–6; and Rival, *Histoire anécdotique*, 97 and 100.

46 David P. Jordan, *Transforming Paris: The Life and Labors of Baron Haussmann* (New York: The Free Press, 1995), 269; Stéphane Frioux, *Les batailles de l'hygiène: villes et environnement de Pasteur aux Trentes Glorieuses* (Paris: Presses Universitaires de France, 2013), 23.

47 Csergo, *Liberté, égalité, propreté*, 213–14.

48 Jean Fourastié et Françoise Fourastié, *Histoire du confort* (Paris: Presses Universitaires de France, 1973), 65 and 72.

49 Merriman, *The Margins of City Life*, 57. Also Frederick Simms, *A Winter in Paris, being a few Experiences and Observations of French Medical and Sanitary Matters Gained during the Season of 1865–6* (London: John Churchill and Sons, 1866), 146.

50 Cited in Léonard, *Archives du corps*, 96.

51 On Lille, see Pierrard, *La vie ouvrière à Lille*, 51; on Rouen, see Jean-Pierre Chaline, *Les bourgeois de Rouen: une élite urbaine au XIXe siècle* (Paris: Presses de la Fondation Nationale de la Science Politique, 1982), 194; on Nevers, see Thuillier, *Pour une histoire du quotidien*, 16; and on Limoges Merriman, *The Red City*, 100.

52 Judith Flanders, *Inside the Victorian Home: A Portrait of Domestic Life in Victorian England* (New York: Norton, 2003), 128; Steven Johnson, *The Ghost Map: The Story of London's Most Terrifying Epidemic—and How it Changed Science, Cities, and the Modern World* (New York: Riverhead Books, 2006), 12; Richard J. Evans. *Death in Hamburg: Society and Politics in the Cholera Years* (New York and Toronto: Penguin, 1987), 146.

53 Frances Trollope, *Paris and the Parisians in 1835*, vol. 1 (London: Richard Bentley, 1835), quoted in Csergo, *Liberté, égalité, propreté*, 221.

54 M. Bret, "L'alimentation de Paris en eau," *Annales des Ponts et Chaussées* (1902): 251. All these figures seem indicative rather than exact.

55 Cabanès, *Moeurs intimes du passé*, 3.

56 Monique Eleb and Anne Debarre, *L'invention de l'habitation moderne: Paris 1880–1914. Architectures de la vie privée, suite* (Paris: Éditions Hazan et Archives d'Architecture Moderne, 1995), 216.

57 Merrien, *La bataille des eaux*, 72.

58 Corbin, *Archaïsme et modernité en Limousin*, 81–2 and 85.

59 Léonard, *Archives du corps*, 144.

60 AN F8 Police Sanitaire, carton 212, "Logements insalubres, 1881–1896": M. Dunoyer, report on the projet de loi relative à l'assainissement des logements et habitations insalubres, June 21, 1886, 60–1.

61 Louis-Narcisse Girard [Inspecteur général adjoint des Travaux de Paris], *Le nettoiement de Paris. Conférence faite aux ingénieurs des travaux publics de la Ville de Paris, le 6 janvier 1923* (Paris: Librairie de l'Enseignement Technique, 1923), 14–15.

62 Pierrard, *Vie ouvrière à Lille*, 54. Also see Colin Heyward, *Childhood in Nineteenth-Century France: Work, Health and Education among the 'Classes Populaires'* (Cambridge: Cambridge University Press, 1988), 165.
63 Girard, *Le nettoiement de Paris*, 12–15.
64 Kalff and Lemaître, *Le logement insalubre*, 101.
65 Rochard, *Traité d'hygiène publique et privée*, 416–19.
66 Gustave Jourdan [chef de bureau à la Préfecture de la Seine], *Étude sur le projet de revision de la loi concernant les logements insalubres* (Paris: Berger-Levrault et Cie., 1883), 3. De Melun cited in Faure and Lévy-Vroelant, *Une chambre en ville*, 126–7; also see the report, "La question du taudis dans les différents pays et le moyens mis en oeuvre pour y rémédier," in Ministère de la Santé Publique, *Recueil des Travaux de l'Institut National d'Hygiène: travaux des sections et mémoires originaux*, tome IV, vol. 1 (Paris: Masson et Cie., 1950), 290 and Frédéric Moret, "Le logement et la question sociale (1830–1870)," in Marion Segaud, Catherine Bonvalet, and Jacques Brun (dirs.), *Logement et Habitat: L'état des savoirs* (Paris: Éditions la Découverte, 1998), 21–2.
67 See the letter addressed to the prefect of the Seine department in Archives de Paris (hereafter cited as AP) V 15: Département de la Seine. Ville de Paris, *Commission des logements insalubres* (Vichon: Imprimeur de la Préfecture de la Seine, 1851), 14.
68 Ernst Monin, *La propreté de l'individu et de la maison* (Paris: Au Bureau de la Société, 1886), 26.
69 Kalff and Lemaître, *Le logement insalubre*, 65–72.
70 Département de la Seine. Ville de Paris. Commission des logements insalubres, *Rapport Générale sur les travaux de la commission pendant les années 1862, 1863, 1864, et 1865* (Paris: Typographie de Chales de Mourgues Frères, 1866), 10, in AP DM 5 0017.
71 Kalff and Lemaître, *Le logement insalubre*, 65.
72 Commission des logements insalubres, *Rapport général* (1852), 4–7.
73 See the discussion in Jenner, "Follow Your Nose," 335–51. For a more speculative and doubtful reading, see Constance Classen, David Howes, and Anthony Synnott, *Aroma: The Cultural History of Smell* (New York: Routledge, 1994), 4: "The powerful denigration of smell by Europe's intellectual elite has had a lasting effect on the status of olfaction. Smell has been 'silenced' in modernity."
74 Merrien, *La bataille des eaux*, 108.
75 Kalff and Lemaître, *Le logement insalubre*, 78–9.
76 These numbers come from Ville de Paris. Commission des Logements Insalubres, *Rapport général sur les travaux de la Commission pendant les années 1890–1891–1892* (Paris: Imprimerie de l'École Municipale Estienne, 1895), 11; also see Jourdan, *Étude sur le projet de révision de la loi*, 5.
77 Pierrard, *La vie ouvrière à Lille*, 92–5.
78 Victor Fournel, *Paris nouveau et Paris futur* (Paris: J. Lecoffre, 1865), 166.
79 Simms, *A Winter in Paris*, 135–6.
80 Monin, *La propreté de l'individu*, 26–7.
81 Département de la Seine. Ville de Paris. Commission des logements insalubres, *Rapport général sur les travaux de la Commission pendant les années 1857, 1858, 1859* (Paris: Charles de Mourgues Frères, 1860), 6.
82 On the activities in one department, see Conseils d'Hygiène Publique et de Salubrité du Gers, *Procès-verbal, 1864, 1865, 1866, 1867* (Auch: F.-A. Cocharaux, 1868), 217.

83 Commission des logements insalubres, *Rapport général* (1868), 29; also see Département de la Seine. Ville de Paris. Commission des logements insalubres, *Rapport général* (1866), 4.
84 On the Cité Napoléon, see Fabienne Chevallier, *Le Paris moderne* (Rennes: Presses Universitaires de Rennes, 2010), 41; and Csergo, *Liberté, égalité, propreté*, 95–6.
85 Chevallier, *Le Paris moderne*, 55.
86 Donald Reid, *Paris Sewers and Sewermen: Realities and Representation* (Cambridge, MA: Harvard University Press, 1991), 29.
87 This discussion of Haussmann's reforms comes principally from Jordan, *Transforming Paris*, 268–76. All otherwise unattributed citations come from there.
88 Kalff and Lemaître, *Le logement insalubre*, 83; also see Commission des logements insalubres, *Rapport général* (1860), 20.
89 Reid, *Paris Sewers and Sewermen*, 57–8.
90 Chevallier, *Le Paris moderne*, 33–4; also Csergo, *Liberté, égalité, propreté*, 227–9.
91 See Matthew Gandy, "The Paris Sewers and the Rationaization of Urban Space," *Transactions of the Institute of British Geographers NS* (1999): 40n.
92 Georges-Eugène Haussmann, *Mémoires de Baron Haussmann, vol. 1* (Paris: Havard, 1890), 514–15.
93 Simms, *A Winter in Paris*, 146–7.
94 Different authors cite different numbers for the length of sewer created. Jordan, for example, writes that there were 217 kilometers in Paris and 188 kilometers in the *faubourgs*: *Transforming Paris*, 270; Reid counts 153 kilometers of sewers in 1853: *Paris Sewers and Sewermen*, 27. According to Gabriel Dupuy and Georges Knaebel, there were 560 kilometers by 1871, not counting the newly incorporated arrondissements, in *Assainir la ville hier et aujourd'hui* (Paris: Dunod-Bordias, 1982), 6. But all agree that the increase was exponential.
95 Will Hunt, "Going Souterrain," *The Economist* (June 14, 2013): 18.
96 Simms, *A Winter in Paris*, 139–40.
97 Gandy, "The Paris Sewers," 30; also see Lionel Kesztenbaum and Jean-Laurent Rosenthal, "Income versus Sanitation: Mortality Decline in Paris, 1880–1914," Working Paper No. 2014-26, Paris School of Economics, July 4, 2014, 14.
98 Paul Hayes Tucker, *Monet at Argenteuil* (New Haven: Yale University Press, 1982), cited in Francis Frascina, Tamar Garb, Nigel Blake, Briany Fer, and Charles Townshend Harrison, *Modernity and Modernism: French Painting in the Nineteenth Century* (New Haven: Yale University Press, 1993), 121.
99 On public urinals, see Barnes, *The Great Stink*, 79–80 and Jones, *Paris*, 398–9.
100 Dufieux, "À propos de l'hygiène," 16–17.
101 Pierrard, *La vie ouvrière à Lille*, 109.
102 On Brittany, see Rochard, *Traité d'hygiène publique et privée*, 246; on Lille, Pierrard, *La vie ouvrière à Lille*, 53; and on Limoges, the *Rapport du Conseil départemental d'hygiène* (1857), is cited in Corbin, *Archaïsme et modernité en Limousin*, 82, n. 41.
103 For his discussion of the sewers as an active metaphor, see Gandy, "The Paris Sewers," 23–44 *passim*.
104 We have already seen Kalff and Lemaître, *Le logement insalubre*, make the same point: "This relation between cleanliness and health," they write, is a result of "a civilization offensive launched by the state" and the permeation of society by bourgeois ideas and sensibilities, 79.

105 Gandy, "The Paris Sewers," 34 writes:

> In bourgeois French society, women were relegated to a dichotomous olfactory universe of the "foul" and the "fragrant," which became manifest in the cultural and aesthetic discourses of urban design above and below ground. The relegation of women to an opposite world of nature and unreason had an increasingly powerful hold over the prevailing political and intellectual outlooks of nineteenth-century Paris, where the dichotomous cultural representation of women reached its apotheosis with the flow of water through urban space. The public face of water in the lakes and fountains in imperial Paris was to be a celebration of the female form for the pleasure of the male citizen. Water-based sculptures and architectural forms allowed a symbolic continuity with classical themes based around nudity and human physical perfection. By the 1870s, the Renaissance emphasis on the male nude as ideal human form was increasingly supplanted by the female nude and the imposition of a new body aesthetic. The ornamental public fountains of Haussmann's Paris exemplified the combination of water with the control of women's sexuality in the most expensive Belle-Epoque neo-Fontainebleau style favored by Napoleon III.

106 Reid, *Paris Sewers and Sewermen*, 3–5.

4

The Republic of Hygiene I—Dirt and Defense

The Civilizing Mission

No one would blame the debacle of 1870–1 on poor hygiene. Yet it is fair to say that the Third Republic was born in both dirt and defeat, or more particularly in the way the nation's new leaders put these two disagreeable facts together: a simple syllogism that linked slovenliness to economic backwardness, social turmoil, political instability, and military disaster. A strong Republic, the founders believed, although they rarely said so explicitly, required citizens who were civilized; that is, whose political thoughts and actions were guided by a patriotism grounded in history and reason, not by the blind passions of class and religion that had destroyed the first two Republics. It required, in other words, citizens who were *modern*.[1]

Accordingly, they set out to invent and adapt the institutions that, in molding modern French men and women, would lay the foundations for democracy, economic growth, and civil order. The army and the schools became, in the words of folklorist Françoise Loux, "the sites of a civic apprenticeship, of socialization. To that end, these institutions focused on the body, preached the importance of its conservation, battled lice, cut hair short, denigrated whatever was not ordered and neat, and condemned disorder as 'savagery.'"[2] This crusade against degeneration and squalor had to be waged, "not in the interest of individuals, but in the social interest, as an act of high morality and the primary duty of public servants." In the words of historian David S. Barnes, this effort represented "a battle of civilization against backwardness and of the secular republic against intractable reactionary enemies," as well as a means to fend off the "decline of the race."[3]

The best known explication of this idea comes from Eugen Weber, whose book *Peasants into Frenchmen* (1976) explores the way the new Republic sought to cultivate the peasantry—*republicanizing* them, in effect.[4] A generation of historians following Weber, especially those who have focused on education, have added depth and detail to his insight, investigating the way that Republican schools, following the expansion of free and more or less universal primary education in the 1880s, taught young French boys and girls to read and to write and to figure. These skills then became the basis of an education in good citizenship. Pupils learned history and civics. They learned to speak proper French. They learned of their rights and duties in a free republic. As historian Rebecca Rogers put it, "Republicans predicated the triumph of democratic institutions and practices on the moral reform of the middle-class home."[5]

It seems unlikely that many architects of the new Republic overtly ranked hygiene near the top of their list of qualities that defined the ideal citizen—alongside literacy, love of country, and hatred of tyrants. Yet, as the institutions that transformed peasants and other so-called backward elements into "Frenchmen" began to crystallize in the decades following the fall of the Second Empire, hygiene found a surprisingly important place in the process. To be sure, the lessons in propriety taught to young and not-so-young French citizens in the last quarter of the nineteenth century were not up to twenty-first-century standards, and even those lessons were mostly honored in the breach. For a long time, until germ theory really took root in the culture, they were not even based on any particular scientific understanding. They stemmed rather from that same intuitive sense that informed the rest of the republican curriculum; that a successful Republic demanded a more *civilized* sort of human being; and that cleanliness, like literacy and sobriety, marked the difference between the sort of people ruled by kings and emperors and those who ruled themselves.

Dirt and Revenge

In the wake of the calamity of 1871, one element in this syllogism became especially germane to those who were planning the renaissance of the French army; specifically, that sickly, unkempt young men made poor soldiers. Better schoolchildren today make better soldiers tomorrow, wrote public education officer A. Féret:

> Let us develop our children with a thoughtful physical education; let us prepare them for their future responsibilities as soldiers; because, whatever their good will and their efforts, if we are not careful, when the time arrives for these challenges, they will not be ready. . . . How many of these values are lacking, to the current despair of our generals. What a danger for the Fatherland![6]

Why did the Prussian Army lose the Battle of Valmy (1792), asked Dr. Félix-Paul Codvelle, in his inaugural lecture to the medical faculty at Val-de-Grâce military hospital in 1935? It was not the patriotic valor of the French, he replied. It was the poor hygienic condition of the Germans after "they had dragged themselves through the mud for three weeks, soaked by incessant rain . . . their bodies racked with dysentery, the famous *courée prussienne*." In what other campaigns, Codvelle wondered, had disease, filth, and fatigue played the pivotal role in deciding the outcome? Moreover, he added, this was not just a matter of comfortable barracks, decent food, and careful training. Military hygiene was largely an extension of social hygiene, of the condition of young soldiers who come out of the civilian population.[7] Codvelle was speaking of the French Revolutionary Wars, but his analysis would have applied equally, with the victorious and defeated parties reversed, to the Franco-Prussian War, which the French fought with soldiers in various states of physical decay—troubling evidence, for the era of social Darwinism, of the "decline of the race."[8]

The circumstances described in the preceding chapters—the crowded, humid, verminous, smoky homes; the lice-ridden heads and skin scaled in dirt; the itchy, uncomfortable, unwashed, and unchanged clothes—left an indelible mark on those who endured them. Hygiene, or more properly, the lack of it, was written on the bodies of the past, even on the soldiers. "It is impossible," observed Lionel Decle, the young middle-class recruit, "to conceive how men can live in the state of filth which seems natural to French soldiers."[9]

Direct evidence about those bodies is thinner than historians might wish. Anecdotal testimony can speak to the disproportion of lameness or scrofula, the incidence of kyphosis (hunch back), or the occurrence of deafness or blindness in this or that region. But in a predominantly pre-statistical world, it is difficult to track the general state of bodies—and, by implication, the sensibilities and practices that affect them—or to trace them across time.

Happily, there exists one such continuous, comparatively reliable, and much discussed series of figures: statistics compiled by French military authorities on the number of young Frenchmen recruited into or exempted from the army annually, department by department, most dependably from the end of the Bourbon Restoration through the Second Empire. These numbers may be more indicative than precise, but they are useful nonetheless—especially in the absence of more abundant and meticulous numbers—for the story they tell about the physical state of what should have been the sturdiest, healthiest slice of the population: young men.

Draft boards had long remarked on "the extraordinary filth in which countrymen wallowed," which they saw every year when a substantial portion of the nation's twenty-year-olds presented themselves for induction.[10] In Rozier, a rural commune not far from Clermont-Ferrand, near the end of the Napoleonic Wars, the army had rejected fully 57 percent of recruits for a "lack of height" or other physical deformities. It focused in particular on the "lack of care for their bodies that accounted for the early mortality and revealed the fragile health" of these young men. "These conscripts," the army observed, "are often weak, with delicate constitutions and some grave disability"; that is, completely unsuited to the military profession.[11]

The physical state of the population, as measured by exemptions for height, could vary substantially, even within regions. In his study of the Beauce, Jean-Claude Farcy found that at the end of the First Empire, the fraction of young men deemed unfit for service in the Grande Armée ranged from 10 percent on one side of the territory to more than 20 percent on the other. The proportion of recruits falling below the departmental average of 5'3" (1.600 meters) ran between 40 and 49 percent in the best cantons to more than 65 percent in the worst. A similar picture emerged from a look at those excused from military service under the vaguer rubric of "weak constitutions": 10–12.4 percent in the healthiest cantons and more than 20 percent in the sicklier ones. "To obtain the necessary number of two hundred thousand capable men," wondered a Parisian newspaper, "how many young invalids will have to be passed over?"[12]

Over the next two generations, the army recorded the combination of progress and inertia that it found imprinted on the bodies of young recruits. In 1845, for example, army physician Théodore Garnier-Léteurrie emphasized the progress he had witnessed, writing that, "Soldiers today are too clean to be verminous." Dr. Garnier admitted that there remained recruits who carried this "stigma of the most disgusting filth," but maintained that these came only from "the most unfortunate villages in France." Yet almost a quarter century later, near the end of the Second Empire, a letter from the sub-prefect to the mayor of La Ferté-Bernard (Sarthe) proposed that all potential recruits from that commune be washed before being examined by military authorities because, "Despite recommendations renewed each year, a certain number of young men present themselves to the draft boards in a state of dirtiness that makes their examinations painful [to the doctors]."[13]

Naturally, military doctors were concerned, not primarily for aesthetic reasons—as unpleasant as the job of examining these young men might be—but because there was such a compelling link between feeble recruits and weak soldiers, as the Conseil de Santé had complained to the War Ministry in 1839, à propos of the exceptionally high mortality in the Lyon garrison. Dirty, scrawny conscripts, as so many were, could not support the physical demands of soldiering, especially during the winter. Concerns about the grubby and weakened state of young Frenchmen did not disappear in the years running up to the Franco-Prussian War. Instead, they seemed to grow alongside France's increasingly parlous security situation.[14]

Different observers drew different lessons from the army's singular experience of French demography. Military surgeon Jean-Christian-Marc Boudin, writing in 1863, addressed widespread fears that France's demographic decline would undercut its military preparedness. "For several years now," he said,

> It has been one of the favorite themes of the foreign press to represent France as a decadent country, from the perspective of its eligible population, to the point that the composition of its army is being seriously compromised by both its short stature and its dirtiness.[15]

Boudin's history of morphology and military aptitude outlined the literal ups and downs of height requirements for the French army. An ordinance of 1701 fixed the minimum at 1.624 meters (5'4"). From the Revolution to the Treaty of Amiens (1802) it was 1.598 meters (5'3"), lowered to 1.544 (4'9") with the return to war in 1804. The Restoration required its soldiers to be at least 1.57 meters (4'10") tall, while the army of the July Monarchy, less in need of cannon fodder, was at first prepared to accept recruits who were merely 1.54 meters (5'1"); although it raised the bar slightly to 1.56 meters in 1832. Between 1818 and 1828, Boudin found the mean height among recruits was 1.657 meters (5'5"), and the army rejected an average of 25,515 men every year for being too short, which number fell to 15,325 after the height requirement was lowered. This represented an "unfit" group of between 4 and 28 percent of the recruiting class, depending on the department. Potential conscripts—that is, the general population of young Frenchmen—were getting shorter. Even reducing the size requirement in 1832 by 3 centimeters produced only 7,804 extra recruits (Table 4.1).[16]

As Table 4.1 demonstrates, however, after 1831, the situation began to turn around. With few exceptions, the number of conscripts exempted for insufficient size fell every year for the next thirty years, from 928/10,000 in 1831 to 594/10,000 in 1860, meaning that every batch of 1,000 recruits yielded thirty-three more men fit for military service.

Table 4.1 The Number of Military Exemptions for Insufficient Height out of 10,000 Men Examined, 1830–61

Class	Exempt	Class	Exempt	Class	Exempt
1831	928	1841	726	1851	596
1832	899	1842	729	1852	618
1833	874	1843	706	1853	560
1834	842	1844	686	1854	687
1835	831	1845	678	1855	688
1836	827	1846	603	1856	630
1837	791	1847	858	1857	638
1838	758	1848	706	1858	617
1839	717	1849	666	1859	580
1840	784	1850	623	1860	594

Source: Jean-Christian-Marc Boudin, *Études ethnologiques sur la taille et le poids de l'homme chez divers peuples et sur l'accroissement de la taille et de l'aptitude militaire en France. Deuxième mémoire* (Paris: Victor Rozier, 1863), 6.

Of course, the vigor of young Frenchmen was not evenly distributed across the country. The departments of the north and east produced the highest proportion of tall-enough conscripts: Doubs, Haute-Marne, Côte d'Or, Jura, and Pas-de-Calais. The Vosges, according to Boudin, was the tallest department in France, with 90 percent of recruits between 1.896 meters (almost 6'1") and 1.922 meters (6'3")—although, in truth, it is difficult to believe the Vosges was turning out such a race of giants.[17] At the other end of the scale lay the remotest parts of *la France profonde*: Haute-Vienne, Corrèze, Hautes-Alpes, Ardèche, Puy-de-Dôme. Boudin compared these figures to those he cited for the British Army, which set a minimum height of only 1.62 meters (5'4") and where only 57 out of every 10,000 recruits surpassed 6 feet. Scottish recruits were shorter, and the Irish shorter still. However, research on the height of British troops during the Napoleonic Wars suggests an average height of about 5'8" (1.68 meters)—at least for Wellington's Foot Guards.[18]

Georges Morache, the doctor who wrote the guidelines on military hygiene, likewise looked at the proportion of recruits rejected for being too short between 1844 and 1868 and came away with the same conclusions. Beginning at 84.1 out of every thousand in 1844, rejections reached a maximum of 108.4 in 1847 and a low of 50.6 per 1,000 in 1868, with a more or less steady decline through the 1850s and especially the 1860s. It is perhaps significant that the numbers of conscripts *exemptés* for *infirmité* did not follow a similar trajectory, hitting a high of 404.7 per 1,000 in 1846 and a low of 312.6 in 1853, but mostly fluctuating in a seemingly random manner.[19]

Boudin's statistics are imperfect, and some of his conclusions are problematical—not only about the height of young men in the Vosges, for instance, but also in his assertion that soldiers in the Belgian army continued to get taller between the ages of twenty-five and thirty. Nonetheless, they served in his mind as sufficient proof that the French population was getting taller and stronger through the July Monarchy and the first decade of the Second Empire, which made Boudin an optimist on the question of France's martial and demographic destiny. He accepted that "below a certain height, which varies according to race and nationality, young men are fundamentally unfit for the military profession." Yet he insisted that "our country occupies the top rank," when it comes to exemptions for insufficient height and other infirmities. He pointed out that in 1831, 37 percent of conscripts had been rejected for physical insufficiencies, whereas the percentage had fallen to under a third by 1850. Conditions had gotten worse in only eleven departments, while they had improved in seventy-five.[20]

Boudin also had a second, and perhaps more important, demographic point to make. A consideration of the distribution of the heights of young conscripts, and the number exempted from military service for other reasons, he stressed, belied any correlation between their size and their poverty (Maps 4.1 and 4.2). "[It] shows," he wrote, "contrary to what has been previously believed, how much height is independent of well-being and misery and to what extent, on the contrary, it is strictly correlated with *race*; in other words, how connected it is to heredity."[21]

That is to say, France did not suffer from any general biological decadence, but merely from the distribution of different "races" throughout the country. If the Bretons were short and weak and the Normans tall and strong, he reasoned, this likely had more to do with the difference between Gauls and Franks than between buckwheat *galettes* and real wheat bread. The pioneering anthropologist Paul Broca, working with the statistical evidence amassed by Boudin, concurred. And he used this finding to argue against long-term military service on demographic grounds: since it concerned

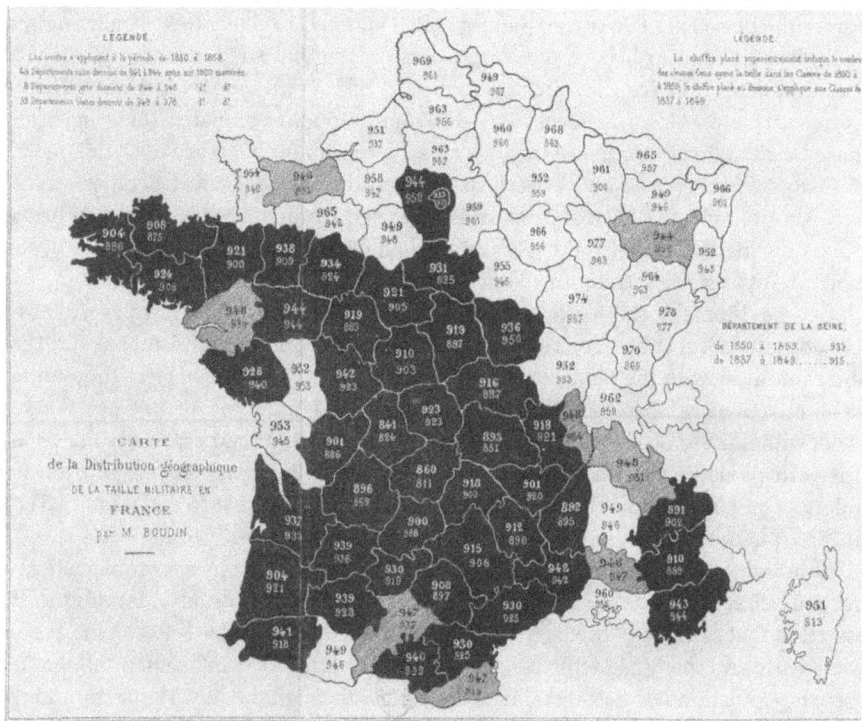

Map 4.1 Geographical distribution of military heights in France. *Source*: Boudin, *La taille et le poids* (between pages 12 and 13).

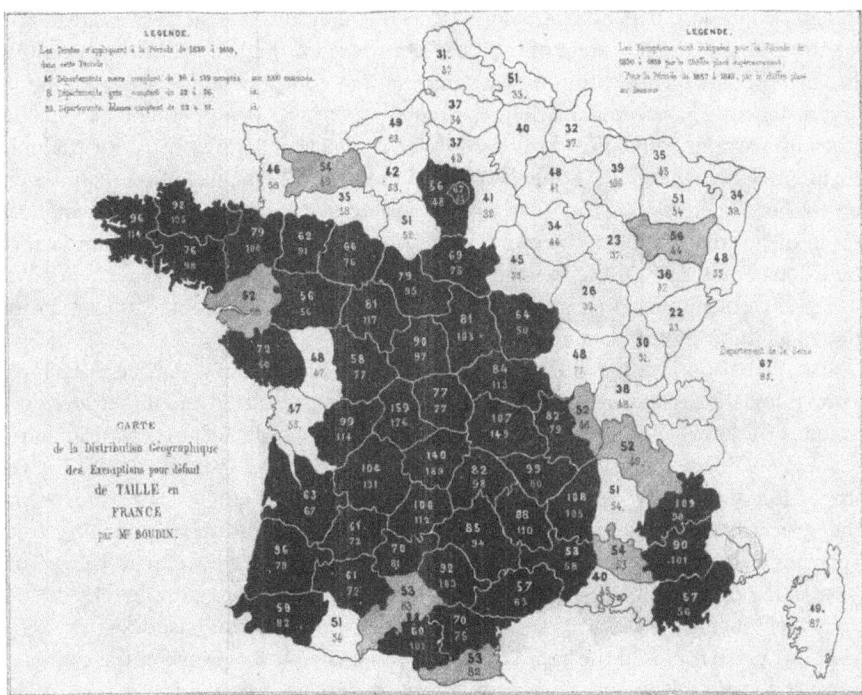

Map 4.2 Geographical distribution of exemptions for insufficient height. *Source*: Boudin, *La taille et le poids* (between pages 12 and 13).

principally the healthiest elements of the population, it was bad for the French race, as it condemned those robust young men to seven years of celibacy. Meanwhile, those who were too short or too sickly to serve were free to marry and propagate.[22]

Today, most of us would accept that there is some hereditary component to height, even if we would reject the nineteenth-century *racialization* of that biological fact. What remains true in any case is that, for our purposes, height, weight, and other exemptible deformities can serve as decent proxies for the general health of a population. Questions of race aside, therefore, they are worth a closer examination.

The various studies of the height and health of French soldiers confirm the general impression left by Boudin. But there are anomalies, and it is not always clear what the numbers tell us. Historian Odile Roynette, for example, writes that in 1862 only 3 percent of conscripts were rejected for some sort of disease or physical incapacity. Clearly, a rate of 3 percent stands out as exceptional, given the figures cited above and below. But Roynette cautions that this number referred to recruits following their first physical exam *after* having been inducted; that is, *in addition* to the 20 or 30 percent who were normally exempted from service for this or that defect. Besides, she adds, the low number of *exemptés* could also reflect a lack of doctors to examine inductees or evidence that the army could simply not be too picky about whom it called to the colors. And, in fact, these numbers rose substantially when the army was reorganized, beginning in 1872.[23]

Figures are less dependable before 1815, but they broadly suggest a substantial variation in the physical state of military recruits from the late seventeenth century through the nineteenth. Minimum height requirements rose and fell, depending on circumstances—in particular, whether France was at war or at peace, since smaller peacetime armies could afford to be choosier in their conscripts. Thus, for example, the infantry demanded that soldiers be 1.705 meters (5'7") in 1691. That requirement fell to 1.651 meters (5'5") in 1776 and to just under 5 feet in 1813 (1.52 meters), which meant that Napoleon's army at Waterloo would have been a head shorter than the troops Louis XIV sent to besiege Cuneo, in northern Italy, in the Nine Years' War (1688-97). The minimum height rose a bit under the largely peaceable Restoration and dipped a bit during the Second Empire.

It is worth noting that the map of exemptions in the nineteenth century looks more or less the same from study to study, with the most isolated and underdeveloped regions of France—Brittany, Dordogne, Auvergne, Périgord: Gustave Lagneau, at the Academy of Medicine called them the "black departments"—producing the highest proportion of young recruits turned away for "insufficient height" or other infirmities. The sturdiest stock, on the contrary, tended to grow in an area stretching from Normandy down through the Isère. Army physician Georges Morache drew from these statistics conclusions similar to those of Boudin and Broca, although he did not completely dismiss the effect of environment on morphology. Thus, drawing on the work of Dr. Bertrand on the Indre department, he cited the example of the canton of Levroux—fertile, clean, prosperous, only fifty recruits per thousand were rejected for service *pour infirmités*—and the counterexample of the next-door canton of Mezières, with its swampy and unproductive land, and its "miserable" population, where 145 out of every 1,000 young men were exempted from military service.[24] At the same time, Morache wrote that "the principal cause of variations in height is no other than the race from which [these populations] issue," and by which he meant, once again, the distinction between "Celts" and "Germans."[25]

We may well doubt that "race" accounts primarily for the regional variations in the physical state of young Frenchmen in the first half of the nineteenth century and imagine that environmental conditions play a larger role than heredity in explaining why twenty-year-old males were taller and stronger in the Ardennes or the Jura than they were in Finistère or the Lot.[26] Nonetheless, we can accept that these statistics on the height, weight, and infirmities of army conscripts—relatively reliable and continuous after 1830—provide important and otherwise unobtainable evidence about the general health of the population.

Three facts leap out of every discussion of these statistics. The first is the extraordinary proportion of men in the prime of their lives rejected for some substantial physical disability. In the worst department, the Haute-Vienne, between 1850 and 1858, more than 300 of every 1,000 recruits were exempted for "insufficient height" or "infirmity." But even in the most robust department of the Doubs, the army rejected more than 20 percent of conscripts. A separate study, by the physician and anthropologist Gustave Lagneau, showed virtually the same geographical distribution of exemptions for cause, and a higher number of them—reaching almost 480 per 1,000 conscripts in 1844. The second, as suggested in the departmental figures, is that, by and large, the poorest, most economically backward parts of the country produce the shortest, weakest, and most disabled young men. A dozen departments were rarely able to fill their quota of recruits. Conversely, three departments—Seine, Rhone, Vaucluse—filled their quota every year between 1844 and 1868. Third, and cutting in the opposite direction, while the situation might have looked dire by later standards, the physical state of young Frenchmen eligible for military service was improving between the exile of Charles X and the exile of Napoleon III. That said, according to historian Julia Csergo, of the 325,000 twenty-year-olds called to the colors after the defeat of 1870–1, 18,000 stood less than 1.45 meters (4'9") tall; 30,524 were dismissed for "weak constitutions"; 15,998 were categorized as "disabled, motley, or rheumatic." The authorities counted 9,100 hunchbacks or flatfooted, 6,934 with serious trouble hearing, seeing, or breathing. Mortality rates in the French army remained stubbornly higher than those in the British or German armies. Every class of recruits, wrote professor of medicine Jules Courmont, contained tens of thousands of "illiterates"—a much higher number than in other parts of "civilized" Europe.[27]

Perhaps Morache, Boudin, Broca, and their colleagues were correct. Perhaps young French men were getting a bit taller on average in the first seventy years of the nineteenth century. Perhaps there were fewer hunchbacks and lice, less illiteracy and feeblemindedness. Perhaps a significant gap was beginning to open up between the "primitive state of man" and the typical pool of annual recruits to the French army. Yet any broad optimism about the demographic and military state of the nation was dashed by the crushing defeat in the Franco-Prussian War. Such a national humiliation always seems to generate a search for explanations and culprits, along with a rash of strategies for making the country stronger and along with the country, the army.

Hygiene and National Revival

As those concerned with national revival reflected on the causes of military disaster, they found two ready narratives. The first pointed to the weaknesses of French politics and, in particular, to the divisive and infantilizing institutions of dictatorship and empire. The second centered on the deeper problem of the moral and material primitiveness of much of the population. The answer to the first question was the construction of a more inclusive and durable Republic; to the second, it was, in effect, the *modernization* of the French people themselves.

The military naturally approached the question of national strength from its own point of view, which involved, at its most basic, building an army that could defeat Germany next time around. This was the thrust of the military reforms in the period between 1871 and 1914 that eventually produced a system of universal, short-term conscription—a citizens' army in a way that the pre-1871 army, with its long term of service, replacement system, undemocratic officer corps, and illiterate peasant soldiers could never be.[28]

The constant adjustments in the minimum height necessary to serve in the French army suggest that military authorities did not suddenly discover in 1871 the unfortunate physical state of the recruitable population. They had long realized that crude personal habits were largely to blame. "The men in our ranks today," wrote Dr. Garnier-Léteurrie in 1845, "are clean enough to be rid of vermin. And if some of our new conscripts still bear this most disgusting stigmata of filth, it is because they come to us from the most backward villages in France"—and no doubt the fruit of the popular wisdom that "treated filth as a sign of virility." The army had therefore been trying for some time to teach its soldiers to behave in a more "civilized" manner, alongside their training in the martial arts. Beginning in the 1850s, for example, it began to substitute individual tins for the *gamelles communes* (common mess kits), so that an entire barracks of men were no longer dipping their spoons, and even their fingers, into the same collective cans when they ate. And Dr. Garnier's 1845 comment on military life insisted that new recruits be subject to haircuts and instructed in the necessity of changing their shirts "pretty often."[29]

Among the elements of propriety that soldiers lacked, Garnier cited pocket-handkerchiefs, wool socks for the winter and cotton socks for summer. They knew nothing of soap or toothbrushes. In fact, they arrived for induction with virtually no culture of personal hygiene whatsoever. Garnier, a military doctor ahead of his time, wrote of his singular disgust at the habit he found among many of the men, who rinsed their mouths with the same water they then used to wash their hands.[30] The prevalence of such primitive and unhygienic practices was precisely what led Garnier, back in the days of the July Monarchy, to champion the cause of a cleaner army. He advocated short haircuts, both because they were "the healthiest, the most convenient, and the most warlike" style and because they would protect heads from overheating—which threatened soldiers with "cerebral congestions" and led to fainting. Likewise, he prescribed frequent washing of head, face, and hands. Eyes, ears, noses, and mouths had to be the object of special attention, because they are "the agents of our senses." A dirty mouth, Garnier continued, led to the loss of teeth, gangrene of the gums, scurvy, cancer of the lips and cheeks, and foul breath. He recommended that soldiers brush their teeth at least twice a week and that, when the weather permitted it, soldiers bathe themselves in the nearest river. At the same time, he warned against soldiers bathing alone, which frequently led to drowning, or plunging themselves into a cold river when they were hot and sweaty, or "when the nervous system is weakened by a long march that has exhausted their powers of resistance." Both of these violations, he urged, should be punishable by imprisonment.[31]

Garnier, moreover, was hardly the only one to recognize the need to clean up the army. An 1840 circular from François Malapert, a military surgeon and secretary to the conseil de santé des armées, had warned of the dangers of "miasmatic poisoning" in overcrowded and unhygienic barracks. Dr. Malapert also called on the army to replace its thick wool uniforms, which looked good on parade, but which were heavy and impractical on the march or in battle, with lighter uniforms made of cotton and linen—especially, he wrote, "as troops change their linen only once a week." In the same vein, an unsigned 1868 note to the Bureau de la Correspondance Générale et des Opérations Militaires urged military authorities to require all officers and noncommissioned officers to master, and to teach their subordinates, the rudiments of hygiene. This note expressed the confidence that the habits learned by young recruits would make them better soldiers and would soon percolate down to "a population ignorant of the subject [of cleanliness]."[32]

> What advantage would we gain, from the perspective of popular health [asked Dr. Villedary] from the inculcation in the military of the love of *true cleanliness*, the habit of bathing frequently that a young man will retain forever and bring back to his village, along with the other qualities that good soldiers pick up in the army, such as neatness, honor, dignity, devotion to duty, bravery, etc.? (emphasis in the original)

These were not easy virtues to teach young men sprung from the backward countryside, noted Dr. Codvelle. But the army had the great advantage of military discipline, since "prescriptions for better hygiene alone are not likely to follow merely from the good will and approbation of these individuals." And it had some effect. By the middle of the nineteenth century, writes Eugen Weber, even in the backwoods of the Limousin, "young men who had returned from military service stood out as less habitually dirty than their peers."[33]

Toward Cleaner Soldiers

However, a great distance remained between good advice and its fulfillment, even after the shock of defeat convinced military experts of the need to make lessons in personal hygiene a basic element of military education. Thus, in 1878, even as he looked toward the cleaner future, Dr. Villedary complained about the slow progress of military hygiene. "It is enough," he wrote, "to have seen the bodies of these sad creatures [the conscripts] to recognize how dirty they are, how covered in filth, and what need they have to wash."[34] The soldiers' teeth were no cleaner than the rest of their bodies, according to military dentist M. Sapet, who wrote that "dental care long remained a dead letter in the army." Before the Great War, extraction was the most common treatment for rotten, caries-filled teeth, themselves common enough in the mouths of men who were ignorant of the most rudimentary dental care.[35]

Lionel Decle, a university graduate and one-year volunteer, had a shock in 1880, when he appeared for his army training:

> We were called up by batches of twenty-five, and shown by gendarmes into a room, around which stood long benches with pegs above them. A red-hot stove was burning in a corner of this room, and as there was no ventilation of any kind, and more than one hundred unwashed ruffians had already undressed and dressed there, the smell was abominable. A gendarme then ordered us to strip off all our clothing, barring our socks, and when we had done so—what a sight we were!—he called each one of us in turn and placed us under a measuring gauge. He first took our height with our socks on, and then without them—except in the case of those who possessed no such garment and who formed the majority.[36]

It was said that two traditions marked a young man's military service: his first cleanup as a new recruit, "naked as a worm," and the pleasure of a "baignade militaire," in the river with his comrades. Nonetheless, the military's campaign against dirt and sloth proceeded slowly because it ran into two obstacles. In the first instance, the army confronted the primitive social practices that conscripts brought with them from their villages and small towns. We have already had a look at some of those: the filthy homes, dirty clothes, and encrusted bodies; the absence of any regular washing or understanding of healthy diets. It would be fascinating to know how many young men arrived in the barracks without ever having seen a fork or defecated indoors. As Weber points out, a significant proportion of them spoke only the most imperfect French—if they spoke it at all.[37] It was no simple matter to turn around such cultural inertia.

More to the point, it was one thing to talk about having soldiers wash their hands, change their socks, use a modern latrine, and keep their beds clear of bedbugs. It was quite another thing to provide them with the necessary facilities. After all, the post-1871 army, whatever its ambitions, was forced to house its recruits in barracks inherited from preceding regimes in buildings that often dated back to the days of Vauban. Garnier had complained in 1845 of spaces polluted by the breathing of the inhabitants, added to "the odor of shoes, of clothes, of food [that] penetrates first the lungs and then the blood," making soldiers sick and weak, even if it doesn't kill them. Thirty years later General Véron de Bellecourt deplored the conditions: "humid, badly ventilated [buildings], haunted by the awful stench of repulsive outhouses, in spite of all the measures employed on behalf of cleanliness."[38]

Once again, Decle provides a most pungent description—this time of his first visit to his cavalry barracks:

> I cannot possibly give an adequate idea of the horrible stench which caught me by the throat when I opened the door of "my" room. Imagine the odour of 80 human beings, 79 of whom had not had a bath within the last three months, add to that the emanations from 160 pairs of boots which had been in use for an average of three years, sheets that had not been changed for a month, and crown the mixture with a smell of stables rising through the floor (our room stood over a stable containing 100 horses), and you will perhaps be able to gather a faint idea of what the place smelt like.[39]

Even at the end of the century, most soldiers lived in surroundings that were less than ideal. The pace of building new barracks was held back by cost and the ever-precarious state of government finances, and so recruits continued to breathe fetid air (all the more so since regulations dictated that windows be closed for the 11 hours of "lights out" between 7:00 p.m. and 6:00 a.m.) and to sleep on horsehair mattresses, with wool blankets and sheets that were changed once a month and that constituted a veritable nest for vermin—against which the battle went on continuously. Maurice Brillaud recalled that the fiercest fight during military service (1906–16) did not come on the Marne or at Verdun, but in an old abbey repurposed into barracks:

> As throughout the Rivaud barracks, bedbugs reigned sovereign, countless numbers of them in the floorboards, in the storage cubbies, in the door and window frames,

the bread boards, and even in the joints of the iron bedframes. The struggle against these little beasts involved two classic military measures: the offensive, which meant painting everything made of wood or metal with gasoline; the defensive, which consisted of removing the storage racks from underneath the top bunks, so that the bedbugs would no longer fall on the faces of sleeping bunkmates—a tactic at which the bugs excelled. Offensive or defensive, the results were the same: the bedbugs nibbled us incessantly.[40]

Military regulations dating to 1879 enjoined soldiers, every morning when they woke up, to brush their hair, rinse their mouths, and carefully scrub their faces and hands—adding that every man should have his own towel, which he was not permitted to share with anyone. Underwear was to be changed once a week.[41] A flood of advice from hygienists attached to the army, laid out in manuals, and presumably enforced by orders from noncommissioned officers directed the men living in the barracks to wash their feet, their heads, and their *parties génitales*. Beginning with the turn of the twentieth century, such instructions even included the use of soap: do not shake off your dust indoors, spit or smoke in the barracks. Brush your hat, clean your shoes but don't wear them in bed or use your bedsheets to wipe them off. Whitewash the barracks walls with lime twice a year. These were the customs universally preached by military hygienists.[42]

Lionel Decle discovered the difference between theory and practice when he asked about the lavatory in his new quarters. "It's quite true," he was told, "lavatories do exist in the barracks, but they have never been utilized since '70 [ten years ago] and are now used for storing straw." He was advised to go into the yard and use the pump.[43]

Latrines presented a special problem for a reforming military, "since," as Dr. Morache put it, "the works of modern science have shown the crucial influence that the collection of fecal matter beneath the barracks has with respect to the insalubrity, the propagation of epidemics, and on the mortality of the inhabitants."[44] In the days before sewer systems became common, this meant an effective system of *fosses fixes*; that is, of cesspits. "In all collective living spaces—and barracks are no exception," observed Jules Rochard in 1897, "latrines are inevitably the most disgusting and worst maintained element."[45]

Moreover, the "latrine question" was especially difficult to answer because it involved not small, relatively cheap fixes, like providing soap and towels, but substantial building and infrastructure costs. Experts wanted soldiers to have easy access to washing and to relieving their natural needs. This meant new building, and it meant finding a way to flush out heavily used urinals and toilets. Latrines, as Dr. Charles Viry indicated, needed to be built outside, but not far away from, and downwind of, the barracks. They had perforce to be well ventilated and to empty into a large and sturdy *fosse fixe*. That was for the daytime. A ministerial circular of March 1885 also stipulated that there be a "night latrine," with a urinal and a sitting toilet on every floor of the barracks, and it prohibited "wooden urinals, detestable devices, leaky, smelly, and repulsive in every way, which must absolutely disappear from all military buildings." The process of installing satisfactory conveniences was not yet complete in 1907, when Joseph Rouget and Charles Dopter, both officers and professors of medicine at the Val-de-

Grâce military hospital, were still insisting on the need "to put night-time facilities [*cabinets pour la nuit*]" inside, because you don't want the soldiers having to go outside in adverse weather, and you don't want them avoiding that by urinating against the side of the building.[46]

Experts differed on some of the details, in particular on whether the modern military toilet should require soldiers to sit or, on the contrary, provide them with facilities "à la turque"; that is, latrines used while squatting. Drs. Rouget and Dopter favored the latter setup, since "usage has demonstrated that in the former case toilet seats are constantly soiled and that the men instinctively squat on top of the toilet seats, despite the surveillance and the posted instructions."[47] It is not clear that the army ever took a definitive position on this issue. What is clear, however, is that it was acutely aware of the need to improve the infrastructure of barracks life and was making uneven progress in that direction—to the point where, in Dr. Viry's view, "we can discern the moment, not far off, when privies will cease to be a continual menace to the health of the troops."[48]

Washing All the Troops

If the army cared about these things, it was because it had begun a campaign to transform—in effect, to modernize—the way young Frenchmen thought about and treated their bodies. At the center of these new habits, of course, was the simple but largely neglected matter of washing. Dr. Villedary's report on the state of things in the barracks at the end of the 1870s was not encouraging. "In the army," he wrote,

> Nobody *ever* washes. The soldier, sad to say, spends eight months of the year without moistening his body with a single drop of water. During these eight months, from October to June, the soldier is not led even once to the public baths; he performs not the least ablution, neither does he receive a sponge with which he could, from time to time, scrub his body a bit.

Although he added that this was beginning to change.[49]

It is simple to trace the evolution of military thinking on the matter. From encouraging various regimes of partial and intermittent washing—a cold rinse of hands and face every day; of "private parts" more or less regularly; of feet every few weeks—the military came to demand more frequent and more thorough ablutions. Cleaner bodies would produce both a more agreeable and a healthier environment. This in turn would make for fewer miasmas and thereby reduce the incidence of such emblematic barracks diseases as typhoid fever and tuberculosis.

If getting soldiers to wash more often, and in more places, was the problem, baths were the ultimate solution. Unfortunately, wrote Sorbonne professor of hygiene Aimé Riant in 1877, French army barracks had no facilities that would allow the men to immerse themselves and to wash *à grande eau*, "whereas this critical element of hygiene is completely assured in *every foreign army*, not only in the barracks but in military camps as a whole" (emphasis in the original).⁵⁰ In England, according to Viry, the majority of barracks already had bathtubs in 1896. In Dutch barracks, the rule was a half-hour bath for each soldier every week. In Dresden, meanwhile, the Germans had set up showers that could accommodate 100 soldiers an hour and permit everyone to enjoy a shower per week.⁵¹ The French army struggled to keep up. What was missing was not the will but the way.

The old practice of sending soldiers off to the local river or stream in the summer months obviously did not suffice for an army that wanted to be clean the whole year round or lodged in urban dormitories. It was a dauntingly expensive project, however, to build dozens of new barracks with modern plumbing and to retrofit the old ones. It was a matter, moreover, not simply of water, but of *hot* water. These conflicting imperatives—to promote propriety and to do it at the lowest possible cost—produced an interesting course of trial and error: a contest, in effect, between immersion and aspersion.

Dr. Villedary summarized the process in 1878.⁵² In 1861, the military physician Major Lécard had tried using the heat produced in the camp kitchens to heat water for a pool, where soldiers could bathe every month. That same year, Dr. Grellois picked up the idea but offered a more detailed plan for bathing the regiment, taking costs into consideration and figuring in the size of the bath and the temperature of the water. Villedary notes, as an aside, that Grellois did not entirely endorse the prospect of having twenty filthy men washing in the same water at the same time—"a repulsion" even more justified by Grellois's proposal, in order to save money, to follow the first group of bathers with a second group, *using the same water*. Other military hygienists thought the contradiction between cleanliness and cost could be overcome with steam baths, followed by "some vigorous rubbing." Villedary saw several difficulties in this solution. Steam baths would accomplish only "a very incomplete cleansing" and have an enervating effect on the soldiers; moreover, it would require more than two months to steam bathe a regiment.

To surmount these difficulties, the military engineer Marchand, in 1866 and again in 1871, suggested a procedure that followed the steam bath with soaping, scrubbing, and a tepid shower. Marchand claimed it could wash forty men in an hour and a half at a cost of under 3,000 francs per regiment—although the danger remained that steam would soften up soldiers who needed to be hardened. At about the same time, physician Major D. Riolacci put in place for the men of the 13th battalion of *chasseurs à pied* (light infantry) a system using tubs and capable of washing his men every two or three weeks, overseen by a sergeant at an affordable cost. One drawback of the *système riolacci* was that it required a barracks served by a public water system, since it was too cumbersome to haul all that water in from outdoor pumps.

In the end, the search for an efficient affordable organization of military baths had to cede to a different practice, "lavages par aspersion"; that is, showers. The first military shower seems to have been set up in 1857 by General Cortigis, the commandant in Marseilles. NCOs stood by to make sure the men soaped up from head to toe and rinsed thoroughly in 3 minutes. The strict organization of changing and toweling-off space meant that Cortigis was able to clean 350 soldiers between noon and 4:00 p.m. "without fatigue, without disorder, with the maximum of decency and the certainty that each soldier emerged perfectly clean." One drawback of this system was that the water was not heated up, which meant that showers needed to cease in the winter, when the water was too cold.

In fact, the system of mass showers was already being perfected in that other institution of involuntary mass living, the prisons, where according to Julia Csergo, with perfect Foucauldian logic, they were used by the authorities to "discipline" the souls of the proletariat. In Rouen, experiments in *aspersion* went forward under the supervision of Dr. François Merry Delabost (1836–1918), who is sometimes credited as the inventor of the shower.[53] The prisoners, explained Villedary, were washed once a month in winter and twice in summer. Each one used just 20 liters of water, whereas an ordinary bath required 200 or 300 liters. The water did not need to be very hot—indeed, some argued that cold showers better fit the military constitution—or stay on for very long: a few seconds to get wet, followed by a scrubbing, and then a few seconds of water to rinse, using about a centime's worth of soap per man. Consulting for the military, hygienist Dr. Émile Vallin proposed in 1877 that the army adopt the Merry Delabost system. He reckoned that, once soldiers got used to the routine, an entire company of 100 men could shower in 2 hours. At two companies a day, this meant that an entire regiment could be washed in at most ten days and that every soldier could have two *aspersions* a month—an altogether unprecedented level of cleanliness.[54]

Speed and cost eventually led the army to adopt collective showers as its preferred means for washing its soldiers. Formal regulations and the recommendations of manuals on military hygiene cannot, however, be taken for the actual state of things. Military standards might dictate basins, sinks, and personal towels for recruits in every barracks; prescribe showers every fortnight; and prohibit urinating against the outside of the barracks. But all of these improvements required funding, and this was generally insufficient to the needs of an expanding and ambitious military. In the meantime, what the barracks could not provide could often be found in the *bains-douches*—the public baths. Odile Roynette writes that one regiment near Lille recorded 441 visits to the municipal baths in 1878. Soldiers across the country were likewise assembled and paraded into town for their monthly cleanup. Hygienists Henri Napias and A.-J. Martin offered a very optimistic assessment of the progress that had been made in providing hot, soapy, cost-effective showers to the mass of recruits. "In the majority of barracks," they wrote in 1883, "the means for washing is assured today."[55]

The experiences of Lionel Decle, however, once again illustrate just how far the army had to go to fulfill its ambitions. When Decle joined his cavalry regiment in 1880, the army's manual laid down a rigorous standard of personal hygiene: "Troopers are sent to the swimming-baths in the summer, and are allowed to have tepid baths in winter, in order to scrape off the deposit formed on the surface of the body by perspiration and dirt." Yet regulations, Decle found, were one thing and actual living conditions another. "I must add," he wrote,

> that, as in many other cases, theory and practice differ vastly, for in my time [1880–1881] there existed but one dilapidated bath in the whole of our barracks, where 1600 men were quartered. No appliance for admitting hot water into the

bath existed, so that, when it had to be used for a sick man, hot water had to be carried from the nearest kitchen 300 yards away!

And later in his service year, when he had occasion to spend ten days in the hospital, he was unable to get a bath the whole time. "When I suggested taking one the doctor laughed at me, and the Sisters considered me a kind of lunatic to want a bath when I had a sore throat."[56]

Decle, however, was a Parisian and an educated bourgeois, not at all representative of the general attitude toward the standards of hygiene he encountered in the army. It is therefore worth asking about the attitude of the great majority of conscripts toward the army's campaign of moral and physical improvement, of which they were the objects. After all, recruits, even if they were poorly educated, did not come to the military life without their own notions of proper hygiene and ideas about, for example, the usefulness of immersing themselves in a tub of hot water or of taking off all their clothes in the presence of more or less perfect strangers. We have already seen how deeply the suspicion of water and skepticism about the virtues of washing were lodged in French popular culture. Recruits commonly hailed from cultures where, as Françoise Loux put it,

> It was a matter of decorum and modesty to cover every bit of the body, aside from head and hands; it was thus indecent to expose one's chest and bare arms, legs without stockings and feet without shoes; indeed, it was opposed to the laws of God, to uncover those parts of the body that both Nature and Decency require to remain always hidden.[57]

Thus, while the army might want to civilize what it considered primitive practices, there is no reason to imagine that the men simply did what they were told without trepidation or resistance, or that conscripts looked forward to collective showers as a pleasure, rather than as an ordeal.

Some experts worried, moreover, that *aspersion*, even apart from its limits as a method of cleaning and reviving the skin, could be dangerous, "provoking nervous afflictions and leading to heart attacks." In their 1908 book *Hygiène*, doctors Maurice Debove, who later became Dean of the Faculty of Medicine at the University of Paris, and Albert-Faron Plicque cautioned that "Showers are not a simple matter of hygiene and cleanliness. They can lead to very serious reactions and should not be taken at random or without proper medical supervision." Thus, even where they were used, showers were sometimes thought to require protective equipment; for example, rubber bonnets to protect the skull from "l'attaque du jet."[58]

Odile Roynette tells a story suggesting that army took these hazards seriously: in 1903 in Douai, a gunner in the 27th artillery regiment was led, along with his mates in the battery, to the city baths for the regulation shower. Singled out by his commander for his dirtiness, this soldier literally had to be forcibly held beneath the shower, under his sergeant's orders, since "he refused to wash himself because he was scared of water." Eight days later, this soldier was dead, without any of his superiors being able to determine the exact cause of his death. However, the inquest that ensued insisted on the link between his demise and his forced shower. And even if they failed to explain cause and effect precisely, exemplary sanctions were nonetheless taken against the officers and NCOs who were implicated in this affair. That is, it was assumed that the shower had somehow traumatized the young recruit sufficiently to cause his death. At the very least, Roynette concluded, "while it may be impossible to say with certainty why he died, it is important to underline how the horror provoked by the effect of running water on the body leaves a distressing mark on the psyche of these young soldiers."[59]

In spite of the occasional shower fatality, the military pressed on with its civilizing mission. Little by little it provided the tools for washing more often and more comprehensively. Increasingly, it welcomed young men into the service with a haircut, a change of socks, a towel, a toothbrush, and a smallpox vaccination[60] (Figure 4.1). Of course, as with showers, it was not sufficient simply to provide conscripts with the tools of hygiene. Military dentist M. Sapet told the following story to illustrate how difficult it could be to inculcate these new habits:

> In 1913, being in the service, I had in my regiment the son of an important manufacturer of toothbrushes and toothpaste. This young man was not a military professional, but in a bid to be noticed by his superiors, he furnished to the chief doctor, for each man, a toothbrush and a box of dental paste. He even gave a little lecture in the common area on the rationale for these objects and the proper way to use them. Several days later, the toothpaste boxes could be seen strewn around

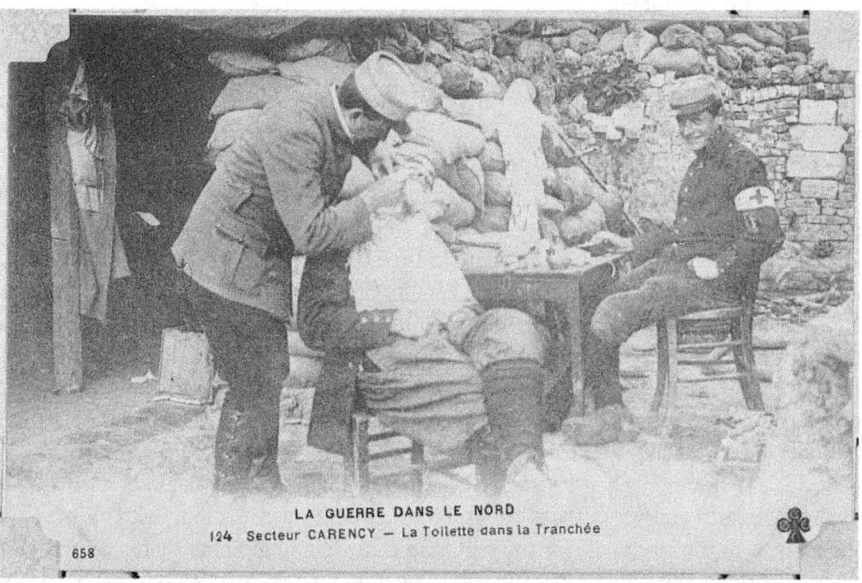

Figure 4.1 *Hygiene in the Trenches. A Soldier Being Shaved* (1916). Charles Colas et Compagnie, Cognac. Courtesy of the Archives départementales du Pas-de-Calais, Cote 12 J 356/122.

the barracks, whereas the brushes had received a warm welcome . . . as it turned out, the men were using them to grease their rifles.⁶¹

That same year the French parliament set up a committee to look into the state of hygiene in the army. The Lachaud Commission, named after the deputy who chaired it, recorded the ambiguous successes of the military's efforts to wean young Frenchmen from the coarse and unhealthy practices they brought with them to the barracks. The responses the committee received to its questions—"Are the billets clean?" "Are there water closets on every floor?" "Are the latrines close to the kitchens?" "Are there shower facilities?"—suggest that much ground remained to be conquered. A report from the camp commander in Compiègne complained of having too few latrines, which besides were sited right next to the kitchens; meanwhile, the portable toilets that made up the difference were neither well sealed nor connected to any source of water for flushing. A doctor with the garrison in Angoulême had a similar set of complaints. In particular, he noted that in order to use the night latrines the men had to descend three floors and walk across a large yard, that in the washroom there was only one faucet for every twenty-five men and in the showers only eight nozzles for 2,000 recruits. This was a typical summary.

Sometimes the reports were more upbeat. At the camp of the 9th Infantry Regiment in Valence, the buildings were hooked up to the city water system in nearby Agen—although, unfortunately, that meant that the camp's faucets also delivered the typhoid fever that had infected the city's water supply. If the barracks did not have a W.C. on every floor, at least the camp's latrines were located away from the kitchen. At the same time, wrote the commandant, there was a public urinal that sat against the exterior wall of the barracks and opposite the kitchen window, which received its noxious vapors.⁶²

In fact, there was worse. A review of the situation in the *Revue Scientifique* (1913) by Dr. Puissan, the army's chief medical officer, noted that sleeping and living quarters still lacked ventilation and natural light; that the battle against dust and germs had not been won; that "the French soldier remains dressed as badly from a hygienic as from an aesthetic point of view"; and that, in general, the army did not provide the water, the soap, and the towels necessary to achieve its vision of a clean, healthy soldiery.⁶³

Did the Army Lose the War for Hygiene?

The temptation is to judge this evidence of slovenly, insalubrious facilities on the eve of the Great War more harshly than the historical context merits. The conditions in which the French army lived and trained before it headed off to execute Plan XVII were deplorable by later standards. But we should not ignore the progress that had been made. Even Dr. Puissan found some cause for optimism. Soldiers in 1914 were eating better than they had in previous decades and a good deal better than their civilian counterparts. One letter to the Lachaud Commission from the First Battalion in Limoges provided a menu that contained lots of meat, vegetables, and potatoes. Soldiers ate only twice a day. But on Wednesday, February 18, 1914, their two meals consisted of:

- MORNING: cabbage soup, boiled beef, and French fried potatoes;
- EVENING: fish stew, fried fish, and green beans with tomato.

The men also received regular rations of coffee and rum—all in all a far more varied and nutritious diet than most of their families were eating at home.[64]

They also had better clothes. The turn-of-the-century French soldier, in his thick wool jacket and trousers, was poorly dressed for march and for battle. Wool was hot in the summer, difficult to keep clean, and hospitable to lice. Hygienists unanimously condemned the lack of extra clothing that would allow soldiers to change their socks and underwear regularly—"at least once a week . . . twice [a week] in summer," in the view of Rouget and Dopter, who listed the standard issue in 1907 as three flannel shirts, two pair of cotton drawers, two handkerchiefs, and two hand towels. "Regrettably," they noted, socks were not regulation. Ideally, every garrison had a *buanderie*, a laundry. Reality inevitably fell short of that ideal. Yet French soldiers in 1914 were better clothed than their fathers had been in the 1890s. Moreover, with sturdy outerwear, shoes, socks, and the occasional change of body linen, most of them remained significantly better dressed than they would have been in civilian life, as well as less dirty.[65]

Not only less dirty, but also less susceptible to epidemic disease than the civilian population, despite the promiscuity of army life. In large part this reflected the improved access to water in the barracks. The city of Paris in 1907 furnished each of them with 120 liters a day for every man and each horse, on top of what was needed for latrines, urinals, and sewers. When it could, it set up systems of "dual canalization": one set of spigots for potable water, the other for "river water," and other sources of "eau dangereuse." Even if this fell short of what the army would have liked to provide for its soldiers, it was far better than the 6 liters a day per soldier laid out in the 1856 regulations, with drinking water, far less reliable in supply and purity, coming from wells and fountains at the garrison. The effect of clean water is dramatically visible in the statistics supplied by Rouget and Dopter on the incidence of typhoid fever, of all maladies, the one that weighed most heavily on army mortality. "As we can see," they wrote:

> The rate of morbidity and mortality for typhoid fever declined rapidly from the first moment that the troops began to receive good quality water in their barracks. To be sure, typhoid has not completely disappeared from the army, but the reason is easy to see: the men do not drink only at the barracks. They drink in town. They drink in the countryside when out on maneuvers, and in the villages where they go when they're on leave.[66]

We should not understate the dimensions of this victory for the French army, which resulted in a steady retreat for a voracious killer of young men. Rouget and Dopter's numbers show that incidence of typhoid fever in Parisian barracks fell by 65 percent between 1888 and 1903, from 13.17 to 4.62 per 1,000 soldiers. The death rate followed a similar trajectory, declining by almost two-thirds, from 2.45 to 0.87 per 1,000. This marked a dramatic improvement from the years 1875 to 1880, when

Table 4.2 Typhoid Fever: Morbidity and Mortality, 1888–1903

Years	France	France	Military Government of Paris	
	General morbidity p. 1,000	General Mortality p. 1,000	Morbidity p. 1,000	Mortality p. 1,000
1888	11.15	1.82	13.17	2.45
1889	9.60	1.56	11.22	2.18
1890	8.44	1.31	5.89	1.11
1891	7.92	1.28	7.93	1.64
1892	10.53	1.62	6.90	1.35
1893	7.41	1.15	5.43	1.14
1894	6.42	1.05	8.88	1.79
1895	6.12	1.02	5.40	0.52
1901	4.30	0.52	2.79	0.34
1902	3.70	0.52	2.29	0.39
1903	5.00	0.72	4.62	0.87

Source: "La statistique médicale de l'armée," cited in J. Rouget and Charles Dopter, *L'hygiène militaire* (Paris: Librairie J.-B. Ballière et fils, 1907), 189.

typhoid fever had accounted for 36 percent of deaths occurring in the French army. Professor of pathology at the University of California Frederick P. Gay cited Minister of War Charles Louis de Freycinet, who estimated that reforms in 1888, tightening controls on water filtration and personal hygiene in the barracks, had led to a 36 percent reduction in the number of typhoid cases that year and 49 percent in the following year (Table 4.2).

The French army's success in this campaign mirrored a similar effort, with an even more dramatic impact, in the German army. The situation in Germany resembled that in all Western nations in the middle of the nineteenth century: mortality from typhoid fever was higher among soldiers than it was among the general public. From 1855 to 1869 German cities averaged 204 deaths per 100,000, while in the garrisons the rate was 840. Between 1876 and 1881, however, these numbers had decreased and the contrast flattened out: 57 per 100,000 in the cities and 190 in the army—resulting almost exclusively from "the full recognition of water contamination from sewage as the source of transmission ... and the consequent introduction of pure and safeguarded water supplies." In the Munich garrison, the death rate from typhoid fever plunged from 1,110 per 100,000 solders during the 1850s to 567 in the 1860s, 466 in the 1870s, and 19.8 in the 1880s. For the entire German army, mortality from typhoid fever fell from 170 per 100,000 the year before the Franco-Prussian War to 8 during the first decade of the twentieth century. Compare this peacetime progress to the catastrophic situation during the war of 1870–1, when the two sides suffered 73,396 cases of typhoid fever and 8,786 deaths—"supplying *sixty percent of total mortality during this period* ... [due to] the carelessness of camp hygiene and to the difficulty of securing a constant pure water supply" (my emphasis).[67]

* * *

Looking back then at the two generations that separated French soldiers at the Marne from their grandfathers at the Battle of Gravelotte, in August 1870, there can be little doubt that the army of the Third Republic had made significant progress in its drive to clean up and strengthen the defenders of the nation. During their terms of service, conscripts who had never taken a bath or seen a fork acquired at least a passing familiarity with the modern objects of civility—toothbrushes, soap, cutlery, handkerchiefs, cotton underwear, and a change of socks. They had learned the virtues of a varied diet and the occasional bath. Sources suggest that progress in the navy, the bigger more modern ships having vastly superior hygienic accommodations, was even more impressive:

> Air and water, both fresh and sea, circulate through a system of pipes to all parts of the vessel, thus facilitating the cleaning and maintenance of latrines and kitchens. The bathrooms are largely furnished with big compartments filled with seawater, where the men can bathe when they want . . . and [most of the newer ships] have sinks and showers.[68]

Soldiers or sailors, it was universally conceded that they brought this knowledge and these practices back with them when they returned to their villages—ideally passing a portion of their training in civility along to their families and neighbors.[69] Some of this training surely rubbed off in the transition from military back to civilian life, and material conditions at home did not always permit the same dedication to clean water and fresh linen. But progress is always partial and irregular, and these former conscripts had been infused with those habits they would conserve forever and, in their turn, bring to their villages: "cleanliness, respect for honor and personal dignity, love of duty and valor."[70] Military service had transformed them into the avatars of a new France.

Notes

1. Patrice Bourdelais, *Les hygiénists: enjeux, modèles et pratiques (XVIII-XXe siècles)* (Paris: Belin, 2001), 16.
2. Françoise Loux, *Pratiques et savoirs populaires: Le corps dans la société traditionnelle* (Paris: Berger-Levrault, 1979), 81.
3. André Rauch, *Histoire de la santé. Que sais-je?* (Paris: Presses Universitaires de France, 1995), 78; also David S. Barnes, *The Great Stink of Paris and the Nineteenth-Century Struggle against Filth and Germs* (Baltimore: Johns Hopkins University Press, 2006), 3 and 169.
4. Eugen Weber, *Peasants into Frenchmen: The Modernization of Rural France, 1870–1914* (Stanford: Stanford University Press, 1976), 147.
5. Rebecca Rogers, *From the Salon to the Schoolroom: Educating Bourgeois Girls in Nineteenth-Century France* (University Park: Penn State University Press, 2005), 206.
6. A. Féret, *Études sur l'hygiène scolaire et d'intérêt général, 1900* (Paris: A. Féret, 1900), 25.

7 Félix-Paul Codvelle, "Hygiène militaire et hygiène sociale," [Leçon inaugurale de cour d'hygiène du Val-de-Grâce], *Revue d'Hygiène* 57, no. 4 (April 1935): 246–7.
8 Barnes, *The Great Stink of Paris*, 169.
9 Lionel Decle, *Trooper 3809, a Private Soldier of the Third Republic* (New York: Charles Scribner's Sons, 1899), 69.
10 By the late nineteenth century, although young men were conscripted at age twenty, they generally did not enter the army until they were twenty-one. Volunteers were eligible to join at age eighteen: see Dr. Alphonse Laveran, *Traité d'hygiène militaire* (Paris: G. Masson, 1896), 2.
11 Weber, *Peasants into Frenchmen*, 149; Gérard Berger, *Le pays de Saint-Bonnet-Le-Chateau (Haut-Forez) de 1775 à 1975: flux et reflux d'une société* (Saint-Étienne: Presses Universitaires de Saint-Étienne, 1985), 395.
12 Jean-Claude Farcy, *Les paysans beaucerons au XIXe siècle*, vol. 1 (Chartres: Société Archéologique d'Eure-et-Loir, 1989), 360.
13 Théodore Garnier-Léteurrie, *De l'enseignement de l'hygiène dans les corps de troupe. Pour compléter l'instruction réglementaire du soldat* (Rignoux: Imprimeur de la Faculté de Médecine, 1845), 25; the sub-prefect's letter is cited in Jacques Léonard, *Archives du corps. La santé au XIXe siècle* (Rennes: Ouest France, 1986), 129.
14 Archives of the État-Majeur de l'Armée de la Terre. Service Historique (hereafter cited as SHAT): 1 M 2200—Commission d'hygiène. Conseil de santé, December 1939.
15 Jean-Christian-Marc Boudin, *Études ethnologiques sur la taille et le poids de l'homme chez divers peuples et sur l'accroissement de la taille et de l'aptitude militaire en France. Deuxième mémoire* (Paris: Victor Rozier, 1863), 1–3.
16 Ibid. *Première mémoire*, 2–6.
17 Ibid., 19.
18 Barbara Chambers, *The Men of the 1st Foot Guards at Waterloo and Beyond* (Letchworth Garden City: B.J. Chambers, 2003), 30–4. According to Robert Burnham and Ron McGuigan, the average height of a soldier in the 1st Foot Guards was 68 inches, with the tallest at 74.5 inches and the shortest, a drummer, at 56 inches: *Wellington's Foot Guards: The Men Who Saved the Day Against Napoleon* (London: Frontline Books, 2018), 30.
19 Georges Morache, *Traité d'hygiène militaire* (Paris: Librairie J.-B. Ballière et fils, 1874), 101–3.
20 Boudin, *La taille et le poids de l'homme*, 8.
21 Ibid., 13, 35 and 44–5.
22 Paul Broca, *Mémoires d'Anthropologie* (Paris: Éditions Jean-Michel Place, 1989 [1871]), 17.
23 Odile Roynette, *"Bon pour le service": L'expérience de la caserne en France à la fin du XIXe siècle* (Paris: Belin, 2000), 226.
24 Dr. Bertrand, *Études statistiques sur le recrutement dans le département d l'Indre de 1838 à 1864* (1865), cited in Morache, *Traité d'hygiène militaire*, 89.
25 Morache, *Traité d'hygiène militaire*, 93, 98.
26 Sociologist David Weir considers the relationship between height and other factors: "Another perspective on heights and living standards . . . sets the mean height of a birth cohort against the level of per capita GDP prevailing around its tenth birthday. In France, the scatter of observations traces a very regular and nearly linear relationship between per capita income and height. From the British data after 1860 it appears that the British height advantage at any given date was only partially due to higher British per capita incomes. Other additional factors, including possibly

genetic differences, contributed to the gap. Heights in northern France were systematically higher than in the south, so the British-French differences may be an extension of the same phenomenon," in Weir, "Economics and Physical Well-Being in France, 1750–1900," in Richard H. Steckel and Roderick Floud (eds.), *Health and Welfare during Industrialization* (Chicago: University of Chicago Press, 1997), 173–6.

27 François-Antoine Sistach, "Études statistiques sur les infirmités et le défaut de taille, considérés comme cause d'exemption du service militaire," in *Recueil de mémoires de médecine et de chirurgie militaire*, 3e. série, tome VI (1861): 353; Gustave Lagneau, *Remarques ethnologiques sur la répartition géographique de certaines infirmités en France*, in *Mémoires de l'Académie de médecine*, t. XXXIX (1869–1870) (Paris: J.-B. Ballière et fils, 1871), 293; Morache, *Traité d'hygiène militaire*, 241–2; and J. Rouget and Charles Dopter, *Hygiène militaire* [part of a series, *Traite d'hygiène*, edited by Paul Brouardel and Ernest Mosny] (Paris: J.-B. Ballière et fils, 1907), 19–20. Also see Jean-Paul Aron, Paul Dumont, and Emmanuel Le Roy Ladurie, *Anthropologie du conscrit français d'après les comptes numériques et sommaires du recrutement de l'armée, 1819–1826* (Paris: Éditions de l'École Pratique des Hautes Études, 1972), 73; Julia Csergo, *Liberté, égalité, propreté: La morale de l'hygiène au XIXe siècle* (Paris: Albin Michel, 1988), 135–6; Jules Courmont, *Précis d'hygiène* (Paris: Masson et Cie., 1914), 143.

28 On the history of military reforms between 1871 and 1914, see Roland André, *Nos beaux militaires! De la Belle Époque à la Grande Guerre* (St.-Cyr-sur-Loire: A. Sutton, 2005); Jean-Jacques Becker and Stéphane Audoin-Rouseau, *La France, la nation, la guerre* (Paris: SEDES, 1995); Henry Contamine, *La Revanche, 1871–1914* (Paris: Berger-Levrault, 1957); and Dorit Geva, *Conscription, Family and the Modern State: A Comparative Study of France and the United States* (Cambridge: Cambridge University Press, 2013). Decle, *Trooper 3809*, begins with a look at the laws on recruitment and service in 1889, 1–8.

29 Garnier-Léteurrie, *De l'enseignement de l'hygiène*, 25 and Csergo, *Liberté, égalité, propreté*, 136; also Roynette, "Bon pour le service," 141.

30 Garnier-Léteurrie, *De l'enseignement de l'hygiène*, 34.

31 Ibid., 37–44.

32 See Dr. A. F. Malapert, "Considérations hygiéniques sur l'habillement des troupes, et sur les causes de maladies qui existent dans l'armée," Paris, February 13, 1840 and "Observations relatives à l'adoption pour l'armée d'un Réglement sur l'Hygiène," September 9, 1862: both these documents are in SHAT, 1M 2200, Commission d'Hygiène. Conseil de Santé.

33 Codvelle, "Hygiène militaire," 256 and Weber, *Peasants into Frenchmen*, 300.

34 This and the previous quote from Léon Villedary, *Essai sur la question du lavage des soldats dans les casernes* (Paris: A. Parent, 1878), 11, 51.

35 M. Sapet, *L'hygiène dentaire dans l'Armée. Conférence faite à l'École de Perfectionnement des Dentists militaires* (Étampes: La Presse Dentaire, 1927), 7.

36 Decle, *Trooper 3809*, 35.

37 Weber, *Peasants into Frenchmen*, 253. On the illiteracy of recruits from the Hérault, see Frédéric Rousseau, *Service militaire au XIXe siècle: de la résistance à l'obéissance. Un siècle d'apprentissage de la patrie dans le departement de l'Hérault* (Montpellier: États-Sociétés-Idéologies-Défense, 1998), 163.

38 Cited in Roynette, "Bon pour le service," 138; also Garnier-Léteurrie, *De l'enseignement de l'hygiène*, 62.

39 Decle, *Trooper 3809*, 60.

40 Maurice Brillaud, *Souvenirs de guerre et d'avant guerre (1906–1916)* (Niherne [Indre]: Éditions Nivoit, 2004), 13–14.
41 Léonard, *Archives du corps*, 130; also see [Capitaine] Edouard Gillon, *Le nouveau soldat du service obligatoire* (Paris: E. Dentu, 1873), 186–7.
42 Dr. Georges-Henri Tellier, *La santé du soldat. Manuel d'hygiène pratique à l'usage des hommes de troupe* (Paris: Henri Charles-Lavauzelle, 1903), 14–17 and 24–36.
43 Decle, *Trooper 3809*, 68–9.
44 Morache, *Traité d'hygiène militaire*, 403–4.
45 Jules Rochard, *Traité d'hygiène publique et privée* (Paris: Octave Doin, 1897), 888.
46 Dr. Charles Viry, *Principes d'hygiène militaire* (Paris: L. Bataille et Cie., 1896), 124–44 passim and Rouget and Dopter, *Hygiène militaire*, 199–200.
47 Rouget and Dopter, *Hygiène militaire*, 200.
48 Viry, *Principes d'hygiène*, 124.
49 Villedary, *Essai sur la question du lavage*, 7.
50 Aimé Riant, *L'hygiène et l'éducation dans les internats* (Paris: Hachette, 1877), 138, n. 1.
51 Viry, *Principes d'hygiène*, 424–5.
52 See Villedary, *Essai sur la question du lavage*, 13–51 passim.
53 On Delabost, see Jules Arnoud, *Nouveaux éléments d'hygiène* (Paris: J.-B. Ballière, 1881), 700; François Merry Delabost, *Les bains douches à bon marché à Bordeaux et à Rouen* (Rouen: La Normandie Médicale, 1896), 263; and Ambroise Tardieu, *Dictionnaire d'hygiène publique et de la salubrité*, tome 1 (Paris: J.-B. Ballière, 1852), 126–34.
54 For a survey of the process by which the army came to rely on showers for its soldiers, see Alphonse Laveran, *De quelques procédés de lavage des hommes dans les casernes. Archives de médecine et de pharmacie militaires*, tome IX (June 1887), cited in Viry, *Principes d'hygiène*, 426.
55 Henri Napias and André-Justin Martin, *L'étude et les progrès de l'hygiène en France de 1878 à 1882* (Paris: G. Masson, 1883), 121–2.
56 Decle, *Trooper 3809*, 90–1 and 184–5.
57 Loux, *Pratiques et savoirs populaires*, 83.
58 Csergo, *Liberté, égalité, propreté*, 72–3.
59 For this story, and the statistics about the Lille regiment, see Roynette, *"Bon pour le service,"* 161–2; also see Maurice Debove and Albert-Faron Plique, *Hygiène* (Paris: C. Delagrave, 1907), 244.
60 According to Elsbeth Kalff and Lucie Lemaître, using figures from Henri Monod, the great "hygienist et solidarist" of the fin-de-siècle, in 1899 approximately 23,000 French conscripts were treated for smallpox, as opposed to 400 German conscripts in the same year, *Le logement insalubre et l'hygiénisation de la vie quotidienne. Paris (1830–1990)* (Paris: L'Harmattan, 2008), 137.
61 Sapet, *L'hygiène dentaire*, 12.
62 See the letters to the Lachaud Commission from Compiègne, March 14, 1914, from Major Bertele in Angoulême, March 13, 1914, from Valence (no date), along with many other such letters in the dossier concerning the parliamentary inquiry: SHAT 1 M 2200—Commission d'Hygiène. Conseil de Santé. Also see the discussions of general health issues in the military in SHAT, 9N 85—Statistiques Médicales (1909) et Divers.
63 *Revue d'Hygiène et de Police sanitaire* (1914): [review of an article by Dr. Puissan, médicin principal de l'armée, in *Revue Scientifique*, (1er semester 1913): 683] 48–50, available in the library of the Archives de Préfecture de Police, Paris.

64 SHAT, 1 M 2200—Commission d'Hygiène. Conseil de Santé, letters to the Lachaud Commission.
65 Rouget and Dopter, *Hygiène militaire*, 68–9 and 122–3; Tellier, *La santé du soldat*, 9–10.
66 Rouget and Dopter, *Hygiène militaire*, 189–90.
67 These and the following numbers, along with the quotations above, come from Frederick P. Gay, *Typhoid Fever Considered as a Problem of Scientific Medecine* (New York: Macmillan, 1913), 14–22.
68 Napias and Martin, *L'étude et les progrès de l'hygiène*, 118.
69 See, for example, the report of Drs. Lemoine and Dupuich, on the "Causes de l'absence d'épidémies de fièvres éruptives dans le 1er corps de l'armée et de son bon état de sanitaire général," in *Comptes rendu des séances du Conseil d'hygiène publique* (1914): 358.
70 Villedary, quoting Major Riolacci, in *Essai sur la question du lavage*, 51.

5

The Republic of Hygiene II—In the Schools

Teaching Hygiene Before Ferry

Many young recruits in the first years of the new Republic would have encountered the lessons and objects of good hygiene as the most extraordinary novelties. Underwear, soap, toilet seats, hot showers, and the other rudiments of a cleaner France would surely have represented a new—and not always congenial—world of practice and sensibility. By way of contrast, the generation of conscripts who went to war in 1914 would all have arrived at the barracks familiar with the rationale for and the tools of *propreté*, because, with the Ferry Laws that expanded and regularized the system of primary education in France, the Republic had opened a second front in the war against dirt in the schools. "There is reason to hope," wrote the housing commission to the city of Paris, "that children will learn in our schools, under the influence of these measures, and thanks to the good efforts of their teachers, habits of order and cleanliness, and will become part of a generation better disposed to respect the rules of hygiene."[1]

Just as the French army had not suddenly discovered the military virtues of good personal habits with the military disaster of 1870–1, the education system already had some experience of teaching pupils the importance of neatness and cleanliness before the Ferry revolution.[2] Even under Napoleon I, boarding schools for girls sought to attract pupils with advertisements that stressed their "cleanliness" and "excellent air." Girls' education, which promised to produce "tender and obedient girls who will become virtuous wives and good mothers," was especially likely to contain instruction on "practical hygiene and domestic economy"—at the school run by the nuns of the Société du Sacre-Coeur, for example, or at the *école professionnelle* for women in Paris, founded by Elisa Lemonnier in 1862, whose basic curriculum included "physics, chemistry, hygiene, and linear drawing."[3]

Historian Anne Quartararo's study of normal schools in the nineteenth century found that hygiene had long had a place in both the curriculum and the training routines for aspiring teachers. When Louis XVIII was still king of France, young men in the normal school in Metz were being taught hygiene, alongside the staples of reading, writing, arithmetic, and natural history. A decade later, in the mid-1830s, boarding students at the normal school in the Yonne department were subject to a military-like discipline that, much as in the army at the time, placed little emphasis on personal hygiene. In contrast, at the normal school in Périgueux, Dordogne, "Students had to wash themselves . . . and comb their hair every morning. Even if it was a superficial exercise, they were at least expected to wash their hands before meals. Instructors also supervised bimonthly footbaths."

Under the Second Empire, normal schools paid even more attention to hygiene, according to Quartararo. "Although precautions against illness were still very limited at midcentury," she writes,

> Students were at least taught some rudimentary health-care practices and developed a little respect for cleanliness. At Carcassonne, the normal school director made his students wash their face every morning and have their hair cut once a month. Every second Thursday his students took footbaths. The Carcassonne normal school also had a regular bathtub, but it was used particularly for "medicinal purposes." ... In the Manche, standards at the men's training school were slightly more demanding. Students took footbaths once a week and a regular bath every three months. School regulations even stipulated how frequently students should change their socks in winter (once a week) and in summer (twice a week).

To the extent that normal school institutions followed similar procedures, Quartararo concludes, "their hygienic practices were far in advance of those of the general population in the 1860s."[4]

There, however, lay the problem. What distinguished these early efforts was not their absence but their irregularity, which was hardly surprising in a country where education still brushed the peasantry and the working classes only lightly—and women almost not all. Agricole Perdiguier was born in 1805 and grew up in a village near Avignon, speaking principally Occitan. His father wanted him to have some education, even though he was bound to be a joiner, and sent him to the village school—although only in the evening after chores and only in winter, and despite the fees (one franc for children learning to read and one and a half francs for those studying both reading and writing) and the schoolmaster's brutality. "We had either to take our beatings or remain completely ignorant," he wrote.[5] Unusually, Perdiguier *père* also sent his daughter to school. But such opportunities and such dedication to education were not common in the countryside.

Focusing on the Nivernais, historian Guy Thuillier found a more profound and wearing ignorance among women. There were fewer schools for girls that might challenge old customs and chip away at "the idiocy of rural life." Whereas the Nièvre department had 5,757 boys in school in 1833, it had only 1,720 girls. Numbers grew somewhat more equal thereafter, and by 1857, 19,043 boys and 14,646 girls were in school in the department. Still, illiteracy remained widespread well into the Third Republic: out of a department of 340,000, Thuillier estimated that 85,000 men and 94,000 women could neither read nor write in 1872. A further 9,600 men and 11,400 women could read but not write.[6]

An 1848 survey of young men and women in the high mountains of the Maurienne similarly found that 58 percent of the boys and only 31 percent of the girls could read and write; a fifth of the former and a third of the latter could neither read *nor* write. Illiteracy was common among the soldiers who went to war in 1870. According to

Henri Baudrillart, in the Anjou a barely existing educational system before mid-century left peasant ignorance and superstition untouched. "The peasant who failed to feed his cow properly attributed her wasting away and lack of milk to witchcraft. Entire stables," he noted, "were considered bewitched."[7]

For the first half of the nineteenth century, popular education was largely the province of religious authorities. It is important not to overstate the quality and reach of this system. Nonetheless, historians Patrick Harrigan and Raymond Grew write that Republicans exaggerated the depth of ignorance produced by a system of bigoted and half-educated nuns and priests for their own political purposes. Harrigan and Grew cite recent scholarship painting a much happier picture of declining illiteracy in the first half of the nineteenth century, especially among girls—and even if the schools' first priority was to educate good Christian mothers and wives. In 1837, 70 percent as many girls as boys were registered for primary school. And the Falloux Law of 1850, which permitted "unauthorized congregations" to establish schools, helped expand the reach of education for girls and virtually to eliminate the gender gap in primary education even before the Ferry Laws.[8]

The National Convention had proclaimed the arrival of free and universal primary education. Yet the French Revolution had left the country's system of primary education largely untouched; schools remained every bit as religious in their orientation and local in their organization in 1815 as they had been in 1789. The work of centralization fell to succeeding regimes and to the particular work of Guizot (1833), Falloux (1850), and Duruy (1865-8). A geography of literacy in France in the mid-nineteenth century would have traced a pattern similar to that captured in the map of the army exemptions, with the country divided along a line that ran roughly from Saint-Malo, in northwest Brittany, to Geneva—between a more prosperous and modern north and a poorer, shorter, more ignorant, and dirtier south. The most literate departments sat in the north and the east. By 1866, over 90 percent of draftees from the five soon-to-be-lost departments of Alsace and Lorraine could read and write—almost 98 percent in the Meurthe, as against a national average of 77 percent. Counting the proportion of conscripts who could read and write, rates of literacy rose steadily across the country from the 1820s to the 1860s: from less than 50 percent at the end of the Restoration in 1830, to over 64 percent in the years between the fall of the July Monarchy and the ascent of Napoleon III (1847-51), to almost 70 percent in the years immediately preceding the Duruy laws. Although not as high in absolute numbers, female literacy showed the same distribution.[9]

While reading and writing are not themselves the point here, the link between schooling and hygiene is an obvious one. Even in these early days of mass education, before the Republic explicitly set out to turn "peasants into Frenchmen," schoolmasters were instructing their pupils about "the physical and moral advantages of personal hygiene."[10] The Second Empire made a particular priority of improving the *propreté* of young French boys and girls, as part of its larger project for national improvement. Thus, an 1858 arrêté required "intense but inoffensive" lighting in all schoolrooms and went so far as to set the minimum dimensions for a healthy classroom: a square meter of space for each child and a ceiling at least 11 feet high. A rectangular room 6.5 by 8 meters was the perfect space for overseeing the tuition of fifty students.[11]

In the mid-1860s, the ambitious minster of education Victor Duruy initiated a series of attempts to make primary education both obligatory and free, as well as to expand the reach of secondary education.[12] His instructions from 1864 note that in the primary schools "it is important to give the child the habits of cleanliness that the man will conserve and to respect the outside of the person, which leads to the respect of the inside"; the law of June 21, 1865, imposed instruction in hygiene, both "theoretical tuition" and "practical training," throughout the educational order. Meanwhile, the secondary schools were urged to focus on "the propriety of bodies, as on healthy food, drink, and exercise."[13]

Even the crèches attracted government notice, as the places where young working-class children could get the care and training their working mothers could not offer and where they could receive "the hygienic and moral care that [they] require." According to an 1862 law, the crèches were obliged to provide a washroom, with hot water and enameled washbowls; separate W.C. for the children and the staff; and such *objets de toilette* as combs, brushes, and towels—each one "labeled with the child's number and placed in an individual, numbered locker."[14]

One of the more fascinating artifacts of this effort comes in the form of a grade-school primer written for young peasant children. Louis Fortoul's *Farm Vigils: Elementary Notions of Agriculture and Rural Hygiene* (1868) aimed to counter "the recent tendency of rural populations to abandon [farm] work for new occupations in the cities," which was producing "population imbalance" and "social malaise."[15] The didactic story focuses on a Monsieur Anselme, who travels around his village with old Maître Jean, exemplary owner of Cherry Orchard Farm, dispensing advice to the children. In the chapter "Seventh Vigil: Hygiene and Farm," the two men come upon a "poor dwelling." They open the front door to see the six-year-old François sitting in front of an old dog. His mother and father, off to fetch the retting hemp from a nearby pond, have left him alone in the house. François is sweet and polite, but he apparently isn't well; he is small for age and clearly suffering from fever. And it is not hard to see why—having been born and raised in this miserable hovel, next to a swamp "whose pestiferous vapors are carried by the breeze into this poor home." The two men's observation becomes a brief lesson on the importance of fresh air for a "robust constitution."

There is worse. The manure piles, "soaking in a foul liquid" in front of the windows, fill the house with noxious fumes—all the more so, since the windows are "few and narrow" and are normally closed while the family is out working. The whole family sleeps jammed into a low corner of the one room, beneath walls "covered in saltpeter," and surrounded by peelings and rotting debris of all sorts and buckets of stinking water that pollute the air. Maître Jean and M. Anselme comment to readers that it is not very hard to use whitewash and bleach the interior walls, with a marvelous effect on salubrity. The two men see dirty clothes piled in a corner, which, they point out, need to be hung up in some dry spot, even if they are not washed. Further observations allow them to extoll the virtues of summer baths in the river, loose wool clothing—critical because changes in temperature are the chief cause of sickness and wool absorbs the sweat than can lead to chills. They go on to recommend a proper diet, including meat in winter and vegetables in summer, along with clean drinking water. Wine, they note, is strengthening, but not in excess; *eau de vie* should never substitute for wine and always be mixed with lots of water: "To be sober," they tell their young readers, "is not itself a great virtue, but it is a great defect not to be [sober]."

Jean and Anselme reflect on the qualities of healthy sleep: nine hours for young children and eight for older ones, and avoiding feather mattresses, "which retain a harmful heat"; they prefer moss, which does not attract vermin. When the parents return, and the men get to talk to the mother, who explains that this house is on a small corner of their land and that they also suffer from fever. The retting pond is a source of both profit and health for the whole village. This gives Fortoul, by way of his two protagonists, an opportunity to expound on the virtues of a clean and orderly life, even in the countryside—precisely the lesson that an improving Imperial regime wanted to impart to its subjects.

As was often the case for a government with grand ambitions and limited means, when it came to cleaning up young French boys and girls, the Second Empire's reach exceeded its grasp. This was particularly true of the education infrastructure. The Commission des logements insalubres in Paris praised the condition of the capital's school buildings in 1865, reporting that only 78 out of the 1,403 it visited required substantial work on their *salubrité*. Most contemporary commentary, however, pointed in the opposite direction. For example, a list of grievances delivered to the minister of education in 1861 by a group of schoolteachers complained about the deplorable state of the buildings in which the schools were forced to operate—usually dilapidated old structures rented by the state. "Many of our schools," hygienist Dr. Aimé Riant told a conference at the Sorbonne in August 1878, "are little better than stables."[16]

In Paris, the 1867 inquiry initiated by education minister Duruy and headed by the celebrated hygienist Dr. Maxime Vernois found that the ideal conditions envisioned in circulars and ordinances went largely unmet in practice. Vernois's report on the city's lycées found that few of the schools he looked at had adequate facilities, and those few that did often failed to follow official guidelines on their use. Boarding schools, for the most part, the lycées did not have the means to bathe their students on any regular schedule. Water was distributed "with parsimony" and often did not reach "certain shameful regions," due to a "ridiculously exaggerated sense of modesty" on the part of both students and teachers. Meanwhile, a fear of humidity made schools loathe to put sinks and other watery objects in the dormitories themselves; anyway, without sufficient heat, it was dangerous to get the boys wet.[17]

Romuald Gaillard, *officier de l'Académie* and economics professor at the Imperial Lycée at Vesoul, carried out a comprehensive study of hygiene in the empire's schools in 1865.[18] He was particularly concerned with the critical matter of latrines and urinals, a part of the school building commonly treated with "small-minded economy and an often shocking negligence likely both to damage the health of the students and to offend their sense of dignity and modesty." For one thing, Gaillard found that few schools had enough latrines for the children and that the ones they did have were poorly situated, shoddily built, and badly maintained. Official guidelines called for "outhouses, as many as possible, in a covered courtyard, isolated, facing north, properly ventilated, and sited so that the teachers could keep an eye on them." The search was for the optimum compromise between convenience and discreet distance. It was better to have these amenities attached to the main building, so that students did not need to go outside during the winter. But that raised questions about how to segregate the offending smells.

Like his colleagues in the military, Gaillard weighed the respective advantages of the two models, the *système à la turque* and the *système avec sièges*; that is, between squatting and sitting. As came to be the case in army barracks, the authorities in general concluded that seats were more civilized. On the other hand, a commission set up to study this question had noted that not enough had been done to put an end to "the students' bad habit of squatting on top of the seats" and of thereby "turning the lavatories into cabinets of permanent filth." The latrines, along with whatever urinals existed, required a constant stream of water sufficient to flush all this waste into the cesspits. Unsurprisingly, under the circumstances of the 1860s these basic requirements of good hygiene were hardly ever satisfied. Hence, Gaillard's conclusion on the sordid conditions faced by most students: "repulsive in their dirtiness and stench, they are also unhealthy because of the draughts that run through them and attack the children in a state of immobility and nakedness."

On a more positive note, Gaillard laid out best practices for the dormitories: cotton or linen sheets changed at least once a month; bed clothes laundered twice a year; covers, quilts, and pillowcases aired out from time to time. He further insisted on chamber pots made of porcelain and washed out regularly with water, and on accessible sinks with plenty of fresh water. As to the students' clothing, Gaillard wanted them to have clean socks and underwear, made of cotton or flannel, essential to protect the lower body against chafing and to compensate for the rare washing of trousers. He was particularly concerned that students learn early on the virtues of washing. Face, neck, and hands needed to be scrubbed every day; feet at least once a week in winter and every day in summer; teeth every morning and after every meal. Hair needed to be brushed every day and checked regularly for lice. Gaillard sampled the wisdom on baths and found widespread agreement on their necessity at least once a month—a routine that did not become common in France until after the Second World War. He apparently did not read the 1852 recommendation from the Conseil d'hygiène de Nantes, which warned that "Bathing is an immoral practice, whose sad revelations have taught us about the moral hazards of spending an hour naked in a bathtub."[19] Otherwise, what is most striking about Gaillard's recommendations is both the high standard of cleanliness they uphold and the all-but-universal failure to live up to these standards.

A decade after Gaillard, Dr. Riant, professor of hygiene at the University of Paris, took up a similar tour of boarding-school facilities. Despite a government circular of September 1872 that formally placed hygiene on lycée curricula, Riant's inquiry convinced him that "hygiene is poorly known and badly practiced in France." In the dormitories he visited he found overcrowded sleeping quarters, where a pathological fear of draughts prevented any decent ventilation. Only the largest and richest schools had their own bathing facilities. Riant thought that other lycées could bring their students regularly to the municipal *bains-douches*—or at least to provide them with tickets, to allow them to go individually in their spare time and at the state's expense. Not every school had public baths nearby, however, and Riant worried that teacher surveillance was difficult in them—which could lead to students scalding themselves in hot water or worse. For the rest, he preached the same habits of cleanliness that Gaillard had and suffered the same disappointment with existing practices—although he painted an even more unsavory picture of the threat to health and comfort contained in the outhouses and cesspits that served the students' natural functions: cramped, unflushed holes in the ground for toilets, connected to leaking, stinking, splashing *fosses fixes*.[20]

There is no better illustration of historian David Barnes's remark that the moralizing agenda of nineteenth-century hygienists was expressed with a vocabulary and grammar of disgust.[21] There was more to this agenda, however, than morality or offended bourgeois sensibilities. For an era that still believed in the power of miasmas to cause disease, overheated, airless dormitories, poisoned by the emanations of dirty clothes and dirty bodies, and punctuated with the stench of latrines and cesspits wafting in from the courtyard represented the constant menace of murderous epidemics. Strengthening the nation meant first of all keeping its boys alive until they were old enough to serve in the army.

Hygiene in Republican Schools

Education placed high on the priority list of the Third Republic, as it would for any regime that counted on the good sense and support of a politically empowered citizenry. For a decade, Republican governments tinkered with the educational apparatus they had inherited from the well-intentioned but unfortunate Second Empire. Beginning in the 1880s, however, with a moderate government comfortably in power, the new regime began to construct its own model of education for a new France. Under the leadership of the solid Republican warhorse Jules Ferry, as minister of public instruction, the National Assembly passed legislation—that has come to be known as the Ferry Laws—that made universal primary education in France free (1881), mandatory (1882), and secular (1882).[22]

"No one can deny," wrote the hygienist Élie Pécaut, "the urgency of bringing simple and precise ideas about hygiene" to the masses. In that spirit, the ministerial *arrêté* of January 1881 specifically required the introduction of hygiene into the curriculum of the primary schools.[23] A simple survey of the manuals, textbooks, and government orders makes it clear that, as the new republican curriculum came together, hygiene found a place alongside reading, grammar, civics, arithmetic, and moral formation. It is more difficult to recover the substance of lessons on hygiene: Did teachers do less or more than the manuals required? Did they know their subject well? Did students pay as close attention to lectures on hygiene as they did to those on grammar and history? Did teachers care?

At any rate, it was not for the most part the inclusion of lessons on hygiene that distinguished the Ferry curriculum from what had gone on in the classroom in the time of Guizot, Falloux, and Duruy. These schools had also encouraged their young charges not to pick their noses or chew their pencils or drink alcohol to excess.[24] Rather, where the Third Republic bent the historical arc was in the scope of its ambition and the strategic place of hygiene in its overall civilizing mission. *All* French children were to be taught these rules, and this was meant to be part of a flourishing and democratic modern society. "The respect of a person for his body," wrote Léon Angot in his 1897 primer on morality, "demands the most scrupulous propriety. Conversely, a clean body leads to respect for others and for one's family; it promotes health and develops qualities of order and economy. So let us be clean in our clothing, in our bodies, in our homes."[25]

Not only would the children themselves learn to be civilized citizens of a self-governing France, but they, like conscripts returning to their villages, would bring modern standards of hygiene back to their homes and their parents. For Dr. Louis Depouilly, the schools could reverse the bad habits learned at home, especially for working-class kids: "Subject to long hours in the almost always filthy lodgings of their parents, they can acquire in school habits of propriety that they will never lose." In other words, the schools would reverse the traditional ways of socialization, and the child would become the means for educating the mother. "Four or five million of [our] children go to school each year," Dr. Riant told a conference at the Sorbonne. "Teach them the value of cleanliness, and through them you will bring better practices to their families."[26]

Ideally, the civilizing process (and the reduction in childhood mortality) would begin with the youngest children in one of the small but growing number of *crèches* being established by reformist municipalities. The first crèches had appeared in the 1840s, with the aim of giving working-class children the training that their mothers had neither the time nor the culture to provide them. This structure was reinforced by an 1862 law, and the Société des Crèches was recognized by the Second Empire in 1869. According to the eminent hygienist and Interior Ministry official, Dr. Henri Napias, 141 communes had crèches in 1891; by 1895, the number had risen to 172, and Paris alone had 58 of these day nurseries. Of course, this represented only a tiny fraction of the more than 37,000 communes in metropolitan France, and they were not a formal part of the educational structure established by the Ferry Laws. But their number grew steadily, and with that their role in teaching young children the value of cleanliness. Indeed, what is striking in the conversations about the crèches is the place of hygiene in their concerns. There was no formal training for the toddler-pupils, as there was for children in the primary schools and beyond. Yet there was a widespread vision that the crèches would be places where very young children would learn propriety through experience. For the school inspector A. Féret, the ideal crèche was impeccable from a hygienic point of view: well ventilated, with linoleum floors, where each child had a "perfectly made up bed" for resting and his or her own *objets de toilettes*—combs, brushes, towels, and so on. Napias noted that the law itself insisted that all crèches have a separate room for washing, fed with hot water, and two W.C.: one for the children and one for the personnel.

Dr. Charles Batallie, a professor at the medical school in Rouen described with enthusiasm a model crèche in his city. The crèche Elisabeth et Marguerite Brière accepted children from fifteen days old to three years and placed them in clean, modern surroundings. The facility had a laundry and drying room in the basement. The main floor had one space for sleeping and another for playing, a kitchen, a nursery, and a bathroom with sinks and a flush W.C. with seven seats. It had two bathtubs—a small one for the children and a big one for the personnel, since "each attending woman was required to have a bath every month." Most crèches would certainly have fallen far short of these exceptional standards. The one in Saint-Harmony, described by Napias, lacked a sufficient number of sinks and washed all of its children with one sponge out of a single bucket of water. "Naturally," he added, "contagions were common." By way of contrast, he praised the crèche in the town of Séruliac, in the old department of Sambre-et-Loire, for its many sinks, its immaculate numbered cubbies for the children to store their things. However well respected, the standards themselves reflected the importance that the French were increasingly placing on keeping their children clean.[27]

At the next level, the *écoles primaires* (primary schools), the messages became more explicit. Ten years before the first Ferry ministry, Louis Cyprien Descieux, professor of hygiene at the agronomy institute in Grignon (Côte d'Or), published *Leçons d'hygiène à l'usage des enfants des écoles primaires* (*Lessons in Hygiene for Primary School Children*). Descieux was a practicing Catholic who offered *hygiénisme* spiced with references to Scripture and laced with Christian moralism; that is, based on science that had not quite broken free of religion and with a notion of sickness still grounded in miasmas. But his basic primer came with the same advice as the more secular and scientific manuals that followed: eat and drink in moderation, protect the body from extremes of heat and cold, keep the home sunny and airy and free of the corrupting smells that mix with the blood and lead to disease, wash regularly—which for Descieux meant two or three baths during the summer, feet once a week, hands and face every day. Cleanliness, he told his young readers, was an element of morality: "A dirty and unkempt person is the sign of a soiled soul."[28]

Subsequent textbooks for a secular Republic dropped the religious perspective and increasingly integrated a more scientific view of the relationship between good hygiene and good health. They presented cleanliness as a matter of morals, one of the Republican rights and duties they had toward themselves and others. But they proposed more or less the same set of practices. Thus, the 1875 primer encouraged dental care with an illustration of a Shirley Temple-like girl with a toothbrush in her mouth. The caption told readers that they needed to care for their teeth because "the smile is the foundation of our empire."[29] The 1902 program taught students "the three precepts that most of their parents don't know: clean your fingernails, wash your hands *before* you eat, brush your teeth *after*."[30]

The 1909 program approved by the city of Bayonne included instruction of the virtues of meticulously clean skin and hair. It directed that students be taught to clean their ears and brush their teeth when they get up and when they go to bed; to wash—with soap—their feet once a week and their hands several times a day; to change their underwear twice a week and their handkerchief once; and to spit, if they must, in that handkerchief and not on the floor.[31] Indeed, in a society where tuberculosis was one of the principal causes of death, the control of spitting stood to make a significant contribution to the mortality rate. As the country teacher Théodore Chalmel told his students: "The germs of this disease live in these expectorations. That's how they spread. Every sputum that lands on the ground, the floor, the rug, the mat, the sidewalk, the car, the wagon, etc. is an agent for the spread of TB."[32]

As students advanced through their school years, the pro-hygiene curriculum changed in orientation and sophistication but not much in its basic message. "The goal of hygiene," Adrien Seignette told his readers, "is to teach us not only to conserve but to improve our health."[33] The ordinance of August 1881 carved out two spaces for hygiene education in secondary schools: Under "Historique," which also included lessons on the legal changes associated with 1789, 1848, and 1875, *la propreté* (cleanliness) found a place next among the "limits" of national sovereignty; it was also listed as a field of study under "Zoologie and Hygiène," which included a section on "Propreté de corps—Bains" (Clean bodies—Baths). An 1885 ordinance from the Education Ministry mandated lessons on "individual" and "public hygiene" under the rubric of "Domestic Economy and Hygiene" for fifteen-year-olds.[34] Seignette, who was also inspector general for *enseignement primaire*, included hygiene among hard sciences like physics, chemistry, and geology. Rural schools required something a little different than their urban counterparts, so each section of the science textbook for eleven- and twelve-year-olds contained a lesson on "applications to hygiene and to agriculture."[35]

Historian David S. Barnes reproduces a secondary school hygiene curriculum from 1890, which incorporated the subject as part of instruction on anatomy and physiology. Lectures focused on the importance of clean water, air uncontaminated by dust and swamp gases, the dangers of adulterated food, contagious diseases, vaccinations, housing conditions, and the "sanitary control of animals." Barnes remarks that, "Curiously, the late nineteenth-century crusade for cleanliness paid relatively little attention to the cleansing of the human body itself"—all the more curious, since contemporary authorities recognized that "Frenchmen bathed less often and less thoroughly than they should." Probably, this reflected the priority of the fight against epidemics above that for aesthetics. However, we have already seen that the primary schools spent plenty of time urging better habits on their students—admittedly with less than complete success. For older students, whose lessons in hygiene were formally part of a program in rhetoric and philosophy, the angle of instruction had changed.[36]

It hardly needs saying that French boys and French girls received slightly different tutelage in hygiene. At twelve or thirteen, boys' textbooks for boys' education stressed the dangers of alcohol, as the main vector of bad health and social dysfunction "that jeopardizes the future of our country and our economy." Their textbooks contained lessons on cesspool management and animal husbandry. Girls were trained above all to be good mothers, wives, and housekeepers, studying safe cosmetics, clothing, and childcare. Their contribution to the nation's destiny lay in their ability to provide healthy homes to help create productive workers and strong soldiers. Jeannine Martay's text offered comprehensive advice on proper grooming, with descriptions of the various sorts of baths and the rules pertaining to each, alongside a catalog of the proper techniques for cleaning hands, feet, mouths, eyes, ears, nostrils, hair, and those "intimate" places that, because of "excessive modesty," often get neglected.[37]

An archetypical bit of pedagogy can be found in the 1892 primer for young girls: "*Tu seras ouvrière*" (*You will be a Working Girl*). A didactic tale of social mobility, it tells the story of Jeanne, a peasant girl who, with no assets beyond her own wisdom and competence, rises to become a successful shop owner in Paris. "Your parents were working people," she is told by a patronizing teacher, "and there is a 100 percent chance that you will be a worker, too." Jeanne defies this prediction and along the way receives all sorts of lessons on sewing, on phylloxera, on the biographies of famous men and women, and on the virtues of good hygiene.[38]

There can be no doubt that the boys and girls who received these lessons in propriety needed them. The students, observed Ernest Monin, secretary of the Société Française d'Hygiène (SFH), "are, it has to be said, extremely grubby." Dr. Pierre Aubert's survey of Lyon schoolchildren in 1879 concluded that only one in ten arrived at school with no history of lice and nits, which is one reason why the Commission d'hygiène des écoles, created by an ordinance of January 1882, established a network of doctors to supervise the regular inspection of young students.[39]

Dr. Henri Gourichon, a medical inspector of primary schools, responsible for some 250,000 students in Paris, described the routine:

> In accordance with regulations, the teacher checks [the pupils'] propriety at the beginning of every class. If the child is dirty, he is sent to the washroom to clean up or sent home to his family. Despite all our observations and these urgent measures, it is far from rare, especially in the outlying districts, to meet students sent to school by negligent parents, in soiled and torn clothes, face and hands black with filth, un-brushed hair full of dandruff and nits. In the name of the public interest, poverty cannot be accepted as an excuse. Cleanliness is required of everyone.

Louis Dufestel described a routine where students in Paris were required to hang their "outdoor" clothes outside the classroom. The rules prohibited scarfs and kerchiefs inside. Children who arrived with unwashed faces were handed off to a woman who would take them off and give them an "energetic" going over with clean water and a sponge.[40]

Pierre Manse remembered his own youth in the small Languedoc village of Meriheu (300 inhabitants) lining up for the morning inspection parade past the teachers—the children,

> berets under their arms, showing their open hands and exposing their necks. Upon a barely perceptible sign [the student] left the line and went off to clean up at the trough of cold, murky water at the end of the courtyard. He returned quickly, presenting himself humbly for a new examination wiping his hand, now more red than clean, on his pants.

Among the children, Manse continued, were those covered in lice. The teacher told them to cut their hair short and expressed his satisfaction when they arrived the next Monday with their heads shaved—thanks to one of the local peasants who played village barber on Sundays.[41]

More often, the teachers and inspectors often found themselves at a loss to compensate for the negligence and poor habits that so many children brought from home. The ideal, thought Gourichon, was to give the schools the facilities to clean the students up—sinks and showers fed by hot water. In 1894, for example, the city of Paris imposed the *bain hebdomadaire* (weekly bath) for students who needed it

Fig. 39. — Bains en cuves (système de Carl Hanssons).

Figure 5.1 *Washing the Students:* "In the Carl Hansson's system, students are immersed in vats containing 90–100 liters of water." Photograph in Henri Méry and Joseph Génévrier, *Hygiene scolaire* (Paris: J.-B. Bailliere et fils, 1914), 63.

(Figure 5.1). This of course was fanciful, since schools never had the means to follow through on the requirement. In the meantime, wrote Gourichon, it was critical to show both children and parents the compelling need for cleanliness, along with the pathological consequences of the neglect of personal hygiene, though assignments in class and at home, by informal talks on the part of the teachers, and by handing out informational brochures. Students were not permitted to attend school if they had mouth or eye infections. They were passed along to the school doctors, who would send them back to their parents with information and instructions about how to treat the condition. However, Gourichon noted, this system did not work very well, as it often ran into the ignorance, insouciance, and suspicion of the parents. As one inspector for nursery schools in the Nivernais told her superiors, "Many mothers, through ignorance or carelessness, remain deaf to the teachers' solicitations on this subject."[42]

What this all suggests is that raising a crusade is not the same as winning one. Anne-Marie Sohn, in her marvelous history of nineteenth-century women in the private sphere, warns readers "not to overestimate the influence of the schools," at least at the beginning of the Third Republic. Louis Théron de Montaugé agreed. All the "happy influence" of the advances in education, he wrote in 1869, had not killed the old superstitions, where in the most backward areas, especially up in the mountains, people still believed in vampires and ghosts and looked to magic to solve their problems. A year after Jules Ferry had made primary education obligatory and secular, Napias and

Martin could still regret that "in fact, virtually no part of the country could boast a complete education in hygiene."[43]

The project of transforming peasants and other "pre-modern" folk into "Frenchmen" had always faced considerable cultural and economic headwinds. It was easier to write about the necessity of better plumbing and cleaner latrines at school than to find the money to build them, easier to publish manuals that described the proper routines for washing and bathing than to assure that children with no access to clean water followed them, and easier to send noncompliant students home than to make sure that their parents followed through on the school's instructions. To put the matter simply, the hygiene revolution requires a certain level of wealth and technology: education is crucial. Republican citizens need to understand why propriety was better for them, in spite of the cost and the effort, than dirtiness. But education in itself does not buy soap or socks or bedsheets or even a decent place to live. The vision of a cleaner France, free of the itch of lice and the mortal threat of endemic diseases tied to filth, was unquestionably a noble one. The schools of the Third Republic undoubtedly helped to move the country closer to that goal—but by inches rather than by yards.

In fact, the teachers sent as missionaries of modern hygiene often found themselves living like the natives. The published memoirs of late nineteenth-century *instituteurs* and *institutrices* unanimously depict the crudest conditions of life and work in the dilapidated shacks that ordinarily served for both schoolhouses and living quarters. Intended as "temples of hygiene" and barricades against epidemic disease—or, as historian Fabienne Chevallier writes, "the battleground for modern doctrines of public health"—the architecture of education was slower to develop than the pedagogy. Of course, there were notable successes, like the Lycée Lakanal, built in the Paris suburb of Sceaux and opened in 1885. It had a washroom with thirty sinks for each dormitory and a bathroom with tubs for 800 students, fed by the nearby Bièvre river and evacuated by modern plumbing—which meant, above all, avoiding narrow pipes prone to clogging and then to smelling. Nonetheless, the evidence speaks overwhelmingly of the decrepitude of the physical plant of education.[44]

Conditions in the countryside remained particularly dire. One young teacher, arriving at a small farming village in the Aube at the turn of the last century, found no hint of plumbing in his new home. "If the farmers or anyone else had their pump or their well, the worthies of the commune had not thought them necessary for the school." Likewise, Ernest Monnot, who, upon graduation from his teacher-training school in Besançon in 1885, took up his first posting in the village of Russey, at a school located in a very solid structure built in 1823 that had previously housed the village hall and then a brigade of mounted gendarmes. In 1867, it was converted to a school, with two classrooms and an apartment for the director. After two years in Russey, the education authorities sent Monnot to the farming community of La Bosse. His lodgings in the converted town hall, built in 1836, were far from terrible, he wrote: five rooms, "three in a decent state and two in a passable one," with a garden. He stayed there until 1930. But the building never had running water, and Monnot depended on the village fountain, like everyone else. The schoolroom was lit with kerosene lamps. Marcel Lignières, for his first posting in Saint-Chinian (Hérault), received a small empty room in the building below the director's apartment. For ten years he lived with a table, a chair, a straw mattress, a jug, and a small tub.[45]

When Théodore Chalmel came to the Breton village of La Fontenelle (Ille-et-Vilaine) in 1886 as the deputy teacher, he confronted a dismal living situation. His director granted him one small room, out of the five he reserved for himself. For thirty-five francs a month in rent, Chalmel had no fire and furnishings that consisted of a short, narrow bed. When Chalmel checked out his small classroom, he found thirty-seven students waiting for him. The courtyard was littered with a heap of kindling wood and, under a shallow cover, several yokes for the local plow horses. There is no reason to believe these stories were exceptional for teachers in village schools.

Under these unpromising conditions Chalmel took up his lessons, among them "Hygiene and cleanliness." But his civilizing mission was made more difficult for being a secular teacher in a very Catholic part of France. Suspicious of the Republic and its anticlerical inclinations, the town even refused to provide inkwells or firewood for the school—or to clean out the latrines, "which spread a nauseating smell across the neighborhood"—under the pretext that the students did not all live in the commune. Despite these difficult circumstances, from 1885 to 1935, Chalmel pressed on with the curriculum: reading, arithmetic, history, geography, alongside lessons on savings banks, museums, and morality. He preached hardest of all about the dangers of alcoholism—the source of most of the vices he saw around him.[46]

Chalmel does not estimate the effect of all his efforts to educate the peasant youth of Brittany. Did they wash more and spit less? Across the country, it is equally difficult to weigh the impact of the hygiene curriculum on the lives of French schoolchildren and their families. School inspector A. Féret sat among the optimists. Speaking to the SFH in December 1893, Féret reflected on the distance traveled in a generation. He expressed satisfaction with the dramatic improvement in the well-being of schoolchildren, even as he recognized that "personal habits and proper dress" required further efforts on the part of educators.[47]

The writer Henri Vincenot, born in 1912, who won a Goncourt Prize alongside other literary honors, also believed that the schools had helped create a "generation gap" in hygiene. Vincenot remembered his grandfather's advice that "crasse et cuirasse" (dirt and breastplate) rhymed for a reason. Following his own counsel, the senior Vincenot, reputedly "the best walker in four cantons," *never* washed his feet. And when Henri's mother encouraged him to wash under his arms, the grandmothers simply shrugged their shoulders: "Under your arms? Why not between your thighs while you're at it?"[48]

At the same time, there is plenty of evidence to suggest that the schools continued for a long time to fire well short of their target. Jeanne Bouvier, born into a skilled working-class family in 1865 and sent off to Catholic boarding school, recalled that "twenty-five pupils used to wash their face and hands in the same bowl. Once a month they proceeded to wash their feet, but they never washed anywhere else."[49] A 1910 survey by the Academy of Dijon found four boys' lycées that had *bains-douches*, one boy's and two girls' lycées that had no such facilities; not one of the fifteen boys' and thirteen girls' *collèges* in the region had them. According to a report to the city council of Nevers (1900), the girls' school did have some showers, but the dormitories themselves did not have running water; neither did the infirmary or the privies. In the Nivernais, writes Guy Thuillier, this "old regime" of *salubrité* that lasted into the 1930s, due to "the lack of running water and local habits," brought the teachers' good intentions to nothing. A report to the Conseil Général of the Nièvre on the state of school toilets made the point without mincing words:

> The state of the water-closets is generally deplorable. The schools, which should be at the center of teaching the population how to be clean, offers its children only latrines in the courtyards, without water, without sunlight, without being able to shield users from the wind. Even schools for adolescents and young boys and girls lack the necessary facilities. I can point, in particular, to the departmental agricultural school in Corbigny, which still has a "W.C." consisting of only two holes in the ground![50]

Things were hardly better in the capital. The lycée Janson-de-Sailly, in the very bourgeois 16th arrondissement of Paris, counted only ten showers for its 2,000 students. Dr. Depouilly, examining young students in "one of the least working-class quarters of Paris" in 1900, found that only fourteen of the forty had any experience of a bathtub. Twelve knew what a sponge was for; the others had never washed anything more than their hands and faces.[51] In some cases, teachers tried to compensate for the poor facilities in their schools by taking their students to the local public baths. But this was not always either possible or practical.

Students in the lower grades across the country had to confront the same disjunction between lessons on cleanliness and the dirty schools where they were delivered. Dr. Dufestel was confident that, in theory, the schools could change habits by giving pupils access to the amenities they did not enjoy at home. But he had to admit that schools were rarely providing these amenities. The departmental health commission in Nancy came to the same conclusion about the state of plumbing in the schools under its jurisdiction. The hygienist Dr. Jayle reported to the departmental council of the Nièvre during the First World War that, "At school, children do not receive the necessary education in hygiene, not because their *ex cathedra* lessons are meaningless, but because of the habits imposed by the [inadequate] sanitary facilities." He was particularly critical of the "mostly deplorable" W.C. he saw. Well into the new century, complained the school inspector in the Finistère, a large portion of children arrived for class "barefoot, in shabby clothes, their face and hands black with dirt." No wonder a medical inspection in 1903 found an excessive incidence of "genital diseases, which the children seem to neglect completely," made worse by the general habit of wearing the same linen day after day.

As for the instructors themselves, they were prepared for the lack of amenities in the schools where they later taught by their experiences in the *écoles normales* where they had learned to teach. It could not have helped that many young women "had little understanding of or appreciation for personal hygiene before they entered" these teacher training programs. Indeed, they often arrived with a deep-seated suspicion that, as Alain Corbin put it, the "moral as well as physical benefits [of water] were overestimated." Of course, there was discernible progress here and there. At the women's normal school in Clermont-Ferrand, for example, young trainees were graduating from weekly foot baths to a monthly trip to the public *bains-douches*, while one *directrice* in the Finistère made her charges bathe every three weeks. And every year more and more of these institutions acquired the means to wash their students in house. But these were the exceptions, rather than the rule.[52]

Reporting on conditions in 1877, Dr. Riant noted a "flagrant contradiction" between what students were taught in the normal schools and what they saw. In the Aude department, school inspectors were surprised to find that students, especially young women, did not bathe *at all* in winter—a reflection of the local culture, where public facilities for bathing were not even open during the winter months. The women's teacher-training school in the Aveyron did not acquire a bathtub until 1907.[53] Even where the facilities for keeping clean existed, there was nothing very deluxe about them.

The same was true for boys. When Ernest Monnot arrived at the *école normale* in Besançon in 1882, he was subject to a rigorous routine of hand- and neck-washing. But there were no baths, no toothbrushes, no hot water.[54] Even at the École Normale Supérieure in Paris, where the most elite minds in the country were formed, students suffered the same discomforts as their less privileged counterparts in the provinces. Without sinks and showers, they had to make due with a simple basin on a shelf next to their beds.

"Let us hope," observed the physician Louis Dufestel,

> that we are on the threshold of a time when the hygiene of childhood and adolescence will be methodically and effectively organized. School doctors in France, in all civilized countries, will oversee the hygiene of students in day and boarding schools. They will look after the salubriousness of buildings and monitor the growth of their young charges, they will direct their physical education and protect them from contagious diseases. The health records [compiled by the schools] will keep track of the important moments of their well-being and their physiological development.[55]

There is reason to think that Dufestel was premature in his optimism. The evidence from the schoolroom, like that from the barracks, testifies to the fact that the Republic's civilizing mission was a slog, rather than a sprint. And yet, from year to year and generation to generation, the practices and sensibilities of the past were giving way to those of the future.

Notes

1 Département de la Seine. Ville de Paris. Commission des logements insalubres, *Rapport général sur les travaux de la commission pendant les années 1862, 1863, 1864 et 1865* (Paris: Charles de Mourgues Frères, 1866), 10.
2 Catherine Rollet, "History of the Health Notebook in France: A Stake for Mothers, Doctors, and the State," *Dynamis* 23 (2003): 143–6.
3 Rebecca Rogers, *From the Salon to the Schoolroom: Educating Bourgeois Girls in Nineteenth-Century France* (University Park: Penn State University Press, 2005), 51,

56, 174 and 181–2; also see Jacques Léonard, *Archives du corps. La santé au XIXe siècle* (Rennes: Ouest France, 1986), 131–2.
4 Anne T. Quartararo, *Women Teachers and Popular Education in Nineteenth-Century France: Social Values and Corporate Identity at the Normal School Institution* (Newark: University of Delaware Press, 1995), 34, 49, and 69.
5 Agricole Perdiguier, "Memoirs of a Compagnon," in Mark Traugott (ed.), *The French Worker: Autobiographies from the Early Industrial Era* (Berkeley: University of California Press, 1993), 119.
6 Guy Thuillier, *Pour une histoire du quotidien au XIXe en Nivernais* (Paris: École des Hautes Études en Sciences sociales, 1977), 139 and 148, note 33.
7 Placide Rambaud and Monique Vincienne, *Les transformations d'une société rurale: La Maurienne, 1561–1962* (Paris: A. Colin, 1977), 216; Jules Courmont, *Précis d'hygiène* (Paris: Masson et Cie., 1914), 143; Henri Baudrillart, *Les populations agricoles de la France. 2e série: Maine, Anjou, Touraine, Poitou, Artois, Picardie, Île-de-France passé et présent* (Paris: Libririe Guillaumin et Cie., 1888), 58.
8 Patrick Harrigan, "Women Teachers and the Schooling of Girls in France: Recent Historiographical Trends," *French Historical Studies* 21, no. 4 (Autumn 1998): 594–5 and 597–9.
9 Stephen L. Harp, *Learning to be Loyal: Primary Schooling as Nation Building in Alsace and Lorraine, 1850–1940* (DeKalb: Northern Illinois University, 1998), 7–24.
10 Léonard, *Archives du corps*, 131–2.
11 Dr. Alfred Collineau, *L'hygiène à l'école: pédagogie scientifique* (Paris: J.-B. Ballière et Fils, 1889), 12.
12 On the Duruy reforms, see Jean-Charles Geslot, *Victor Duruy. Historien et ministre (1811–94)* (Villeneuve d'Ascq: Septentrion, 2009); Jean Rohr, *Victor Duruy ministre de Napoléon III. Essai sur la politique de l'instruction publique au temps de l'Empire libéral* (Paris: Librairie général de droit et de jurisprudence, 1967); also the classic Ernest Lavisse, *Un ministre. Victor Duruy* (Paris: Armand Colin, 1895).
13 Julia Csergo, *Liberté, égalité, propreté. La morale de l'hygiène au XIXe siècle* (Paris: Albin Michel, 1988), 114 and Csergo, "Propreté et enfance au XIXe siècle," in Didier Nourrisson (dir.), *Éducation à la santé, XIXe-XXe* (Rennes: Éditions ENSP, 2002), 47–50.
14 Dr. Henri Napias, *Règlementation des crèches publiques et privées, rapport présenté par M. le Dr. Henri Napias, le 21 décembre 1896* (Melun: Imprimerie Administrative, 1896), 5–15.
15 Louis Fortoul, *Les veillées de la ferme: notions élémentaires d'agriculture et d'hygiène rurale* (Paris: Librairie Classiqe de Paul Dupont, 1868), i and 88–102.
16 Collineau, *L'hygiène à l'école*, 2; Camille Lagnières, *La vie d'un instituteur centenaire de la IIIe République* (Uzès: Éditions Henri Peladan, 1982), 27 and Dr. Aimé Riant, *Conférence sur l'hygiène de l'école, faite à la Sorbonne le 29 août 1878* (Paris: Librairie Charles Delagrave, 1878), 12.
17 On the failures of hygiene in the schools, see Maxime Vernois, *État hygiénique des lycées à l'Empire en 1867: extrait du rapport présenté à Son Excellence le Ministre de l'Instruction publique* (Paris: J.-B. Ballière, 1868); Csergo, *Liberté, égalité, propreté*, 118; Lucien Gretelly, *De quleques progrès de l'hygiène dans les pensionnats* (Macon: Imprimerie de Protat frères, 1897), 58.
18 Romuald Gaillard, *Hygiène des lycées, collèges & des institutions de jeunes gens, composée d'après les documents les plus autorisés, conformément à l'arrêté ministériel du 15 février 1864 sur les commissions d'hygiène, et aux instructions et circulaires relatives à cet arrêté* (Vesoul: A. Suchaux, 1868), *passim*.

19 Csergo, *Liberté, Égalité, Propreté*, 77.
20 Dr. Aimé Riant, *L'hygiène et l'éducation dans les internats* (Paris: Librairie Hachette, 1877), 51 and *passim*.
21 David S. Barnes, *The Great Stink of Paris and the Nineteenth-Century Struggle against Filth and Germs* (Baltimore: Johns Hopkins University Press, 2006), 92–3.
22 There is a vast literature on the Ferry Laws. See especially the review essay Barry H. Bergen, "Primary Education in the Third Republic France: Recent French Works," *History of Education Quarterly* 26, no. 2 (Summer 1986): 271–85. Also see Pierre Chevallier, *La séparation de l'église et de l'école: Jules Ferry et Léon XIII* (Paris: Fayard, 1981); Danielle Delhome, Nicole Gault, and Josian Gonthier, eds., *Les premières institutrices laïques* (Paris: Mercure de France, 1980); Robert Gildea, *Education in Provincial France, 1800–1914: A Study of Three Departments* (New York: Oxford University Press, 1983); Raymond Grew and Patrick Harrigan, *School, State, and Society: The Growth of Elementary Schooling in Nineteenth-Century France: A Quantitative Analysis* (Ann Arbor: University of Michigan Press, 1991); Dominique Maingueneau, *Les livres d'école de la République, 1870–1914 (discours et idéologie)* (Paris: Éditions le Sycamore, 1979); Jacques Ozouf and Mona Ozouf, *République des instituteurs* (Paris: Gallimard, 1992); Mona Ozouf, *L'école, l'église et la République, 1871–1914* (Paris: A. Colin, 1963); and Antoine Prost, *Histoire générale de l'enseignement et de l'éducation en France, tome III: 1789–1930* (Paris: Nouvelle Librairie de France, 2004).
23 Henri Napias and André-Justin Martin, *L'étude et les progrès de l'hygiène en France de 1878 à 1882* (Paris: G. Masson, 1883), 47; Élie Pécaut, *Résumé du cours d'hygiène, à l'usage des classes élémentaires* (Paris: Hachette, 1883), 1; for a more extensive exposition of his ideas, see Pécaut, *Cours d'hygiène* (Paris: Hachette, 1882), *passim*. Also see Mary Lynn Stewart, *For Health and Beauty: Physical Culture for Frenchwomen, 1880s–1930s* (Baltimore: Johns Hopkins University Press, 2001), 2.
24 See Brigitte Sandrin Berthon, *Apprendre la santé à l'école* (Paris: Édition Sociale Française, 1997), 9.
25 Léon Angot, *L'enseignement moral à l'école primaire* (Paris: Paul-Auguste Godchaux & Cie., 1897), 61.
26 Riant, *Conférence sur l'hygiène*, 36–7; and Dr. Louis Depouilly, *L'eau dans les logements ouvriers*, thèse de médecine (Paris: A. Depouilly, 1900), 62.
27 On the crèches, see A. Féret, *Études sur l'hygiène scolaire et d'intérêt général* (Paris: A. Féret, 1900), 199; Henri Napias, *L'assistance publique dans le département de Sambre-et-Loire* (Paris: L. Bataille et Cie., 1893), 30–1; and Napias, *Règlementation des crèches*, 3–15; Charles Batallie, *La crèche Elisabeth et Marguerite Brière* (Rouen: Émile Deshays, 1892), 1–5.
28 Dr. Louis Cyprien Descieux, *Leçons d'hygiène à l'usage des enfants des écoles primaires* (Paris: Librairie Classique de Paul Dupont, 1871), 62.
29 Lise Bésème-Pia, *Folklore des dents en Champagne-Ardenne, à l'usage des dentists, des patients et des petits enfants* (Langes: Éditions Dominique Guéniot, 2010), 101.
30 Léonard, *Archives du corps*, 132.
31 Ville de Bayonne. Bureau Municipal d'Hygiène. Inspection médicale des établissements scolaires, *Le propreté de l'écolier: conseils pratiques aux parents* (Bayonne: Imprimerie Lamaignère, 1909), 3–10.
32 Théodore Chalmel, *Les mémoires d'un instituteur rural, 1885–1935* (Saint-Père-Marc-en-Poulet: Association Théodore Chalmel, 1999), 108.
33 Adrien Seignette, *Sciences usuelles et agriculture. Anatomie et physiologie de l'homme, hygiène, physique, chimie, zoologie, botanique, géologie et agriculture. [Cours supérieur:*

80 leçons, 289 figures, 96 sujets proposes au Certificat d'études et au Brevet Élémentaire, avec Lexique explicative] (Paris: Librairie de l'Enseignement, 1913), 38.

34 *Réglements et programmes d'études des écoles normales d'instituteurs et d'institutrices* (Paris: Imprimerie Nationale, 1886), 37, 56, and 97.

35 A. Lepigoché and Charles-Joseph Seltensperger, *Le livre unique de sciences et d'agriculture, d'hygiène et d'économie domestique à l'école rurale. Notions scientifiques. Notions agricoles. Applications à l'hygiène et à l'économie domestique. Résumés par leçons. Expériences simples. Rédactions. Problèmes. Promenades scolaires. 337 gravures* (Paris: Delaplane, 1913), 23, for example.

36 Barnes, *The Great Stink*, 176 and 209–10. He took the curricula out of "Arrêté du ministère de l'instruction publique, fixant le nouveau programme de l'enseignement secondaire classique dans les classes de lettres (28 janvier 1890)," in *Recueil des lois et actes de l'instruction publique*, année 1890, premier semester, 105–6 and "Circulaire relative à une nouvelle répartition des matières de l'enseignement scientifique dans les classes supérieures des lettres (12 août 1890)," in *Circulaires et instructions officielles relatives à l'instruction publique*, vol. 11: June 1889–December 1893 (Paris: Delalain Frères, 1894), 280. Also see Dr. E. Laplane, *Leçon d'ouverture du cours d'hygiène, fait à l'école de Médecine de Marseille* (Marseille: Barlatier et Barthelet, 1890) and Adrien Proust, *Douze conférences d'hygiène, rédigées conformément au plan d'études du 12 août 1890*, 2nd ed. (Paris: G. Masson, 1895). On the inclusion of sex education, see Dr. Lucien Mathé, *L'enseignement de l'hygiène sexuelle à l'école* (Paris: Vigot Frères, 1912).

37 Association de l'An 2000, *Quelques chapitres de la vie d'Émile, Ernest Monnot: instituteur à la Bosse, de 1887 à 1928, un petit village du Haut-Doubs et son école* (Le Bizot: Association de l'An 2000, 2002), n.p.; also see Berthon, *Apprendre la santé à l'école*, 9; Jeannine Martay, *L'hygiène dans les soins de toilette chez la jeune fille et chez la femme* (Paris: Librairie des Annales, 1909), 201; also Linda L. Clark, *Schooling the Daughters of Marianne: Textbooks and the Socialization of Girls in Modern French Primary Schools* (Albany: SUNY Press, 1984), 16 and 93; and Stewart, *For Health and Beauty*, 71.

38 Louis-Charles Desmaisons, *"Tu seras ouvrière": simple histoire. Livre de lecture courante à l'usage des écoles de filles. Leçons de choses—Hygiène—Travail manuel—Économie domestique—143 gravures* (Paris: A. Colin, 1892), iv. Also see Simone de Kéranflech-Kernezne, *Hygiène de la ménagere rurale (conseil pratiques)* (Saint-Brieuc: R. Prud'hommes, 1909), 1–3 and Ernestine Wirth, *La future ménagère: Lectures et leçons sur l'économie domestique, la science du ménage, l'hygiène, les qualités et les connaissances nécessaires à une maîtress de maison: À l'usage des écoles et des pensionnats de demoiselles* (Paris: Hachette, 1882), 385–91.

39 Dr. Ernest Monin, *La propreté de l'individu et da la maison* (Paris: Au Bureau de la Société Française d'Hygiène), 34; Pierre Aubert, *Un point d'hygiène scolaire. Les poux et les écoles* (Lyon: Association Typographique, 1879), 2; "L'hygiène à l'école et par l'école," in Patrice. O. Bordelais, et al., *Les nouvelles pratiques de santé: acteurs, objets, logiques sociales, XVIIIe-XXe siècles* (Paris: Belin, 2005), 215; and André Rauch, *Histoire de la santé. Que sais-je?* (Paris: Presses Universitaires de France, 1995), 63.

40 Louis Dufestel, *Hygiène scolaire* (Paris: Octave Doin et fils, 1909), 147.

41 Pierre Manse, *Meriheu de mon enfance* (Pau: Éditions Marrimpouey Jeune, 1988), 13–16.

42 Dr. Henri Gourichon, *Hygiène de l'enfant à l'école. Rapport présenté à la Société des Médecins-Inspecteurs, au nom d'une commission composée de MM. Toledano, Toureil et H. Gourichon, rapporteur* (Paris: Imprimerie Typographique Jean Gainche, 1905),

5–6 and 12; also see Léonard, *Archives du corps*, 132; Thuillier, *Pour une histoire du quotidien*, 54.

43 Napias and Martin, *L'étude et les progrès de l'hygiène*, 452–3; Anne-Marie Sohn, *Chrysalides. Femmes dans la vie privée (XIXe-XX siècles)*, vol. 1 (Paris: Publications de la Sorbonne, 1996), 303; and Louis Théron de Montaugé, *L'agriculture et les classes rurales dans le pays toulousain depuis le milieu du dix-huitième siècle* (Paris: Librairie Agricole de la Maison Rustique, 1869), 456.

44 Aimé Riant, *Hygiène scolaire, Influence de l'école sur la santé des enfants* (Paris: Hachette, 1874) and Fabienne Chevallier, *Le Paris moderne: Histoire des politiques d'hygiène (1855–1898)* (Rennes: Presses Universitaires de Rennes, 2010), 206.

45 *Nous les maîtres de l'école* [autobiographies d'instituteurs de la Belle Époque présentées par Jacques Ozouf] (Paris: Gallimard, 1983), 43; Association l'An 2000, *Quelques chapitres de la vie d'Emile*, n.p.; Camille Liginières, *La vie d'un instituteur centenaire de la IIIe République* (Uzès: Éditions Henri Peladan, 1982), 70–1.

46 Chalmel, *Les mémoires d'un instituteur rural*, 11, 18, 20, 32–3, and 71–2.

47 Féret, *Études sur l'hygiène scolaire et d'intérêt général*, 134.

48 See Claudine Vincenot, *Le maître de Bonheur: mon père, Henri Vincenot* (Paris: Librairie Générale Française, 1997), 297.

49 Jeanne Bouvier, *Mes mémoires ou cinquante-neuf années d'activité industrielle, sociale et intellectuelle d'une ouvrière* (Niort: L'Action Intellectuelle, 1936), 22.

50 Nevers. *Conseil général*, 1904, 165 and 1905, 318: cited in Thuillier, *Pour une histoire du quotidien*, 58, note 11; also Département de la Nièvre. Conseil Général, *Rapport du préfet et procès-verbaux des délibérations. Session d'août 1916* (Nevers: Mazeron Frères, 1916), 260. Also see André Burguière, *Bretons de Plozévet* (Paris: Flammarion, 1975), 294; and Dufestel, *Hygiène scolaire*, 10.

51 Csergo, "Propreté et enfance au XIXe siècle," 57.

52 Alain Corbin, "The Secret of the Individual," in Michelle Perrot (ed.), *A History of Private Life*, vol. 4 (Cambridge: Belknap Press, 1999), 482.

53 Quartararo, *Women Teachers*, 141; Riant, *L'hygiène et l'éducation*, 131.

54 Association l'An 2000. *Quelques chapitres de la vie d'Émile*, n.p.

55 Dufestel, *Hygiène scolaire*, 2.

6

Water in, Water Out

1900: Taking Stock

The architects of the Third Republic had learned important lessons from the failures of 1792 and 1848: neither an enlightened constitution nor the native virtue of the people was enough to sustain a Republic. That is why they put so much effort, through the army and in the schools, into giving citizens the habits of mind and body that would support a strong, prosperous, and modern nation, and why they made hygiene a key part of that civilizing mission, alongside literacy and patriotism.

Practices and sensibilities always advanced hand in hand in this campaign—although, as practical matter, practices walked slightly in front. Students and recruits were taught the rudiments of hygiene and given, at least in principle, the necessary tools to lead cleaner, healthier lives: socks, toothbrushes, soap, linen, urinals, and *lieux d'aisance* (latrines) with water and seats. It was assumed that new instruction would change old habits and that, once young French men and women had gotten used to being free of vermin and pong, they would develop a preference for *salubrité* and an intolerance for the unwholesome ways they had lived before. Lessons learned in the classrooms and the barracks would be carried through families, neighborhoods, and villages. Habits picked up in the cities, always a bit more advanced, would be brought back to the countryside—just as nurses trained in the small town of Bogros, studied by the geographer J. Levainville, became "the vectors of modernity" across the Morvan and the Savoie—as seasonal migrants brought new practices back to their old villages. Historian Anne-Marie Sohn notes that before 1914 one French woman in four was or had been a domestic servant. That represented a lot of cultural exchange.[1]

As earlier chapters have pointed out, this noble mission ran into significant obstacles. It moved forward unevenly across time and space, and with varying degrees of success between individuals. Then again, the question is not whether the conditions of 1900 would meet twenty-first-century expectations but to what extent the old regime of hygiene had begun to give way to something more modern.

Dr. Boell (de Baugé) was buoyant on this count. "Hygiene has come a long way in this century," he wrote in his 1896 treatise on rural standards of *propreté*. Boell, an officer in the Académie Chevalier du Mérite agricole, was certainly not wrong; although this confidence clashed with the descriptions that followed his upbeat preface. To take only the most shocking bit of his analysis, Boell, writing a full seventy-five years after Louis-August Maréschal's grim depiction of Breton *puériculture*, pointed to the same dangerous customs of baby care—such as feeding infants indigestible food

Table 6.1 Infant Mortality Rates in Diverse Industrial Countries, 1906–10 (per 1,000 Live Births)

Norway	69	Denmark	119
Sweden	78	United States	121
Netherlands	114	**France**	**128**
Switzerland	115	Italy	152
England	117	Germany	174

Source: Alain Norvez, *De la naissance à l'école: santé, modes de garde et préscolarité dans la France contemporaine* (Paris: Presses Universitaires de France, 1990), 65.

and using tainted milk bottles—that continued to sustain a premodern rate of infant mortality. Fifty infants out of a hundred raised on a *biberon* die in their first year, he claimed, whereas infant mortality for breastfed babies was only 10 percent. Aside from the individual tragedies, Boell added, this hecatomb was enhancing the demographic advantage of the "Prussians."[2]

In fact, according to Jules Courmont, professor at the Lyon medical faculty, French rates of infant mortality in 1909 were better than German rates: 14.3 deaths per 100 births in France, as against 17.8 in Germany—although they were higher in France than in England, Switzerland, Sweden, and Norway.

As Table 6.1 implies, the real demographic advantage for Germany was not its infant mortality rate but its vigorous birthrate, adding 800,000–900,000 souls a year to the population, whereas the French birthrate was flat. Still, Courmont calculated that if France could lower its infant mortality to the levels of England or Scandinavia, it could increase its population substantially. That is why he worked so hard on behalf of better hygiene: the defense of the country depended on it.[3]

Whether the efforts of schools, barracks, and hygiene commissions to clean up the country appeared to be paying big dividends or lagging behind expectations depended partly on where one looked and which half of the phrase "slow progress" one emphasized. The evidence cut in both directions. Few would have been as positive in their assessment as historian Fabienne Chevallier, who writes that the second half of the nineteenth century "witnessed the attainment of . . . cities armed with all the attributes necessary to achieve a salubrious existence for their inhabitants."[4] Still, many observers found reasons for optimism. For instance, A. Féret, a teaching inspector, speaking to the SFH in December 1893, reflected on the distance traveled in a generation. He expressed satisfaction with the dramatic improvement in the well-being of schoolchildren, even as he recognized that "personal habits and proper dress" required further efforts on the part of educators.[5] In one indirect measure of the success of the Republic's hygiene offensive, the army class of 1893 produced recruits who, at 5' 5 ½", were an inch taller on average than their grandfathers had been.[6]

Water In

The limited success of the Republic's mission to clean up its citizens points over and over to one essential truth: there could be no hygiene without water. "The preoccupation with water," remarks historian Emmanuel Le Roy Ladurie, "is at the heart of the religion of progress."[7] Dr. Louis Depouilly agreed. "The agendas of all those organizations concerned with public health," he wrote, "are unanimous in affirming the fundamental importance of water."[8] In the countryside it was polluted and, in the warm summer months, often unavailable. If anything, the situation was worse in the towns, which could rarely manage to provide enough water to their inhabitants. Even in Paris, where the housing commission in 1865 could salute the progress that had been made since the last days of Louis XVIII, and which enjoyed a special place in state priorities, water remained inconvenient, expensive—laced endemically with typhoid and occasionally with cholera.[9]

The SFH concurred, and its 1882 report insisted that "Water must be abundantly available in every public and private home, for cleaning every building, every dwelling, everybody. Whatever obstructs this project is condemnable."[10] Reformer Émile Cheysson called water "la question primordiale" for civilization. Without it "there is neither cleanliness, nor hygiene, nor health . . . nor virtue." It was as essential to political stability as to hygiene, he added. For democracy to survive in France, access to water "cannot be the exclusive privilege of wealth."[11] Historians Jean-Pierre Goubert and Georges Vigarello tell us that water has always had important ceremonial and sacred functions.[12] In the battle for better hygiene, however, what mattered in the history of water were not its magical but its functional qualities. In the schools, in the barracks, in their homes, people's ability to keep themselves and their environment clean and healthy rose in direct proportion to the amount of water at their disposal. The schools and the military could preach the virtues of *propreté*, but if the schoolhouse has no running water; if the army cannot provide sinks and showers, so that soldiers can wash after a hard week's march in high summer, or flushable latrines and *urinoirs* for hundreds of young men; if people living in rough country houses or crowded urban apartments need to fetch and carry water into their homes, then the mission will inevitably come up short of its goals.

As these institutions implicitly recognized, the mere supply of water was not enough. Although habits broadly followed technical advances, as Julia Csergo cautions, culture sometimes disrupted that process. "Despite the spread of running water," she writes, "to use it for keeping clean [long] remained contrary to peasant customs and to the economizing spirit of the poorer classes."[13] True enough. At the same time, however, one of the principal lessons of this story is that, as people gained access to more water, they sooner or later learned to use it. And they never went backward.

Buried in the footnotes of Eugen Weber's brilliant book of essays, *France: Fin-de-Siècle*, is a remarkable statistic: "[U]nder Napoleon III a successful medical man living in the center of Paris paid his water hauler 72 francs a year for 14,000 liters of water; at the turn of the century the same sum paid for 206,000 liters of tap water."[14] This represents an almost fifteenfold reduction in price in the course of fifty years of the resource most precious to the human condition. Moreover, the precipitous drop in the cost of water does not in itself speak to the other key elements of the water revolution of the modern era: the greater ease of getting and disposing of it and the substantial improvement in its quality. "A gift from the sky and the earth," writes Jacques Léonard, "[water] was more and more sought out, captured, pumped, piped, and purified."

Usage tripled.¹⁵ And even where the water did not run through pipes, there was more of it. For example, in the town of Châtellerault (Vienne), where there had been three fountains in 1861, there were twenty-five in 1866, thirty-seven in 1875, fifty-two in 1889, and fifty-eight in 1900.¹⁶

Evidence from across the country tells the story of the progress made under the Third Republic. In 1879, the city of Nancy still depended on local and insufficient sources of water. But in the 1880s it began to bring in water from the Moselle—enough for 400 liters per day for everyone, with one household in two directly connected to the water system by the 1890s. In the same decade, Nantes extended its water distribution system into working-class districts. The 1894 Foville Report on housing conditions around the country noted that Lille had a functioning municipal water service. "Wells have disappeared almost everywhere [and] water is distributed in abundance."¹⁷ Even the notoriously backward city of Rennes got a municipal system of *adduction* in 1883, brought in from as far as 42 miles away—although much of that water still went into wells and not into buildings.¹⁸ In the eastern city of Troyes, the switch to piped-in spring water in the late 1890s cut the number of typhoid cases in half.¹⁹

Still, the forward march of the water supply left a lot of people behind. In 1892, of the 691 French towns with more than 5,000 residents, only 290 had running water systems, and those served only 127,318 subscribers. In Nevers, writes Guy Thuillier, "Water on every floor was rare before 1914," and the whole system remained "very archaic into the 1920s." In Avignon, "the city of popes," 30,000 people were still hoisting their water out of wells in 1914.²⁰ In Rouen, where a modern system of water distribution was installed in 1881, even the bourgeoisie were slow to hook up to "les adductions municipales." In view of "deep-rooted habits and the widespread employment of domestics in this milieu," writes Jean-Pierre Chaline, "the advantages of city water, costly to connect to and requiring a pricey subscription, were not obvious. . . . That is why, in so many of the great houses . . . wells remained common throughout the nineteenth century."²¹

Whether it came out of fountains or wells or kitchen faucets, the purity of water remained a constant concern of public authorities. A 1906 report on the state of the water supply across the country spoke of the "épidémies de puits" (contaminated wells) that made typhoid fever a constant menace.²² At the local level, responsibility for looking after the water supply fell to the hygiene councils, but these functioned unevenly. And their job was made more difficult, noted Dr. Courgey, attached to the hygiene bureau in Ivry-sur-Seine, by the population's tendency to dissemble. "How many grocers, bakers, and small merchants of all sorts," he asked, "who have a child with measles or diphtheria, beg their doctors not to report them, fearing that this would scare away their business?"²³

An 1889 study of hygiene councils' activities found that in the department of the Nord the council examined no fewer than 150 cases of suspected water pollution. At the other end of the spectrum, the councils in the Correze, in the Lozère, and in Corsica never met at all. In all, fifty-six departmental councils did not hold the minimum of four meetings a year prescribed in the law. Predictably, the incidence of official oversight conformed to the usual geographical logic: the most backward regions of the country, where hygienic standards were weakest and public health most fragile, had the least active program of *hygiène publique*. It seems, wrote Gilbert Ballet, vice-president of the council in the Indre-et-Loire department, to the prefect, evidence of "a regrettable insouciance." "Every year," said Ballet, "we see the same epidemics carry off new victims. It seems like everyone considers himself safe from the diseases that strike his neighbors and with a complete disinterest in the most elementary rules of hygiene."[24]

Similarly, an 1885 report by the deputy Dunoyer to the National Assembly on a social reform project—the so-called Nadaud Law, named after its chief sponsor—praised the work of hygiene councils in the areas around Lille, Paris, Rouen, Versailles, Bordeaux, Nantes, La Rochelle, Nancy, Épinal, and Caen. Conversely, noted the report, where water quality was neglected, typhoid fever and cholera flourished.[25] The action of *pouvoirs publics* was therefore crucial.

We find an exemplary instance of the way that an energetic system of public oversight might function in Nancy, where, in early 1908, the local hygiene council sent an inspector out to investigate a complaint by a Madame Pigeon that her well water was being polluted by the leaky cesspit of her neighbor, Monsieur Maury. The inspector did not find Maury's *fosse* at fault, although it was true that the neighbor was dumping manure into a pit only 10 meters from the sump belonging to Mme. Pigeon. He concluded rather that Pigeon's well was being polluted principally by rainwater. The council nevertheless ordered the neighbor, M. Maury, to stop his dumping.[26] In a similar fashion, the departmental hygiene council of the Yvelines was convoked to investigate reports of water pollution coming from runoff in Versailles, subsequently making recommendations to clean up the local streams. In the Var, the prefect empowered the hygiene council in Toulon to do something about garbage removal, polluted water, defective *fosses d'aisances*, and public toilets. The council also acted to shut down private slaughterhouses, "dangerous from a public health perspective," and to construct public state-of-the-art abattoirs—all with a positive effect on public health. These were all virtuous exceptions to the rather lax rule.[27]

Paris was in a category of its own, given its size and its weight in national affairs. Despite the progress owed to the efforts of Haussmann and Belgrand, the capital continued to suffer from the same problem: there wasn't enough water to meet the demand, and the existing supply was often polluted or worse. Well into the 1890s, moreover, the system continued to depend on the old points of distribution. Wallace fountains, named after the English philanthropist Richard Wallace (1818–1890), still delivered drinking water to thousands. So did the many *bornes-fontaines* (standpipes) that opened around the city (Figure 6.1). A census carried out by the housing commission in 1892 counted some 4,000 wells operating through the capital. Most stored water of dubious quality. The last porters carting water across the city from the Seine and the Ourcq disappeared only in 1890. In 1900, a million Parisians still had no running water in their homes.[28]

It is hard to say where that placed Paris, contrasted with other cities. "Among the great works undertaken in a certain number of cities in the last few years," noted Henri Napias, the well-known physician and hygienist, in 1883, "Paris ranks at the very top."[29] The precise numbers vary from source to source; all, however, agree on the trajectory. Thus, an article in the 1902 volume of the *Annales des Ponts et Chaussées* reported that water usage in Paris had grown from 5 liters per person in 1830 to 30 in 1850 to 360 liters per person in 1902. According to Julia Csergo, daily

Figure 6.1 *It is hot in Paris. A little girl takes some water at a standpipe during a hot summer day in Paris (France) in 1921.* Courtesy of the Bibliothèque nationale de France.

usage rose from 20 liters per person in 1860 to 95 by the mid-1890s. Jean-Claude Daumas writes that daily water consumption rose from 13.3 liters per person in 1800 to 249 liters in 1900. Not all that water, he notes, was used directly by individuals: typically 12–15 liters a day. The rest of it went to industry or to public sanitation efforts.[30]

Comparing Paris to London, Émile Vallin, *médicin-inspecteur* in the army and on the medical faculty of the University of Paris, wrote in 1883 that there remained 30,000 houses without direct access to water in the French capital; Paris, however, provided on average more water per capita to its inhabitants than London: 185 liters in the French capital, as opposed to 150 liters across the channel. Paradoxically, though, in London 80 percent of that total was used by individual households. In Paris it was only 25 percent, while the rest went to public services.[31] Historian Steven Johnson, in his brilliant study of cholera epidemic in Chelsea in 1856, which served to prove that cholera was in the water, not in the air—"swallowed and not inhaled," as he put it—paints a rather different picture of French accomplishments. He cites estimates that the average London household used 160 gallons of water a day in 1850; and by 1856, largely thanks to the runaway success of the W.C., it was using 244 gallons.[32] This clearly dwarfs water consumption anywhere in France.

Writing at the end of the 1880s, Georges Bechmann, *polytechnicien* and chief engineer for the construction of Paris's second metro line, connecting the Place de l'Étoile to the Place de la Nation across the north of the city, reckoned daily water consumption for eighty-four cities in France and across the world at 185 liters per person. Naturally, this average hid considerable differences between urban centers. For example, where Rome provided 100 liters, Madrid provided only 15. French cities, he wrote, compared favorably with the others. Marseille and Paris were at the top of the table, with the Marseillais enjoying 500 liters a day and Parisians 300. (These figures seem outlandish.) Of the eighty-four cities he mentioned, only twenty-four supplied their inhabitants with more than 200 liters a day; twenty-two delivered less than 100, which Bechmann considered the minimum; anything below that would do real damage to public health. He added that there remained serious issues of waste from leaky pipes and dripping faucets—a problem exacerbated by the general absence of water meters that would make people responsible for what they consumed. "We should not be too severe with landlords hesitant about connecting their buildings to the water system," a Monsieur Kern told a meeting of the Paris hygiene council. "Few of them recoil at the initial expense, but what they do fear are the ongoing costs of water consumption. We need to protect them from the [expenses of] spillage, which are considerable."[33]

Historian Richard Evans's study of the 1892 cholera in Hamburg leads him to a parallel discussion of the water system in Imperial Germany. By 1890, he writes, Hamburg was more or less even with Paris. It had over 400 kilometers of pipes and almost every building in the city had at least one tap inside or in the courtyard. This went well beyond standards in Prussia generally where, as late as 1895, 58 percent of towns with more than 2,000 inhabitants still depended on wells, springs, and river and rainwater, although almost all the biggest cities in the empire had a central water supply. In 1875, only 43 percent of Berlin houses were connected to the city's water system; by 1890, Evans estimates that number had risen to 93 percent. In a book about cholera, Evans has much to say about water quality, and here the difference between Hamburg and Berlin was consequential. Whereas Berlin's water, taken from the Spree river, was purified by a sand-filtration system, Hamburg's, taken directly from the Elbe and stored in reservoirs, was subject to no such purification. Cholera thrived.[34]

In 1889, demographer Paul Brouardel and bacteriologist Léon-Henri Thoinot published a study of typhoid fever in the port city of Le Havre. Typhoid was endemic in Le Havre, as in so many cities, but numbers had spiked in the previous few years. Brouardel and Thoinot wanted to explain why, and their book reads like a survey of an urban hygiene catastrophe before the arrival of modern water and sewer systems. The first problem was the "absolutely insufficient" quantity of water available to the inhabitants of Le Havre: an average of 99 liters per person daily. The lack of hygiene that derived from the poor water supply was then multiplied by the careless handling of potentially infected material—in particular, the widespread practice of simply dumping garbage and excrement in places where they could leach into the wells and groundwater. They cite one egregious example, a restaurant, especially crowded on Sundays, where the *matières fécales* of the inhabitants of the building and the clients of the restaurant were simply collected in pails and emptied into a nearby field, without any further treatment. This was no isolated incident.[35]

Le Havre had four networks of sewers, but they were limited in length (only 37 kilometers) and lacked both the volume of water and the pitch to be properly flushed out; besides, they were meant to drain the streets and not to contain raw sewage. *Déjections* (excreta) that did not end up in a field or a stagnant sewer system found their way into the cesspits (*fosses d'aisances*) that lay, as elsewhere, around and below most of the buildings. In principle, an army of *vidangeurs* pulling *tinettes mobiles* (carts for transporting excrement) picked up all this material and carted it away to be dried and sold as fertilizer to local farmers. But everyone knew how badly the system worked, particularly in the poorest and most neglected parts of the city. The *fosses* were sometimes located not in the courtyards but in the buildings themselves, were not emptied frequently enough, and exuded a poisonous miasma. Alternatively, the *eaux vannes* ("blackwater," i.e., urine and excrement) were simply poured into the sewers or directly into whatever stream ran through the neighborhood. In other words, the whole arrangement functioned as a delivery system for typhoid. Periodic outbreaks of epidemic were overdetermined.

It is not surprising then that the question of quality and waterborne epidemics appeared on the agenda of virtually every meeting of the Paris public hygiene council. Typhoid fever remained a constant concern of the health authorities, although it almost never came close to killing as many Parisians as tuberculosis and other respiratory diseases. A survey of the city's demography conducted by the Conseil in 1900 documented the toll of these endemic killers, month by month and *quartier* by *quartier*. For example, statistics collected in the 16th arrondissement for 1900 show 15 deaths from typhoid, 23 each from measles and flu, 113 from cancer, and 331 from tuberculosis and other respiratory ailments. Predictably, conditions got worse and the toll higher in the outlying parts of the city and in the suburbs. In general, the poorer the area, the more crowded the living conditions, the bigger the gap between death-by-lung and death-by-everything-else.[36]

Even in the best-heeled neighborhoods, however, the council found that water could be dangerously polluted. This was especially true in places where water came from both potable and non-potable sources and where the faucets were not well marked and therefore easily confused. Even in the relatively swank 8th arrondissement, in the majority of schools, students were told never to drink the school water during the day, and the *robinets* (taps) were shut tight. Children who ate their lunch at school, as well as those in nursery school, were given only water that had been boiled beforehand. Dr. Léon Colin, president of the Permanent Committee on Epidemics, went further. He advised the council that it would be prudent "*for the entire population of Paris* to drink only water that had first been boiled" (my emphasis).[37]

It comes as no surprise that aggregate numbers on water consumption conceal a significant amount of inequality in the Paris water economy. As running water arrived slowly in individual flats, faucets first appeared in the kitchen, above the sink. In the middle- and upper-class homes, the plumbing increasingly brought it to other parts of the house: boudoirs, bathrooms, and most crucially W.C., where "a strong flush of water prevents any fetid emanations."[38] Moreover, until the completion of a comprehensive infrastructure of pipes and pumps, well into the twentieth century, not everyone received the same water. The supply consisted, in varying proportions, of water from faraway springs, from the Seine and the Ourcq, and from local wells of uneven quality. A part of the population, for example, got its water from the Montsouris reservoir, which was served by water from the Vanne, itself subject to runoff from "farm wells," and which carried typhoid fever into the city.[39] The city's central and more middle-class districts were hooked up to the water system well before its outlying working-class neighborhoods, whose population still had to fetch their rations from nearby wells and public fountains.

By 1891, almost 96 percent of "bourgeois" neighborhoods in the capital had access to piped water, as against 71 percent in the *quartiers populaires*; although, as in Rouen, among the better-off classes, not everyone elected to pay the subscription for running water, if they could have their servants go retrieve it for free. And even where buildings were connected to that system, water usually did not reach the upper floors, inhabited by the poorest tenants.[40] The census of *habitations* launched in 1894 by hygienist Paul Juillerat and sociologist Jacques Bertillon, which took eleven years to complete, uncovered precisely these discrepancies. In 1897, for example, all the buildings on the rue de Penthièvre, in the bourgeois 8th arrondissement, were hooked up. All the buildings on the rue Rochechouart, in the middle-class part of the 9th arrondissement, reached that milestone by 1912. This was a long way from the state of things in 1876, when drinking water on the street had depended entirely on (often polluted) wells—as it still did in 1895 on the rue de Rigoles, in the working-class commune of Belleville.

By 1914, notes Colin Jones in his "biography" of Paris, 90 percent of Parisian buildings were receiving piped water, although that figure was considerably lower in the suburbs. This massive infrastructure project had been financed through a combination of usage charges on landlords, taxation, and direct public spending.[41] This did not quite put the matter of adulteration to rest. As Paul Brouardel told the Congress of International Hygiene and Demography in 1900, the purest water still remained under the threat of pollution at some point along its journey, frequently through the "excretions of people and the animals around them." At the end of the nineteenth century, cities still contained huge numbers of beasts for various purposes. In 1885, the 13th arrondissement alone remained home to some 500 head of cattle.[42]

Brouardel might have cited the complaints of the hygiene council in Mantes (Seine-et-Oise), down river from Paris, that its own water supply was being poisoned, as the capital pumped its sewage into the Seine; or the council in Cognac, its water infected by abattoirs and sewers feeding into the Charente. Félix Launay, Paris's chief engineer in charge of drainage, agreed with Brouardel that "the protection of potable water from all contamination is one of the main tasks of hygiene and one of the first duties of the public authorities." Sadly, he added, the state of French law made it hard for communities to shield themselves from others who would contaminate their rivers and reservoirs.[43]

The military played an important role in the development of urban water systems. There was hardly a town of more than 10,000 inhabitants without a *caserne* (barracks) and, as we have seen, the army had a compelling interest in keeping its recruits clean and typhoid-free. Wherever the army had a presence, therefore, military doctors "exercised a close oversight and the sanitary condition of the garrison" and pushed local authorities to increase the supply of clean water.[44]

In the countryside, the battle for water generally progressed more slowly than in the towns. Historian Jacques Léonard takes the optimistic view, writing that in the second half of the century a steady increase in the supply of water improved the existence of both men and beasts. In the Dombes, according to Henri Napias, beginning in 1854, the meres were drained and thirty-two new public wells were dug, "deep enough to procure an abundance of pure water." The proof of better hygiene lay in the fact that "mortality [in the region] declined by half, and the number of military exemptions for physical disabilities dropped from 52 to 9 percent."[45]

Of course, most villages did not get piped running water for a long time. It was simply too expensive to extend the infrastructure network, often over considerable distances, to such a dispersed population. The authorities complained, moreover, that country people did not want it because they hated to spend money on collective goods: "To save a hundred francs," observed *La Technologie Sanitaire* (1901) with more than a little condescension, "a peasant would sell his soul to the devil and poison his whole commune."[46] Where public works depended on local enthusiasm, therefore, not much happened.

Occasionally, in some places an old system worked well. A note from the hygiene council in the Var from June 1908, for instance, reported that the commune of Saint-Moutier had but one fountain with potable water for its 250 citizens, fed by a local *source* (spring). Yet it noted that "there has never been a single complaint about the water" and that a chemical analysis carried out in nearby Toulon deemed it "of excellent quality."[47] Even so, the difference between the purity and volume of water and the labor involved in fetching it remained, and the water that flowed into the village fountain from the mountains or some local spring still preserved the *corvée féminine*—of women having to haul the water from fountain to home. Moreover, where people still got their water from wells, the old problems of leaky walls and pollution often remained. And even where systems of adduction existed, the pipes remained "unprotectable, without excessive expenditures."[48]

In places where modern water systems had not yet arrived, people nevertheless coped and invented. Edouard Bled, for example, lived with his family in the far Paris suburb of Saint-Maur, in the early years of the new century. There was no municipal water supply, but Bled, who was an engineer, managed to jerry-rig a system with a motor that would pump water out of the nearby well and distribute it through the house. The setup included a stove with a *bain-marie* that kept 12 liters of hot water ready at all times, along with bathrooms on both floors.[49] Obviously, not many families had the imagination or the means to imitate the Bleds and solve the water problem on their own.

However patchy the modernization of the French water system between 1875 and 1914, it nonetheless represented an unprecedented improvement in the lives of millions of citizens and a substantial, if qualified, success for the young Republic. This great historic endeavor made water a weapon in two separate but overlapping crusades. In the first, water was the foundational element of hygiene, the practice of which required the self-discipline and refined sensibilities that were at the core of Republican virtue. In the second, it became, even before the triumph of germ theory, the focus of efforts to fight epidemic disease and promote public health. Clean water was the enemy, not just of dirt, but of mortality. In effect, national defense, social order, and economic prosperity all rested on the ample supply of water safe for drinking and washing.[50]

There was, as we have seen, nothing new in the need for copious amounts of clean water, but previous efforts to provide these had always come up against the limits of know-how and finance. Now, as the nineteenth century approached its end, a new ecology of water was made feasible by technical innovations in metallurgy and by the mass production of pipes, joints, faucets, *comptoirs*, and the refinement of the steam engines that ran the pumps. The construction of water systems was planned and directed from the top down. This did not simply reflect that fact that the scale of the undertaking required state participation, although it undoubtedly did. Huge amounts of capital were needed to finance the miles of digging, the laying of water lines, and the construction of purification facilities. Legislation had to be passed to coordinate these efforts and to coerce the recalcitrant. While experts had to be recruited to instruct and guide the politicians and to organize the means of enforcing the rules.

Professional reformers and state agents took the lead, while the great majority of citizens remained detached from the effort—at least on the demand side. Local governments, pushed by crusading hygienists, joined reforming prefects and, responding to a population now more likely to vote than to raise barricades, began to lay water pipes and build purification facilities. Starting in the mid-1880s, localities with more than 5,000 people were required to have their plans evaluated by the national Comité consultative d'hygiène. The assignment got off to a slow start, and in 1891, the number of dossiers submitted was "none or virtually insignificant." Fifteen years later, however, the committee had looked at some 1,500 of them. In its 1906 report to the interior minister, the Guilhaud Commission presented a table of "projets d'adduction d'eau" that had been tendered to various *conseils d'hygiène* and *commissions sanitaires* that identified 345 such projects from the Ain to the Yonne. Almost all of them, it noted, received an *avis favorable* (the go-ahead) from local authorities.[51]

Compared to the Anglo-Saxon countries, writes historian Stéphane Frioux, whose book *Les batailles de l'hygiène* provides the most thorough examination of the process, French towns and cities often saw "feeble" levels of popular activity tied to "questions of hygiene." Political and commercial interests drove the project forward. According to Frioux, before 1914 most reforming city councils tended to be on the left and center-left. But their projects did not always succeed, and their constituents were not always enthusiastic for the reforms. It was said that there was neither left nor right in the politics of urban reform and, at the local level, these battles were more personal and technological than ideological and bounded by financial considerations. That is, municipalities practiced caution, given the costs of the undertaking and in view of the untested efficacy of many of the techniques involved. Projects took years—decades— to move from proposal to functioning system, and this was especially the case for purification, with its competing and largely unproven technologies. Plans first presented in the late 1880s or early 1890s commonly became operational only in the new century.[52]

The water revolution, as it played out in metropolitan France, was part of an international effort that spanned the developed world and involved both cooperation and competition. International conferences met in Switzerland, Scandinavia, and England—"English supremacy in matters of hygiene," writes Frioux, was internationally recognized—to explore the best ideas for bringing pure water to thirsty, grimy citizens.[53] In spite of popular inertia and in the face of daunting costs, dozens of towns and cities took out loans and issued bonds to fund these expensive projects, and they were able to do so because the progress of the Industrial Revolution had made France a richer country.

Between the will and the way, however, the water revolution encountered several roadblocks. First, the technical path forward was not always clear. Experts disagreed, to take just one example, about which system of purification was best and most economical; sand and chlorine were the principal contenders. In addition, when it came time to do business, politicians naturally disagreed about who should get the contracts to build these facilities. For their part, hygienists complained that, once the decision to build a water system was made, the job was handed off to the engineers, who worried more about the volume of water than its quality, while they were shoved to the side.[54]

Second, while almost everyone agreed on the benefits of ample, epidemic-free water, there was less agreement on who was going to pay for it—or, indeed, whether it should be paid for at all. In the view of the *Echo de Paris* (1898), "It is no more permissible to dicker [over the price of] clean water than over the price of fresh air or good bread."[55] Yet the "battle for water" in Rennes was handicapped both by the poverty of the city and the hesitations of the conservative elites who ran it.[56] In the Nivernais, reformers consistently bumped into the apathy of mayors, the reluctance of elites to vote "les centimes nécessaires," and the unwillingness of the locals in both town and country to pay for subscriptions. The urban bourgeoisie, writes Thuillier, were the first to sign on to these projects, "but the masses remained indifferent into the 1890s—through misery, ignorance, or indifference."[57] The water revolution was not driven from below.

The apportionment of costs was especially contested in the cities, where landlords and tenants found themselves on different sides of the issue. Municipal authorities in Paris tried to push landlords into joining their buildings to the city's water system. Landlords pushed back, afraid that the expense of providing water to their tenants would continue to rise, and they would never be able to raise rents sufficiently to cover those expenses. "We should not be too severe," argued one member of the Paris hygiene council,

> with those landlords who worry about connecting their buildings to the water lines. Few of them recoil at the costs of the hookup itself. What gives them pause is how much water will be used afterward. They need to have some sort of guarantee against the frightful cost of waste.[58]

This standoff was complicated by two things. First, Paris contained a number of "private" streets, whose owners were not subject to municipal authority until the twentieth century. Thus, whatever rules the city laid down would not apply there. Second, the fact that a building's inhabitants shared a common spigot meant there was no reliable way of getting everyone to pay for what they actually used. Buildings necessarily had water meters, but they measured only the volume of water coming into the building, which had to be paid for either directly by the landlord or collectively by the residents, and not by household consumption. The predictable result, as landlords explained, was an economy of waste and overuse—the classical tragedy of the commons.[59]

The obvious solution was to install individual meters for individual users. How would that work, however, when only a minority of inhabitants had water delivered directly to their flats, or even to their floors, and when the majority of tenants took their water out of collective faucets? The matter came up in the 1900 meeting of the Société de Médecine Publique, which included some of the most eminent hygienists in the country. Professor Pierre-Inès de Prompt, of the Paris medical faculty, suggested to his colleagues that it would make sense to have a water meter for every consumer, as was done for gas. Georges Bechmann added that Paris was "one of the rare cities in Europe fed by spring water" that still measured water by building, instead of by dwelling. Émile Vallin disagreed, arguing the high cost of all those *comptoirs* made them impractical. Landlords did not want to be stuck with paying for and installing them, while residents had no incentive to pay for what they used.

In any case, the council was merely consultative, and no decisions were taken. Over the next decade, the Paris government moved steadily toward requiring water meters by apartment or by floor. But, of course, where the water source to a building served multiple households, and even businesses, which was widely the case, there remained no way to measure and regulate individual consumption.

The bottom line, according to Frioux: whereas in 1919 American cities typically gave inhabitants 400–500 liters of water a day, the average in French cities—Paris being the giant exception—was closer to 50 liters.[60]

Water Out

To get water into the cities and *into* people's homes was to solve only half the puzzle. Once it was drunk or used to cook or to clean or to wash out a *cabinet d'aisances* (latrine), where was all this water to go? There were effectively two possibilities. Household waste could be tossed out the window, where it ended up in the gutter, ideally to drain into an existing sewer system and be flushed under the streets and out of town, but often just sitting in stagnant puddles or turning the streets into "a permanent , putrid, scourge."[61] Alternatively, poured down evacuation pipes, it liquefied the excremental mess in the *fosses*; that is, the cesspits that every building was obliged to have. This made the *fosses* more disgusting, more difficult and dangerous to muck out, more likely to overflow and to leach into the ground water and nearby wells. Clearly, to continue to increase the volume of water coming into a city, without being able to get rid of it effectively, threatened both public health and the quality of urban life.

Dr. Jules Courmont, professor of hygiene at the Lyon medical faculty, estimated that the average individual produced 48.5 kilograms of fecal matter and 438 kilograms of urine a year. To contain this enormous volume of raw sewage, Paris at the end of the nineteenth century still had some 80,000 *fosses*—which meant approximately 1.6 million cubic meters of feces sitting in the city's basements.[62] Indeed, the real situation was uglier than this. At the start of the Third Republic, the capital, out of its 68,000 buildings, counted 7,690 with no dossier filed at the prefecture; that is, getting rid of their "refuse" in God-knows-what illicit fashion.[63] The same situation was repeated on a smaller scale in cities and towns throughout the country. It all constituted a sort of ecosystem of excrement, including residents, landlords, *vidangeurs* (those who emptied the *fosses*), and the peasants who eventually bought what the *vidangeurs* carted off to the countryside: "Everyone lived close to shit," observed the writer Annie Ermaux.[64] As a system, however, as we noted for an earlier period, this one worked imperfectly.

The cesspits, which were supposed to be sealed, often were not. Landlords balked at the costs of frequent *vidange*. Residents were careless about what they threw into their *fosses*. Moreover, as the century progressed, the small improvements resulting in better technology and the pressure brought to bear on landlords by public authorities were often overwhelmed by growing populations who used more water than ever.

Gruesome descriptions of the resulting mayhem are not hard to find. Dr. Octave du Mesnil has left us this image of the cité Jeanne d'Arc, a cheap housing project on the edge of the 13th arrondissement, built at the end of the 1870s. The filtering mechanisms for the cesspits are badly maintained and overflowing, he wrote, leaving the cellars covered in fecal matter. At the same time, "Without any drainage, residents habitually spill their wastewater into the courtyard, accompanied by garbage thrown from every floor."[65]

"In the big *fosses* attached to the boarding schools," wrote Aimé Riant, professor of Hygiene in the Paris faculty of medicine, "we find reservoirs of putrid matter almost always flowing back into the *cabinets*, the courtyards, and the neighboring apartments—a source of contamination for the soil, for the walls in contact with the ground, and for the whole neighborhood." Historian David Barnes confirms this picture in his study of the crisis of August 1880, when "a pestilential stink suddenly invaded Paris":

> Nearly every aspect of the existing system of human waste disposal was a source of concern for Parisians in 1880. Cesspits under the residential buildings, the drainage and transportation of their contents, the suburban treatment plants that turned wastewater into fertilizer and other chemical by-products, and the sewers of the city all operated defectively and hazardously.[66]

In an age that had not quite left behind miasmatic theories of disease, the stench was broadly taken as a leading indicator of epidemic.

As noted in Chapter 3, there exists an academic literature, anchored in cultural studies, that treats sewers and sewage as a literary trope and an aestheticized strategy of bourgeois domination.[67] On the ground, though, confronted by the rising tide of public filth, few citizens, and even fewer public authorities, would have denied the need for a dramatic *practical* response to the problem. The solution that modern cities like Paris found to their excrement challenge was what came to be called the *tout à l'égout*.

We have already examined the state of the French sewer system as reconstructed by Haussmann and Belgrand, but the *tout à l'égout* were something different. The old sewer system was built to accommodate street runoff, allowing for bits of rags and the odd horse carcass. But the decision had been made before, and was reaffirmed by Haussmann, that the rivers running under the city would not include *eaux vannes*—the "blackwater" made up of raw sewage. That responsibility continued to fall on the system of *fosses*. As that system increasingly failed to meet the demands of public hygiene, however, the *tout à l'égout* was offered as "le système plus simple et plus rationnel."[68]

All the "experts, engineers, and hygienists"—almost everyone, in fact—agreed on the need to get rid of the *fosses*. The fate of the modern city, wrote Dr. Albert Calmette, a pioneer of social medicine at the Institute Pasteur, depended on it.[69] The question was how to do it in an expeditious and affordable manner, and the matter had a more or less permanent place on the agendas of the municipal council and the high commission for sanitation throughout the 1880s. The Paris director of public works, commenting on a series of reports to the prefecture, suggested that the solution lay in allowing *eaux vannes* into the existing sewer system, whence they could be flushed into the Seine. The city's chief engineer, Alfred Augustin Durand-Claye, demurred, warning that, in order to accommodate all that solid waste, the sewers would need sufficient pitch and water flow, which they did not have. This put him in agreement with hygienist, Louis Havard, who argued that pouring sewage into the existing sewers, "defective and with insufficient water flow," would have more "pernicious" effects than keeping the cesspits. Léonce Levraud, president of the municipal council, simply called the idea, "a monstrosity."[70]

As opinion coalesced around the need to build a system of *tout à l'égout*—that is, devoted to the material that otherwise would pour into the *fosses*—perhaps tracking but physically separate from the old sewer system, public authorities confronted two further questions: What to do with all that sewage? And how to pay for what promised to be a very expensive undertaking? Doctor Joseph Gabalda considered the difficulties: you needed to get the *eaux vannes* from people's apartments and the *cabinets d'aisances* (toilets) into the *tout à l'égout*, which required buildings that did not already have them to install evacuation pipes. Then you needed a way to flush them out of town, then a place to flush them to. It would not do to pour all that sewage into the nearest river, thereby polluting much of the water supply. That was initially true in Paris, where the law of April 4, 1889, provided funds for construction that would send the effluence of the city's sewers up the Seine beyond Saint-Germain, propelled by pumps in Clichy. Not surprisingly, this solution provoked a complaint, like the one, cited above, from the hygiene council in Mantes that its own water was being poisoned "by the sewers of Paris and its suburbs in proportion to the increasing practice of *tout à l'égout*."[71]

But even if a city managed to carry all that sewage to a place where it could be treated—sewage farms, in effect—that required both a reliable method of treatment and the facilities to accomplish the task. In the meantime, Gabalda asked, how was all the decomposing sewage to be prevented from seeping into the ground water, and how were the neighbors to be protected against the foul smell? Gabalda liked the idea of giant incinerators that would both destroy the sewage and provide a source of heat to power industry. This idea never caught on, and the search for the most effective and cost-effective method of sewage treatment continued with the expansion of *tout à l'égout* across the country.[72]

The departmental hygiene council in the city of Troyes, in the Champagne region department of the Aube, for example, had provided 3,000 francs in 1903 to study the issue of municipal sewage and to come up with recommendations to resolve it.[73] It presented its findings at the end of October 1909, endorsing a system much like the one that was being constructed in Paris. In effect, it said, Troyes faced two sewage problems. The first pertained to the runoff of street water, the second to the removal of *eaux vannes*; that is, the excreta-filled sewage discharged by thousands of *cabinets d'aisances*. The council had considered putting both flows through one set of sewers, as was being done in other places. The thinking was that the volume of rainwater was so much greater, it would mostly nullify the effect of the "blackwater." However, as the hygienists on the council pointed out, when washed into the river, it would still pollute the water supply. They preferred a system where the pipes for the *tout à l'égouts* followed the sewer tunnels, but the two streams were kept separate—the first sent off to be purified, while the second spilled directly into the river—carrying the occasional dead cat, but not a constant load of excrement.

In effect, the council and the Troyes authorities found themselves having to make a very expensive bet. As to the "best system," there was no consensus on the matter among hygienic engineers. Moreover, the council was told that, "these installations being very new in France," it would be best to learn from the broader German experience, which suggested that the dual system of sewer-*tout-à-l'égout* was the most effective, but it was also the most expensive. This was the dilemma that faced all efforts to effect this revolution in public health. The documents do not say precisely what decisions were made in Troyes or how much money was allocated to the project—except to suggest that the "sewer question" continued to be debated into the interwar period.[74]

Wherever public authorities launched a campaign of public works, they ran into resistance from those who would have to pay for it. The director of public works in Paris told the municipal council that the 300 kilometers of new sewer lines would cost around thirty-five million francs. In fact, the law of July 10, 1894, which made the connection to the *tout à l'égout* obligatory, authorized the city to borrow 117,500,000 francs, at 4 percent interest, to help finance these improvements. Even if payment was deferred, however, the cost would still fall eventually on landlords, tenants, and taxpayers.[75]

The first *chutes* [evacuation pipes], of which some 206,000 were already connected into the *fosses*, began spilling *eaux vannes* into the sewers in 1886. Despite the state's attempt to hurry reforms along, progress was slow, both in building the *tout à l'égout* and in linking them to the buildings. Landlords had to pay sixty francs per year for each connected downpipe. Given the average value of total rent per building, this was a sizeable fee. Even when the fee was reduced to thirty francs, this added up to double the cost of maintaining a septic tank.[76]

So, landlords dragged their feet as other incentives also pointed in the direction of resistance. At the April 1885 meeting of the Paris municipal council, convened to discuss "la suppression des *fosses d'aisances*," the council heard the landlords' side of the story. It is impossible, their representative told the council, "to get rid of the collective *lieux* on every floor of the workers' houses. Where," he asked, "would you find the space [in every apartment] to put it? How would you light it? How would you ventilate it?" Besides, he went on, what the councilors were suggesting would involve "an almost total demolition of the building" in many cases. And what is going to happen to rents, if all these expenses are imposed on landlords? Neither did he believe that a transition from *fosses* to *tout à l'égout* would inflect the incidence of disease. Quite the contrary, he averred: "the mortality of typhoid would only increase with the number of downpipes [*chutes à l'égout*]." The reality, however, was different. Statistics showed that the presence of sewers—with high rents as a proxy—added four years to Parisian life expectancies.[77]

The city tried to push the process forward with regulation. Thus, in 1887, Eugène Poubelle, the prefect of the Seine Department, issued an *arrêté*, laying out new specs for *cabinets d'aisances* and the pipes that would attach them to the *tout à l'égout*. In 1894, the city passed a law obliging all buildings on streets that had *tout à l'égout* to connect to them within three years. In 1902, it extended the obligation to buildings on ostensibly "private" streets. According to historian Roger-Henri Guerrand, whose left-wing politics might color his judgment on the matter, landlords continued their "passive resistance" against this new demand on their finances from a figure (Poubelle) whom they considered a "crypto-socialist."[78] It is perhaps worth noting, as Stéphane Frioux does, that, for their part, renters did not much insist on the zealous pursuit of recalcitrant landlords. After all, better amenities meant higher rents.

Nonetheless, municipal efforts may be counted a qualified success. To cite the numbers produced by the *censier Juillerat*—the census of Paris buildings carried out beginning in 1893 under the authority of Paul Juillerat, the director of the Paris sanitation authority—at the end of 1910, 48,450 buildings, about 60 percent of the total, were directly hooked up to the *tout à l'égout*. Predictably, landlords with tenants, who could pay higher rents to offset the expense of installing modern plumbing, moved first, while the unconnected houses were almost all in working-class neighborhoods. Progress was therefore not only slow, it was discriminatory, as the better-off classes hooked up to the sewers while the hoi polloi continued to pour their sewage into the *fosses* just as they continued to fetch their water from fountains or from collective taps in the courtyards. On the rue de Rigoles, in the *quartier populaire* of the 20th arrondissement, the 1910 census showed the majority of buildings served by the city water system. But the *tout à l'égout* did not arrive on the street until 1944. On the other hand, on the middle-class rue Rochechouart (9e), the 1897 census showed *all* the buildings with *fosses*. By 1914, most of these had been replaced by the *tout à l'égout*.[79]

Lavatories, Good and Bad

At the top end of the downpipes that poured wastewater into the sewers were the tens of thousands of *cabinets d'aisances* and sinks. The *cabinets*, in particular, endured not merely as a threat to public health, but as an offense to decency, comfort, and sensibility. We might imagine that, where repulsive odors were such a pervasive and unavoidable part of the environment, people might have gotten used to them. All the sources tell us that they did not, and disgusting privies remained the principal source of complaints to the Paris Hygiene Commission. "The majority of cases referred to the commission," it reported in 1892, "concern the *cabinets d'aisances*":

> They are too small or too dark or poorly ventilated, too far from people's homes, and badly constructed—either the seats or the *chutes* or the evacuation pipes. As a consequence, the filth accumulates. The liquid does not flow away—or, even worse, backs up. The walls are indecent, and the whole gives off mephitic gases that permeate the hallways and the apartments.[80]

Ten years later, the hygiene commission's survey of conditions across Paris turned up the same descriptions of shit-stained outhouses, with defective toilets and stuffed-up pipes, completely devoid of water for flushing them out.[81]

Complaints about and descriptions of the horrifying conditions in which hundreds of thousands of people dispatched their natural functions could be cited literally in the dozens. But a few will serve as examples of the rest. The tireless Octave du Mesnil once again left us this memorable picture of a typical outhouse outside a building off the avenue de Choisy, in the 13th arrondissement: "The causes of the dirtiness of the courtyard cesspool," he wrote,

> lay in the arrangement of the *cabinet d'aisances* currently in use. It consists of a shallow hole in the ground, surrounded by three wicker partitions. Above the hole are placed two planks, about a foot [20 centimeters by 25 centimeters] apart. When this improvised *fosse* is filled, which happens frequently, given its lack of depth, the whole thing is picked up and placed around a newly dug pit, until the whole area is saturated. Thanks to this mobile *cabinet*, moved around several times in the life of the building, the ground of the entire neighborhood is poisoned.[82]

These *cabinets* commonly had no toilet paper—for which people substituted rags, leaves, bits of straw, hay, old linen, and shreds of cotton, and, with the arrival of the popular press, newspaper.[83] The wooden seats, for those outhouses that actually had seats, were themselves vectors of filth and disorder. Perhaps most significantly, until the water revolution of the 1890s, which began in Paris but took decades to encompass all regions and all classes, the majority of *cabinets* lacked any means of flushing away the excrement deposited there; besides even if they had had more water, the sewers would not yet have been able to handle the runoff.[84] In the working-class quarter of Sainte-Anne, in Nantes, the water used to clean out the public latrines—the only such option in the neighborhood—flowed under the nearby buildings and directly into the Loire. Even when they were cleaned out (more or less) the runoff ended up in the gutter, where it flowed into the sewer or sat in the street, producing a poisonous mud.[85]

For the Universal Exposition of 1889, in addition to the main attraction, Eiffel's new tower, the city of Paris built an exhibition that compared two types of houses, the one insalubrious and the other neat and clean, "exaggerating the defects of the first and the benefits of the second." The dirty house had cheap walls that sweated dampness and plumbing that leaked. But the centerpiece of insalubrity was the *cabinet d'aisance*: "A low seat. The almost complete absence of water and a badly sealed evacuation pipe that soon rusted, stuffed with paper and garbage so that it backed up, and when it was being used, was completely open to the pestilential fumes coming up from the *fosse*." All the visitors must have been disgusted, but not a few would have been reminded of their own circumstances.[86]

René Michaud was born after the exposition had closed, but he described similar conditions in his old boyhood lodgings at 24, rue Charles Berthaud, not far from the ill-starred avenue de Choisy:

> There was one outhouse for the sixty inhabitants of number 24. Sewers were a luxury for the rich. For the rest of us, the little people, worse than the discomfort, it was the

intense stink that made us miserable. The reek of all the accumulated excrement followed around all the inhabitants of number 24, permeated their clothes, already stained and infused with the smell of work and sweat and unwashed bodies... and for good reason![87]

As Michaud's memoir suggests, the absence of plumbing combined with overcrowding to make the average working-class *cabinet* a repulsive disaster. According to the urbanist Yankel Fijalkow, using numbers collected by the 1891 census on housing conditions, directed by Jacques Bertillon, there were some 911,000 *logements* in Paris. Of these, 743,000 did not have *cabinets particuliers*; that is, reserved for a single family. The people who lived in those dwellings used collective toilets, located on stairwells, at the ends of the corridors, or even in the courtyards. The distribution of *particuliers* followed a predictable pattern of geography and class. They were concentrated in the bourgeois parts of the city: in the 7th, 8th, and 16th arrondissements. Conditions deteriorated nearer the periphery of the French capital—at the fringes of the 13th and 15th arrondissements, at the southern edge of town, and throughout virtually the whole of *quartiers populaires* of the northeast. Comparing amenities across the city, the Juilleret census found that, in the working-class neighborhood of Belleville, there were twice as many collective W.C. as private ones, and that even the so-called private *cabinets d'aisances* served an average of nine people on the rue de Rigoles (20e)—as against six on the middle-class rue Rochechouart (9e) and three on the relatively elite rue Penthièvre (16e). Even within neighborhoods, the quality of these *conforts* varied by street and by building, and within the buildings themselves some tenants enjoyed amenities that others did not. Bigger apartments on the lower floors were more likely to have their own toilets. The apartments got smaller and the *cabinets* increasingly *collectifs* as one climbed the stairs (Table 6.2).[88]

Moreover, if almost three-quarters of dwellings in France's most important city did not have their own bathrooms, the situation was worse elsewhere. A Labor Ministry study, cited in a 1918 book on the "scourge" of substandard housing, looked at the incidence of *cabinets particuliers*—a source of "health, dignity, and a well-ordered

Table 6.2 Apartments without Private Bathrooms by Floor, Paris 1871

Story	Number of Buildings	Percent w/o private W.C.
Ground floor	10,380	1.40
First floor	47,736	6.42
Second floor	68,607	9.23
Third floor	100,121	13.47
Fourth floor	138,949	18.69
Fifth floor	177,524	23.88
Sixth floor	180,135	24.23
Seventh floor and above	197,79	2.66
TOTAL	743,501	100.00

Source: From an 1891 census of Paris *logements*, cited in Yankel Fijalkow, *Mesurer l'hygiène urbaine: logements et îlots insalubres, Paris, 1850–1945* (Villeneuve d'Ascq: Presses Universitaire du Septentrion, 1994), 126.

household"—in other big cities and discovered a sobering reality: 83 percent of families in Rouen, 89 percent in Nantes, 92 percent in Saint-Étienne, and 95 percent in Lille were condemned to share *cabinets communs*.[89]

How many toilets should a building have? Should every apartment have its own? Opinion among the experts differed. The Paris Sanitation Commission took up the question in its February 1885 meeting. There was consensus on the commission that it would be best, in theory, if every apartment could have its own private bathroom. Some members argued, however, that there was not enough water yet to make this feasible, especially on the upper floors of a building. *Chambres de bonne*, the garrets where the bourgeoisie lodged their domestic servants, presented special problems, since they normally packed a lot of individuals—Dr. du Mesnil, a member of the commission, estimated that there were 300,000 of them spread through the city—into a lot of tiny rooms. One commissioner recalled the dangers to public health, during the last cholera epidemic, when "a single *cabinet d'aisance* had served up to twelve or fifteen *chambres de domestiques*." Another thought that one cabinet for every two rooms would be best. A third demurred, saying that it made no sense "to multiply to infinity the number of *chutes*."

At any rate, 1885 was too early in the hygiene revolution to make it feasible to reorganize the plumbing in the *chambres de bonne*; it remained too early even a generation later. When the Society for Popular Art and Hygiene—presumably in the business of social betterment—issued a report on the conditions of urban life in 1909 and called for modern bathrooms be installed for *chambres de bonne*, it thought that one *cabinet d'aisance* for every five or six rooms was an adequate number.[90]

Naturally, squalor accumulated in shared outhouses, in a classic illustration of the free-rider dilemma. In the working-class slums of Nantes, for example, the Union de la Paix Social found that, while families were supposed to take turns cleaning out the latrines, many were negligent. This in turn discouraged the more responsible families from doing their share of the work. Meanwhile, the filth piled up—the more so, the Union noted, because these *cabinets* were not connected to any sewer, and there was therefore no convenient way of carrying away all the fecal matter. This unfortunate social drama must have played itself out in thousands of cases across France. As one contributor to the international congress of hygiene and democracy (1901) concluded: "Every *cabinet* shared by several families is doomed to irresponsible abuse and to filth" and every individual to personal degradation. Or, as Monsieur Guichard told his colleagues on the hygiene commission, "Nobody wants to clean up his neighbor's garbage or to become, in effect, his maid."[91]

At the same time, there were successes to register. Thus, the Paris Hygiene Commission, in its 1900 survey of the city, noted that, while the majority of complaints to the commission in the 14th arrondissement still focused on the reeking, filthy latrines, "since the installation of the *tout à l'égout*, there has been a substantial diminution in their numbers." Elsbeth Kalff and Lucie Lemaître go a step further, suggesting that, as the atmosphere changed, so did sensibilities, with polite euphemisms replacing old habits of plain talk. "In removing the sight and smell of garbage and sewage," they write,

> the *tout à l'égout* simultaneously lowered the threshold of tolerance and moved the boundaries of propriety, to the point of altering the language. Thus, while in the

1860s people spoke frankly of "shitwater" [*eaux vannes*], by the end of the 1870s they were referring more politely to "dubious liquids."[92]

Modern plumbing, it appears, was as much a matter of culture as of infrastructure, bringing people not only more comfort but more delicacy. As such, it represented an important victory for the Republic and for its domestic civilizing mission.

Notes

1 Anne-Marie Sohn, *Chrysalides. Femmes dans la vie privée (XIXe-XXe siècles)*, vol. 1 (Paris: Publications de la Sorbonne, 1996), 133; J. Levainville, *Le Morvan, étude de géographie humaine* (Paris: A. Colin, 1919), 228.
2 Dr. Boell (de Baugé) [Officier d'Academie Chavalier du Mérite Agricole], *L'hygiène du paysan: traité populaire d'hygiène rurale* (Angers: Imprimerie Gaston Pare, 1896), 2.
3 Jules Courmont, *Précis d'hygiène* (Paris: Masson et Cie., 1914), 30.
4 Fabienne Chevallier, *Le Paris moderne: Histoire des politiques d'hygiène (1855–1898)* (Rennes: Presses Universitaires de Rennes, 2010), 11.
5 A. Féret, *Études sur l'hygiène scolaire et d'intérêt général, 1900* (Paris: A. Féret, 1900), 134.
6 David Wier, "Economic and Physical Well-Being in France, 1750–1900," in Richard H. Steckel and Roderick Floud (eds.), *Health and Welfare during Industrialization* (Chicago: University of Chicago Press, 1997), 174.
7 Emmanuel Le Roy Ladurie, "Introduction," in Jean-Pierre Goubert, *La conquête de l'eau: l'avènement de la santé dans l'âge industriel* (Robert Laffont, 1986), 7.
8 Dr. Louis Depouilly, "L'eau dans les logements ouvriers," *Revue d'Hygiène et de Police Sanitaire* 22 (November 28, 1900): 1085.
9 Département de la Seine. Ville de Paris. Commission des logements insalubres, *Rapport général sur les travaux de la commission pendant les années 1862, 1863, 1864 et 1865* (Paris: Charles de Mourgues Frères, 1866), 17.
10 Henri Napias and André-Justin Martin, *L'étude et les progrès de l'hygiène en France de 1878 à 1882* (Paris: G. Masson, 1883), 173.
11 M.-E. Cheysson, *Le confort du logement populaire [extrait du Bulletin de la Société française des Habitations à bon marché]* (Paris: Imprimerie Chaix, 1905), 3.
12 See, for example, Goubert, *La conquête de l'eau*, 7.
13 Julia Csergo, *Liberté, égalité, propreté. La morale de l'hygiéne au XIXe siècle* (Paris: Albin Michel, 1988), 279.
14 Eugen Weber, *France: Fin-de-Siècle* (Cambridge, MA: Harvard University Press), 256, note 26. The original citation is to Georges d'Avenel, *Le nivellement des jouissances* (Paris: E. Flammarion, 1913), 210.
15 Jacques Léonard, *Archives du corps. La santé au XIXe siècle* (Rennes: Ouest France, 1986), 148; Jean Fourastié and Françoise Fourastié, *Histoire du confort* (Paris: Presses Universitaires de France, 1973), 65.
16 Geneviève Cerisier-Millet, *Un siècle de bains et lavoirs: Châtellerault, 1830–1930* (Châtellerault: Cerisier-Millet, 2003), 68.
17 Monique Eleb and Anne Debarre, *L'invention de l'habitation moderne: Paris 1880–1914. Architecture de la vie privée, suite* (Paris: Éditions Hazan et Archives

d'Architecture Moderne, 1995), 216; G. Heurtaux-Varsavaux. Unions de la paix sociale, groupe de Nantes, *Enquête sur la condition des petits logements dans la ville de Nantes. Rapport présenté par M. Heurtaux-Varsavaux* . . . (Paris: Au Secrétaire de la Société d'économie sociale, 1888), 22–3; Alfred de Foville, *Enquête sur les conditions de l'habitation en France. Tome I: les maisons-types* (Paris: Ernest Leroux, 1984), 23.

18 François-Xavier Merrien, *La bataille des eaux: l'hygiène à Rennes au XIXe siècle* (Rennes: Presses Universitaires de Rennes, 1994), 122–4.

19 Jules Robin, *Questions de salubrité urbaine et spécialement de l'amenée d'eau pure dans les agglomérations* (Paris: Imprimerie Nationale, 1901), 18.

20 Jean-Claude Daumas, *La révolution matérielle. Une histoire de la consommation: France XIXe-XXIe siècle* (Paris: Flammarion, 2018), 119; also Guy Thuillier, *Pour une histoire quotidienne en Nivernais* (Paris: EHESS, 1977), 16 and 337, note 20.

21 Jean-Pierre Chaline, *Les bourgeois de Rouen: une élite urbaine au XIXe siècle* (Paris: Presses de la Fondation Nationale des Sciences Politiques, 1982), 194.

22 République Française. Ministère de l'Intérieur et des Cultes. Conseil supérieur d'hygiène publique de France, *Rapport général sur les travaux des conseils départementaux d'hygiène et des commissions sanitaires pendant l'année 1906, par M. le Dr. Guillaud, secrétaire du Conseil Supérieur d'Hygiène publique de France* (Melun: Imprimerie Administrative, 1910), 34.

23 Dr. S. Courgey, *Les bureau d'hygiène: des bureaux d'hygiène et des rapports des médicins practiciens avec les bureaux d'hygiènes* (Paris: A. Maloine, 1912), 25.

24 Dr. Gilbert Ballet [Professeur agrégé à la Faculté de Médecine], République Française. Ministère de l'Intérieur. Comité Consultatif d'Hygiène Publique de France, *Rapport général sur les travaux des conseils d'hygiène publique et de salubrité pendant l'année 1889* (Melun: Imprimerie Administrative, 1892), 6–10.

25 See the discussion of the so-called Nadaud Law, which took aim at the general filthiness of housing and public hygiene in Archives Nationales (hereafter cited as AN), F8 Police Sanitaire, carton 211: Rapports de la Commission des Logements Insalubres.

26 Jules Dorez , *Compte-rendu des travaux du Conseil d'Hygiène départemental et des commissions sanitaires. Année 1908—Tome XLIV* (Nancy: Imprimerie Berger-Levraut, 1909), 1er commission sanitaire, séance du 7 février 1908, 68–9.

27 AN, F8, Police Sanitaire, dossier II.3: "Projet de loi relative à l'assainissement des logements et habitations insalubres, 21 juin 1886," rapport par M. Denoyer. Also see Archives Départementales (hereafter cited as AD), Seine-et-Oise, 7M 2: Conseil départemental d'hygiène, 1868–1873, délibérations du Conseil central d'hygiène et de salubrité publique, du 26 mai 1869 au 30 avril 1873: séance du 26 mai 1873; and AD Var, 5M 18.

28 Ned Rival, *Histoire anécdotique du lavage et des soins corporels* (Paris: Jacques Grancher, 1986), 99–100; Jules Rochard, *Traité d'hygiène publique et privée* (Paris: Octave Doin), 1897, 246; Ville de Paris. Commission des Logements Insalubres, *Rapport général sur les travaux de la Commission pendant les années 1890–1891–1892* (Paris: Imprimerie de l'École Municipale Estienne, 1895), 27; Mary Lynn Stewart, *For Health and Beauty: Physical Culture for Frenchwomen, 1880s-1930s* (Baltimore: Johns Hopkins University Press, 2001), 66.

29 Napias and Martin, *L'étude et les progrès*, 163.

30 On the water supply to Paris, see M. Bret, "L'alimentation de Paris en eau," in France. Conseil Général des Ponts et Chaussées, *Annales des Ponts et Chaussées. Mémoires des*

documents relatifs à l'art des constructions et au service de l'ingénieur. Lois, arrêtés et autres actes concernant l'administration des ponts et chaussées. Personnel (Paris: Dunod, 1902), 251; Csergo, *Liberté, égalité, propreté*, 276; Daumas, *La révolution matérielle*, 119.

31 Émile Vallin, "L'hygiène à Londres," *Revue d'hygiène et de police sanitaire*, séance du 22 mars 1882, no. 4 (1882): 330–1.
32 Steven Johnson, *The Ghost Map: The Story of London's Most Terrifying Epidemic—and How it Changed Science, Cities, and the Modern World* (New York: Riverhead Books, 2006), 12.
33 Depouilly, "L'eau dans les logements ouvriers," 1091. Also see Georges Bechmann, *Salubrité urbaine, distribution d'eau, assainissement* (Paris: Baudry, 1888), especially chapter 6, "Époque actuelle," 66–76.
34 Richard Evans, *Death in Hamburg: Society and Politics in the Cholera Years* (New York: Penguin, 1987), 146–51.
35 On the water situation in Le Havre, see Paul Brouardel and Léon-Henri Thoinot, *Enquête sur les causes des épidémies de fièvre typhoïde au Havre et dans l'arrondissement du Havre en 1887–1888* (Melun: Imprimerie Administrative, 1889), *passim*.
36 Préfecture de Police. Conseil d'Hygiène Publique et de Salubrité du Département de la Seine, *Rapports sur les Travaux des Commissions d'Hygiène du Département de la Seine et des Communes de Saint-Cloud, Sèvres et Meudon en 1900. Rapport général du Conseil d'Hygiène de la Seine par le Docteur A. Le Roy Des Barres* (Paris: Imprimerie Nationale, 1902), *passim*.
37 Préfecture de Police de Paris, *Revue d'Hygiène et de Police Sanitaire*, no. 22 (1900): 1171.
38 Dr. Jules Rengade, *Les besoins de la vie et les éléments du bien-être: traité pratique de la vie matérielle et morale de l'homme* (Paris: Librairie Illustrée, 1887), 152.
39 Robin, *Questions de salubrité*, 7 and 17.
40 Daumas, *La révolution matérielle*, 119.
41 Colin Jones, *Paris: Biography of a City* (New York: Viking, 2004), 365; Elsbeth Kalff and Lucie Lemaître, *Le logement insalubre et l'hygiénisation de la vie quotidienne. Paris (1880–1990)* (Paris: L'Harmattan, 2008), 148–50; also see Lionel Kesztenbaum and Jean-Laurent Rosenthal, "Income versus Sanitation: Mortality Decline in Paris, 1880–1914," Working Paper No. 2014-26, Paris School of Economics, July 4, 2014, 8.
42 Roger-Henri Guerrand, *Les lieux: histoire des commodités* (Paris: La Découverte, 1985), 13.
43 Congrès International d'Hygiène et de Démographie, *Compte-rendu du Xe Congrès International d'Hygiène et de Démographie à Paris en 1900* (Paris: Masson et Cie., 1901), 213–15; also see Ballet, *Rapport général sur les travaux*, 13–15.
44 Stéphane Frioux, *Les batailles de l'hygiène: Villes et environnement de Pasteur aux Trentes Glorieuses* (Paris: Presses Universitaires de France, 2013), 183; also see Joseph Rouget and Charles Dopter, *Hygiène militaire* (Paris: Librairie J.-B. Ballière et Fils, 1907), 171–2 and Chevallier, *Le Paris moderne*, 77.
45 Napias and Martin, *L'étude et les progrès*, 242.
46 Quoted in Frioux, *Les batailles de l'hygiène*, 150–1.
47 AD Var, 5M 18, letter of June 13, 1908.
48 Georges Augustins and Rolande Bonnain, "Maisons, mode de vie, société," in Isaac Chiva and Joseph Goy (dirs.), *Les baronnies des Pyrénées: Anthropologie et histoire, permanences et changement*, tome I (Paris: Éditions de l'EHESS, 1981), 46; Tina Jolas, Marie-Claude Pigaud, Yvonne Verdier, and Françoise Zonabend, *Une campagne voisine: Minot, un village bourguignon* (Paris: Éditions des Sciences de l'Homme,

1990), 16; and Max Le Couppey de la Forest, *Alimentation en eau potable dans les campagnes* (Paris: Imprimerie et Librairie A. Munier, 1904), 7.
49   Edouard Bled, *J'avais un an en 1900* (Paris: France Loisirs, 1987), 133–4.
50   On the evolution of urban mortality rates in the nineteenth century, see Weir, "Economic Welfare and Physical Well-Being in France," 178.
51   Conseil supérieur d'hygiène publique, *Rapport général* (1910), 98–106; in Limoges, see John Merriman, *The Red City: Limoges and the French Nineteenth Century* (New York: Oxford University Press, 1985), 206.
52   Frioux, *Les batailles de l'hygiène*, 158, 209–14, 221–2.
53   Ibid., 73–4.
54   See, for example, "Compte rendu des séances du Conseil d'Hygiène Publique," Paris, March 30, 1900, 124.
55   Cited in Csergo, *Liberté, égalité, propreté*, 234.
56   Merrien, *Bataille des eaux*, 21–2.
57   Thuillier, *Pour une histoire du quotidienne*, 14–15.
58   The discussion appears in the *Revue d'Hygiène et de Police Sanitaire* no. 22 (1900): 1090–3.
59   Cheysson, *Confort du logement populaire*, 6.
60   Frioux, *Les batailles de l'hygiène*, 226.
61   See, for example, the complaints of landlords in Paris's 13th arrondissement to the Commission des logements insalubres in Préfecture de Police, *Rapports sur les travaux des commissions d'hygiène* (1902), 120; also see Pierre Pierrard, *La vie ouvrière à Lille sous le Second Empire* (Paris: Bloud et Gay, 1965), 52. Local authorities received continuous complaints from the inhabitants and shopkeepers of small towns in the Var about sewage-filled streams flowing down the street past their homes and businesses: AD Var, 5M 38 (logements insalubres).
62   Courmont, *Précis d'hygiène*, 323. Also see Archives de Paris (hereafter cited as AP), DM5 0001, Préfecture du Département de la Seine. Conseil Municipal de Paris. Discussion sur le projet relative à la réforme de vidange, extraits du compte rendu des séances du Conseil Municipal, 7 avril 1885. The same discussion is available in AN, VI[5] Article I: Police et Hygiène, dépenses communales.
63   Jacques Lucan, *Eau et gaz à tous les étages. Paris: 100 ans de logement* (Paris: Édition de Pavillon de l'Arsenal, 1992), 21–2.
64   Annie Ermaux, *Les années* (Paris: Gallimard, 2008), 39.
65   Octave du Mesnil, *L'hygiène à Paris: L'habitation du pauvre* (Paris: Librairie J.-B. Baillière et fils, 1890), 103 and 107.
66   David S. Barnes, *The Great Stink of Paris and the Nineteenth-Century Struggle against Filth and Germs* (Baltimore: Johns Hopkins University Press, 2006), 23–4; Kalff and Lemaître, *Logement insalubre*, 106. Also see Aimé Riant, *L'hygiène et l'éducation dans les internats* (Paris: Librairie Hachette, 1877), 148 and Rochard, *Traité d'hygiène*, 416–18.
67   Donald Reid, *Paris Sewers and Sewermen: Realities and Representation* (Cambridge, MA: Harvard University Press, 1991), 3–5. Also see Mary Douglas, *Collected Works: Purity and Danger. An Analysis of Concepts of Pollution and Taboo* (New York: Routledge, 1996), 2; William A. Cohen, "Introduction: Locating Filth," in Cohen and Ryan Johnson (eds.), *Dirt, Disgust, and Modern Life* (Minneapolis and London: University of Minnesota Press, 2005), xx; and Dominique Laporte, *History of Shit* (Cambridge, MA: MIT Press, 1993), 13. For a particularly egregious example of this

approach to public hygiene, see Constance Classen, David Howes, and Anthony Synnott, *Aroma: The Cultural History of Smell* (London and New York: Routledge, 1994), 4. They give us this bit of meaningless tripe:

> The suggestion is rather that smell has been marginalized because it is felt to threaten the abstract and impersonal regime of modernity by virtue of its radical interiority, its boundary-transgressing propensities and its emotional potency. Contemporary society demands that we distance ourselves from the emotions, that social structures and divisions be seen to be objective or rational and not emotional, and that personal boundaries be respected. Thus, while olfactory codes continue to be allowed to reinforce social hierarchies at a semi- or subconscious level, sight (as the most detached sense (by Western standards), provides *the* model for modern bureaucratic society.

68 The phrase is Rochard's, *Traité d'hygiène*, 425. Also see Georges Knaebel, *Assainir la ville hier et aujourd'hui* (Paris: Dunod-Bordas, 1982), 6.

69 Albert Calmette, "L'assainissement des villes et les procédés modernes d'épuration des eaux d'égout," *Revue Pratique d'Hygiène Municipale Urbaine et Rurale* 7 (1905): n.p.

70 See AN, F8 Police Sanitaire, carton 211: Rapports de la Commission des Logements Insalubres; AP VI[5] Art. 1: Police et Hygiène: Préfecture du Département de la Seine. Direction des Travaux de Paris. Comission Supérieure de l'Assainissement de Paris, séance du 15 janvier 1885; and AP DM5 0017: Préfecture du Département de la Seine. Conseil Municipal de Paris. Discussion sur le projet relatif à la réforme de vidange, extraits du compte-rendu des séances du Conseil Municipal, avril 7, 1885. Also, Louis Havard, *La maison salubre et la maison insalubre à l'Exposition Universelle de 1889. Étude sur l'exposition du Service de l'Assainissement* (Paris: Imprimerie de Charles Noblet et fils, 1890), 11.

71 Ballet, *Rapport général sur les travaux*, 15; AP, D1 S8: Affaires Générales et Collectives. Préfecture de la Seine. Service technique des eaux et de l'assainissement, *Assainissement de la Seine. Lois et decrets* (Paris: Imprimerie Chaix, 1911), 9–10.

72 Joseph Gabalda, *Les plans d'aménagement et d'extension des villes—de leur nécessité au point de vue de l'hygiène urbaine* (Lyon: A. Rey, 1913), 81–5.

73 This discussion can be found in AD Aube, 5M 40, Santé publique et hygiène: minutes of the meeting of the conseil d'hygiène départemental, janvier 10, 1906 and of the 1ère commission sanitaire de l'arrondissement de Troyes, octobre 27, 1909.

74 AD Aube, 5M 40: "Arcis-sur-Aube. Désinfection des immeubles inondés. Installations de cabinets d'aisances avec fosses étanchées," Lecture des Rapports, février 10, 1919.

75 AP, DM5 0017: Préfecture du Département de la Seine. Conseil Municipal de Paris, Discussion sur le projet relatif à la réforme de vidange, April 7, 1885.

76 Keszstenbaum and Rosenthal, "Income versus Sanitation," 14.

77 AP, VI[5] 1: Préfecture du département de la Seine. Conseil Municipal de Paris. Discussion sur le projet relative à la réforme de vidange, extraits du compte-rendu des séances du Conseil municipal, 7 avril 1885. On sewers and life expectancy, see Kesztenbaum and Rosenthal, "Income versus Sanitation," 17.

78 Roger-Henri Guerrand, "Aux origines du confort moderne," in Lucan, *Eaux et gaz à tous les étages*, 22–6.

79 Frioux, *Les batailles de l'hygiène*, 163–4 and Eleb and Debarre, *Invention de l'habitation moderne*, 415. On the 1902 law, see AP, DM5: Santé publique et hygiène, XIII-1929 (1804–1929), carton 13, Préfecture de la Seine. Commission du Règlement Sanitaire. Rapport de M. Paul Strauss, Sénateur, re: projet de règlement sanitaire (selon la loi du 15 février 1902), manuscript, 14–15 and D1 S8 1: Affaires Générales et Collectives,

"Bulletin Officiel du Minstère de l'Intérieur," publication mensuelle, août 1912: Lois et decrets, juillet 29, 1912, 380–1. On the number of buildings directly connected to the *tout à l'égout*, see Kesztenbaum and Rosenthal, "Income versus Sanitation," 14–15 and Lucan, *Eau et gaz à tous les étages*, 5. On the rue de Rigoles, see Kalff and Lemaître, *Logement insalubre*, 151.

80 Commission des logements insalubres, *Rapport général* (1895), 15; also see the report ". . . concernant la ventilation des fosses et l'assainissement des cabinets d'aisances," in Département de la Seine. Ville de Paris. Commission des logements insalubres. *Rapport général sur les travaux de la commission pendant les années 1862, 1863, 1864 et 1865* (Paris: Typographie de Chales de Mourgues frères, 1866), 52–7.

81 Conseil d'Hygiène Publique, *Rapports sur les travaux des commissions d'hygiène* (1902), 52, 71–2, and 137–8, to mention only a few instances.

82 Du Mesnil, *L'hygiene à Paris*, 31–2.

83 Léonard, *Archives du corps*, 118.

84 AP, VI⁵: Art. 1: Police et Hygiène, dépenses communales, Préfecture du Département de la Seine, Direction des Travaux de Paris. Commission Supérieure de l'Assainssement, séance du 15 janvier 1885, *Procès-verbal*, report of the 2e sous-commission: Rapport sur les dispositions intérieures des cabinets d'aisances et de l'évacuation, 3; and Annexe No.2: Projet de règlementation et projet de loi relative à l'assainissement de Paris, discussion sur le Projet relative à la réforme de la vidange. Extraits du Compte-rendu des séances du Conseil municipal, séance du 10 avril, 48.

85 M. Heurtaux-Varavaux [Unions de la Paix Sociale—Groupe de Nantes], *Enquête sur la condition des petits logements dans la ville de Nantes* (Paris: Au Secrétariat de la Société d'Économie Sociale, 1888), 8. Also see Dorez, *Compte-rendu des travaux*, 2e commission sanitaire, séance du 25 janvier 1908, 31.

86 Havard, *Maison salubre*, 3 and 15. Also see Préfecture de Police, Paris. Conseil d'Hygiène Publique et de Salubrité du Département de la Seine, *Rapports sur les Travaux des Commissions d'Hygiène du Département de la Seine et des Communes de Saint-Cloud, Sèvres et Meudon en 1900. Rapport general au Conseil d'Hygiène de la Seine par le Docteur A. Le Roy Des Barres* (Paris: Imprimerie Nouvelle, 1902): 13th arrondissement, 120.

87 René Michaud, *J'avais vingt ans. Un jeune ouvrier au début du siècle* (Paris: Éditions Syndicalistes, 1967), 23.

88 Yankel Fijalkow, *Mesurer l'hygiène urbaine: logements et îlots insalubres, Paris, 1850–1945* (Villeneuve d'Ascq: Presses Universitaires du Septentrion, 1994), 109–27. By way of comparison, plumbing in the most bourgeois parts of Paris in the mid-1890s was substantially worse than in the richest parts of Hamburg, where 50 percent of households had indoor bathrooms: see Evans, *Death in Hamburg*, 171.

89 Fénélon Gibon, *Le fléau du taudis. Le premier remède: les habitations ouvrières* (Paris: Fénélon Gibon, 1918), 11. Gibon was the secretary of La Société Générale d'Éducation et de l'Association pour le Repos et la Sanctification du Dimanche.

90 AP, VI⁵, Art. 1: Police et Hygiène, Préfecture de Police, Commission supérieure de l'Assainissement, procès-verbal du séance du 26 février 1885, 22–7. On the matter of *chambres de bonne*, also see (Drs.) Henry Thierry and Lucien Graux, *L'habitation urbaine. Chambres de domestiques, cuisines et loges de concierges. Rapport adopté par la Société d'Art Populaire et d'Hygiène* (Paris: Imprimerie de Saint-Denis, 1909), 22.

91 Heurtaux-Varavaux, *Enquête sur la condition des petits logements*, 507; also Congrès International d'Hygiène et de Démographie, *Compte-rendu du Xe Congrès international d'hygiène et de démographie, à Paris en 1900*, 282; and AP, VI⁵, Art. 1:

Police et Hygiène, Préfecture de Police, Commission supérieure de l'Assainissement, procès-verbal du séance du 26 février 1885, 30.
92 Kalff and Lemaître, *Le logement insalubre*, 12 and Préfecture de Police, Paris, *Rapports sur les travaux des commissions d'hygiène* (1902): 14th arrondissement, 129.

7

The Lived Environment of the *Fin-de-Siècle*

The New Century

The *cabinets d'aisances*, along with water and sewer lines, were components of a more comprehensive structure of the lived environment, of which the keystone was housing. At the most fundamental level, individuals' ability to keep clean and to stay healthy depended on the surroundings where they slept, ate, washed, and, in general, lived out their lives.

The Third Republic hardly discovered this fact. Social reformers in the 1830s knew how much filthy, damp, overcrowded dwellings perverted morals and added to the grim reality of mortality figures. The Second Republic created the commissions des logements insalubres (housing commissions) for precisely this reason, and the empire tried its best to follow up on this initiative, without having much more success.

Something was different about the Third Republic, however. In part, it was the political context of social reform. The republic was a democracy, not only at the national level, but at the local level, where the war against *insalubrité* was largely fought. Politicians who met their constituents' needs were more likely to keep their jobs than those who did not. It did not require socialism to get public authorities to worry about the plumbing, only a normal set of democratic incentives and a bit of good faith. Equally, the Third Republic was the first French regime to inherit a world where growing wealth and technological advances made a significant improvement in the conditions of urban life feasible: pipes, pumps, sidewalks, sophisticated ways of purifying water and treating sewage, and the wealth to afford all this. There was not enough money to pay for *all* the reforms that were needed, of course. Per capita GDP was not in 1890 what it would be sixty or seventy years later; neither was the machinery of hygiene. But the Industrial Revolution had advanced far enough to make visions of material comfort for everyone better than a utopian dream. It made sense, therefore, for hygienists, politicians, and even slum-dwellers to believe that, finally, French society could provide domestic comfort for everyone.

The Housing Conundrum

There is reason to believe that French housing at the turn of the twentieth century was better than it had been in the days of the barricades. Then again, "better than an early industrial city" was a very low bar for housing stock, and most people still lived within four wretched walls. Haussmann's reconstruction of Paris had improved some things, but not housing for the masses, who were mostly pushed out of hovels in the center of the city to hovels on the periphery.[1] The commissions created by the law of 1850 continued to try to police the state of housing in the capital, pursuing thousands of cases a year—a total of 51,468 between 1870 and 1892.[2] They might have been able to nibble at the edges of housing reform, but they were in no position to effect large-scale transformation. The two-volume study of *logements* in France, carried out by the economist and statistician Alfred de Foville in 1885, detailed progress in many towns and small cities. He found, for example, workers in Elbeuf inhabiting homes with several rooms and having "un bon aspect," or proletarian housing in the Brie Champenoise providing "a degree of comfort and luxury," at least compared to the farmhouses in the region. In Lille, no one lived in caves anymore. Historian Anne-Marie Sohn's broad-based investigation into women's day-to-day lives revealed the multiplication of household furnishings, which themselves stood as evidence of "the desire to live better, basic to improving domestic hygiene."[3]

Better, however, was not good, and the miserable state of French homes remained among the chief concerns of politicians and hygienists (not to mention of the poor people who had to live in them)—a ticking time bomb of epidemic, social dysfunction, and moral turpitude. To stir up support for a new campaign against *logements insalubres* reformers adopted two tactics: they counted the devastation, and they described it.

The first *censier sanitaire* (housing census) was launched in Le Havre in 1879 by Jules Siegfried, who was mayor at the time, with the aim of expanding smallpox vaccinations and attempting "to determine the characteristics of epidemics by their distribution on the map."[4] The model was brought to Paris in 1892 by the prefect of the Seine, Eugène Poubelle, best known for his introduction of the eponymous garbage bins, who handed the job off to the bureau d'assainissement, directed by the well-known hygienist, Paul Juillerat. The object of the census was to provide a full and "objective" picture of housing conditions in Paris by measuring the number of buildings, their height, the density of their population, and the incidence of disease. Juillerat was particularly concerned to follow the path of tuberculosis, the leading killer of the age, through the apartments and garrets and *garnis* of the capital. He was assisted in this vast undertaking by the sociologist and statistician Jacques Bertillon. The battle against *logements insalubres* was, as noted, an old one, but these new efforts reflected the recent influence of germ theory and the understanding that tuberculosis was not inherited, it was caught.

There exists a substantial literature on the *censier sanitaire*, but it is worth noting here a couple of salient points.[5] The first is that Juillerat, who was a prodigious investigator, had not quite given up the miasmatic model of disease and wanted to prove, in effect, that tuberculosis was caused by the dwellings themselves—what he referred to as *maisons tuberculeuses*—a consequence of sordid, cramped conditions. In this, Juillerat disagreed with his collaborator Bertillon, who as a sociologist emphasized the impact of poverty and overcrowding and believed that "Fresh food and rest count for more than *salubrité*, whereas pure air has no power to neutralize the effects of deep deprivation." In the end, Juillerat came around to his partner's way of seeing things.[6]

The second is that, while Juillerat was dedicated to compiling statistics, he did not make much contribution to debates about policy.

His numbers, however, in many ways spoke for themselves, and they more or less confirmed what everyone knew; that the state of housing in France was deplorable. In Paris, a substantial proportion of the 884,335 households Juillerat and Bertillon counted were small, dirty, and overcrowded. Thirty percent lacked heating. Six percent had no window. Fifteen thousand dwellings had neither heat nor window. Dr. André-Alfred Dumont wrote that Paris in 1905 contained 25,000–30,000 households where five or six people shared one room—and sometimes with more than one species. Octave du Mesnil, with his sharp eye for squalor, noticed that on the rue du Chateau des Rentiers, deep in the 13th arrondissement, "animals and men lived together in the most complete and horrible intimacy."[7]

Of course, the state of *logements* varied dramatically across neighborhoods, and even from street to street, in predictable ways. The airier, newer, and more bourgeois *quartiers* in the west of the city generally provided better housing for their residents. Calculating living space per person, the *censier* concluded that each inhabitant of the 3rd arrondissement enjoyed on average 33 square meters, as against 27 square meters in the 19th, on the city's northeast edge. But even the posh *seizième* (16th arrondissement) had its share of substandard buildings. At the other end of the scale, Juillerat identified a number of *îlots insalubres* (slums), with high buildings and narrow streets, where people lived in the most unspeakable degradation: Saint-Merri (4th), Saint-Gervais (4th), Saint-Victor (5th), Plaisance (14th), Combat-Villette (19th), and Sainte-Marguerite (11th and 12th). These accounted for some 1,600 houses and 59,000 inhabitants, with double the average rate of mortality for the city.[8]

The *censier sanitaire* did not provide proof of the existence of *maisons tuberculeuses*, as Juillerat had suspected. It did, however, find substantial differences in the distribution of mortality linked to tuberculosis across the city. In general, mortality was lower in the center-west of the city than on the periphery or along the narrow streets of central Paris. For example, between 1894 and 1908, the per capita rate of deaths from tuberculosis was four times higher in the 20th arrondissement than in the 8th. The figures also showed a strong correlation between overcrowding and morbidity/mortality rates, as Bertillon had predicted. Du Mesnil estimated the impact of crowding on life expectancy beyond tuberculosis, writing that households with five to ten persons per room succumbed to infectious disease at a rate 50 percent higher than those with only one or two persons per room: forty-seven years for 1–2 persons, thirty-nine years for 2–5 persons, thirty-seven years for 5–10 persons, and thirty-two years for more than 10 persons.[9]

Bertillon counted 26 percent of *logements* in Paris as *surpeuplés*. According to Catholic social reformer Fénelon Gibon, 341,000 Parisians, over 14 percent of the population, had less than half a room of living space. In the cité Jeanne d'Arc, the slummy housing project along the city's southern edge, for example, families of four or five people lived in "one room, two meters by three . . . without heat or any amenities." Sociologist Jacques Valdour, a Catholic and a royalist, described a small furnished room in the grimy suburb of Menilmuche "where the childrens' and parents' beds were pressed together, and the family took its meals in corner of the congested space." The

Justice of the Peace in Suippes (Marne) heard testimony from a widow, who lived with her three children in "a rabbit hutch," 45 square feet of floor space and not quite 5 feet high—"a refuge of misery, the fruit of laziness and drunkenness."[10] The majority of working-class families inhabited apartments with one or two rooms, where "curtains, screens, and partitions" were used to break up the narrow, undifferentiated spaces, to separate parents from children and girls from boys. As historian Michelle Perrot remarks, "fragmentation was substituted for enlargement."[11] This meant, according to the Association for the Improvement of Workers' Housing, that only 18 percent of families had a room where someone did not sleep. This propinquity came with moral hazard, meaning that "boys and girls often slept out of necessity in the same room"—although, it added with relief, "rarely in the same bed." In fact, according to the economics ministry, looking back, while the proportion of "overcrowded" dwellings rose slightly throughout the nineteenth century, it began to fall—to around 7.5 percent—in the years preceding the First World War.[12]

Naturally, the crowding problem was worst for larger families in poorer neighborhoods. The association provided statistics for all the principal working-class arrondissements, noting average rent (by the proportion of income), square meters per person, average family income, minimum necessary income per person, distribution of apartments by the number of rooms, average rent per room, and the number of children under the age of fifteen for every 100 dwellings. It illustrated these numbers with personal stories:

- Of a tile cleaner, who lived with his wife and five children in one furnished room in the 10th arrondissement, "where a single window looks out on a sad little courtyard that serves as a dump for all the garbage in the building [and where] the breach in the outhouse, right next to the *logement*, emits mephitic gasses."
- Of a family in the 16th arrondissement expecting their eighth child who lived in two rooms of 35 square meters. In one room the parents slept in a big bed, with a two-year-old daughter in a crib, while four sons (ages fifteen, thirteen, eleven, and four) shared a second bed, head to toe. In the second room, two daughters (nine and seven) shared a bed.
- Of a family in the 20th arrondissement where "the father, who has had a stroke and the mother, who has TB, lived with their five children, ages thirteen to one year, in one of the filthiest buildings in the area, before they were thrown out for having too many children."
- Of another family in the 20th with nine children in a "house of the most repulsive dirtiness [where] rag merchants sell their wares amidst the most fetid odors."[13]
- and so on.

What was true for the capital was also true for provincial cities. In the Saint-Jean quarter of Toulon, the average was three beds per room; in Saint-Omer, 6–8 persons per room was normal. In 1886, the majority of dwellings in Nantes had one room, 30–35 square meters housing six or seven people. An inquiry in Lille around the turn of the century showed that three working-class families in four lived in one or two rooms. The 1905 study by Émile Cheysson found that for fifty cities (out of the 616 in the census), the average was eleven inhabitants for ten rooms. A number of those cities had considerably higher density rates. The proportion of households living in only one room reached 20 percent in Saint-Étienne, 22 percent in Puy, 42 percent in Brest, and 60 percent in Concarneau, in the Finistère, which must have had the worst housing in the country.

Frightening as these numbers are, French cities were hardly more teeming than other major cities on the continent: Berlin, Prague, Krakow, Saint-Petersburg, Vienna, and so on.[14] Indeed, there is another way to look at the problem: what the proliferation of contemporary studies of working-class housing seems to imply is that while living conditions remained awful for the mass of French families—and when had they *not* been?—society was beginning to expect something better.

As the numbers and the stories suggest, housing was a particular problem for *familles nombreuses*, as landlords resisted the sort of crowding and chaos that hordes of children brought with them. One consequence was to push the most desperate families into unsavory boarding houses, where police visits were frequent and the children hung out with the lowest sorts, and where they naturally become "Apaches"—that is, violent delinquents. Alternatively, in order to find a place to live, some large families took to hiding their members. The organization for the improvement of worker housing L'Amélioration du logement ouvrier—ALO), which had launched its own survey of housing for *familles nombreuses* in 1911, cited one instance where a family with five children declared only two of them to the landlord and sneaked in the others in sacks.[15]

More fundamentally, the survey found that many large working-class families simply could not afford the rent for more spacious apartments. In the middle classes, noted the ALO, rent consumed a fifth of family income. For working-class families, fixed costs, as for food, ate up a much larger portion of their income, leaving only a sixth of a meager salary—or even an eighth—to pay for housing. This situation got worse in the Belle Epoque, as migration to the cities pushed up rents at the bottom of the housing market by 20 percent between 1900 and 1914. The problem was sharpest in Paris but affected cities across the country. Roger Merlin, graduate of Sciences Po and archivist at the Musée Social, wrote that in 1910, rents rose in seventy-five departments and fell in only ten. Unsurprisingly, rent rises pinched more at the lower end of the scale than at the top. The landscape was painfully clear: there just was not enough decent and affordable housing for the working classes, who constituted well over half the urban population.[16]

Paris also housed a considerable populations of foreign immigrants, and these were, in general, even worse off, often living in *garnis* [furnished rooms]—"nests of bedbugs and all sorts of vermin"—whose impoverished inhabitants came and left with virtually no personal possessions. "The cabinet [where people live]," observed housing reformer Cyril-Berger, "is a narrow room often without any opening to the outside, where a bed and a chair suffice to fill up the space. It is often a miserable attic or a loft, where even to get in requires climbing a ladder and opening a hatch with your head." The police kept a close eye on the *garnis*, seeing them as dens of crime and prostitution. So did the housing commissions, in their higher-minded struggle against shabbiness and depravity. In spite of official suspicions and oversight, but reflecting tide of immigrants into the cities, the population of *garnis* kept growing—quintupling between 1850 and

▲ 15 rue Liancourt, quartier de Plaisance, circa 1910

Figure 7.1 *Garnis: 15, rue Liancourt* (~1910). Archives de Paris, 11 Fi 3660.

the early 1880s from 50,000 to 250,000 and expanding into the twentieth century (Figure 7.1 and Table 7.1).[17]

In sum, the sources do not lack for depictions of the ghastly surroundings in which millions of lives played out during the Belle Epoque. There were so many run-down buildings and seedy apartments to describe, after all. And from the reformers' perspective, these tableaux of degraded human existence served only to pique the conscience and

Table 7.1 Foreigners in *Garnis* (Boarding Houses) in Paris, 1876–1936

Year	Number of Foreigners in *garnis*, Paris	Proportion of Foreigners in *garnis*, Paris
1876	20,276	14.3
1881	36,313	17.9
1886	32,973	18.7
1891	27,432	16.8
1896	26,408	15.4
1936	42,867	21.6

Source: Alain Faure and Claire Lévy-Vroelant, *Une chambre en ville: hôtels meublés et garnis à Paris, 1860–1990* (Paris: Créaphis, 2007), 13.

spur it to action. To take one example, Dr. du Mesnil's description of conditions in the cité des Kroumirs delivered to the International Congress of Hygiène in 1878:

> The houses are set on either side of a narrow street, where the sun's light never shines. If it happens to be a private street, which is often the case in the poorest districts, with their many passages, alleys, courtyards, etc. The ground is uneven, pockmarked with holes, where rainwater and wastewater mix, and covered in mounds of decomposing garbage. Go into one of these houses, and you come upon some dark alleyway, with an open-air gutter where residents from all the floors toss their *eaux ménagères*. The stairway is gloomy, the walls are dirty. On every floor one breathes the most nauseating air and discovers *cabinets d'aisances* in a state as incompatible with decency as with sanitation. They are built with porous materials; the liquid waste spills over; the loo seat is an open hole; elsewhere, everyone throws their waste into ducts with no cover, which continuously emit mephitic odors into the stairwell.

As to the apartments themselves,

> [They are] often ventilated only by the poisonous air of the hallways, and they are dark; their walls are covered in tattered paper; the cracked and uneven floors are impossible to clean, and the insouciance of the human beings who inhabit these slums does the rest. If there is a window, it often opens directly above a small courtyard where the flow of air, rather than ventilating the apartments, merely carries infectious miasmas around and through the building. On the upper floors, the uninsulated roofs make apartments torrid in summer, glacial in winter, and soaked in humidity all year round. We should add to this the complete absence of water, essential to the most rudimentary hygiene of the inhabitants and the building.[18]

Conditions were similar in the neighboring slums of the cités Doré and Jeanne d'Arc—large complexes of small, crowded apartments built on narrow lanes "with the most absolute contempt for hygiene." Jules Rochard called them "barracks for civilians."[19] Built originally to house the poor in wholesome environments, they quickly deteriorated. Dr. Lafont, who had spent much of his career treating the poor inhabitants of the cité Doré, described "hovels as wretched as in the cité des Kroumirs, only more cramped. There is no water to rinse the gutters. Scrofula and lethargy run rampant among the children, who were also subject to passing epidemics of smallpox, measles, and diphtheria; typhoid fever is not rare." He added damningly that he "would rather live in a tent in the Kroumirs than live in one of the nicer flats of the Doré."

The Jeanne d'Arc was perhaps worse; one social worker wrote that its children were the most deprived in the capital. The buildings in the cité had been constructed by the railroad company for single men. By the early twentieth century, however, apartments were typically home to entire families, largely Bretons, with each 6-meter square room filled by four or five people and utterly without amenities, a den of disordered families, rape, and incest.[20]

Philanthropist and social reformer Georges Picot described eight buildings with 1,200 dwellings, dark stairways more dangerous than any public street in the middle of the night. "Their foulness defies description," he concluded. The poet Jean Richepin portrayed the Jeanne d'Arc as "gloom, sticky with dirt, and humidity, that form themselves into a sort of past [with] corridors that smell like cesspits. The scent of ammonia and sulfur hydroxide remind one of a garbage dump. Entire families crowded into one room with a single tiny window."[21]

That was 1883. Twenty-five years later René Martial, a member of the Paris medical faculty, still found working-class apartments that were

> dark, dirty and reeked of the outhouses located in the courtyard or on the staircase landing. . . . Where, on the rare occasion when the house is washed, the humidity remains and continues to poison it. It must be said besides that those who own and rent these houses are not themselves any cleaner than the walls that encase them. The tenants, even more pitiable than the landlords, are often Italians who care nothing for hygiene. They eat with their fingers—a piece of bread, a herring, a bit of cheese—chewing and spitting everywhere, or they smoke an old pipe and sleep on a pallet, without a thought, stupefied with fatigue.[22]

Things were no better in the working-class suburbs. In Saint-Denis, for example, where Jean-Paul Brunet recalled his childhood surroundings on the eve of the First World War: "In the dark lobby, open to the elements, one is seized by the throat by the stinking outhouses, stuck in the tiny courtyards or on every landing." "The reek of the accumulated excrement," he continued, "followed the inhabitants, infecting their clothes, which were already stained by sweat and hard labor and unwashed bodies." The odor seeped into the apartments, where it mixed with the scents of oily coal and urine. More than the discomfort, Brunet added, "It was the intense stink that oppressed us."[23] Similarly in Villejuif, whose *cités* compared unfavorably with "the most miserable Neapolitan *fondacos* [housing projects]."[24] It is sometimes suggested that the people get used to the disgusting smells. It appears, they do not.

Roger Merlin, librarian and archivist at the Musée Social, put the pieces together, describing, the shortage of housing units, leading to a hike in rent, overcrowding, dirtiness, alcoholism among fathers escaping the their miserable homes, abandoned children who gather in the streets, [elevated] infant mortality—in sum, the slums, the difficulties of big families finding a place to live, and, as a reaction, lower rates of childbirth, and the general discontent produced In working-class households that make them enemies of a society that is indifferent to their fate.[25]

Amid the general unpleasantness, inhabitants lived with an almost complete lack of amenities [*conforts*]. Examining the *scellés*, postmortem inventories of working-class lives, Anaïs Albert's survey of the 10th arrondissement at the turn of the century found only two *cabinets de toilette* in the sixty-one apartments mentioned. Nationally, a 1906 survey of worker housing in fifty cities by the labor ministry counted private and semiprivate W.C., along with rooms, windows, and fireplaces; although the survey limited itself to dwellings with between one and four *pièces*, which left out the most dismal and crowded. In a few towns—Fougère, in the Ille-et-Vilaine, and Bessèges, in the Gard, for instance—virtually all residences had (semi-) private toilets. Overall, though, it found that two *logements* out of three had no W.C., adding that "there are cities where practically every dwelling lacks one. Instead, W.C. were to be found in the courtyards, proportional to the number of families in the building." Moreover, 10 percent of rooms lacked a window and 25 percent a fireplace.[26]

The Bourgeois Household

It is no surprise to learn that many among the poor and working classes lived in ruin and discomfort.[27] More surprising is the fact that the French middle and upper classes often inhabited their own version of *insalubrité*. This fact conflicts with one of the familiar tropes of the history of hygiene, which portrays a "bourgeoisie" attached to cleanliness as a strategy of power; that is, as a means both of domesticating a volatile working class and of marking their superiority—a way, in the words of Julia Csergo, "to wash the bodies to cleanse the spirits [of] a dreaded proletariat, made up of depraved, dirty peasants who have un-learned obedience and respect." That is why, in her view, "The history of hygiene is above all a political history."

Architect Philippe Dard speculates on the politics, not of hygiene per se, but of smells. Like Csergo, however, he sees improved hygiene as the victory of "bourgeois morality" over the stronger and earthier scent of the lower classes and their environments— the aroma of "cemeteries, garbage, and human excrement"—that fixed the difference between "good" and "bad" smells and demanded the suppression of the latter. Adding a bit of Freudian spin to a Marxist pitch, the architect Monique Eleb asserts that the bourgeoisie was attached to order and cleanliness not merely as a strategy of power, but from "complex relations of morality, anchored in the idea of sin" and that hygiene was an artifact of repressed sexuality and a rejection of pleasure. There is no evidence behind any of these propositions.[28]

Historian Alain Corbin offers a more down-to-earth view of the political and symbolic elements concealed in *propreté*. Poor hygiene, he writes, became a kind of synecdoche for poverty, a living counterpoint to bourgeois cleanliness and virtue. In the same vein, sociologist Olivier Le Goff adds that "The bourgeoisie, *without indulging in a systematic caricature* enjoyed a certain comfort, made up of order and *propreté*, at least in appearance, from which they derived their sense of moral superiority" (my ironic emphasis).[29] From different angles, all agreed that cleanliness, far from making working-class lives better, served as a tool of social hegemony and political control.[30]

Hygiene for the masses may or may not have been a tool of oppression. My own view is that it was not. In either case, the evidence points to the fact that, while the upper and middle classes lived in more capacious accommodations, their commitment to modern standards of cleanliness has often been exaggerated. True, *conforts*—running water, electricity, gas, bathrooms, and elevators—arrived first at the most exclusive addresses and, soon after, in the homes of the solid middle classes. At the top of the pyramid, Paris elites lived in vast apartments on smart avenues, where rents could run to 5,000 francs a month, 25 percent of the most ample family budgets.[31] Still, it is easy to overstate the neatness and comfort of even bourgeois circumstances. "It must be said," wrote hygienists Henry Napias and André-Justin Martin in 1883, "that the cause of domestic hygiene progresses very slowly." The material elements of domestic *propreté*—bidets, sinks, bathtubs—remained expensive in an age before they were mass produced. It was not cost, however, but a certain cultural conservatism that explains the resistance to change among the privileged.[32]

Looking not at amenities but at décor, Charles Jeanselme saw a modern concern for hygiene in a growing "revulsion" toward the deployment of fabric in bourgeois apartments. "It is no longer a matter," he wrote, "of decorating a dwelling by crowding together rugs, wall hangings, and curtains and enveloping it from one end to the other with fabrics, which modern concerns about cleanliness and hygiene reject with good reason.... We would not," he concluded, "go so far as to say that fabrics have completely disappeared from interior decorating, but they occupy only a limited place."[33]

Insofar as plumbing remained the key element in the advancement of domestic hygiene, the nineteenth-century "bourgeoisie" were not very modern. Even in 1900, while every middle-class flat had a washroom, not all had a *salle de bain* and even fewer an actual bathtub. According to Georges Vigarello, when the composer Hector Berlioz died in 1869, he left an apartment with two washrooms but no bathtub. Estimates of the presence of bathtubs vary, since the census did not yet count such things, but they are all low—4 percent according to Mary Lynn Stewart; 3 percent, according to Peter Ward, citing the work of Csergo and Thuillier—and not all of these had the hot-water heaters that would have made bathing practical. Predictably, these amenities were rarer outside the capital. Most of the time, when the occasion demanded it—and it did not demand it very often—middle-class families rented a tub and had it carried, along with the hot water, up to their *cabinets de toilette*. As for the majority of bourgeois households, Thuillier describes them as typically rather dirty. This was true, wrote Napias and Martin, even in the newest, richest, and most spacious homes, where the *salubrité* was often more apparent than real.[34]

American historian Nicole Rudolph observes that it was not cleanliness so much as "order" that defined the bourgeois *ménage*.[35] It was therefore ironic that the small army of domestics necessary to maintain this order themselves introduced a very un-bourgeois element of disorder and dirt. Increasingly, these young women, who did most of the domestic labor and whose presence represented a sort of working-class intrusion, were exiled to the *chambres de bonnes*—"these sordid attics," where even the imperfect cleanliness of middle-class apartments disappeared.[36]

Mlle. Célestine R, the fictional author of Octave Mirabeau's novel, *Journal d'une femme de chambre*, described her own "sordid attic":

> a tiny room under the eaves, open to the four winds, too cold in the winter and hot in the summer. No other furniture than an iron bedstead and a mean armoire in white wood, which wouldn't close and where I wasn't able to put my things... [and] no other light than a candle that smokes and burns out in the copper candlestick. It was pitiful.[37]

The two urban reformers, doctors Thierry and Graux, added their expert critique of servants' housing, based on their investigations of servants housing:

> These tiny rooms with low ceilings almost never have chimneys and seldom have windows. Light and air come in through a transom or skylight, above a narrow courtyard, from which waft up the insipid and oily smell of dirty sinks, garbage bins, and outhouses. Coming upstairs late from their labors, exhausted, the servants are cold in the winter and hot in the summer.... If you visit these rooms in the daytime, you are seized at first by the sickening smell of close spaces filled with unwashed clothes, unmade beds, and basins of dirty water than haven't been emptied. The girls brush off their clothes and fill the air with dust.[38]

It is no wonder, they concluded in their 1909 survey of *habitation urbaine*, that the provincial girls who come to work in these garrets, "disoriented, overworked, and often malnourished," made easy prey for tuberculosis. More frightening still, these young women, "disdainful of all hygiene and repugnant in their aspect," brought the general sociopathy of their class down the back stairs and into the very homes of their employers.[39]

Those other working-class intruders, the concierges, brought a similar element of proletarian "disorder" into middle-class buildings. Dr. Jean Lahor, a proponent of housing reform, painted a grim picture of the typical concierge's flat:

> a narrow gallery, one room, no light, no window, a French window opening on an unlit passage at the end of a hall [where] the gas burned all day long. The cesspit [it was 1905], which was not connected to the *tout à l'égout*, opened on to the passage in front of the casement letting in whatever light and air are able to get in.

In Lyon, 80 percent of the 300 concierge *loges* inspected by the housing commission "were uninhabitable, due to the insufficient supply of air."[40]

The Illusion of Social Housing

The principal focus of reform, however, was not on the margins of middle-class housing but on the appalling deprivation in which the urban masses lived. A 1912 survey of Lyon, for example, found that a full 10 percent of its 20,000 buildings were *insalubres*—and 700 or 800 of those "were in such a state of degradation that they do not seems susceptible to renovation."[41] At this level of French society, the fundamental issue was not, as with the better-off classes, cultural conservatism but poverty. E. Fichaud, director of the École communale in Paris, told his students that it made no sense to economize on housing, because "in harming one's health, a dirty home will entail a higher cost than if one had spent the money to live in *conditions hygiéniques*." Maybe so, but more salubrious accommodations required money up front, and *that* was something most working-class families did not have.[42]

To judge by the proliferation of studies and conferences dedicated to the problem of *habitations ouvrières*, not to mention the continuing efforts of local hygiene commissions, the crusade against *logements insalubres* became one of the defining issues of the Belle Époque. As the architect, Monsieur Lacaud, told the Congress on International Hygiene and Demography in 1900: "The hygienist knows how grave and compelling are these questions [of public health], and he will not have done his duty if he does not share this conviction with the public.... It is only when everyone has heard this message that no serious obstacles remain to its perfect and effective application."[43] But serious obstacles did remain.

Naturally, the reforming spirit found its way into legislation. On the national level, the so-called Nadaud Law first appeared on the legislative agenda in the early 1880s. Nadaud, the young stone mason and revolutionary who became a member of the Chamber of Deputies, saw in his project the means to finish the work begun by the 1850 law on *logements insalubres* by imposing government controls on building construction and renovation and by expanding the work of local hygiene commissions. This "absolutely necessary" project went through several iterations but had not yet become law when Nadaud's parliamentary career came to an end in 1889, with a second-round defeat to his conservative opponent.[44]

Nadaud's forced retirement from politics, notwithstanding, reform was in the air, and more legislation followed. The law of November 1894 on *Habitations à Bon Marché* (HBM) provided for public funds to be used to furnish decent homes for the masses at affordable prices. Motivated by the notion that "to sanitize is to moralize," the Siegfried Law, as it was called, after its chief sponsor, Jules Siegfried, the industrialist and deputy, eased fiscal burdens on landlords; made it easier for the state to pour money into new housing; and set standards for the provision of water, space, and access to sewers. It quickly led to the formation in cities across the country of associations to lobby for the construction of HBM and spawned a postcard campaign to promote the achievements of the social housing movement.[45]

We can infer from similar legislation that followed that the Siegfried Law, however well intentioned, did not much change the trajectory of public housing. It was revised in 1902, with new rules, sponsored by the deputy Paul Strauss, that made it easier to condemn, and even to expropriate, old, substandard housing and to finance new construction. The 1902 law sponsored the creation of local boards of hygiene and made housing on *voies privées*—that is, private streets—subject to the same standards that applied to public thoroughfares. It added tighter but more generous requirements that, for example, prohibited people from living in cellars and regulated the height of ceilings, increased the minimum size of courtyards, and widened staircases. This did not finish the matter. The Loi Ribot (1908) and the Loi Bonnevay (1912) expanded the field of government action to support the building of *logements sociaux*. As Alexandre Ribot, the four-time prime minister, put it: "The time has come to pose the question of workers' housing. The situation is urgent, because in France we are so far behind. . . . The state of our housing is unworthy of a civilized nation."[46]

It is hard not to be impressed by the energy and optimism reflected in all the laws and studies and on-the-ground campaigns aimed at providing the working people of France a decent place to live. Yet, despite the spur from below and the determination from above, the gap between the demand for social housing and its supply did not narrow very much before 1914. Between the passage of the Siegfried Law in 1894 and the outbreak of war, only 50,000 HBM units were built—"feeble results, in fact no results at all," as the preface to the Loucheur Law of 1928 observed.[47]

There is little in the way of hard numbers, but the scattered and casual observations all tell the same story: some new building, but far short of what was needed. Alfred de Foville described the progress made in the city of Lille. Half a century earlier portions of the poor population were still living in caves, but that was no longer true. The tireless local housing commission had forced the closure or renovation of the filthiest and most verminous buildings. Foville wrote that the enterprising industrial city had begun to construct a number of model working-class habitations, whose residents were able to share such modern conveniences as clean water, kitchens, laundry rooms, and *cabinets d'aisances*, but he gave no indication of how many of these were erected.[48] In a similar fashion, the city of Lyon, led by progressive mayor Edouard Herriot, claimed to have built no fewer than 1,700 housing units and two "restaurants économiques" between 1886 and 1909, but this was not even close to being adequate. Besides, none of those apartments had a bathroom, apart from some larger homes intended for factory foremen and engineers.[49]

In Rouen, a philanthropic effort in the mid-1880s put up six buildings of four stories each, with three apartments of one and two bedrooms per floor, where the fortunate inhabitants enjoyed "unheard-of comfort: gas, flush toilets, garbage pickup, sewers, laundry, and an infirmary." The project received a gold medal at the 1889 Exposition Universelle. Still, it comprised a mere 100 units. In Mulhouse, as Will Clement writes, the Société mulhousienne des cités ouvrières erected more than 1,200 houses between 1853 and 1895, which were sold by annuities to the workers of the town of Mulhouse. Innovative architectural features and financing, along with the fact of workers' ownership, brought these efforts international notoriety. At the end of the day, however, local conditions in Mulhouse proved impossible to replicate. Anyway, 1,200 units was a long way from solving the housing crisis.[50] As for Paris, the city was building 100,000 dwellings a year before 1914—not all of them *logements sociaux*, while the prefecture had concluded that the city needed to build a minimum of 137,000 two-bedroom units per year. But even that was a significant underestimate of the demand for apartments at the lower end of the market.[51]

Various laws and local initiatives sought to close this gap. The Siegfried Law (1894) and those that followed facilitated the power of the authorities to seize private property in the public interest. They provided more money to compensate those who suffered eminent domain expropriations and permitted state subsidies for private construction. Here and there employers built *logements* for their employees. In Montceau-les-Mines, for example, the Creusot Company had been housing their employees since the 1830s, even giving workers interest-free loans to buy their homes, which could be paid back through future paychecks. A doctor Laroche visited the town in 1920. What he found was "a succession of small houses lined up down long, wide streets, usually surrounded by a garden," with every household having one or two bedrooms—spacious, airy, and well-lit—where "the worker and his family can breathe fresh air and live in a clean environment." Laroche noted, however, that construction was not always first rate and that "sufficient attention had not always been paid to the evacuation of waste." The company had dropped its paternalistic policies following strikes in 1899 and 1901. But the housing was still good enough that Montceau-les-Mines had one of the lowest mortality rates in the country. In any case, Creusot was a huge enterprise with enormous resources and a relatively stable work force. Few businesses were in a position to copy it.[52]

In 1888, Paris authorities made plans to build a new HBM in the dilapidated shadow of the Jeanne d'Arc project. Plans included thirty-five apartments "pour des familles supposées nombreuses" with two rooms each, with a W.C. and a small kitchen in no more than 29 square meters. According to architectural historian Marie-Jeanne Dumont, the building rapidly filled up with *petits bourgeois* and workers dedicating "between a seventh and an eight of their incomes [to rent]," which was normal for the time. Overall, though, the project was a failure. For one thing, the finances did not work. It earned about 4 percent return on investment in its first year, which declined thereafter, illustrating the principal reason the HBM never became an important factor in the normal housing market; they were never able to pay for themselves in the long run, "despite the most scrupulous management." And once again, the scale of the operation was insufficient. The housing shortage would not be solved thirty-five apartments at a time. But that was all the government could afford.[53]

Historian Pascal Mory sees politics as the proximate cause of the lack of social housing in Paris. "The loss of city hall by the left in 1909," he writes, "explains in part the *immobilisme* of the city when it came to new building."[54] This is simply wrong. The problem was not that the new Paris government lacked the social conscience of the old one. It was rather that HBM, even at a modest level of *conforts*, were expensive to build. Local governments did not have the funds and neither did charitable interests. Rules requiring new buildings to provide more amenities—like W.C. in each apartment, hookups to the sewer system, and even showers—only made them more expensive. An ordinance of August 1894 dictated that "all new construction should provide a *cabinet d'aisances* for every apartment or home, or for every three rooms let separately." But this was a pipedream. As René Martial, physician and hygienist, told the Paris public health council, discussing a report on the question of "Maisons à bon marché et salubrité," in 1914: there is *no such thing* as cheap, clean, housing. This was a fundamental error in all the recent housing legislation: "It is impossible," he continued, "to construct a house using passable materials . . . large enough for a family . . . according to accepted standards of comfort and hygiene for less than 7.000 francs." "It remains certain," Martial summed up, "that 'cheap' excludes hygienic."[55]

This was no mere casual observation. It pointed rather to the most basic fact in this whole story: hygiene costs money. The need to include amenities made HBM more expensive to build, just as refitting old buildings with new plumbing imposed new outlays on landlords. Naturally, builders and proprietors attempted to recover these costs, and this, in addition to the general shortage of housing, drove up rents. The supply of cheap housing dwindled alongside the supply of miserable housing. Perversely, then, the campaign to improve the housing stock did not so much improve the living conditions of the poor as drive them to the worse slums of the suburbs; and even there, rents rose steadily before the war. The net gain to hygiene was small.[56]

How Clean Were the Popular Classes?

There is always reason to treat middle-class descriptions of working-class deficiencies with skepticism. Nonetheless, just as landlords complained to the housing commissions that the decent apartments they rented were spoiled by the slovenly practices of the tenants, urban reformers often disparaged the ability of working-class families to profit from better housing. Even E. Hatton, president of a foundation dedicated to building HBM, felt the need to declare that "It is equally against indifference, against lack of any habit of cleanliness and hygiene [among the tenants], that we have to struggle." The architect Henry Provensal was of the same regrettable opinion. "Unfortunately," he observed, "the habits of *propreté* find no place in many workers' households.... No improvement in a worker's home will have any effect, if we cannot advance the coarse understanding of the simplest elements of hygiene and of the use of the sources of regeneration that are within his reach."[57]

Proponents of social housing disagreed among themselves about the best and most efficient way for the working classes to clean themselves up. The authorities, mostly middle class themselves, tended to favor baths, since that was what they had in their homes, insofar as they had anything. As a practical matter, baths were too expensive, and so architects, builders, and those who paid the bills, and exactly as the military had done, planned for showers instead—and often *collective* showers, on the ground floor and overseen by the concierge, since putting even showers in individual apartments would break the budget.

The sad truth in this observation was made plain in a letter of January 1914 from the Administration Générale de l'Assistance Publique, responding to a query from the prefect of the Seine, who asked how many *bains-douches* had so far been installed in the local HBMs: "[Not] a single building either built or being built by *Assistance publique* has any facilities of that nature," the A.G. replied.[58] In the end, therefore, the question of whether the working classes were ready for low-cost housing with modern amenities was beside the point. There was not enough profit in building social housing to attract investors, and state did not have the funds to do it alone.

When Mory lauds the important contribution that architects made to the cause of working-class hygiene, therefore, the optimism of his question reflects both his political bias and the blind spots of his sources, which focus on laws, blueprints, and the curriculum at the École d'Architecture. To take one example: a regulation of June 1904, based on the Strauss law of 1902 and on the advice of consulting architects, imposed minimum standards for space and light and *conforts* for HBM. In practice, so few of them were ever built before the First World War that this advice was superfluous, and the architects' impact on working-class hygiene was tiny.[59]

Cleaner Streets

If the authorities' attempts to bring modern hygiene into people's homes consistently came up short, they found more success in clearing the filth out of city streets. Reformers had long called for measures to battle the most obvious evidence of urban decay—public spaces littered with trash, roads where horseshit turned into mud, and all-purpose landfills like the Montfaucon. The Montfaucon became an icon of urban renewal. Located in the half-developed northeast of Paris, the site had served, during the Middle Ages, as one of the city's main execution sites and into the middle of the nineteenth century as one of its "principal sewage dumps," the end of the line for worked-to-death horses and a haven for the city's small army of rag-pickers. The July Monarchy had already entertained a plan to close it down in the 1840s. But it was only with the full-scale renovation of the city under the Second Empire that the most repulsive corner of the capital was transformed from a huge rubbish tip into a landscaped public park, the Buttes-Chaumont, under the watchful eye of the engineer and designer Jean-Charles Alphand.[60]

The Third Republic accelerated efforts to rid city streets, alleys, courtyards, and streams of garbage, industrial pollutants, and dead animals with their "excremental flair."[61] The impetus to clean up the urban environment was an old one. Cities stank. There is reason to believe that, as people began to experience and to believe in the possibility of things getting better, they became, in fact, less tolerant of terrible conditions and more anxious "to live in an environment devoid of bad smells, sewage runoff, and the torture of emptying cesspits."[62]

Malodor, however, was not simply a matter of sensory discomfort. Both science and common sense continued to conflate noxious odors with miasmas and to see miasmas as the source of disease. The multiplying externalities of rapid urbanization threatened to make things worse. The work of Robert Koch and Louis Pasteur in the early 1880s identified germs and demonstrated that it was not the stench itself that was toxic; in the long run, the "everything-that-stinks-kills" school was doomed. Powerful old ideas die hard, though, and the prescientific intuition that filth polluted air and thus caused disease did not disappear overnight. Furthermore, while germ theory put a new twist on an old narrative, it did not much change the implications for public policy.[63]

At the same time, there was more at stake than lethal smells and threat of epidemics. Some part of the drive for urban cleanup, as historian Fabienne Chevallier proposes, was propelled, as much as anything, by a self-conscious commitment to "modernity"; that is, "to progress in the conditions of human life in the cities." "This progress," she continues, was "defined by a scale that runs from survival, when the collectivity has mastered the plague of epidemics, to household comfort, accompanied by facilities and institutions designed to care for the sick and provide food for the population."[64] The future, it was widely felt, would be more sanitary, and this became, over time, a self-fulfilling prophesy.

The particulars of urban sanitation were straightforward: collect the trash and dispose of it, pave the streets, clean up the horse manure,[65] curb spitting and public urination, push manufacturing activity and abattoirs to the edge of town; pass the laws to make this happen, and enforce them. Existing legislation, noted a 1904 report to the Commerce Ministry, "belongs to another age."[66] The Nadaud project, which had sat on the legislative docket throughout the 1880s, never became law, and the more ambitious Strauss law of 1902 remained, for the most part, a dead letter, at least on the national level.[67]

This left the initiative to local authorities, who generally did their best with limited means. Public works projects never regained the frantic pace of the Haussmann years but proceeded in a slower and more piecemeal fashion. The nineteenth century had brought sidewalks, an English invention, and gutters to French cities. Asphalt first appeared in 1837 and became common in the urban renewal projects of the Second Empire—replacing cobblestones, which had not only proved useful for making revolution, but which were an enduring source of dirt. The first mechanical sweepers, with rotating brushes, appeared on Paris streets in 1876. Since it quickly became clear that sweeping dry dust served only to redistribute it, the city introduced pressure washing in the 1890s, to be carried out in the middle of the night, so as to cause the least disruption. By the early 1920s, the city was dusting and washing 17 million square meters of streets and sidewalks nightly—although by then it had replaced the old horse-drawn *machines-balayeuses* with sweeper trucks.[68]

Of course, dust was hardly the only thing littering public spaces. The courtyards next to or behind the façade of almost every building had long been *véritables puits d'infection*, places where the garbage pitched out by the inhabitants mingled with mud and sewage, polluting the apartments that surrounded them.[69] This was private squalor, for the most part outside the ken of the *Propreté de Paris* and analogous services in other cities, but it was part of the same ecology of garbage. In addition, trash that did not end up in these vacant lots was simply tossed out front, where it became part of that mix of mud and excrement that covered the streets of Paris—"powdery in the summer, gluey and viscous in the winter," as Jules Rochard described it.[70]

None of this was new to the late nineteenth century, and cities had long before evolved makeshift systems for dealing with all this detritus. For general sorts of refuse, for instance, most towns provided dumps (*voiries*) on the edge of town. But that arrangement had its limits. As Louis-Narcisse Girard, inspector general of public works for Paris, observed: "We know the Parisians' character too well to believe that they conscientiously brought their trash there." They mostly dumped it in front of their neighbor's door or in some other public spot. The imperfect arrangement of the *voiries* was supplemented by the work of the rag-pickers (*chiffonniers*), who selected out of the mountains of debris "whatever had some commercial value: linen, paper, fabrics, metal, etc." In fact, municipal authorities wanted to get rid of the *chiffonniers*, because their practice of triage tended to leave a mess. But reform ran into the staunch defense of their corporate privileges.[71] Regardless, the system of rag-pickers and town dumps still left most of the rubbish behind.

Like the Water Question, there was nothing new about the Garbage Question. And also like the Water Question, the Third Republic not only recognized the problem, but also found the will and the means to do something about it. Little by little, public authorities began to clean up the streets and to levy the taxes to pay for the service, the price of which could be steep. A letter sent to the prefect of the Seine by the Compagnie Anglo-Française responsible for cleaning up one dump of more than 200,000 cubic meters of garbage toted up the costs: horses, workers, tools, employees, plus 5 percent interest on capital—the city-owned company 1,150,000 francs.[72] In 1884, the prefect of Paris, Eugène Poubelle, famously imposed on landlords and their concierges the obligation to collect their building's trash and to place it in the bins that still bear his name. The containers had to close, so that rats and other vermin would be sealed off, and the trash had to be collected every day, with the greatest possible care for sanitation, and carted off by vehicles—carts and trams—that would then be disinfected. After the turn of the century, much of it began to be incinerated.

How much garbage? Inspector general Girard estimated that the volume of household rubbish and street debris to be removed in Paris every year amounted to 2 million cubic meters and weighed approximately a million tons. If it were collected at the Place de la Concorde, he added, it would create a hill the size of the Buttes Montmartre. This did not count, moreover, the 150,000 tons taken away by *chiffonniers*, even before the garbage trucks arrived, or the 50,000 tons that disappeared into the sewers. The cost of all this cleaning up was enormous. Girard estimated forty-eight million francs a year for trash collection and thirty-eight million for street cleaning.[73]

Success in the capital was repeated imperfectly across the country. Besançon, "one of the foulest cities in France," developed a powerful new interest in municipal "de-stinking." Lyon likewise began to make some headway in cleaning up its public spaces, and Rouen put in place a new regime of garbage removal. Reports from the hygiene council of the Meurthe-et-Moselle show an exceptional diligence in pursuit of public sanitation in both the towns and the countryside. As always, progress was spotty. In the Limousin, for example, the authorities were less energetic, and the old dirt remained. Moreover, the reach of municipal efforts did not as a rule extend to the suburbs, which generally remained more polluted than the adjacent cities. According to the journal *Le Matin*, the city of Saint-Denis, abutting the north edge of the capital, remained "one of the ugliest and dirtiest [of the Paris suburbs]: the air and the soil encrusted in black smoke, the grubby population, the lack of water for street cleaning and proper sewage." But Saint-Denis was not significantly worse than other makeshift slums outside the *Périphérique*.[74]

Back in the towns, meanwhile, those who worried about the urban environment confronted bad habits, as well as bad structures. Two of the worst were spitting and public urination. The conscientious hygiene commission of the 16th arrondissement expressed its concern that the rain was introducing all these dangerous expectorations into the sewers, while busy brooms swept them across the roads and sidewalks. The Strauss Commission, for its part, wondered about the practicality of including in the 1902 law a prohibition against spitting in the street, attaching "the highest priority to the disappearance of a despicable practice that contributes to contagious disease, most notably tuberculosis." Alas, it concluded, such an interdiction was probably impossible, given "the actual state of our manners." The best that could be done was to encourage people to spit into what it called pocket spittoons or at least into the gutters, instead of onto the sidewalk. An article in the *Revue d'Hygiène et de Police Sanitaire* (1900) by Dr. Rouget recommended that, since it is now considered "reprehensible" to spit into your pocket handkerchief and a menace to public health to spit on the sidewalk or in a building or a tram, Parisians should make liberal use of *crachoirs*, both collective and personal; individual cuspidors could be carried as "elegant and convenient little bottles." As for the collective models, Rouget laid down some practical rules: they should be high enough that people won't miss them when they spit and stable enough that they won't get knocked over; and they should be covered, even though this might put off "certain excessively delicate temperaments, who would find it repugnant to have to lift the cover of a *crachoir collectif*."[75]

The old habit of public urination proved equally recalcitrant. Naturally, Paris was comparatively favored, when it came to the disposition of public urinals. Haussmann had sought to make them part of the "street furniture" of a modern Paris, and by 1914, some 4,000 public urinals had been built in the capital (Figure 7.2). Nonetheless, municipal authorities continued to receive scores of complaints about this common offense to hygienic sensibilities, while, in less fortunate places like Limoges, where the city lacked the water resources to wash the streets and had built not a single public latrine, stone bollards still served for the relief of natural functions, unshielded from public view. Meanwhile, even the *pissotières* of Paris offered little relief to women.[76] They required more elaborate plumbing and would have to wait.

Figure 7.2 *"Vespasienne" with three stalls made of slate, with a street lamp. Avenue du Maine, Paris* (1865). Charles Marville, photographer. Collections de la Bibliothèque d'État du Victoria, Australia.

Notes

1. Octave du Mesnil, *L'hygiène à Paris: L'habitation du pauvre* (Paris: Librairie J.-B. Baillière et fils, 1890), 22–3.
2. Ville de Paris. Commission des Logements Insalubres. *Rapport Général sur les Travaux de la Commission Pendant les Années 1890–1891–1892* (Paris: Imprimerie de l'École Municipale Estienne, 1895), 810 and Roger-Henri Guerrand, "Aux origines du confort moderne," in Jacques Lucan, *Eau et gaz à tous les étages. Paris: 100 ans de logement* (Paris: Édition de Pavillon de l'Arsenal, 1992), 20.
3. Alfred de Foville, *Enquête sur les conditions de l'habitation en France. tome I: Les maison-types* (Paris: Ernest Leroux, 1894), 33 and *tome II: Les maisons-types, avec une étude historique de M. Jacques Flach* (Paris: E. Leroux, 1899), 118. Also see Anne-Marie Sohn, *Chrysalides. Femmes dans la vie privée (XIX-XXe siècles)*, vol. I (Paris: Publications de la Sorbonne, 1996), 115.
4. Pierre Bourdelais and Yankel Fijalkow, "French Cities and the Origins of Medical and Social Policy: Late-19th-20th Century France," in Laurinda Abreu (ed.), *European Health and Social Welfare Policies* (Brno: Campostela Group of Universities, 2004), 365–6.
5. David S. Barnes, *The Making of a Social Disease: Tuberculosis in Nineteenth-Century France* (Berkeley: University of California Press, 1995), in particular, Chapter 4: "Interiors." Also see Isabelle Backouche, *Paris transformé: Le Marais, 1900–1980* (Paris: Créaphis Éditions, 2016), 163–6 and Yankel Fijalkow, "Mesurer l'hygiène urbaine en épargnant les propriétaires : Le casier sanitaire des maisons de Paris," *Les Annales de la Recherche Urbaine* 53 (1991): 73–8.
6. Quoted in Elsbeth Kalff and Lucie Lemaître, *Le logement insalubre et l'hygiénisation de la vie quotidienne. Paris (1880–1990)* (Paris: L'Harmattan, 2008), 130.
7. André-Alfred Dumont, *Les habitations ouvrières dans les grands centres industriels et plus particulièrement dans la région du Nord: étude d'hygiène sociale*, thèse pour le doctorat en médecine (Lille: Masson, 1905), 9–10; du Mesnil, *L'hygiène à Paris*, 38.
8. Fijalkow, "Mesurer l'hygiène urbaine," 130–4, 147–52, and 165–7.
9. The table accounting tuberculosis deaths by arrondissement is in Conseil Municipal de Paris, "Rapport au nom de la 6e commission sur les îlots insalubres de Paris," presented by Ambrose Rendu, conseiller municipal, 1909, 54. Also see du Mesnil, *L'hygiène à Paris*, 164. On mortality rates in crowded housing, see Alliance d'hygiène sociale, *Congrès de Roubaix, 19–22 octobre 1911: De la ville-taudis à la cité-jardin* (Agen: Imprimerie Moderne, 1912), 274–6.
10. AD Marne, 6 U 686, procès-verbal du justice de paix, Suippes, novembre 9, 1894. Also see Fénelon Gibon, *Le fléau du taudis. Le premier remède: les habitations ouvrières* (Paris: Fénelon Gibon, 1918), 12; Yvonne Knibiehler, ed., *Nous, les assistantes sociales. Naissance d'une profession, témoignages présentées par Y. Knibiehler* (Paris: Aubier, 1980), 131; and Jacques Valdour, *De la propinque à Menilmuche* (Paris: Spes, 1924), 111.
11. Michelle Perrot, *Histoire des chambres* (Paris: Seuil, 2009), 291.
12. Amélioration du logement ouvrier, *Une enquête sur le logement des familles nombreuses à Paris* (Paris: Imprimerie Veuve Denis, 1912), 12. Also see Ministère de l'Économie Nationale. Service Nationale des statistiques. Direction de la Statistique Générale. Études Économiques. No. 1. *Documents sur le problème du logement à Paris* (Paris: Imprimerie Nationale, 1946), 68.
13. Ibid., the statistics and the descriptions can be found, 13–26.

14 Cited in Roger Merlin, *La crise du logement et les habitations à bon marché* (Paris: Commission d'Action Sociale, 1913), 13–14. On overcrowding in Paris and other French cities, see Dumont, *Les habitations ouvrières, passim.* Information on foreign cities comes from a report by Arthur Fontaine, director of Labor at the Ministry of Commerce and Industry, based on figures collected by Bertillon on other countries' statistics, in *Revue d'Hygiène et de Police Sanitaire* (1900), 929 and Jacques Bertillon, *Essai de statistique comparé du surpeuplement dans les habitations à Paris et dans les grandes capitales européennes* (Paris: Imprimerie Chaix, 1894), *passim*. Also see Jules Rochard, *Traité d'hygiène publique et privée* (Paris: Octave Doin, 1897), 319.
15 Amélioration du logement ouvrier, *Enquête sur le logement*, 4, 24.
16 Ibid., 10. On rents, also see Lionel Kesztenbaum and Jean-Laurent Rosenthal, "Income versus Sanitation: Mortality Decline in Paris, 1880–1914," Working Paper No. 2014-26, Paris School of Economics, July 4, 2014, 8; Merlin, *La crise du logement*, 11–12; and Rochard, *Traité d'hygiène*, 332.
17 The quotes come from Yves Lequin, "Les espaces de la société citadine," in Lequin (dir.), *Histoire des Français, XIXe-XXe siècles: la société* (Paris: Armand Colin, 1983), 363–6 and Victor Cyril-Berger, *Les têtes baissées* (Paris: P. Ollendorff, 1913), 43–4. On *garnis*, also see Amélioration du logement ouvrier, *Enquête sur le logement*, 16; Guerrand, "Aux origines du confort," 17 and André Gueslin, *Gens pauvres, pauvres gens dans la France du XIXe siècle* (Paris: Aubier, 1998), 60.
18 *Compte-rendu du Congrès international d'hygiène de 1878*, tome 1 (Paris: Imprimerie Nationale, 1880), 10–11. Also see the descriptions in Préfecture de Police. Conseil d'hygiène publique et de salubrité, *Rapport sur l'insalubrité de la Cité Doré et de la Cité des Kroumirs (13e arrondissement)* (Paris: Imprimerie Chaix, 1882), *passim* and Gustave Jourdan, chef de bureau à la Préfecture de la Seine, *Étude sur le projet de Revision de la loi concernant les logements insalubres* (Paris: Berger-Levrault et Cie., 1883), 8.
19 Rochard, *Traité d'hygiène*, 332.
20 Yvonne Knibiehler, ed., *Nous, les assistantes sociales*, 131.
21 On the cité Doré, Dr. Lafont cited in Préfecture de Police, *Rapport sur l'insalubrité*, 13. On the cité Jeanne d'Arc, see Georges Picot, *Les logements d'ouvriers, un devoir social* (Paris: Calmann-Lévy, 1885), 38 and Jean Richepin, *Paysages et coins de rue* (Paris: Librairie de la Collection des Dix, 1900), 107.
22 René Martial, *L'ouvrier: son hygiène, son atelier, son habitation* (Paris: Doin et fils, 1909), 302.
23 Jean-Paul Brunet, *Saint-Denis, la ville rouge: Socialisme et communism en banlieue ouvrière, 1890–1939* (Paris: Hachette, 1980), 98.
24 Bibliothèque de la Préfecture de Police de Paris, Commission des Logements Insalubres, "Rapports, 1851–1892: Rapport sur les Travaux des Commissions d'Hygiène du Département de la Seine et des communes de Saint-Cloud, Sèvres et Meudon en 1888," 11.
25 Merlin, *La crise du logement*, 9.
26 Anaïs Albert, *La vie à crédit. La consommation des classes populaires à Paris (années 1880–1920)* (Paris: Éditions de la Sorbonne, 2021), 48. Also see Lucienne Cahen, "Évolution des conditions de logement en France depuis cent ans," *Études et conjonctures* 10–11 (1957): 1207. A 1946 report from the Economics ministry noted that in both 1891 and 1896 only 25 percent of dwellings had private W.C.: l'Économie nationale, *Documents sur le problème du logement à Paris*, 68–9.

27 For one example, Limoges, see Gaston Ducray, *Le travail porcelanier en Limousin: Étude économique et sociale* (Angers: A. Burdin, 1904), 198.
28 In A. Blanchet, Ph. Dard, and G. Palmade, *Odeurs et Habiter: Études exploratoires, fonctions et significations des odeurs et des sensations de gêne dans les pratiques de l'habitat* (Paris: CSTB, 1981), no page number; Monique Eleb and Anne Debarre, *L'invention de l'habitation moderne: Paris 1880-1914. Architectures de la vie privé, suite* (Paris: Éditions Hazan et Archives d'Architecture Moderne, 1995), 215.
29 Julia Csergo, *Liberté, égalité, propreté. La morale de l'hygiéne au XIXe siècle* (Paris: Albin Michel, 1988), 12, 87, and 288; Corbin, *Le miasma et la jonquille* (Paris: Flammarion, 2016), 67-72 and 167-88; Olivier Le Goff, *L'invention du confort: naissance d'une forme sociale* (Lyon: Presses Universitaires de Lyon, 1994), 36; and Nell Blackadder, "Merde! Performing Filth in the Bourgeois Public Sector," in William A. Cohen and Ryan Johnson (eds.), *Filth, Dirt, Disgust and Modern Life* (Minneapolis: University of Minnesota Press, 2005), 185.
30 "The social benefit of the battle against filth is inestimable," wrote the photographer Christopher Levébure, in the text attached to his collection of photographs of village washhouses [*lavoirs*], "giving reason to hope that the dangerous laboring classes, once cleaned up, will no longer cause trouble, since the worker with clean underwear will have a more peaceful spirit than the worker who is ragged and dirty," in *La France des lavoirs. Photographies de l'auteur* (Toulous: Éditions Privat, 1995), 19. Ariel Beaujot writes of the habit of women wearing clean white gloves that, since dirt was evidence of work, signaled privilege: *Victorian Fashion Accessories* (London and New York: Berg, 2012), 10.
31 Jean-Claude Daumas, *La révolution matérielle. Une histoire de la consommation: France, XIXe-XXe siècles* (Paris: Flammarion, 2018), 112.
32 Le Goff, *L'invention du confort*, 41-3.
33 Charles Jeanselme, reporter, *Exposition universelle internationale de 1900 à Paris. Raports du jury international classe 71. Décoration mobile et ouvrage du tapissier* (Paris: Imprimerie Nationale, 1901), 9.
34 Mary Lynn Stewart, *For Health and Beauty: Physical Culture for Frenchwomen, 1880s-1930s* (Baltimore: Johns Hopkins University Press, 2001), 66. Also see Georges Vigarello, *Concepts of Cleanliness: Changing Attitudes in France Since the Middle Ages* (Cambridge: Cambridge University Press, 1988), 187; Guy Thuillier, *Pour une histoire quotidienne en Nivernais* (Paris: EHESS, 1977), 140; Henri Napias and André-Justin Martin, *L'étude et le progrès de l'hygiène en France de 1878 à 1882* (Paris: G. Masson, 1883), 133; and Peter Ward, *The Clean Body: A Modern History* (Montreal and Kingston: McGill-Queens University Press, 2019), 66.
35 Nicole Rudolph, "'Les peuples soucieux de la propreté sont des peuples supérieurs': The Norm of Order in French Domestic Economy Manuals, 1881-1986," unpublished manuscript, 1997, 3.
36 The phrase is from Csergo, *Liberté, égalité, propreté*, 37.
37 Octave Mirabeau, *Le journal d'une femme de chambre* (Paris: Bibliothèque Charpentier, 1900), 30.
38 Drs. Henry Thierry and Lucien Graux, *L'habitation urbaine. Chambres de domestiques, cuisines et loges de concierges. Rapport adopté par la Société d'Art Populaire et d'Hygiène* (Paris: Imprimerie de Saint-Denis, 1909), 8-10.
39 Also see Raymonde de Ryckère, *La servante criminelle: étude de criminologie professionnelle* (Paris: A. Maloine, 1908), 4. 406.

40 Jean Lahor, *Les habitations à bon marché et un art nouveau pour le peuple* (Paris: Larousse, 1905), 49; Philippe Dufieux, "À propos de l'hygiène de Lyon (1800–1960)," in Conseil d'Architecture, d'Urbanisme et de l'Environnement du Rhône, *Le confort moderne dans l'habitat* (Lyon: CAUE, 2007), 20.

41 Laurent Bonnevay, *Les habitations à bon marché* (Paris: Dunod et Pinat, 1912), 106.

42 E. Fichaux, *Petites leçons d'hygiène, à l'usage des écoles primaires et des classes élémentaires des lycées et collèges: questions—pensées—expériences—exercises pratiques—rédactions du certificate d'études* (Paris: Hachette, 1907), 55.

43 *Compte-rendu du Xe Congrès International d'Hygiène et de Démographie à Paris en 1900* (Paris: Masson et Cie., 1901), 288.

44 *Le Progrès de Lyon* (juin 28, 1893). The story of the Projet Nadaud can be found in AN F8, carton 211: Rapports de la Commission des logements insalubres, Dossier II.

45 On the law of November 1894, see Marie-Jeanne Dumont, *Le logement social à Paris, 1850–1930: les habitations à bon marché* (Liège: Mardaga, 1991), 21; Pierre Guinchat, Marie-Paule Chaulet et Lisette Gaillardot, *Il était une fois l'habitat: chronique du logement social en France* (Paris: Éditions du Moniteur, 1981), 53; Jacques Léonard, *Archives du corps. La santé au XIXe siècle* (Rennes: Ouest France, 1986), 87; and Susanna Magri, "L'émergence du logement social: objectifs et moyens d'une réforme," in Marion Segaud, Catherine Bonvalet, and Jacques Brun (dirs.), *Logement et Habitat: L'état des savoirs* (Paris: Éditions de la Découverte, 1998), 34. Also see the summary of the history of French housing legislation in "La questions du taudis dans les différents pays moyens mis en oeuvre pour y remédier," in Ministère de la Santé Publique, *Recueil des travaux se l'Institut National d'Hygiène: travaux des sections et mémoires originaux*, tome IV, vol. 1 (Paris: Masson et Cie., 1950), 289–99. On the postcards, see Renaud Epstein, *On est bien arrivés: un tour de France des grands ensembles* (Paris: Le Nouvel Atila, 2022), 13.

46 Ribot is cited in Alliance d'hygiène sociale, *Congrès de Roubaix*, 263. Also see AP M 5: Santé publique et hygiène, XIII-1929, carton 13, contains a number of documents relevant to this issue: Préfecture de la Seine, Projet de règlement sanitaire, p. 14, on the details of the 1902 law; on the new rules, see the pamphlet written by the Conseil d'hygiène publique et de salubrité du département de la Seine, "Projets de règlements sanitaires, approuvés par les Commissions d'hygiène des arrondissements de Saint-Denis et de Sceaux," (n.d.); on the Hygiene Boards, see the letter from the interior minister to the prefects, March 23, 1906, "pour l'application des mesures sanitaires sur tout le territoire." Also see AP VI[5] 1, Police et Hygiène, "Proposition de loi relative à l'expropriation pour cause d'insalubrité publique," reported by deputy Jules Siegfried, novembre 18, 1910. In addition, pertaining to this series of laws on HBM, see Alliance d'hygiène sociale, *Congrès de Roubaix*, 218–19; Émile Cheysson, *Le confort du logement populaire [extrait du Bulletin de la Société française des Habitations à bon marché]* (Paris: Imprimerie Chaix, 1905), 7; France. Programme socio-économie de l'habitat. Groupe d'études de démographie appliquée, *L'accès au logement: filières et blocages*, especially chapter 4: "Le logement en France et en Grande Bretagne: Histoire et Politiques" (Paris: Imprimerie Le Clavier, 1995) and Hélène Frouard, "À l'ombre des familles nombreuses: les politiques françaises du logement au XXe siècle," *Revue d'histoire moderne et contemporaine* 57, no. 2 (avril–Juin 2010): 119–20.

47 Yves Salaün [Inspecteur des Finances], *Se loger: construire 20.000 logements par mois est, pour la France, une question de vie ou de mort* (Paris: Imprimerie de Montsouris, 1949), 24; also see Georges Cahen, "Rôle de l'initiative privée en matière d'hygiène

sociale," in Louis Martin and Georges Brouardel, *Hygiène sociale*, vol. XXIII (Paris: J.-B. Ballière et Fils, 1929), 529.
48 Foville, *Enquête sur les conditions de l'habitation en France: I*, 27–34.
49 Christian Legrand, Krysztof Kazimierz Pawlowski, and Bruno Voisin, *Le logement populaire et social en Lyonnais, 1848–2000* (Lyon: Aux Arts, 2002), 90, 101–2, 443.
50 Will Clement, "The 'Unrealizable Chimera': Workers' Housing in Nineteenth-Century Mulhouse," *French History* 32, no. 1 (February 17, 2018): 66–85 *passim*.
51 Daumas, *La révolution matérielle*, 73; Dufieux, "À propos de l'hygiène de Lyon (1800–1960)," 24–5; Foville, *Enquête sur les conditions de l'habitation: I*, 33; F. Roussel, Directeur des Services Municipaux d'Hygiène et d'Assistance Sociale de Vitry-sur-Seine, "La crise du logement et l'hygiène. Le nouveau programme législatif (loi du 13 juillet 1928): Loi Loucheur," manuscript, 3–4.
52 Dr. Laroche, directeur du Bureau d'Hygiène, *Histoire des habitations ouvrières de Montceau-les-Mines* (extrait de la *Revue Pratique d'Hygiène Municipale Urbaine et Rurale*, nos. 7-8, juillet-août 1920), 3–9.
53 Marie-Jeanne Dumont, "L'invention d'un programme: le logement populaire," in Lucan, *Eau et gaz à tous les étages*, 55–6.
54 Pascal Mory, "Architecture et hygiénisme à Paris au début du XXe siècle: L'architect entre savoir médical et pouvoir politique," in Patrice Bordelais (dir.), *Les hygienists: enjeux, modèles et pratiques (XVIIIe-XXe siècles)* (Paris: Belin, 2001), 159.
55 René Martial, "Maisons à bon marché et salubrité," in *Revue d'Hygiène et de Police Sanitaire* (Paris: G. Masson, 1914), 233–47.
56 Merlin, *La crise du logement*, 11–12.
57 The first quote is from Eleb and Debarre, *L'invention de l'habitation moderne*, 237; the second is from Henry Provensal, *L'habitation salubre et à bon marché* (Paris: Schmid, 1908), 72. Also see Jean Taricat and Martine Villars, *Le logement à bon marché. Chronique. Paris, 1850–1930* (Boulogne: Éditions Apogée, 1982), 42.
58 AP DM 5 0017, dossier "Contrôle des bains-douches," letter of January 26, 1914.
59 Mory, "Architecture et hygiénisme à Paris," 146–57. Also see Jean-Paul Lacaze, *Les français et leur logement: éléments de socio-économie de l'habitat* (Paris: Presses de l'École Nationale des Ponts et Chaussées, 1989), 14–15.
60 AP VI[5] 1, "Développement d'un projet, présenté par une compagnie ou la suppression de la voirie de Montfaucon," May 1840; and AP D1 S8 27, "Curage des égoûts départementaux, 1900–1933." Also see Colin Jones, *Paris: Biography of a City* (New York: Viking, 2004), 70.
61 The term belongs to Constance Classen, David Howes, and Anthony Synnott, *Aroma: The Cultural History of Smell* (London and New York: Routledge, 1994), 80–1.
62 Kalff and Lemaître, *Le logement insalubre*, 120–1.
63 Raphaël Blanchard, *Les ennemis de l'espèce humaine, conférence faite le 25 février 1888 à l'Association française pour l'avancement des sciences* (Paris: Administration des deux revues, 1888), 2–3.
64 Fabienne Chevallier, *Le Paris moderne: Histoire des politiques d'hygiène (1855–1898)* (Rennes: Presses Universitaire de Rennes, 2010), 14–15.
65 "It goes without saying," remember Edouard Bonnefous, "that certain parts of Paris in the Belle Epoque smelled like stables and that Parisians never ceased to complain about horses," in Bonnefous, *Avant l'oubli: La vie de 1900 à 1940* (Paris: Laffont/Nathan, 1985), 22.
66 Ministère du Commerce, de l'Industrie, des Postes et des Télégraphes, *Rapports du jury international (de l'Exposition Universelle Internationale de 1900 à Paris): Groupe*

XVI: *Économie sociale-Hygiène-Assistance publique* (Paris: Imprimerie Nationale, 1904), 313–16.
67 On the Nadaud *projet de loi*, see AN F8, Police Sanitaire, carton 212: "Logements insalubres, 1881–1896"; for the Strauss report, see AP DM 5, carton 13: "Santé publique et hygiène, XIII-1929 (1804–1929)."
68 Louis-Narcisse Girard, *Le nettoiement de Paris. Conférence faite aux ingénieurs des travaux publics de la Ville de Paris, le 6 janvier 1923* (Paris: Librairie de l'Enseignement Technique, 1923), 53, 71. Girard's little book offers a wonderfully potted history of public sanitation in Paris.
69 Ville de Paris. Commission des logements insalubres, *Rapport général* (1895), 2.
70 Rochard, *Traité d'hygiène*, 248.
71 Girard, *Le nettoiement de Paris*, 10; Jules Courmont, *Précis d'hygiène* (Paris: Masson et Cie., 1914), 314.
72 AP V^{15} 1, Préfecture du département de la Seine. Conseil Municipal de Paris. Discussion sur le projet relative à la réforme de vidange, extraits du compte-rendu des séances du conseil municipal, avril 7, 1885.
73 Girard, *Le nettoiement de Paris*, 5, 23–9.
74 C. Vivier, "Les actions d'une société sportive en faveur de la santé publique. Le S.N.B. (1865–1930)," in Pierre Leveque (dir.), *Éducation et Hygiène du corps à travers l'histoire. Actes du colloque de l'Association interuniversitaire de l'Est* (Dijon: Éditions Universitaires de Dijon, 1991), 101; also Dufieux, "À propos de l'hygiène de Lyon (1800–1960)," 20–1; *Compte-rendu du Xe Congrès international d'hygiène et de démographie*, 399; Jules Dorez, *Compte-rendu des travaux du Conseil d'Hygiène départemental et des commissions sanitaires* [Meurthe-et-Moselle]. *Année 1908—tome XLIV* (Nancy: Imprimerie Berger-Levrault et Cie.), *passim*; and Maurice Robert, *Mémoire et identité: traverses éthnohistoriques en Limousin* (Limoges: Maison Limousine des Sciences de l'Homme, 1991), 390. On Saint-Denis, see Brunet, *Saint-Denis*, 18–19.
75 On the question of expectoration, see Préfecture de la Seine. Commission du Règlement sanitaire. Rapport de M. Paul Strauss, Sénateur, re: projet de règlement (selon la loi du 15 février 1902), ms., in AP DM 5, carton 13: Santé publique et hygiène; Préfecture de Police. Conseil d'Hygiène Publique et Salubrité du Département de la Seine, *Rapports sur les Travaux des Commissions d'Hygiène du Département et la Seine et des Communes de Saint-Cloud, Sèvres et Meudon en 1900. Rapport général au Conseil d'Hygiène de la Seine par le Docteur A. Le Roy Des Barres* (Paris: Imprimerie Nouvelle, 1902), 149; and *Revue d'hygiène et de police sanitaire* (1900), 892.
76 On the matter of public urination, see David S. Barnes. *The Great Stink of Paris and the Nineteenth-Century Struggle against Filth and Germs* (Baltimore: Johns Hopkins University Press, 2006), 79–80; Alain Corbin, *Archaïsme et modernité en Limousin au XIXe siècle: 1845–1880* (Paris: M. Rivière, 1975), 82; Jones, *Paris*, 399.

8

How Clean Was the Belle Epoque?

What Progress?

The opening of the twentieth century seems like a convenient place to stop and to assess both the successes and the disappointments in the advance of hygiene (Figure 8.1). How much had the practices and sensibilities surrounding this critical aspect of the human condition changed in France between the Second Empire and the First World War? For all the military drills and the school lessons and the investigations of the poor-housing commissions and the *censiers sanitaires* and the countless meetings of local councils and national associations of reformers, was France very much cleaner in 1914 than it had been in 1871?

The first thing to say is that the evidence is neither ample nor dispositive.[1] Doctors of public medicine and professional hygienists produced thousands of pages advising readers how to wash their feet and change their socks; how to practice proper dental care; and what sorts of amenities belonged in barracks, schools, and homes. Prescriptions and publicity aside, though, few sources have anything to say about the *actual* state of infrastructure and routine. It is not difficult to find encouraging anecdotes, as Anne-Marie Sohn does in the archives of the Seine-Inférieure, where, in the area around Rouen in 1905, "it was not rare to find nannies bathing a child twice a week, whereas not long before a demi-tasse of water would have sufficed [to wash that child]."[2] Overall, however, it appears that the real impact of modern hygiene was not up to its ambitions. Facilities for cleaning up soldiers and pupils might have been better in 1910 than they had been a half-century earlier. But everyone agreed that they fell far short of the modern ideal of lavatories, bedbug-free mattresses, proper ventilation, showers, and non-disgusting latrines.[3]

It was the same in other public institutions, where regulations on the proper state of both the furniture and the praxis of *propreté* were strictly aspirational. To be sure, conditions in most places had improved beyond what they had been in the first years of the Third Republic. But official standards were far from being met almost everywhere. When Henri Napias visited a hospital in the Sambre-et-Marne in 1903, he concluded that the personnel still retained "a holy horror of water." Moving on to a nearby orphanage, he found no sinks and only two bathrooms for the whole facility, which had 100 beds. "The sick ones receive baths on a doctor's prescription," the director told him. "The grown-ups never; the orphans once a year, *like me*." Conditions were even more deplorable in the Bon-Pasteur school in Nancy, where the orphans bathed only

Figure 8.1 *Paving the road by hand.* Photograph is from Louis-Narcisse Girard, *Le nettoiement de Paris. Conférence faite aux ingénieurs des travaux publics de la ville de Paris, le 6 janvier 1923* (Paris: Librairie de l'Enseignement Technique, 1923). Courtesy of the Bibliothèque nationale de France.

once a year, while the boarders did not have even that. The children washed their feet once every three months in winter and every six weeks in summer. Without soap or underwear, drying themselves with a dirty rag, they wore the same shirts sometimes for three weeks running. Worse yet, without basins to wash their face and hands, the children had to use their chamber pots.[4]

Did the hygiene lessons taught in the schools and in the army nevertheless leave a substantial mark on comportment? Students and recruits had been told that they needed to wash regularly and bathe occasionally. Did they? Advice was plentiful, especially for women, "who alone have the spirit and good taste to appreciate the importance and utility that a diligent *toilette*, used with discernment, can render to health," and who were therefore the natural targets of efforts to improve the race.[5] But descriptions of people's private lives—especially those parts of their private lives that are both intimate and quotidian—are sparse. The general impression is that era's what-to-do lists of proper hygiene were quite modern, but actual behavior ran two or three generations behind the experts' counsel. Jules Renard remembered that in Nevers, even the bourgeois washed their feet only once a week, although the typical recommendation at the time was once a day.[6]

An especially wide gap separated guidance from custom when it came to oral hygiene. Every grade-school primer or normal-school lesson book told children to clean their mouths on a regular basis. The recipes varied a little. Some hygienists recommended rinsing several times a day with soapy water or vinegar. The Baronne Staffe suggested to her readers a mixture of camphor and myrrh, for sweeter breath.

Otherwise, remarks historian Jacques Léonard, "urine passed for the supreme disinfectant." Past a bit of mouthwash, the advice books insisted on brushing—once a day, after every meal—the particulars varied from expert to expert. All of them, however, mentioned the need for a proper dentifrice. In the absence of toothpaste and the rarity of tooth powder, other abrasives would serve. Staffe recommended carbon powder or quinine. Some people used charcoal, which tended to blacken the gums and wear out the enamel.[7]

The truth of the matter is that at the end of the nineteenth century, the principles of oral hygiene were honored almost entirely in the breach. Recall the story military dentist M. Sapet related about the fate of the toothbrushes he distributed to his fellow recruits in 1913; they were used to clean rifles. And while educator Jeannine Martay told young women to go frequently to the dentist (1909), that was easier said than done. The first diploma for a surgeon-dentist was granted only in 1892, and even a medium-sized city like Nevers had only four dentists in 1907, most of whom were busy making *prosthèses dentaires*. It is no surprise that, as a peasant woman confessed to folklorist Françoise Loux, "[her] husband had brushed his teeth twice in his life: once for his first communion and once for his wedding."[8]

Meanwhile, through much of the countryside, folk dentistry survived intact. In the 1970s, Lise Bésème-Pia, an amateur folklorist, began to collect oral histories in and around her native Ardennes, publishing a study on the folk wisdom surrounding teeth. One man remembered, for instance, having his grandmother place around his neck a small sachet with a mole's paw inside, meant to ward off toothaches. Elsewhere, in Lorraine, in order to facilitate the appearance of the first teeth, babies' gums were rubbed with the milk of a black cow; in the Champagne it was coffee. On the other side of the country, in the Charente, mothers hung a pouch stuffed with slugs around the baby's neck. In the Ardennes region it was said that a bad eyetooth should never be pulled—that would cause blindness, since the canine was connected by nerves to the eye—and peasants still prayed to Sainte-Apolline, martyred by fire in Alexandria in 249 CE while having her teeth pulled out with pincers. More secular folk cures ranged from placing cloves on a sore tooth to "cutting one's toenails every Monday."[9]

Peasant "ignorance on this point is complete," observed Jules Rochard. "In our villages, on our farms," he wrote, people pay no attention to oral hygiene, "like the animals." Ignorance, however broadly and equitably distributed, was not the only factor in the dental geography of France. Tooth decay also varied with local conditions. Food and drink made small differences in dental hygiene that might not have satisfied the experts but nonetheless made some significant difference to the incidence of caries and other sorts of tooth decay among the peasantry.

Gustave Lagneau, a physician-turned-anthropologist, and Émile Magitot, a dentist and prolific author who also became general secretary of the Anthropology Society of Paris, drew up in 1882 a map of military exemptions due to poor teeth. They found the greatest number of exemptions in north and east: French Flanders, Picardy, Normandy, Champagne; and in the west Anjou, Poitou, Vendée, Guyenne, Gascony, and Béarn. The healthiest mouths were located in Brittany and the Centre region, from the Auvergne east to the Alps and south to the Mediterranean. Aside from the bona fides of the authors, it is impossible to know how much credence to give this picture of national oral hygiene—all the more so, since its geography conflicts with the usual distribution of military exemptions and general health. The scattered and partial work of anthropologists and folklorists on the question is not conclusive.[10]

Conclusive or not, one thing is certain: whatever change was occurring sorted itself along predictable lines of class and neighborhood. The lower classes in Edwardian England were dismissed by polite society as "the great unwashed," despite the abolition of the long-standing soap tax in 1853. "At the bottom of our social ladder," wrote Stephen Reynolds, "is a dirty sheet; at the top is fixed not laurels, but a tub! The bathroom is the inmost, the strongest fortress of our English snobbery."[11] It is not unreasonable to think that something similar was going across the channel.

Even if we look with skepticism at dubious assertions about bourgeois "strategies of power," middle- and upper-class urban households in France took the lead in the slow race to a cleaner future. Bigger homes with more amenities allowed for higher levels of cleanliness. Based on her long analysis of death inventories, Julia Csergo concludes that the tools of *propreté* were substantially more common at the turn of the century than they had been in 1850. They nonetheless remained thin on the ground and belonged almost exclusively to the *classes aisées*. "The installation of a bathtub in the dressing rooms of bourgeois apartments marked the progress of hygiene," writes Daumas, in his history of material culture, "but it was reserved to a tiny elite." According to Csergo's count, only 4 percent of households had a bathtub in their inventory. Given that a tub could cost upwards of $200, this is not surprising.[12]

At the same moment, not a single *cabinet de toilette* was inventoried in the 11th, 13th, 19th, or 20th arrondissements, ground zero of working-class Paris. The physician and public health advocate Augustin Cabanès described a conference early in the new century that looked at the working class in the town of Charleville. Out of 100 individuals interviewed by the committee of inquiry, two had the habit of taking a bath in a bathtub; eighteen reported washing their feet when they changed their socks; fifty-two washed their feet twice during the winter, although they washed their face and neck, but not their head, every Saturday; twenty-four never washed anything *ever*.[13]

Csergo sees in these practices not merely ignorance or poverty but a working-class "resistance" to bourgeois norms of *propreté*. Perhaps it is true that some members of the proletariat rejected the hygienic standards of their social betters either because they did not want to give in to the hegemonic aims of the ruling class—or because they preferred to be dirty. In any case, old habits will not change simply because a book or an expert says they should. But the principal barrier was financial: hygiene cost money, and the working classes did not have much of it to spare. We have already seen the quality of housing that blighted working-class lives. Without easy access to water and living in sordid conditions, what was the point of acquiring *objets d'hygiène*?

To be fair, while the era of genuine mass consumerism and modern plumbing for all lay several generations in the future, the fin-de-siècle did see some improvement in working-class standards of living. For one thing, the poor were not as poor as they had been. According to economist Thomas Piketty, average income rose in France by 15 percent between 1900 and 1913, a function of real wage growth and less precarious employment. In particular, the relative cost of food declined dramatically for working-class families, while the variety and nutritional value of their diets improved. In the

Figure 8.2 *A working-class home, rue de Romainville, 20th arrondissement, Paris* (1910). Photograph by Eugen Atget (1857–1927). Courtesy of the Bibliothèque Historique de la Ville de Paris. Cote : 4-EPR-00379.

Limousin, according to Maurice Robert, they increased the weight of bread they consumed by 20 or 30 percent between 1870 and 1914. Meat consumption rose in the same proportion, and even nonelites began to consume commodities like sugar, coffee, pasta, and fruit.[14]

The working classes also acquired larger, more comfortable, and therefore more hygienic wardrobes after 1890. Historian Jean-Claude Daumas cites the case of a supervisor from the town of Guise: his clothing included six hats, six colored shirts, six white shirts, three ties, six handkerchiefs, a dozen pairs of socks, two pairs of everyday slippers, a pair of boots, and—a revealing moment in the history of priorities—only three pairs of underpants (*caleçons*).[15]

Housing was the lagging indicator of working-class life in this period. The price of rent did not rise markedly, even if demand for decent housing did. In fact, the cost of housing in France remained comparatively moderate, at 12.3 percent of a family budget nationally and 15.8 percent in Paris. Since the French could not put up enough new buildings to meet this rising demand, however, lower-class families were compelled to take what they found in an old and dilapidated supply of affordable housing. In other words, the French did not pay more for rent than did their analogs in England or Germany, but they lived worse (Figure 8.2).[16]

How Much Washing?

As Csergo demonstrates, the new material culture of hygiene made its appearance first in the households of the privileged: running water, hot-water heaters, sinks, bathtubs, bidets. Many of Baronne Staffe's recommendations to her presumably elite readers would have made no sense for a working-class audience, who did not have dressing rooms and bathtubs—or even combs and hairbrushes—to follow them. But even the modern apartments of Staffe's imagination had an aspirational edge to them. Well past the turn of the century, *salles de bain* remained exceptional, even in the homes of the upper-middle class—and they were not necessarily for hygiene. The bathrooms Staffe described had walls covered in onyx and marble, silk curtains hiding the tub, shelves filled with perfumes and oils, and a *chaise longue* covered with a white bearskin.[17] It was a space devoted to occasional luxury, rather than to the everyday labor of washing up.

Jean-Pierre Chaline's description of bourgeois apartments in Rouen makes the same point:

> If the end-of-the-century witnessed a multiplication of "cabinets de toilette," small rooms furnished with a basin and a jug of water; bathrooms remained exceptional. At the home of the rich Beaurepaire family, who did not have [a *cabinet de toilette*] in their mansion, they ordered a home delivery from an establishment that specialized in bathtubs and hot water. In the home of the Vaniers [a well-to-do merchant family], there was a tub—employed so infrequently the zinc in it rusted... and no one dared to use this *installation*, which frightened the servants.[18]

Even the Proustian nobility, who could certainly afford it, hesitated on the doorstep of modern hygiene. Pauline de Pange, for example, recalled the moment when, near the turn of the century, the de Broglies had decided to equip their Angevin chateau with heated, running water, "They did not think to hook it up to a bathroom, which seemed a luxury in a hotel and positively reprehensible in a private quarters." In her own home, she remembered the excitement that surrounded her bath: "We spoke about it for days beforehand," the Comtesse wrote. "[Normally] no one in my family took a bath. You washed in a tub with two inches of water, or you sponged yourself over a big basin, but the prospect of plunging yourself into water up to your neck felt pagan... almost shameful."[19] Indeed, the suspicion that there was something louche, and even perilous, about lying in a tub of hot water had not completely dissipated by the end of the nineteenth century. There was little room for error: "An extra minute or a degree too much," the Comtesse de Gencé warned her readers "and one is exposed to all manner of diseases." Author Bill Bryson tells the story of the Duc de Doudeauville who, when asked if he would be installing plumbing in his new house, responded with disdain: "I am not building a hotel."[20]

Where only a tiny percentage of the French had access to private tubs, it made sense for authorities determined to improve popular hygiene to encourage the construction of public baths. But local governments never seemed able to produce enough of them at a price the masses were willing to pay—or to rid them entirely of their reputation for moral compromise. Where it was feasible, privately owned river baths provided an extra (or alternative) supply. Cities also began to build public warm-water pools. These were not meant to function as baths—soap was prohibited, for example—but they often came to be used that way. This did not always add up to a victory for cleanliness, though: a letter to the Paris municipal council in March 1914 from the organization representing the owners of private bathhouses pointed out that the public pool at Ledru-Rollin received 14,000 clients a week but replaced its water only every Tuesday. It would be "audacious," suggested the letter, to claim under these conditions that the bathers [of whom there were almost 400,000 in 1907] "are protected from contagion."[21]

The authorities soon discovered that *bains-douches*, where people would not swim or soak in tubs, but could wash under *aspersion* at a relatively low cost, made the most sense, and these became the facilities most often visited by army recruits and schoolchildren. But visited how often and in what numbers? The dozens of responses from the municipalities surrounding Paris to a questionnaire circulated by the Interior Ministry in 1913–14 paint a less than rosy picture. Most of them wrote that they had "no such facilities" in their towns. Those that did have them often added that they had special prices for students, soldiers, and the indigent. Some businesses distributed tickets for the *bains-douches* to their employees; schools gave tickets to their students. The *bains-douches* offered subscriptions and charged a nominal fee for soap and a towel. In other words, the price of washing was now within reach of all elements of the population. The most striking aspect of these responses, however, is the small number of people who took advantage of these facilities, even where they existed and were subsidized by the local authorities.

In Creteil, in the southeast Paris suburbs, where there were no public baths, the city paid the privately owned facilities of M. Rivaud 600 francs a year to provide services to the local schools. Rivaud had two *cabines* and charged prices ranging from sixty centimes for the general public to fifty for soldiers, and thirty for the poor and schoolchildren—although these last often received free tickets from their schools. In the whole of 1913, out of what must have been a population of thousands, more or less none of whom would have had access to a private bath, Rivaud wrote that only 152 people took advantage of this cut-rate opportunity to bathe. In nearby Sceaux, a *bain-douche* had been built in 1898. It had ten *cabines*, was opened four or five days a week, and averaged *two* customers a week. In Saint-Maur, just the other side of Créteil, the *bains-douches* that opened in 1905 served around five people per day in 1913, although it was free to soldiers, students, and the indigent. The authorities in Sceaux confessed their despair: "It is hard to convince families of the advantages of [these services]," they wrote to the ministry.

Public baths in the capital itself seemed to do a brisker business. Those attached to the pool at Ledru-Rollin delivered 46,387 baths and showers in 1913, up from around 10,000 when it had opened in 1896. Those in the Butte aux Cailles, in the 13th arrondissement, served 95,000 customers in 1913—a 20 percent increase over their four years of existence. In the 18th, the *bains-douches* Hébert welcomed 67,000 customers, and public baths on the rue de Rouvet (19th) 56,409. Overall, the city claimed to have some 7,000 public bathtubs and 850 *cabinets* in *bains-douches*, which provided 2.5 million soakings per year. Other estimates of public bathing were less optimistic. The physician Augustin Cabanès counted fewer than half a million visits to the public baths in Paris in 1903, of which only about one in five were by women. Gustav Tarlé estimated two or three baths per Parisian, per year, but he offered no evidence. Indeed, these numbers all depend on self-reporting and speculations. And even Tarlé was forced to concede that "The tub is not a national institution."

A reasonable guess is that Paris had a respectable number of public baths, and a lot of people used them but not much more than once a year.

On the other hand, the Parisians did not stand out among their compatriots for their aversion to bathing. In fin-de-siècle Lyon, only 150,000 of the locals paid the fifteen centimes that would buy a bath—soap and towel included. Compare French habits to those pertaining elsewhere. Public baths in London served around six million customers in the years before the war, at affordable prices. Austria and Germany had been building public baths for twenty-five years, observed Dr. Courmont. Sadly, he conceded, "the spread of these establishments has been slow to get off the ground in France." It might be more accurate to say that the public baths were there, but the public were not.[22]

In the absence of regular baths, most people practiced *lavage partiel*; that is, they washed some parts and not others with varying degrees of regularity. The most problematical of these parts were the *parties sexuelles*—"this secret domain of primitive practices and venereal disease"—which confounded practical considerations with a lingering culture of modesty (*pudeur*). As folklorist Françoise Loux explains, popular tradition held that "it opposed the laws of God to reveal those secret parts of the body that both nature and modesty require always to remain hidden from sight." Just as it was widely considered indecent to leave shoulders and arms uncovered, legs without stockings, and feet without slippers.[23]

Hygienists and moralists were caught, therefore, between decorum and good health. On the one hand, they worried about a lack of genital hygiene, which they feared might lead to infertility, and on the other about an excess of attention to it, which could pave the road to iniquity. Discretion was called for. And compromise. Thus, when a doctor prescribed a bath to check the fever of the young Comtesse de Broglie, the servants made sure she wore a chemise. Alas, such prudence was no guarantee of sexual reserve in later life. The young Liane de Pougy had also learned as a girl to cover up when she bathed, and she grew up to be one of the Belle Epoque's great courtesans.[24]

The routines of *lavage partiel* and concern with genital hygiene for women led to the growing use of bidets—"the primary necessity for every woman," as Jules Courmont called them.[25] Invented in the early eighteenth century, bidets remained exclusive to the *toilettes* of the well-to-do. And like so many of these *objets de toilette*, they catered as much to luxury as to cleanliness. In the nineteenth century, bidets became increasingly familiar in homes that could afford them, despite having acquired a certain disreputable status, becoming associated with contraception and prostitution, but their use was confined, for the most part, to the urban elites. In the countryside, they remained rare and somewhat exotic—as illustrated in this story recounted by Dr. Cabanès:

> Around 1855 a woman living in the Gers department ordered a bidet from a manufacturer in the capital, which arrived the very day that she was hosting a large dinner party. As a proper hostess, she went to inspect the preparations for the meal before all the guests arrived. What did she find enthroned in the middle the great table, amidst all the other serving dishes, but her bidet sent from Paris! "What's this?" she asked the caterer indignantly, "and what is the meaning of

this joke?" Her interlocuter did not understand her indignation. "It is," he replied ingenuously, "the new soup tureen that arrived for Madame this morning."[26]

Bidets became less exotic, and less misused, as they became more common. By the end of the century, these "ladies' confidants" were appearing in more and more household inventories, and with the arrival of running water, they added the convenience of a *jet d'eau*, which made washing easier. Nonetheless, bidets never became as ubiquitous as their historical reputation might suggest. Mary Lynn Stewart writes that only 5 percent of Parisians owned bidets at the end of the nineteenth century, and, as bathtubs became more common, their importance faded.[27]

Whether they used a bidet or not, women experienced the advance of hygiene differently than men did. In a world of so little salubriousness, generally, it is hard to say who had less of it. There is some reason to think that men visited public baths and pools, and jumped naked into rivers, more frequently than women did, and men clearly benefited more than women from the institutional settings of *bains par aspersion* (i.e., showers) in the military and in the prisons. In poorer and rural households without *conforts*, where the weekly wash happened over a big basin shared by the family, fathers and older sons probably enjoyed precedence over their wives, mothers, and sisters; although young boys and girls were likely treated the same. The Englishwoman, Edith Hall, born in 1908, for example, remembered that in her house, before the First World War, the children bathed first, and then the father, while her mother kept the hot water boiling on the stove. But Hall does not recall her mother ever having bathed, herself. We have no reason to believe that the pecking order was different on the other side of the Channel. Eugen Weber writes that young girls in Orléans visited the public baths only once in their lives, on the eve of their wedding. Charles Rouleau, born in the 1880s, knew of "old women washed only for their burials."[28]

On the contrary, households where water was easier to come by, and especially among the elites, where cleanliness had always been the residue of luxury, the presence of strictly female spaces—*cabinets de toilette* and *salles de bains*—suggests that women spent more time and effort taking care of their bodies; such is the implication of the Comtesse de Gencé's advice to her readers to top off their "ablutions matinales," which would themselves count as a great leap forward, with a few drops of eau de cologne on their lingerie.[29] Obviously, in the great majority of homes, small and without amenities, where the women worked as hard as the men and got just as dirty, and where the "ablutions matinales" consisted of a handful of cold water splashed on the face, the economy of hygiene looked very different. School primers might have told young readers that a proper woman wore clean clothes and had her hair done "even when she was alone." But such advice had little relevance to the lives of the majority of women in fin-de-siècle France.

Cleaner Peasants?

In the history of manners, innovation tends to gestate in the cities before spreading across the countryside. Taking stock of the state of hygiene in France at the turn of the twentieth century, therefore, it seems reasonable to ask how far the hygiene revolution, crawling forward in the towns, managed to reach the villages. The answer, much as we might expect, is ambiguous: meaningful change, on the one hand, and the durability of old structures and routines, on the other.

Théodore Chalmel, teaching in Brittany in the 1920s, was not sanguine on this point. "Throughout the centuries," he wrote, "no one in the village [had] practiced hygiene. People cared nothing for keeping clean. Filthiness reigned everywhere . . . profound ignorance and pernicious practice spread misery."[30] Conversely, historian Jean-Luc Mayaud refers to an imperial survey of 1866 in which peasants described themselves as being "better housed, better fed, better clothed" than in the past.[31]

How much better? It is certainly an exaggeration to talk about any substantial "modernization" of rural France before the Fourth Republic. The water and sewer systems that were changing the landscape of hygiene in the cities were slow to touch the countryside. If the price of soap fell by two-thirds in Paris between 1840 and 1914, where in a village would a peasant buy a bar of soap?[32] "The misery to be found in the villages," wrote the novelist Gustave Drouineau in 1892, "is more heartbreaking than anything seen in the cities."[33] Even so, there is reason to think that the countryside was a healthier place in 1914 than it had been in 1870.

The overall picture of rural hygiene remains complicated. Jules Renard, writing in the 1890s, extolled the rude good health of the peasants, despite their insouciant ways with elementary hygiene: "They are never sick," he wrote.[34] Of course, such broad generalizations are neither right nor wrong. Inevitably, some regions produced stronger bodies than others. In the Touraine, for example, "the very vigorous race of countrymen" led to an exceptionally low incidence of military exemption. On the other hand, an "astonishingly high number of young peasants in the Artois" were excused from military service because of their physical infirmities—rheumatism, pleurisy, and other lung-related frailties.[35]

In the Beauce, infant mortality declined modestly between 1860 and 1890, "due to improved conditions of *accouchement* [birthing]." Although old problems of hygiene, hard work, and poor diet for pregnant women remained and kept the infant mortality rate from falling further. Even as the end of the century approached, a fifth of newborns in the region still failed to reach their first birthday. The mortality rate actually rose for those aged between twenty and sixty, as rampant alcoholism continued to make its particular contribution to the mortality statistics.[36]

We ordinarily think of the countryside as exporters of population and of cities as net killers. The numbers presented by the agronomic engineer, Max Le Couppey de la Forest, however, tell a different story (Table 8.1). Le Couppey explained that while improvements in urban water supplies were reducing the incidence of typhoid and diphtheria, bad water continued to kill people in the countryside. As long as they continued to take their water out of wells, and as long as those wells sat next to dung heaps, Le Couppey observed unsympathetically, peasants would continue to poison themselves—"a sin of ignorance," in the eyes of doctor Henri Henrot, a member of the Reims medical faculty.[37] In its 1915 report to the prefect, the Conseil Générale of the Nièvre tied the rural exodus precisely to the dirtiness of the villages. "How can anyone

Table 8.1 Mortality in France, 1902

Place	Population	Mortality	Rate per 1,000 Inhabitants
Countryside	23,903,191	448,960	19.7
Cities	15,058,754	335,916	19.2
Paris	2,660,559	49,070	18.4

Source: Max Le Couppey de la Forest, *Alimentation en eau potable dans les campagnes* (Paris: Imprimerie et Librairie A. Munier), 1904, 3.

love places," the council asked, "where the streets are never cleaned, there no sewers, the latrines are nauseating, the water is questionable, [and] where medical care and surgery are absent? How can anyone with a taste for hygiene . . . love the countryside?" Certainly, the state would have loved to clean up the water supply in the villages. But pipes and pumps were expensive, and local authorities, who presumably cared more, did not have the money.[38]

There is a tendency in some of the historical literature—we have already seen it in the case of the urban working class—that reads the tenacity of peasant *insalubrité* as an act, not of cultural inertia (or the simple absence of practicable alternatives), but of cultural resistance. "The casual approach to cleanliness," writes historian André Rauch,

> The rejection of water, the tolerance for the bodily odors of people and animals, the peasants' reclamation of excrement and trash become the means by which the popular classes recognize their common identity: The strength of their opposition to the *hygienist* bourgeoisie and its normative measures define their existence.[39]

In other words, by refusing to wash and contaminating their own drinking water the peasants were fighting a rearguard action against the modern industrial world and their own irrelevance.

This purports to explain, as well, why rural France held on so resolutely to its folk notions of dirt and cleanliness. Birthing practices retained a strong element of magical thinking, as did the treatment of newborns. In Haut-Languedoc, mothers still gave birth, not in bed but in a litter in front of the fire, and midwives, when they cut the umbilical cord, made sure it was not touched by fire or water, "lest the child perish by these elements." By the end of the century, newborns were first washed in water that had been boiled but then, in what must have been a widespread custom, they were slathered in lard or oil and swaddled from head to toe.[40] In her study of women's private lives before the Great War, Anne-Marie Sohn discovered dozens of instances of what we would call superstition from across the country—pertaining to cutting children's nails ("It will turn them into thieves") or cutting an infant's hair (which will cause it to fall out); washing a child's face in urine to prevent acne or using lice to prevent sickness.[41]

Adults applied the same casual approach to washing to themselves. "Clean bodies remained unknown," observes Sohn. The peasant, explained Gustave Drouineau, had no fear of dirt and had no notion of the dangers it contained. What then was the sense of washing his hands every time he walked out of the stable? Or of washing his feet today when, amid the dust and mud and shit of the countryside, they would simply get dirty again tomorrow?

Accordingly, out of both habit and practicality peasant *toilettes* remained *sommaires* (summary): a quick dash of cold water out of a shallow *baquet* before heading off to the fields or to school. In turn-of-the-century Limousin, "daily washes are considered unnecessary: no one takes a bath . . . men shave twice a month, and women comb their hair once a week, for church." As for the objects necessary for keeping clean, "There are none." The women, added Drouineau, were no better than the men—despite the fact their hygienic needs were different, and in some respects more acute.[42] Tampons did not exist for menstruating women, and the reluctance to touch these "private places" made these matters worse. Adding insult to injury, note ethnographers Robert Bouiller and Louis Challet, local custom in the Forez region forbade them from coming too near the cooking and the washing, lest their "impurity be communicated to these preparations."[43] Across the French countryside, folklore and departmental archives tell the same story: whatever it said in the grade-school primers and the military manuals, it is hard to conclude that their instruction on hygiene had as yet penetrated deeply into the daily life of the peasantry. The local archives Sohn examines are a compendium of "dirt and vermin" well into the twentieth century; for instance, the child in Troyes "covered in a layer of lice several millimeters thick."[44]

At the same time, the stasis in the countryside can be exaggerated. If the Republic's "civilizing mission" advanced slowly, it advanced just the same. Elementary school lessons and barracks regulations could not effect change overnight, but they planted new ideas about cleanliness in millions of French heads. Weber observes that, if baths were still unknown in the Corrèze in 1913, schoolchildren had learned to wash once a week. Moreover, best practices were supported by the general improvement in the economic circumstances of the peasantry. The twenty-five years between the end of the Second Republic and the consolidation of the Third witnessed a widespread and substantial improvement in rural incomes, rents, and wages.[45] The arrival of the railroads, which helped city culture reach the villages, and the steady rise in agricultural prices and peasant incomes, alongside a helping hand from the Crédit Agricole, put certain improvements within reach of most people in the countryside. The aspirational Strauss law of 1902 required all communes to provide drinkable water to their inhabitants; a companion law of 1903 helped poor communes pay for it. There was not enough money to construct water or sewer systems in the countryside; running water inside peasant homes would have to wait for the post-1945 boom. But country life improved on the margins.[46]

Clothing serves as a leading indicator of this. Sara Hume's study of clothing of rural Alsace near the turn of the century suggests just how much things were changing on this front. Hume's analysis of photographs, museum collections, and personal inventories reveals the growing size and complexity of peasant wardrobes; country clothes increasingly came to resemble city clothes. In most households by 1900, men and women had multiple sets of shirts and trousers and underclothes—representing a certain amount of wealth. Moreover, the quality of the clothes was better and even incorporated elements of fashion. "Rural Alsatians," Hume writes, "did not simply replace their regional dress with urban dress; they participated in the general transformation from nineteenth-century clothing practices to twentieth-century ones."[47]

Alsace probably represented the forward edge of this trend. Abbé Gorse, for example, complained that poorer children in turn-of-the-century Limousin still went out "in winter without hats, socks, or mufflers."[48] Babies across France continued to be swaddled into the Fourth Republic, and reports from the countryside suggest that parents remained less than diligent about changing the swaddling clothes—or washing them even when they were changed: "Soiled 'diapers' were often just hung by the fire to dry. After a while," said one report, "the smell was repulsive." It was said that a "decent" mother would "unwrap" her baby at least once a day. But one woman in the Seine-et-Oise explained to authorities that she *never* changed her son's swaddling, "because it was pointless." On the other hand, once out of swaddling, children changed their clothes with the same frequency as the rest of the family; that is, between once a week and once a month.[49]

Across the countryside, peasant clothing was becoming lighter, more diverse, and more comfortable. Costumes in the mid-nineteenth century had still been heavy and coarse. They were expected to last a working lifetime, and, once dirty, they remained so: "a layer of clayish soil covered the bottom of a farmer's trousers," explained Eugène Bougeâtre, "while his wife's skirts were stained with cowshit. A person's clothes bore the odor of his animals: the carter smelled like a horse, the shepherd his sheep, the cowherd his stable." Even at the turn of the century, remembered Pierre-Jakez Hélias, the Bretons were still wearing hemp shirts, "day and night until they were stiff with sweat and soil." Linen was reserved for Sundays.[50]

Much of this traditional wardrobe was un-washable; it would simply have fallen apart. For the pieces that could be exposed to water and detergent, *lavage* was such a huge undertaking that it occurred only rarely and was limited mostly to the household linen, even in villages that had their own *lavoirs*, the communal washhouses. Peasants asked themselves with reason whether it was worth the bother to wash objects that would be filthy again soon enough.

Cotton arrived in the French countryside beginning in the 1840s and soon began to remake clothing culture. Wool was better for keeping warm, but cotton was more practical for outerwear. It was easy to dye, and it did not fall apart when washed. Best of all, the Industrial Revolution continuously drove down the price of cotton fabric. Peter Ward writes that the price of a yard of plain-woven calico went down by more than 80 percent between 1780 and 1830, and it kept getting cheaper.[51] This meant that people in the countryside could afford more shirts, for example, and could put on a clean one more often. "Every woman," wrote Michelet, "used to wear a blue or black dress that she kept for years without washing it, for fear that it would fall to pieces. Today her husband can cover her in flower-printed cotton for the price of a day's wage." Peasant clothing, wrote Théodore Chalmel, had been transformed: the fabrics are more varied, along with their shape, their colors, and their comfort. "More and more, peasant wardrobes are becoming more modern and losing their local character."[52]

For clothing that touched the body, cotton was a small miracle of comfort, and as it spread, it produced a proliferation of undergarments, even among the poor. Anne-Marie Sohn calls the nineteenth, "the century of *linge* (underwear)."[53] At the beginning of the century, the elites might have worn linen undergarments, and most everyone would have had something in the way of shirts and stockings under their outside clothes. Few women wore *caleçons*—what we would call underpants—which anyway had a scandalous reputation. Layers of petticoats were more common, although early in the nineteenth century, some fashionable women began to wear *pantalons*. Men more often put drawers between their skin and their trousers.

By the middle of the century, however, *caleçons* were covering ever more French bottoms. Naturally, the habit first captured bourgeois women and then slowly worked its way down the social scale. By the end of the Second Empire, according to Philippe Perrot, even working-class women were wearing them.[54] That was in the cities. It took a while for the practice to reach provincial towns and even longer for the peasants to adopt cotton *sous-vêtements*. Still, it is easy to imagine how eagerly both men and women welcomed the end of wool underwear and the age of cotton. And no one who made the switch to cotton knickers ever returned to wool.

As ever, peasant practices chased those that had already taken hold of the urban population. By the beginning of the new century, according to Anaïs Albert, the culture of *lingerie* had changed dramatically. Working from postmortem inventories of working-class possessions, collected in the dossiers called *scellés*, used in the settlement of debts, she finds a "profusion of underclothes"—petticoats, chemises, camisoles, corsets and *caches-corsets*: mostly hardy and practical but sometimes fancy and seductive—the consequence of mass production and sharply declining prices. These were mostly practical garments, made from cotton, flannel, or wool. Although there were rare examples of *sous-vêtements* in silk or trimmed with lace; even the popular classes sought seduction and distinction, so far as they could afford it. *Caleçons* were rare enough to suggest that "The men of the [Parisian] popular classes were hardly ahead of the inhabitants of the Limousin mountains, who began to put on underwear around the same time, 1890–1900"—not a very high standard. Of course, to *wear* underclothes was not the same thing as to *change* underclothes. Evidence suggests it was not out of bounds for men to switch underpants once a month; to change them once a week would have put a man at the outer limits of personal hygiene.[55]

Other elements of the peasant wardrobe also improved. For outerwear, even the rural working class began to give up their smocks (*paletot*) for proper overcoats. "Almost all the prosperous farmers," observed Antoine Desforges of his native Morvan region, "buy themselves a goatskin coat." In Normandy, noted Henri Baudrillart, "*souliers* [shoes], formerly rare, have become common—at least for non-work days," and so had socks.[56] Peter Ward retells a story from ethnographer Yvonne Verdier about a woodcutter's daughter who wore her pinafore to school for a week, then turned it inside and wore it for another week, in order to save her mother the work of washing it. But such behavior became less common in the new century, and this proved a particular blessing for children.[57] More and cleaner clothes meant fewer lice. Exchanging wood *sabots* for shoes meant less deformation of their feet. And lighter clothing meant less itching and sweating and more freedom of movement. The very young of both sexes still wore dresses up to age eight. Jean Cornec, remembering his early youth in the Breton countryside, wore a dress and nothing underneath (called a *cul nu*) "perfect for satisfying his natural functions."[58] Yet French children of the Belle Époque undeniably went to school better clothed and better shod than their parents had done.

Curiously, one expert stood firm against the new styles and the new fabrics—Hans Gustav Jaeger, the German doctor and zoologist who was at the forefront of the "Hygienist" movement of the fin-de-siècle. Jaeger saw in trousers "a dangerous source of pathologies" that exposed legs to chills at the same time as they overheated the abdomen and interfered with circulation, which explained the contemporary epidemic of men with bloated stomachs and what he called "sparrows' feet." He prescribed culottes, carefully closed off at the knee and made from virgin wool, as the cure for this unfortunate condition.[59]

Where people lived could not respond to new demands for comfort as quickly as what they wore. Worn-out houses could not be abandoned and replaced like worn-out clothes. It is self-evidently true, moreover, that life on the farm necessarily remained dirtier than life in the town. The soil and the animals and the manure are not incidental to peasant life; they are its essentials. "Rural hygiene," wrote Drouineau,

> would make no progress without accommodating the needs of life on the land. . . . Conditions are simply not the same city as in the country. The collective urban life does not resemble the isolated life of the rural family or involve the same intimate contact with the domestic animals who are such an important part of their existence—with which they cohabit and work and do business.[60]

The Third Republic was especially interested in the quality of rural housing, as the most basic element of rural welfare, and it sponsored a number of surveys of housing conditions across the country. Economists Alfred de Foville and Henri Baudrillart produced the most comprehensive of these. Baudrillart's three-volume work, *Populations agricoles de France*, appeared in 1885, and Foville's two-volume study, *Les maisons-types. Enquête sur les conditions de l'habitation en France*, was finished in 1899. These two studies became the foundation of a huge literature on both national and regional circumstances. The picture they sketch reveals elements of both progress and stasis.

The principal lines of division ran unsurprisingly through region and class. In the deepest parts of *la France profonde*—up in the mountains of the Savoie, in the Auvergne and the Dordogne, and in proverbially backward Brittany—progress came slowly. Jules Rochard wrote of the Jura that some people still lived in grass-covered huts, like warm-weather Eskimos. Émile Guillaumin, the well-known and peasant writer, born in the Allier in 1873, left this unsentimental picture of dirt and density in the peasant home:

> The [farmhouse] was a mess: crowded, untidy, dark, the earthen floor almost impossible to keep clean, dirt inescapable, when [streets], stable and yard were a mass of muck, gluey and degrading, clinging to clogs and clothes, trailing into the house, denying all hope of freedom from dirt for the house or for oneself . . . the family, sometimes the servants, too, slept several to a bed, sick and well together. Only the very ill, those with a disgusting ailment or taking their time to die, were somehow segregated.[61]

In the Charentais, according to sociologist François Julien-Labruyère, the majority of peasant homes still had dirt floors. Up until the war, farmhouses across the country commonly covered their windows with oil paper, "given the rarity and price of glass." Well past the turn of the century, hygienists and government agents, tramping through isolated villages in the most backward parts of the country, continued to complain about the immovable *saleté* of peasant homes.[62]

Generalizations, however, can be deceptive. First, from top to bottom rural society was steeply differentiated: landless day laborers and domestics, at one end; well-off agricultural entrepreneurs, at the other. Agricultural laborers, remarks Michel Augé-Laribé, lived in a state of "the most complete and permanent misery." The poorest were naturally the worst housed, and descriptions of the ramshackle dwellings of the rural working class at the end of the century recall those of an earlier period: dirt for a floor, thatch for a roof, humid walls, one-room interiors bare of anything but the most essential furnishings, and little separation between man and beast. Augustine Rouvière remembered her house in the Cévennes: "We lived virtually without furniture. A cooker, a table and chairs, a cot for my little daughter and son, who slept in the same room [as my husband and me], a mattress laid on crates and covered by a bedspread: this was our first home."[63]

Daniel Desbois, born at the turn of the twentieth century to a family of peasants near the Ouche river in the region around Dijon, left a similar description of his boyhood home:

> It was a charming house, aside from the fact that it possessed not the least *confort*. Like all country farms and houses, it had no running water. The *commodités* [i.e., the latrine] consisted of a couple of planks of wood, set at a considerable distance from the house, memorable principally for the flies it attracted. Since there was no bathroom, everyone washed up in the bedroom; in the summer, the *toilette* moved outside. A cistern served both animals and people. For decent drinking water, we had to head down the hill to the spring *des Patureaux*, which provided for the village. Comfort and even hygiene seemed completely absent [from our lives].[64]

Laurence Wylie records similarly that at the turn of the century in the Vaucluse village of Roussillon, inhabitants still had to lug their water a quarter of a mile up a steep hill, from the fountain to their homes, or buy it from the waterman, who brought it up in wheeled barrels pulled by donkeys. But Roussillon was lucky to have a progressive mayor, who worked with the local *député* to have water piped into the reservoir above the village, allowing the village to have a system of running water long before its neighbors.[65] Not far away, in the hills of sheep country, shepherds still slept in tiny stone huts, while, on the very lowest rung of this ladder, young farmhands lay their heads on piles of straw in the stables, next to the livestock. Of everyone in France, concluded a study for the labor ministry in 1913, "agricultural workers are the worst housed."[66]

Second, things were changing. For one, the most disadvantaged parts of the rural population were disappearing. According to historian Jean-Luc Mayaud, wage-laborers made up 56 percent of the rural workforce, around four million individuals, in 1862. That number had shrunk to three million by 1900, as emigration to the cities, rising prices for agricultural products, falling prices for building materials, and the increasing exchange between town and country lifted fortunes even for the rural working class. Wages went up. More peasants were able to acquire their own farms and their own farmhouses. The rural exodus meant that a lot of the worst housing now sat empty, and the reshuffling allowed remaining families to "move up," as it were. Peasants, as Ronald Hubscher notes, had always put their animals first. But now, a little further above the line of subsistence, they could also concentrate on "l'amélioration de la condition humaine."[67]

Writing in 1909, geographer J. Levainville traced the evolution of peasant housing in the Morvan, lying between the Nièvre and the Côte d'Or.[68] Most of the homes in this region had only one floor; two-story houses were rare and found only in the more important towns. The quality of construction, he wrote in 1909, had recently begun to improve with the increasing use of cement and limestone imported from the Low Countries, and most peasants had learned to move their *fumiers* and stables away from the main house. On the other hand, he observed, the reputation for filth in the older cottages is "well earned." The main space that served as kitchen, dining room, and bedroom is low, dark, airless; the unfinished walls sweat dampness. The insouciance of the inhabitants makes things worse. They feed their animals—pigs, sheep, goats, and chickens—on the floor, when the beasts come in to escape the winter rain. The large open hearth lets the winter wind into the house, while the smoke necessitates that the door, the sole opening to the outside, be left open. Newer houses, Levainville reported, were much better. Ventilated by five or six windows, with flagstone floors and impermeable walls, they now had three rooms: the largest serves as a kitchen, parents' room, and *salle de reunion*; the second is for the children; the third a storeroom with space for a bed. Generally speaking, the material culture of sleep remained cramped and primitive in the country. This compared unfavorably with the beds and mattresses of the Parisian popular classes that Anaïs Albert identified in the *scellés*. Not everyone in those households had their own bed. But there is no mention in the 1895 inventories Albert examined of the pallets and other makeshift arrangements so common in country cottages.[69]

Still, the modern world was arriving in the Morvan little by little, especially as peasants, particularly those who had been urban nannies, returned to their villages from Paris, bringing with them money and "a better appreciation for elementary laws of hygiene." However closely they followed the laws of hygiene, Levainville remarked that the small and stocky race of Morvaniers is anyway "vigorous enough that centenarians are far from rare."

The map of progress in peasant housing up to 1914 inevitably retraced the patterns of the previous century. Regions that were more linked to national and international markets had higher incomes. The new prosperity fed the creation of a rural middle class, and their standards were copied, insofar as possible, by the lower classes, even as it widened the economic gap between the top and the bottom of village society. The most successful inhabitants in those villages built new homes—or rather, had them built by carpenters, masons, and roofers. Others laid down flagstone floors over the dirt and replaced their thatched roofs with slate or tile. The growing middle class of farmers added upper floors to their houses, increasing the distance between living space and workspace, filling those spaces with furniture, and keeping them clean. They consigned livestock to outbuildings. As for outhouses, notes Albert Goursaud of the Limousin, even the poor were building them—perhaps just a small jerry-built hut, hiding a simple hole with two planks across it, but at least now hidden from plain view.[70]

Pierre Leshauris, a teacher and small holder in the Landais, who dedicated himself in retirement to writing a history of daily life as he had known it, lived in a large multigenerational house, with five rooms and two fireplaces.[71] Most houses in his village of Geloux still had dirt floors up until the Great War, but the Leshauris home—"Lagraulet"—was laid with red tile, "washed every Sunday morning." It was only in 1910 that the house got glass to replace the open, barred windows that had previously linked the interior to the outside, which significantly reduced the cold and humidity inside. The kitchen had a stove, a long table surrounded by chairs and benches, and a slatted dresser-drainer for the dishes. In the great room the fire burned all year round. The house had plenty of furniture, including a grandfather clock made of pine and two armoires for larger kitchenware. A porcelain gas lamp, with lampshade, illuminated the room. Sausages and hams hung from the ceiling. An old gun—"strictly for ornamentation, since there were no hunters in the family"—sat next to the fireplace. An attached out-room was fitted out for slaughtering, laundry, and storing foodstuffs. It also housed a bicycle and a small plow.

There was a bedroom for each couple with daub walls and small windows. The grandparents slept on a four-poster bed with curtains. The others enjoyed somewhat less luxurious accommodations. Leshauris remarks that, "instead of the wool mattresses of bourgeois bedrooms, at Lagraulet, as in the homes of all the local sharecroppers, everyone still slept on *paillasses*." All the beds had hemp sheets and a cotton blanket, and all the bedrooms had an armoire, a sideboard, where the bed linen and clothes were stored, and a couple of chairs.

It was a sign of progress that in the bedrooms of Maria and Germaine, the two married children, "modern innovations brought a new element of comfort: a *table de toilette*, draped in cheap lace, on which sat a water jug, and a flowered porcelain basin—seldom used, since the inhabitants normally washed in the kitchen sink—just like the varnished chamber pot that sat on the nightstand." Neither the text nor the map of the property mentions a latrine among the outbuildings.

Leshauris remarks that Lagraulet had a "reputation for cleanliness." The women washed underwear and napkins once a week, either at the well or the nearby stream. The *grande lessive* of sheets, towels, and cotton covers was a collective bit of heavy labor that occupied the women for a couple of days twice a year, once in spring and once in autumn. This semiannual laundry *corvée* points to an element of "progress" that often gets overlooked. Simply put, expectations of cleaner children and cleaner, better-furnished households meant more work for those who had to take care of them. In this respect, improved hygiene often became the opposite of liberation for the wives and mothers and daughters who needed to make it happen.

Hygiene at the *Fin-de-Siècle*

The enormous majority of French people in the Belle Epoque lived amid material conditions that we would find intolerable, with standards that, by today's measure, seem almost barbaric. Most citizens of the Third Republic in its ripe middle age enjoyed neither running water nor indoor plumbing. They did not have a lot of clothes or comforts and lived in often crushing and crowded conditions, riddled with tuberculosis and other diseases. Every day they drank water that had a decent chance of killing them. Most people were aware of germ theory and may have understood vaguely that hygiene was the enemy of disease; at least that was the lesson they had learned in school and, for the young men, in the army. But cleanliness was far from being the default state of their lives.

Indeed, if there is one truth that leaps out of school primers, hygiene commission reports, and experts' recommendations, it is the chasm between what the French were being told to do and what they were actually doing. Every publication that purported to offer advice on the proper habits of *propreté* contained the same general set of suggestions: wash your hands, your feet, your face, your *parties privées*; take a bath now and then. Keep your outhouse clean. Change your socks and your underclothes regularly and your outer garments a bit less regularly. Don't throw your night soil into the gutter. Don't drink to excess. Don't urinate or spit in the street.[72] The peasantry received their own set of instructions from hygienists and local authorities: Keep your dung heaps away from the front door and the well; keep the animals out of human spaces; lay down a real floor, switch out thatched roofs for slate and tile, maximize light and air, and make sure the smoke goes up a chimney. The experts recognized that country life was bound to be dirtier than city life but insisted, nonetheless, on the importance of homes and persons as clean as possible. This was the civilizing mission to which the Third Republic had committed itself.

It would be three generations and two more Republics before that mission was accomplished. It is more enlightening, however, to think about how far the story of French hygiene had come by 1900, rather than about how far it still had to go. That distance is best measured in mortality statistics and other proxies of health. Life expectancy across the country rose from around thirty-five years (at birth) in 1800 to forty-five years in 1900 and almost fifty on the eve of the First World War. Interestingly, a second proxy of a healthy body, the estimated median height of army recruits between the battles of Austerlitz and the Marne, increased only a fraction: 1 percent (to approximately 5'5"). The number of recruits in the Haut-Forez region, lying between Lyon and Clermont-Ferrand, rejected for military service, fell between the Second Empire and 1890 from 70 percent to 52 percent. Arguably, the fact that over half the young men were too weak or short or deformed or rheumatic to qualify for service was continuing cause for concern. And substantial regional differences also survived: conscripts from the North and East were still persistently taller than those from the South and West. Nonetheless, there is reasonable evidence of some overall improvement in human capital.[73]

Much of the gain in life expectancy can be explained by falling rates of infant mortality. "Monstrously high" at the beginning of the nineteenth century, these came

Table 8.2 Comparative Infant Mortality, 1909

Country	Mortality per 100 births	Country	Mortality per 100 births
Russia	27.2	France	14.3
Austria	20.2	England	12.1
Hungary	19.9	Switzerland	10.8
Germany	17.8	Sweden	7.7
Italy	15.6	Norway	6.7

Source: Jules Courmont, *Précis d'hygiène* (Paris: Masson et Cie., 1914), 30.

down gradually—from almost 200 (per 1,000 live births) in 1800 to around 150 in 1900, which left France more or less in the middle of the European pack (Table 8.2). According to the National Institute of Hygiene, that number dropped by 20 percent between 1901 and 1913—from 142 to 113 per 100,000. Of course, dying infants were unevenly distributed through the country—highest in rural areas, particularly in places where the wet-nursing industry was well established, and somewhat lower in the more developed agricultural regions and in the towns. In 1908, the national toll of infant mortality was 13.7 percent; in Finistère, it was 23.7 percent. Both the high absolute numbers and the relative decline were driven by hygienic practices having to do with childbirth and the treatment of very young babies.[74]

Moreover, the graph describing this notable, if not yet revolutionary, demographic success was jagged, rather than smooth. In years of widespread epidemic, especially cholera, mortality spiked upward, even while it continued its secular decline. On the local level, long-term gains in mortality were often interrupted by brief but deadly irruptions of typhoid fever and diphtheria, or especially cold winters and hot summers. Lungs remained overall, and by far, the most vulnerable organs—tuberculosis and the vaguer diagnosis of *phtisie* (consumption) consistently outpacing other causes of death.[75]

Neither bad water nor tainted air nor infectious diseases like measles and scarlet fever struck the population randomly. They were all tied, to one degree or another, to the human environment. In the countryside, as we have seen, housing got a little better, water a bit more dependable. The abuse of alcohol began to decline—perhaps a success for the schools, which preached relentlessly against the abuse of spirits. The government often helped matters with projects to drain malarial swamps and dig new public wells.[76] In the cities, the rich, who lived upwind and had less polluted air, who had more space and more servants to keep things clean, and who inhabited buildings with better water and sewer connections, lived years longer than their less fortunate compatriots. Those who crowded into the especially repulsive *îlots insalubres* suffered the worst deficit in good health and life expectancy. Mortality rates in the slums of Rouen and Marseille were 25 percent higher than in other parts of those cities. French rates continued to suffer in comparison to cities in England and Germany.[77] All these differences, both within France and across Europe, were clearly a function of vast disparities in access to hygiene. In sum, on the doorstep of the Great War, the job of cleaning up the French remained half done.

Notes

1. For a report on the state of French hygiene generally, see Olivier Faure, "Hygiène, hygiénisme et santé publique en France, XIXe-XXe siècles," in Didier Nourrisson (dir.), *Éducation à la santé, XIXe-XXe siècles* (Rennes: Éditions ENSP, 2002), 23–7.
2. Anne-Marie Sohn, *Chrysalides. Femmes dans la vie privée (XIX-XXe siècles)*, vol. I (Paris: Publications de la Sorbonne, 1996), 307.
3. On the true state of *salubrité* in the military, see Gustave Drouineau, "Hygiène Rurale," in Jules Rochard, *Encyclopédie d'hygiène et de médecine publique*, tome IV (Paris: Veuve Babé et Cie., 1892), 669; Georges-Henri Tellier, *La santé du soldat. Manuel d'hygiène pratique à l'usage des hommes de troupe* (Paris: Henri-Charles Lavauzelle, 1903), 9–36 *passim*; and Charles Viry, *Principes d'hygiène militaire* (Paris: L. Bataille et Cie., 1896), 124, 423–5. On advertisements for dental care, see Anaïs Albert, *La vie à credit. La consommation des classes populaires à Paris (années 1880–1920)* (Paris: Éditions de la Sorbonne, 2021), 66.
4. Dr. Augustin Cabanès, *Moeurs intimes du passé. Deuxième série: La vie aux bains* (Paris: Albin Michel, 1909), 384–5; Henri Napias, *L'assistance publique dans le département de Sambre-et-Loire* (Paris: L. Bataille et Ciel, 1893), 19 and 30; and Henri Méry and Joseph Génévrier, *Hygiène scolaire* (Paris: J.-B. Baillière et Fils, 1914), 64.
5. *Le Confortable. Journal de l'Économie Domestique et Ménagère* (1867), no page numbers.
6. For a sample of advice books, see Dr. Louis Dufestel, *Hygiène scolaire* (Paris: Octave Doin et Fils, 1919); A. Féret, *Études sur l'hygiène scolaire et d'intérêt général. 1900* (Paris: A. Féret, 1900); Jeannine Martay, *L'hygiène dans les soins de toilette chez la jeune fille et chez la femme* (Paris: Librairie des "Annales Politiques et Littéraires," 1909), 11; and Ville de Bayonne. Bureau Municipal d'Hygiène, *La propreté de l'écolier: conseils pratiques aux parents* (Bayonne: Imprimerie Lamaignère, 1909). For advice aimed particularly at upper-class women, see Baronne Staffe, *Le cabinet de toilette. Agencement et ameublement. Soins corporels. Conseils et recettes. Bijoux. Chiffons et dentelles* (Paris: Flammarion, 1893), *passim*; Jules Renard, "Journal d'un bourgeois de Corbigny," *Bulletin de la Société Nivernaise* 30 (1936): 377.
7. Staffe, *Le cabinet de toilette*, 113; Jacques Léonard, *Archives du corps. La santé au XIXe siècle* (Rennes: Ouest France, 1986), 121.
8. Françoise Loux, *Traditions et soins d'aujourd'hui: Anthropologie du corps et professions de santé* (Paris: Interéditions, 1990), 53; also Martay, *L'hygiène dans les soins de toilette*, 72; and Guy Thuillier, *Pour une histoire quotidienne en Nivernais* (Paris: EHESS, 1977), 51.
9. Lise Bésème-Pia, *Folklore des dents en Champagne-Ardenne, à l'usage des dentists, des patients et des petits enfants* (Langes: Éditions Dominique Guéniot, 2010), *passim*.
10. Gustave Lagneau, *La statistique du recrutement de l'armée, considéré sous le rapport démographique* (Orléans: E. Colas, 1882), 38.
11. Stephan Reynolds, *A Poor Man's House* (London: John Lane, 1909), 89, cited in Victoria Kelley, *Soap and Water: Cleanliness, Dirt & the Working Classes in Victorian and Edwardian Britain* (London: Bloomsbury, 2010), 39.
12. Jean-Claude Daumas, *La révolution matérielle. Une histoire de la consommation: France, XIXe-XXe siècles* (Paris: Flammarion, 2018), 20.
13. Cabanès. *Moeurs intimes*, 372, note 2.

14　Maurice Robert, *Mémoire et identité: traverses ethnohistoriques en Limousin* (Limoges: Maison Limousine des Sciences de l'Homme, 1991), 248–9.
15　Thomas Piketty, *Les hauts revenus en France au XXe siècle: inégalités et distributions (1901–1998)* (Paris: Grasset, 2001), 679. On the price of bread, see Jean Fourastié and Béatrice Bazil, *Pourquoi les prix baissent* (Paris: Hachette, 1984), 252. On clothing, see Daumas, *La révolution matérielle*, 178. Also see Lisa Tiersten, *Marianne in the Market: Envisioning Consumer Society in Fin-de-Siècle France* (Berkeley: University of California Press, 2001), 162.
16　Daumas, *La révolution matérielle*, 183.
17　Staffe, *Le cabinet de toilette*, 51–4.
18　Jean-Pierre Chaline, *Les bourgeois de Rouen: une élite urbaine au XIXe siècle* (Paris: Presses de la Fondation Nationale des Sciences Politiques, 1982), 194.
19　Pauline de Pange, *Comment j'ai vu 1900* (Paris: Grasset, 1975), 195–6.
20　Comtesse de Gencé, *Le cabinet de toilette d'une honnête femme* (Paris: P. Pancier, 1909), 61. Bill Bryson, *At Home: A Short History of Private Life* (London: Black Swan, 2010), 224.
21　On this letter, and the discussion of *bains-douches* that follows, see Letter to Messieurs les conseillers municipaux de la ville de Paris, March 25, 1914, from the Syndicat général des propriétaires des bains, in AP, DM 5 0017, dossier "Contrôle des bains-douches."
22　On the issue of bathing in France and elsewhere, see Cabanès, *Moeurs intimes*, 378; Jules Courmont, *Précis d'hygiène* (Paris: Masson et Cie., 1914), 69–70; Roger Leblanc, *Le savon de la préhistoire au XXIe siècle* (Montreuil l'Argile: Éditions Pierrann, 2001), 274; Jules Rochard, *Traité d'hygiène publique et privée* (Paris: Octave Doin, 1897), 64; and Gustave Tarlé, *À propos de l'hygiène du paysan en Bretagne* (Montpellier: Imprimerie Grollier, 1911), 61.
23　Françoise Loux, *Pratiques et savoirs populaires: le corps dans la société traditionnelle* (Paris: Berger-Levrault), 83.
24　The *peignoir de bain*, according to Olivier Le Goff, represented a revealing compromise between modesty and hygiene: Olivier Le Goff, *L'invention du confort: naissance d'une forme sociale* (Lyon: Presses Universitaires de Lyon, 1994), 43; Liane de Pougy, *My Blue Notebooks* (New York: Harper & Row, 1979), 100.
25　Courmont, *Précis d'hygiène*, 67.
26　Cabanès, *Moeurs intimes*, 232–3.
27　Mary Lynn Stewart, *For Health and Beauty: Physical Culture for Frenchwomen, 1880s–1930s* (Baltimore: Johns Hopkins University Press, 2001), 67; also see Fanny Beaupré and Roger-Henri Guerrand, *Le confident des dames. Le bidet du XVIIIe au XXe siècle. Histoire d'une intimité* (Paris: La Découverte, 1997), 87.
28　Edith Hall, *Canary Girls and Stockpots* (Luton: WEA, 1977), 27. Also see Eugen Weber, *Peasants into Frenchmen: The Modernization of Rural France, 1870–1914* (Stanford: Stanford University Press, 1976), 148 and Raymond Doussinet, *Le paysan saintongeais dans ses bots* (La Rochelle: Éditions Rupella, 1963), 368; Rouleau cited in Sohn, *Chrysalides*, I, 303.
29　Comtesse de Gencé, *Code mondain de la jeune fille* (Paris: Bibliothèque des Ouvrages Pratiques, 1910), 95; also Mathilde Salomon, *À nos jeunes filles: Lectures et leçons familières de morale—d'après le programme des jeunes écoles primaires supérieures des jeunes filles* (Paris: L. Cerf, 1896), 127, cited in Nicole Rudolph, "'Les peuples soucieux de la propreté sont des peuples supérieurs': The Norm of Order in French Domestic Economy Manuals, 1881–1986," unpublished manuscript, 1997, 11.

30 Théodore Chalmel, *Une commune rurale à travers les siècles: Saint-Père-Marc-en-Poulet (Ille-et-Vilaine)* (Rennes: Imprimerie Brevetée Francis Simon, 1931), 231.
31 Jean-Luc Mayaud, "Salaires agricoles et petite propriété dans la France du XIXe siècle," in Ronald Hubscher and Jean-Claude Farcy (dirs.), *La moisson des autres. Les salariés agricoles au XIXe-XXe siècles. Actes du colloque international de Royaumont, 13–14 novembre 1992. Rencontres à Royaumont* (Paris: Éditions Créaphis, 1996), 121.
32 Jeanne Singer-Kérel, *La coût de la vie à Paris de 1840 à 1954. Recherches sur l'économie française* (Paris: A. Colin, 1961), 490–1.
33 Drouineau, "Hygiène rurale," 483.
34 Jules Renard, *Journal, 1902–1905*, tome 3 (Paris: Union Générale d'Éditions, 1894), 819.
35 Henri Baudrillart, *Les populations agricoles de la France. 2e série: Maine, Anjou, Touraine, Poitou, Flandre, Artois, Picardy, Île-de-France passé au présent* (Paris: Librairie Guillaumin et Cie., 1888), 147, 365.
36 Jean-Claude Farcy, *Les paysans beaucerons au XIXème siècle* (Chartres: Société archéologique d'Eure-et-Loir, 1989), 354. On alcoholism among the peasants, see, for example, Jules Dorez, *Compte-rendu des travaux du Conseil d'Hygiène départemental et des commissions sanitaires* [Meurthe-et-Moselle]. *Année 1908—tome XLIV* (Nancy: Imprimerie Berger-Levrault et Cie.), 65.
37 Henri Henrot, *Projet d'organisation de l'hygiène publique en France* (Reims: Matot-Braine, 1887), 12.
38 Département de la Nièvre, Conseil Général, *Rapport du projet et procès-verbaux des délibérations, Session d'août 1916* (Nevers: Mazeron Frères, 1916), 260. On the rural water situation, also see A. Lepigoché and Charles-Joseph Seltensperger, *Le livre unique de sciences et d'agriculture, d'hygiène et d'économic domestique à l'économie rurale. Notions agricoles. Applications à l'hygiène et à l'économie domestique. Résumés par leçons. Expériences simples. Rédactions. Problèmes. Promenades scolaires. 337 gravures* (Paris: Librairie Classique Delaplaine, 1920), 31.
39 André Rauch, *Histoire de la santé. Que sais-je?* (Paris: Presses Universitaires de France, 1995), 70–1.
40 Daniel Fabre and Jacques Lacroix, *La vie quotidienne des paysans du Languedoc au XIXe siècle* (Paris: Hachette, 1975), 94 and Eugène Bougeâtre, *La vie rurale dans le Mantois et le Vexin au XIXe siècle* (Cergy-Pointoise: Éditions du Valhermeil, 1996), 121.
41 For secondary sources on the varieties of folk wisdom, see Georges L'Hôte, *La Tankiotte. Les usages traditionnels en Lorraine* (Nancy: Presses Universitaire de Nancy, 1984); Claude Rouleau, *Essai de folklore de la Sologne bourbonnaise* (Moulins: Crépin-Leblond, 1935); and Claude Seignolle, *Le Berry traditional* (Paris: Maisonneuve et Larose, 1969).
42 Drouineau, "Hygiène rurale," 673–4; Sohn, *Chrysalides*, I, 302–3.
43 Robert Bouiller and Louis Challet, *Forez: De la Madeleine au Pilat* (Paris: Christine Bonneton, 1987), 104.
44 AD Aube, 5U 254: Réquisitoire, septembre 26, 1893, cited in Sohn, *Chrysalides*, I, 302.
45 On the wages of farm labor, see Gabriel Désert, "Les salaires agricoles en Basse Normandie au XIXe siècle," in Hubscher and Farcy (dirs.), *La moisson des autres*, 120.
46 On Crédit Agricole, see Bernard Stéphan, *Paysans, mémoires vives: récits d'un monde disparu, 1900–2000* (Paris: Éditions Autrement, 2006), 214.

47 Sara Hume, "The Final Bows: The Evolution and Replacement of Regional Dress in Alsace, 1870–1920," in Maude Bass-Krueger, Sophie Kurkdjian, and Steven Zdatny (eds.), *French Historical Studies* 43, no. 2 (April 2020): 277.
48 Abbé M.-M. Gorse, *Au bas pays de Limousin, études et tableaux* (Paris: E. Leroux, 1896), 31.
49 See the short discussion of swaddling in Sohn, *Chrysalides*, I, 296–7. Also see Paul-Henri Paillou, *Mon village à la Belle Epoque* (Aurillac: Éditions du Centre, 1962), 153 and Charles Talon, *Histoire de la vie rurale en Bas Dauphiné* (Lyon: E. Bellier, 1981), 317.
50 Baudrillart, *Les populations agricoles* (1888), 121. Pierre-Jakez Hélias, *The Horse of Pride: Life in a Breton Village* (New Haven and London: Yale University Press, 1978), 1–2.
51 On the price of clothes, see Baudrillart, *Les populations agricoles* (1888), 444–6 and Hume, "The Final Bows," 289–93.
52 Jules Michelet, *Le Peuple* (Paris: Calmann Lévy, 1877), 34 and Chalmel, *Une commune rurale*, 625.
53 Sohn, *Chrysalides*, I, 118. On the advantages of cotton, see Joan Dejean, *The Age of Comfort: When Paris Discovered Casual—and the Modern Home Began* (New York and London: Bloomsbury, 2009), 206.
54 Philippe Perrot, *Fashioning the Bourgeoisie: A History of Clothing in the Nineteenth Century* (Princeton: Princeton University Press, 1994), 146–9.
55 Albert, *La vie à crédit*, 78–9; Alain Corbin uses the phrase "l'ascension du linge de corps" in "Le grand siècle du linge," *Ethnologie française* 16, no. 3 (juillet–septembre 1986): 299.
56 Antoine Desforges, *La vie dans un coin de Morvan* (Nevers: Les Cahiers du Centre, 1911), 29. Also see Henri Baudrillart, *Les populations agricoles en France. 1ère série: Normandie, Bretagne, passé et présent* (Paris: Librairie Guillaumin, 1885), 620 and Jules Renard, *Nos frères farouches; Ragotte* (Paris: L'Académie Goncourt, 1908), 15.
57 Yvonne Verdier, *Façons de dire, façons de faire. La laveuse, la couturière, la cuisinière* (Paris: Gallimard, 1979), 116.
58 Jean Cornec, *Josette et Jean Cornec, instituteurs* (Paris: Éditions Clancier-Guénaud, 1981), 45.
59 Cited in Farid Chemoune, *Des modes et des hommes: deux siècles d'élégance masculine* (Paris: Flammarion, 1993), 97–8.
60 Drouineau, "Hygiène rurale," 512.
61 Émile Guillaumin, *The Life of a Simple Man* (Hannover: University Press of New England, 1983 [1943]), xi.
62 Rochard, *Traité d'hygiène publique*, 576; François Julien-Labruyère, *Paysans Charentais: Histoire des campagnes d'Aunis, Saintonge et bas Angoulême. Tome 1: Économie rurale* (La Rochelle: Rupell, 1982), 237; Lucien et Marcel Sage, *Un village du Bas Dauphiné. Saint-Jean-d'Avelasne* (Grenoble: Centre Alpin et Rhodanien d'Ethnologie, 1976), 112.
63 Raymonde Anna Rey, *Augustine Rouvière, Cévenole* (Paris: France Loisirs, 1977), 124; Michel Augé-Laribé, *La révolution agricole* (Paris: Éditions Albin Michel, 1955), 299.
64 Daniel Desbois, *Le pays des souvenirs* (Paris: Éditions Lettres du Monde, 1994), 23–4.
65 Laurence Wylie, *Village in the Vaucluse* (Cambridge, MA: Harvard University Press, 1981), 25.
66 L. Duge de Bernonville, "Enquête sur les conditions de la vie ouvrière et rurale en France en 1913–1914," *Bulletin de la Statistique générale de la France* VI, no. II (1917): 61.

On the rural proletariat, also see Albert Babeau, *La vie rurale dans l'ancienne France* (Paris: Didier et Cie., 1883), 12–13; Georges Buisan, *Hier, en vallée de Campan. Vie montagnarde et Communautaire d'un village des Pyrénées centrales* (Tarbes: Éditions Cairn, 2002), 21; and Gilbert Garrier, "L'apport des récits de vie et des romans 'paysans,'" in Hubscher and Farcy (dirs.), *La moisson des autres*, 21–2.

67   Ronald Hubscher, "L'identité de la terre," in Yves Lequin (dir.), *Histoire des Français, XIXe-XXe siècles: la société* (Paris: Armand Colin, 1983), 363–6 and Cyril-Berger, *Les têtes baissées* (Paris: P. Ollendorff, 1913), 25.

68   Capitaine J. Levainville, *Le Morvan, étude de géographie humaine* (Paris: A. Colin, 1909), 220–9.

69   Albert, *La vie à credit*, 86.

70   Albert Goursaud, *La société rurale traditionnelle en Limousin. Ethnographie et folklore du Haut-Limousin et de la Basse-Marche*, tome 1 (Paris: G.-P. Maisonneuve & Larose, 1976), 79. On improvements in *logements* in the Beauce, see Félix Chapiseau, *Le folklore de la Beauce et du Perche* (Paris: Maissonneuve, 1902), 34; for the Normandy *bocage*, see Raoul de Félice, *La Basse-Normandie, étude de géographie régionale* (Paris: Hachette, 1907), *passim*; for the Nord and Pas-de-Calais, see François Bécu, *Le travail agricole et la condition des ouvriers agricoles dans le département du Pas-de-Calais* (Arras: Librairie E. Boileux, 1907), 49; and André Joppé, *Conditions de salaire et de travail des ouvriers agricoles dans le département du Nord* (Lille: Imprimerie C. Robbe, 1910), *passim*.

71   Descriptions of the house are in Pierre Leshauris, *Ceux de Lagroulet: La vie quotidienne d'une famille des paysans landais (1870–1914)* (Toulouse: Éditions Eché, 1984 [1949]), 87–9, 93, 110–12.

72   Arlen Hansen tells a story about the repression of public urinating. One very early morning in July 1923, E. E. Cummings, walking along the street with John Dos Passos and Gilbert Seldes, stopped at the corner of Git-le-Coeur and Saint-André-des-Arts, not far from the Place Saint-Michel, to relieve himself against a wall. This poet was promptly arrested and booked by "a whole phalanx of gendarmes," as "un Américain qui pisse": Arlen J. Hansen, *Expatriate Paris: A Cultural and Literary Guide to Paris of the 1920s* (New York: Arcade Publishing, 1990), 45.

73   David Weir, "Economic and Physical Well-Being in France," in Richard H. Steckel and Roderick Floud (eds.), *Health and Welfare during Industrialization* (Chicago: University of Chicago Press, 1997), table 5B.1, 191. For the Haut-Forez, see *Gérard Berger, Le pays de Saint-Bonnet-le-Chateau (Haut-Forez) de 1775 à 1975: flux et reflux d'une société* (Saint-Etienne: Presses de l'Université de Saint-Etienne, 1985), 400.

74   See Marie-France Morel, review of Catherine Rollet-Échalier, *La politique à l'égard de la petite enfance sous la IIIe République* and of Alain Norvez, *De la naissance à l'école: Santé, modes de garde et préscolarité dans la France contemporaine*, in *Population Studies* 47, no.2 (July 1993): 373 and Secrétaire d'État à la Santé et à la Famille, *Recueil des Travaux de l'Institut National d'Hygiène*, tome IV, vol. 2 (Paris: Masson et Cie., 1952), 736. Also see Louis Dujardin, *Basse-Bretagne et bas Bretons: étude d'hygiène* [thèse pour obtenir le grade de docteur en médecine. Université de Montpellier] (Montpellier: Imprimerie Cooperative Ouvrière, 1912), 59.

75   For example, see the arrondissement-by-arrondissement, plus suburbs, survey: Préfecture de Police, *Rapports sur les travaux des Commissions d'Hygiène . . . en 1900*, *passim*.

76   Henri Napias and André-Justin Martin, *L'étude et le progrès de l'hygiène en France de 1878 à 1882* (Paris: G. Masson, 1883), 242.

77 Ambrose Rendu to the Conseil municipal de Paris, *Rapport au nom de la 6e Commission sur les îlots insalubres de Paris* (Paris: Imprimerie Nationale. 1909), 16. On Marseille and Rouen, see Rochard, *Traité d'hygiène publique*, 334. For mortality statistics for German cities, see Richard Evans, *Death in Hamburg: Society and Politics in the Cholera Years* (New York: Penguin, 1987), 180–4 and 197–8 and Augustin Rey, "La crise de l'habitation française, les grands remèdes," in Alliance d'hygiène sociale, *Congrès de Roubaix, 19022 octobre 1911: De la ville-taudis à la cité jardin* (Agen: Imprimerie moderne, 1912), 97–9.

9

"A Decent Place to Live"

Hygiene at War

No history of life in the trenches fails to mention the ubiquitous squalor. The filth and the lice were as essential a part of the *poilus'* experience as German shelling, endless fatigue, and bloody, pointless offensives. Of course, vermin were less lethal than enemy machine guns. On the other hand, the killing was intermittent; the lice were incessant. One author made an attempt to describe conditions from the official side: André Tournade's *La pratique de l'hygiène en campagne* published by the military press in 1918. Wherever troops settle, he wrote, they need a way to bathe and a barber. In one instance, an officer improvised a shower in a stable, in order to profit from the "central heating" provided by the animals:

> The men, each one with towel and soap, passed through in groups of ten; they squatted one at a time in a tub while two stretcher bearers, promoted to shower specialists [*doucheurs*], poured warm water on them, allowing the men to soap up, after which a second dousing rinsed them off. The entire operation lasted 5 or 6 minutes and required 10 or 12 liters of water per man.

Tournade added instructions for setting up a field *lavoir* to wash uniforms and other amenities for keeping soldiers clean.

These, of course, were suggestions for the rear areas. Conditions in the trenches presented "insurmountable obstacles" to keeping bodies and clothes clean. The men themselves were often unaware of the value of washing their hands, their feet, their mouths, their heads, and their "regions périnéales et interfessières"; that is, their bottoms. But Tournade thought that their officers could serve them well by insisting on these habits. He believed that, in the end, victory was not completely unconnected to decent latrines, showers, and disinfection facilities to restore wearability to filthy uniforms.[1]

Horrible as the war was, however, viewed in the long term, the reduction of millions of twentieth-century European men to conditions that would have disgusted a medieval peasant stands as a parenthesis—a detour along the road to modern hygiene. Obviously, for those in the trenches, and for those who mourned them, it was a personal and national catastrophe. At the same time, the war left other parts of French life, far from the front lines, relatively untouched. Unlike the German Occupation twenty-five years later, when shortages of everything made daily life in France a dirty, hungry struggle, it is difficult to discern the impact of the First World War on the history of *propreté*.

True, if schools continued to imbue students with cleaner habits, efforts to improve the water supply or build social housing had to be shelved for the duration. Money for infrastructure had always been tight; now it dried up almost entirely. Perhaps the price of soap went up a bit, as ingredients were used for military purposes, or young women got dirtier as *munitionettes* than they had gotten as domestics and seamstresses before the war (although probably not). Indeed, the fashion business, although constrained in some respects, flourished during the war, spreading even among young working-class women, whose war experience brought them unprecedented levels of income and autonomy.[2]

In other words, the war had a paradoxical impact on the long-term trajectory of French hygiene. For the moment, the demolition of fields and cities along the battlefields of Flanders, Artois, and Champagne made it harder for people in those regions to keep clean. In the long run, however, this created the opportunity for a wholesale modernization of the infrastructure of *propreté*, as the towns and cities of the northeast, which had to be rebuilt in any case, could now be provided with modern water and sewer systems. This promised to be a very expensive undertaking, though, and it was not clear where the money for reconstruction would come from—although it soon became clear that it would not come from German reparations.

The Damage Done

The first order of business in the job of restoring the devastated regions was to provide survivors with someplace to live (Figure 9.1). As Fénélon Gibon, general secretary of the Society for Education and Association for the Sanctification of Sunday, wrote: "A clean, spacious, airy dwelling" was the foundation of all social values and the most effective weapon against the scourge of alcoholism. "I am persuaded," wrote the architect Émile Malespine, "that most of our political problems would be more or less resolved through wide-ranging and energetic action to bring hygiene into people's homes."[3] Give this to the working classes and they will become civilized, domesticated, *embourgeoisées*. Elementary school texts echoed the message that poor housing—"dirty, humid, dark and airless"—led inevitably to alcohol abuse, tuberculosis, and rickets. Public health and morality, they stressed, depended on conditions in the home.[4]

As we have seen, the shortage of clean, spacious, airy housing was endemic in France. The war merely aggravated the situation. The crisis had two faces. The first was the increasing number of people, especially in the towns, needing accommodations for themselves and their families. France's urban population had swelled throughout the second half of the nineteenth century and into the twentieth: from 24.5 percent of the population in 1846 to 31 percent in 1872, 37 percent in 1891, and 44 percent in 1911. This represented a modest rate of urbanization by the standards of more industrialized neighbors. Even so, the 100,000 logements being added to inventory every year before 1914 was not enough to keep up with the *demand* of working families needing shelter. The National Assembly had passed the Siegfried Law in 1894, in order to set the table

"A Decent Place to Live" 213

Figure 9.1 *Slum of the Poulettes Quarter, Villeurbaine, Lyon* (1930). Jules Sylvestre, photographer. Bibliothèque municipale de Lyôn, cote P0546 SV 0362.

for the construction of HBM; that is, social housing. Subsequent laws over the next twenty years doubled down on that policy. But with what results? "Few, not to say none at all," responded legal scholar and *haut fonctionnaire* Georges Cahen-Salvador. Only 50,000 such units were built before the war.[5]

The "housing crisis" was among the most commented upon problems facing the Third Republic, but neither the efforts of the state nor those of private reform groups had been able to do much about it. And whereas it had been hard enough to finance new construction before 1914, the catastrophic costs imposed by the war made it that much harder. Yves Salaün, inspecteur de finance, tallied up the destruction. He estimated that in the towns along the front lines some 366,000 homes had been partly shattered and 298,000 completely demolished. Comparable figures for the countryside were 160,000 buildings partially and 40,000 totally ruined. Meanwhile, in the recovered territories of Alsace and Lorraine, 21,000 rural dwellings were seriously damaged and 11,000 reduced to rubble. Salaün calculated the losses at 547,000 buildings smashed in part and another 349,000 in their entirety. For a nation already short of livable housing, and now shorter than ever on cash, this was a calamity.[6]

However, France's comprehensive and enduring dearth of suitable places to live was not entirely the work of German artillery. Rural housing stock was old: 110 years, on average. In the big cities the average was only fifty-two years, but almost a fifth of it dated back a century or more. In Paris, the average dwelling had been built during the Second Empire, a quarter of buildings when Louis Philippe was on the throne or before. But both public policy and the demands of constituents made the problem worse. The construction of new residences, which had never managed to match supply with demand, ceased with the shift to a war economy, and it never recovered even the unsatisfactory pace of the prewar years after the fighting stopped. In all of France, estimated Jean-Claude Dumas, only 2.4 million *logements* were built between 1919 and 1939—an average of 114,000 per year and far short of requirements, even for a stagnating population. Indeed, a country in need of labor after 1918 was importing more workers than it could house in the cities—a surge in immigration inflated by postwar upheaval in Central and Eastern Europe. The "penury" of the housing market in Paris, writes Fabienne Chevallier, sent half a million people into the suburbs, where the most primitive and deplorable conditions continued to prevail and where families lived in "the most revolting promiscuity" (Figure 9.1). "In these new neighborhoods," wrote the architect Émile Malespine, the unpaved streets, hardly worthy of the name, "are full of mud and garbage up to your knees. No sewers, no basements, no effective drainage. No water . . . or, rather, wells sitting right next to cesspits." There are laws meant to control this chaos, he added, but builders and landlords did not respect them, and the authorities did not enforce them.[7]

"Despite the succession of legislative measures since the Siegfried Law," complained the urbanist Fernand Bassé-Parton, "we must deplore the nation's failures in the struggle against *insalubrité*." And these failures were not unique to the Paris region. In Bordeaux, for example, as construction costs rose fourfold between 1914 and 1922, the pace of new building declined in proportion. It picked up a bit at the end of the decade; some 300 new houses went up in 1930. But this small boom collapsed with the economic crisis—to only 200 new houses in 1939. Lyon, run by the progressive mayor Edouard Herriot with ambitious plans for urban renewal, was no more successful than Bordeaux. The situation in the Yvelines was so dire in the mid-1920s that departmental authorities considered simply seizing empty apartments from their owners and putting homeless families in them. They also talked about turning old army barracks into private housing. Apparently, nothing came of these ideas, but they are evidence of desperation in high places.[8]

Rent Control

If the French were unable to find a solution to a problem they clearly recognized, a large part of the explanation lies in their devotion to low rents. In 1900, according to historian Susanna Magri, in the capital almost 700,000 dwellings cost less than 600 francs a year; even in 1915, three-quarters of apartments belonged in this category.[9] It might be said that Paris remained an overwhelmingly working-class city, where people did not have a lot of money for rent. At the same time, though, the French paid less for housing than just about anyone else in Europe. Where the English, Italian, and Swiss spent up to a quarter of their household income on rent in 1940, the average French family spent only 6–8 percent (Table 9.1), and that portion had been declining for a century. A 1946 report from the Ministry of Economic estimated that in 1810, the average household budget gave 7.8 percent to rent. That rose throughout the century to 18.1 percent in 1900 and hit a prewar peak of almost 20 percent in 1908. As the hot summer of

Table 9.1 Percentage of Income Devoted to Rent in 1940

Country	Percent of Income Devoted to Rent
England	22–27
Netherlands	20.5
Switzerland	20–25
Australia	15–20
Denmark	13.4
Italy	25
France	6–8

Source: Report by M. Marrane to the Congrès International de l'Habitation et de l'Urbanisme à Zurich, June 1948, in Ministère de la Santé Publique. *Recueil des travaux de l'Institut National d'Hygiène: travaux des sections et mémoires originaux*, tome IV. vol. 1 (Paris: Masson et Cie., 1950), 249.

Table 9.2 Percentage of Family Budgets Devoted to Rent

Years	Rent as a Percentage of the Family Budget	Years	Rent as a Percentage of the Family Budget
1914	16% (est.)	1929	5.0
1919	6	1930	5.3
1920	4.3	1931	6.3
1921	4.7	1932	8.1
1922	5.3	1933	8.8
1923	4.8	1934	9.5
1924	4.6	1935	10.5
1926	5.1	1936	9.5
1927	5.3	1937	7.1
1928	5.5	1938	7.3

Source: Yves Salaün, *Se Loger: construire 20,000 logements par mois est, pour la France, une question de vie ou de mort* (Paris: Imprimerie de Montsouris, 1949), 35.

1914 approached, according to the journal *La Population Française*, the average rent payment represented 16 percent of a typical family income. By way of context, the article added that, "In 1938 the French spent 9 billion francs on *apéritifs* and *digestifs* (not counting wine, beer, or cider) in the half-a-million drinking establishments across the country. In that same year," the article continued, "the total value of all the rent paid by six million renters could be estimated at 15 billion francs," which the journal considered a mordant commentary on national priorities. A social worker reported with some irritation her visit to a working-class family in Saint-Germain-en-Laye. They all lived in one room but had "a radio and a phonograph and numerous records."[10]

The percentage of family budgets given over to rent varied between the wars, according to Salaün's reckonings, between a low of 4.3 percent (1920) and a high of 10.5 percent (1935). These are nominal figures, however. The monetary instability of the interwar years meant that real rents declined by half between 1914 and 1939 (Table 9.2). When it came to paying the landlord, the French remained the stingiest people in Western Europe.[11] Low rents were not, of course, in themselves a bad thing. But insofar as they starved the housing sector of capital for construction and renovation, they had a devastating effect on the availability and quality of housing, especially at the lower end of the market.

As historian Anaïs Albert writes, the moratorium on rent hikes passed by the legislature within days of the war's outbreak in August 1914 "was welcomed eagerly by the popular classes."[12] Yet this understandably well-liked policy, which made some sense at a time of national emergency, in the end turned market failure into public policy and made it virtually certain that the majority of the population would continue to live in crowded, dirty, substandard homes. The initial law seems sensible enough. Rents were frozen, in order to protect families against rent-racking while their breadwinners were off defending *la patrie*, and landlords lost the right to evict tenants whose leases had expired or who simply did not pay the rent. These strictures did not apply to the highest categories of rent: over 9,000 francs a month in Paris, 6,000 francs in other big cities, and 3,000 francs in smaller cities.[13]

The end of the war, however, did not bring the end of rent control. Indeed, according to a 1946 report from the Ministry of National Economics, when the war ended the legislature extended these benefits and even *lowered* rents in some cases. The legislators knew that they were ruining landlords and preventing the expansion and improvement of the housing stock. Yet the public's taste for low rents was too strong to resist—at least for elected officials who wanted to keep their jobs. To be fair, the National Assembly subsequently passed a number of laws aimed ostensibly at softening the effect of rent control on landlords, but they had little effect, assuring, in the words of the National Institute for Hygiene, that "the rent-control legislation enacted in 1914 and continually extended . . . conditioned the French to paying lower and lower rent for their places of habitation."[14]

The report further reflected on the trade-off between low rents and low-quality housing:

> Renters, after having paid an increasing share of their income up to 1914, had, at the price of restrictions on space and comfort, been able to house themselves subsequently at relatively small expense. However, the [resulting] poor housing conditions were directly related to ill health and elevated mortality. In the period between the world wars, the rising cost of building, combined with aggressive rent controls, limited new construction and accelerated the deterioration of the housing supply.[15]

Thus, while the better-off classes began to fill their homes with the tools of modern hygiene, the mass of *locataires* got what they paid for: crowding and shabbiness.[16] How crowded and how shabby? The infamous parricide from the 1930s, Violette Nozière, lived with her parents in a working-class flat on the rue Madagascar in the 12th arrondissement of Paris. The family lived,

> in two rooms that looked out on a courtyard. The door faced the kitchen. To the left there was a bedroom and to the right a dining room. As in the majority of working-class buildings, the WC was located on the landing, although it was exclusive to the Nozières. They also had gas and a shower, although the family

tended to wash up in the kitchen sink, as in the overwhelming majority of urban dwellings.

The Nozières were fortunate. Their rent was effectively subsidized, since the building was owned by the railroad, where her father had worked, until Violette murdered him (and only just failed to murder her mother) with the gas.[17]

Not all working-class Parisians had the Nozières' good luck with their housing. The most common situation found a family of whatever size in a *deux pièces* (one bedroom) in an old building, virtually all of which predated the war and many of which, especially in the inner arrondissements, had gone up centuries before. They were typically chock-a-block with people and sparse in furniture. Social worker Yvonne Knibiehler described apartments in the cité Jeanne d'Arc, supposedly reserved for unmarried employees of the Compagnie d'Orléans railroad, where families of four and five people stuffed themselves into one room of 6 square meters.[18] In Rouen, meanwhile, Gaston Chevereau went to visit his brother, who worked for Tramways Électriques, in 1926. He described the experience:

> an alley and a courtyard and, at the back, a dilapidated building. A narrow staircase, with the distinctive smells of gas lighting, kitchens, old apartments, cat piss, uncirculated air. [My brother] lived on the third floor, the top. The flat was tiny, cramped. [. . .] For my toilette, a small table with a basin, a jug, and a bucket. To have a bath required a trip to the municipal baths. [. . .] The apartment was heated by the cooker, which also served to heat water, which had to be fetched from a nearby fountain. The steep, narrow staircase made it inconvenient, painful and exhausting to lug buckets of water and coal up to the apartment.[19]

Anne-Marie Sohn's research in departmental archives found a woman in Lyon who lived with her three children and her lover, a laborer, in a 10-meter square space without windows, and a family of fourteen in Sablé crowded into one derelict room. Among the poorest tenants, she wrote, children could be found sleeping on sacks, in dresser drawers, and in old soap cartons. Even in the better-off cities of the north, working-class housing tended to be dark and humid. Amenities were scarce. On the eve of the Second World War, although most Paris buildings had electricity, two-thirds had not yet been connected to the sewer system, and only half the population had an inside or unshared toilet.[20]

The Ligue National Contre les Taudis (National League to Combat Slums) offered readers a disturbing tour through these appalling conditions of relentless filth and crowding in 1924:

> On the rue de la Mare (20th arrondissement): The S. family is composed of parents, both in a terrible state of health, and five children aged between eleven years and one year. A sixth is on the way. Two children have already died. These seven people live in one room. There is a bed for the mother and father, a crib for the two babies, a carriage for one of the little ones, a short bed for another child, and a pallet on the floor, where the oldest sleeps. The room is about 850 square

feet, but since it is directly under the roof, much of that space is under the incline. The front door opens on to a disgusting staircase, dominated by the stink of an uncared-for collective toilet. There is no running water.

Îlots Insalubres

George Orwell left us his own dark portrait of the down-and-out "rue du Coq d'Or" (1929):

> It was a very narrow street—a ravine of tall, leprous houses, lurching towards one another in queer attitudes, as though they had all been frozen in the act of collapse. All the houses were hotels and packed to the tiles with lodgers, mostly Poles, Arabs and Italians. At the foot of the hotels were tiny *bistros*, where you could be drunk for the equivalent of a shilling. On Saturday nights about a third of the male population of the quarter was drunk. There was fighting over women, and the Arab navvies who lived in the cheapest hotels used to conduct mysterious feuds and fight them out with chairs and occasionally revolvers. At night the policemen would only come through the street two together. It was a fairly rackety place. And yet amid the noise and dirt lived the usual respectable French shopkeepers, bakers and laundresses and the like, keeping themselves to themselves and quietly piling up small fortunes. It was quite a representative Paris slum.[21]

Thousands of people in Paris, and tens of thousands in towns across the country, lived in such "representative slum[s]." The worst neighborhoods were often populated by immigrants, who found refuge in their miserable flats and cheap furnished rooms, adding elements of anti-Semitism and nativism to the horrified observations of reformers and critics. The lawyer and urban reformer Charles Badini-Jourdin was not the only one to be disgusted by the *îlot insalubre* of Saint-Gervais, in the Marais, full of "these foreigners who know nothing of the rules of hygiene and who swarm together with their compatriots in the most sickening slums."[22]

Native-born inhabitants of city slums hardly lived much better. And what could the missionaries of hygiene do? Céline Lhotte, a nurse and social worker in Le Havre, sometimes despaired of what seemed like an impossible challenge: "Preach hygiene?" she wrote,

> A noble crusade, and how proud we are to be part of it! They are good people and, when I talk, they listen quietly, with weary smiles, instead of just kicking me and my beautiful words out the door. Sunshine, fresh air, sewers, roast beef, etc. Where and how? Open the windows: Onto the courtyard? Wash your linen: In the kitchen? Dry it wherever you can.[23]

Even the best advice cannot change old habits overnight, especially when dirtiness is easy and cheap, while cleanliness is hard and costly (Figure 9.2).

Figure 9.2 *Îlot insalubre number 1: Rue de Venise* (1931). Archives de Paris VD 5, Salubrité Publique. Conseil Municipal de Paris. Rapport au nom de la 6e commission sur les résultats de l'expropriation de l'îlot insalubre no. 1.

These *îlots insalubres* presented a particularly concentrated version of urban misery. They identified themselves, writes Yankel Fijalkow, "by their elevated mortality rates," especially from tuberculosis.[24] The disease that had killed 85,000 French people in 1909 still sent 70,000 to their deaths in 1927, and mortality figures compiled for Paris, 1932–4 showed considerably higher rates in the slummier arrondissements than in the airy and middle-class west of the city (Map 9.1).[25] From 1935 to 1937 the proportion of deaths from tuberculosis was 38 per 100,000 in the neighborhood of the Porte Dauphine, on the western edge of Paris and 508 per 100,000 in the *îlot insalubre* number 3 (Saint-Victor-Sorbonne) along the streets of the Latin Quarter. Other studies found similar conditions in Lyon and Nantes.[26] Naturally, these mortality statistics tracked the geography of overcrowding in the city (Map 9.2).

Other cities were worse. In Le Mans, "the second-worst city in the country for mortality, generally, and the worst by tuberculosis," mortality was twice as high in the *immeubles insalubres* as in other parts of the city. Buildings in the Saint-George district in Toulouse "were considered not only unhealthy but dangerous."[27] In Nantes, the *zone insalubre* of the Marchix quarter experienced mortality rates two-and-a-half times higher than elsewhere in the city. The municipal authorities were not unaware of or unconcerned by these statistics. Thus, in Nantes in 1937, the local conseil d'hygiène launched an extensive investigation of the disaster along the rue Marchix, which was part of a process that aimed at tearing down the slum and putting up affordable public housing. "The filth of [this] neighborhood,"

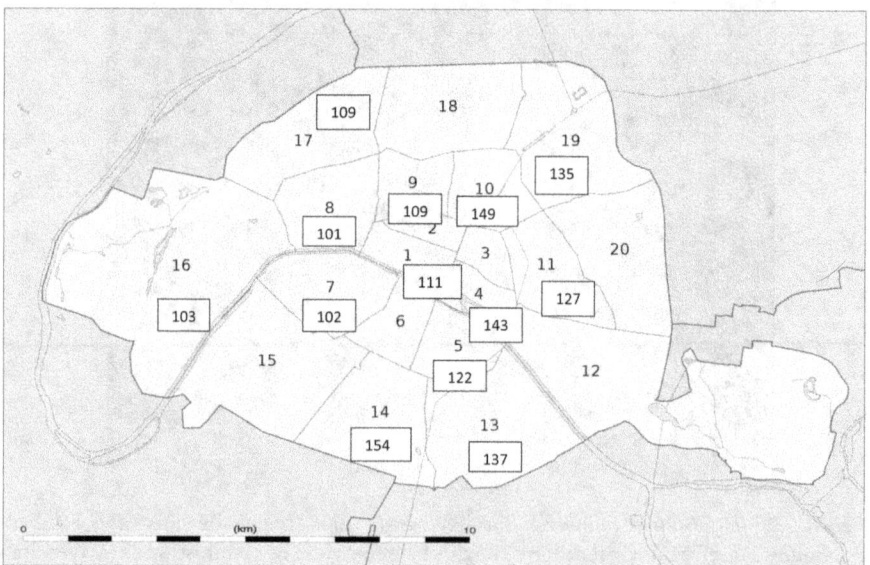

Map 9.1 Deaths per 100,000 inhabitants, 1932–4. *Source*: Ministère de la Santé Publique. *Recueil des travaux de l'Institut National d'Hygiène: travaux des sections et mémoires originaux. Tome IV. Vol.1* (Paris: Masson et Cie., 1950), 216. The source does not include a number for the 15th arrondissement. The report does not include numbers for the 2nd, 3rd, 6th, 12th, 15th, 18th, and 20th arrondissements.

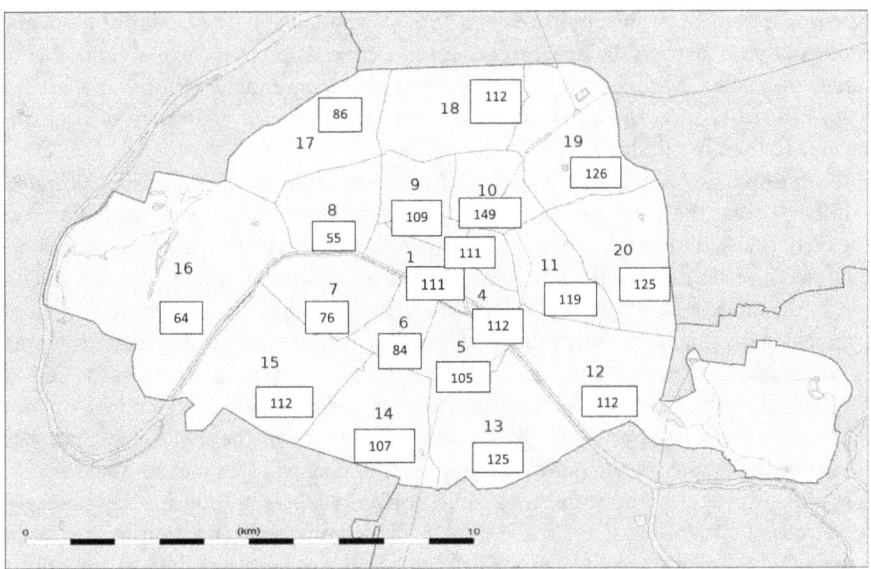

Map 9.2 Index of overcrowding in Paris by arrondissement Paris average = 100. *Source*: Ministère de l'Économie Nationale. Service National des Statistiques. Direction de la Statistique Générale. Études économique No. 1, *Documents sur le problème du logement à Paris* (Paris: Imprimerie Nationale, 1946), 71.

it observed, "is indisputable. Thirty-five percent of the people who live there die of tuberculosis. The street is a virtual abattoir for the inhabitants." In building after building the investigators found

> the low ceilings, the absence and faulty installation of *cabinets d'aisances*, the lack of fresh air and proper shutters, the terrible state of the drainpipes, the absence of bungs and siphons for the sinks and basins in the courtyard. . . . The toilets under the stairs, dark and unventilated, with no flaps to cover the sewer pipes, are in a repulsive state of filth.

In *îlot insalubre* number 6, with twenty-five buildings, the hygiene council found roughly the same conditions. As a rule, they reported, although most buildings were in a general state of disrepair, apartments in the front of the buildings, with windows that opened onto the street, tended to be more livable than those in the back, surrounding the sordid courtyards. In one instance, investigators for the council came upon one of those disgusting privies directly below the window of the bakery room where the bread was being made. The landlord told the council that he had bought the building after the war and had been doing constant renovations. The council voted to condemn it nonetheless.[28]

In other words, there was nothing mysterious about the existence of these *îlots insalubres* or about the dire need to do something about them. In the years after 1918, Paris authorities identified seventeen such areas, comprising over 4,000 buildings, covering 3 percent of the city's area and 186,000 residents, in the center of town and in the outlying districts, in structures that sometimes dated to the age of Louis XIV—often, ironically, "with beautiful facades and an incontestable historic and artistic value." In scale, the razing of an *îlot insalubre* in Paris was the equivalent of knocking down and then rebuilding a city the size of Lille.

According to Colin Jones, the fear of rats and bubonic plague in *îlot insalubre* number 9, near the Porte de Clignancourt, spurred the authorities to quick action in the early 1920s. In the end, 815 new units were built between 1929 and 1933, and about 60 percent of residents were able to return. But the program of urban repair quickly ran into problems in other places.[29] In fact, *îlot insalubre* number 9 was the only one completely overhauled between the wars, and it is easy to see why. Inevitably, the price of reconstruction outpaced the government's ability to pay for it. Thus, in the case of Clignancourt, the buildings were expropriated in order to be knocked down, but at a cost four times what was originally budgeted for. This was the first issue: landlords, whatever the quality of the buildings they owned, needed to be compensated for the loss of their property; the authorities could not simply seize it. Indeed, a series of laws were passed—1915, 1918, 1921, 1935, 1938—facilitating expropriation in the public interest while guaranteeing some "fair" return to the landlords. Good intentions, however, commonly ran into a stone wall when it came to working out the details.

Take the case of the *îlot insalubre* number 1 in Paris: Saint-Merri, the dense slum around the rue Beaubourg. Georges Cahen-Salvador, the high-ranking civil servant, described the place in 1922:

> Along the narrow alleys are decrepit walls and curbs strewn with garbage and dotted with craters gathering dust, trash, and excrement. More or less half the houses offer inexpensive furnished rooms, where there is a perpetual coming and going. Along the street are located dealers in second-hand goods next to shops selling cheap wine. And there is in every house a cabaret or a tavern or some other sanctuary for this miserable population.[30]

Everyone agreed that the neighborhood was unsalvageable. "It is not possible," reported the subcommittee to the Paris municipal council,

> to rehabilitate and to render salubrious those buildings that are, in view of their condition and the narrowness of the streets—or rather the alleys—deprived of light and sun, with their cramped, poisonous courtyards where the light of day hardly penetrates [and which make] such excellent reservoirs for the most virulent and deadly germs to infect the inhabitants and passers-by.[31]

The only option was to raze it and rebuild. This implied not one massive expenditure, but two.

The Paris municipal council heard a report in 1931 on the progress of this project, based on the 1915 law on *l'expropriation pour cause d'insalubrité publique*, itself an extension of the 1902 Strauss law. The legal process, which began with buying the properties so they could be knocked down, had been launched in 1923. The proposal was to demolish 347 structures, displacing a population of 12,653 people. The offending properties needed to be identified, a price agreed, and the funding rounded up. But prices were not so easily agreed between opposed parties, and the higher the prices the more difficult it became to arrange the funding. The main point of disagreement was on the matter of what constituted "a fair price." Unsurprisingly, landlords complained that they were not being offered enough for their property. From the other end, public officials, who believed that landlords were to blame for the deplorable state of their buildings, thought that they should be punished for this antisocial behavior by receiving something less than the market price—whatever that turned out to be—for their property. C. Roéland, author of the 1931 report, accused the landlords of *îlot insalubre* number 1 of acting "in bad faith" and against "the public interest."

However, while the landlords might want more money, they did not set the prices. That, as the law prescribed, was done by so-called *jurys* of experts. And these, as it turned out, had a disagreeable habit—at least from the public authorities' point of view—of setting higher prices than those recommended by the state's experts. In a similar report to the same committee in 1937, the hygiene crusader and municipal counselor Louis Sellier objected that the "indemnities fixed by the *jurys d'expropriation* showed an excessive generosity for the expropriated." The law, he added, "protects the landlord and kills entire families." In this particular case, where the experts for the Saint-Merri *îlot* suggested a price of 1,000–2,000 francs per square meter, the *jury* wanted the city to pay 5,000 francs per square meter—which the commission objected was the price of the best locations in the pricy area around the Porte Dauphine and therefore completely inappropriate to the derelict neighborhood of the Saint-Merri quarter.[32] In the end, the financing never appeared and *îlot insalubre* number 1 survived.

More Better Housing

The patchy success of cleaning up *îlots insalubres* and putting up affordable and hygienic new housing does not, however, signal a lack of good intentions or ambition on the part of reformers and public authorities. The drive to fill French cities with HBM, dormant for the duration of hostilities, sprang back to life with the return to peacetime concerns. Some reformers were moved by the urge to provide housing "that did not compromise the health of its occupants," others by "utopian socialist" ambitions to make better citizens through hygienic, modern standards of living. Either way, noted demographer Alfred Sauvy, the number of *logements* condemned as *insalubres* in Paris rose from 150,000 in 1911 to 2.8 million [*sic*] in 1939.[33]

Almost immediately, Louis Loucheur, a politician drawn from the industrialist class who had served as armaments minister at the end of the war and was the leading economic adviser to the French delegation in the peace talks, proposed legislation, piggybacking on the Siegfried Law of 1894, to facilitate the construction of 200,000 new units of affordable housing—especially of larger apartments for *familles nombreuses*, which was the most pressing unfulfilled need in the housing market. The parliamentary process was slow—not abnormally so for the Third Republic—but the Loi Loucheur finally passed in 1928.

The ambitious new initiative aimed to build 260,000 *logements* in five years, divided between HBM and moderately priced housing, *immeubles à loyer moyen* (ILM). For Paris, the plan was to erect 18,000 units of HBM and 20,000 of ILM, of which half ever appeared. And those, remarks Jean-Claude Daumas, tended to be expensive and "hardly more decent than the old working-class barracks."[34] Still, the new program got off to a promising start. In fact, the number of new units had been increasing, if slowly, through the mid-1920s as the national economy recovered. It continued to grow with the passage of the Loucheur Law, rising to a peak of about 200,000 new units in 1930. Yves Salaün, director general of the Ministry of Urbanism and Reconstruction in 1946, estimated that the French government put more money into housing between the wars than the English, and about as much as the Dutch and Germans. Such a large part of that, however, went into reconstructing the parts of the country flattened by the war—estimates run to about 400,000 units—that it left the rest of the country terribly short of funds to subsidize new construction elsewhere. In 1934, the Paris municipal council voted to borrow 300 million francs to raze six *îlots insalubres*. The government reduced that sum by half. It was not nearly enough money to do the job. Moreover, just as the massive effort in the *régions sinistrées* was almost complete, the Depression dealt a stunning blow to public finances. By 1938, when only 60,000 new units went up, this progress had all but dissipated.[35]

Looking backward from 1950, the National Institute for Hygiene offered a harsh judgment: "The battle against slums between the wars was not pursued with sufficient energy, and it produced very insufficient results [. . .] compared to what was accomplished in other countries"—which did not necessarily have more resources but simply considered decent housing a higher priority. Moreover, even in that limited number of instances when decrepit buildings were knocked down and new ones actually put up, this did not necessarily help the unfortunate residents. The people moved out of the slums often could not afford even the reduced rents of the new apartments and never returned to their old neighborhoods.[36]

Salaün lays out the dimensions of the international comparison (Table 9.3). Although he admits that his statistics are more indicative than precise. Clearly, according to these numbers, French efforts look pale compared to those in England and Germany—to say nothing of the incomparable US experience. What is particularly noteworthy, he points out, is the trajectory of building across the interwar years. England suffered a decline in new construction in 1922 and 1923. It picked up steam in the mid-1920s, languished with the arrival of the Depression, and then climbed significantly from about 225,000 units in 1932 to almost 360,000 in 1934. Similarly, Germany reached a high of 320,000 units in 1929, plummeted to 130,000 at the depth of the economic crisis in 1932, and took off again under the Third Reich, reaching about 370,000 units a year in 1938. Meanwhile, construction of new *logements* in France increased modestly through the 1920s and trailed off markedly in the 1930s. What is more, in England and Germany the construction of new housing was accompanied by the destruction of the

Table 9.3 Number of Housing Units Built, 1918–39

Country	Number of Dwellings Built between the Wars (in Thousands)	Existing in 1939 (in Thousands)	Percentage of New Dwellings	Population in 1939 (in Thousands)
Etats-Unis	10,000	37,000	26	131,669
Allemagne	4,600	20,000	23	70,000
France	1,600[a]	13,300	12	41,900
Angleterre	4,200	11,525	40	41,460
Pays-Bas	800	2,100	40	8,830
Suisse	228	1,111	20	4,195

Source: Yves Salaün, *Se loger: construire 20,000 logements par mois et, pour la France, une question de vie ou de mort* (Paris: Imprimerie de Montsouris, 1949), 53.
[a]These figures do not include war reconstruction, which it can be estimated included around 400,000 new *logements*. Thus, total number of new *logements* is on the order of two million (15 percent).

Table 9.4 Public Subsidies for New Housing, 1918–39

Country	Number of Dwellings Constructed between the Wars (in Thousands)		
	Total (Not Including War Reconstruction)	With Public Subsidies	Percent
Etats-Unis	10,000	(several thousand)	<1
Allemagne	4,600	2,000	43
France[a]	1,600	325	20
Angleterre	4,200	1,600	38
Pays-Bas	800	150	19
Suisse	228	38	16

Source: Yves Salaün, *Se loger: construire 20,000 logements par mois et, pour la France, une question de vie ou de mort* (Paris: Imprimerie de Montsouris, 1949), 57.
[a]Does not include reconstruction in the war-devastated areas.

worst old housing, which did not happen in France, where the *îlots insalubres* mostly remained standing.[37]

In large part, as the National Institute for Hygiene remarked, this reflected a less vigorous effort of public finance in France, compared to England and Germany—the United States, the Netherlands, and Switzerland relying much more on unsubsidized private efforts—which built almost three times the number of *logements* with a substantially larger public investment (Table 9.4).

If parlous public finances and the rent-paying public's willingness to trade poor conditions for low housing costs explain much of the French failure to put more of its population in decent living quarters, a substantial share of the blame has to fall on the government's ill-conceived, if popular, rent-control policies that removed all the incentives for profit-seeking business to build affordable habitations for the working classes. Édouard Bonnefous, future minister of transportation in the Fourth Republic, wrote that, in order to cover the costs of construction, rents would have had to rise by a factor of ten. The law prevented this. In a word, ideology piled on top of shortsighted self-interest, as the renunciation of market-based solutions to the housing problem reflected a widespread and deep-seated aversion to markets in French culture, especially on the reform-minded left. Confidence in capitalism was at low ebb.

The author of a report to the Ministry of Public Health, "The Question of the Slum in Different Countries and How to Fix the Problem," put the matter plainly: "The construction of dwellings with rents low enough for former slum-dwellers to afford," he wrote, "will never be profitable."[38] He therefore concluded that the housing crisis could only be relieved through massive public expenditure. But the state did not have the money; and neither, thanks to rent control, did landlords and developers. This effectively assured that existing infrastructure would continue to degrade and progress in the service of national hygiene languish. It is also worth noting that rent control privileged people who already had a place to live, while ceilings on prospective rents, preventing new building, made it more difficult for younger families to find livable quarters. One final perverse consequence of the rent-control regime was that private money continued to flow into construction, but almost exclusively to provide larger apartments for the more well-to-do.[39]

Moreover, even those units that did go up failed to serve the cause of better living conditions as well as they might have done. For one, the lack of new space for building in Paris chased much new construction into the suburbs, where infrastructure was lacking and municipal oversight weaker. Colin Jones reckons that up to 90 percent of new building in the *région parisienne* happened on the far side of the Périphérique.[40] For another, HBMs that were built often ran into their own market snafus. For example, incomes were such among those eligible for subsidized public housing that there was a disjunction between the apartments that people needed and those they were able to afford. That is, there was an incentive to build small apartments—*deux pièces*, largely—because that is what the working classes could afford or perhaps what they were willing to pay for. However, these young families, more or less *nombreuses*, needed *bigger* apartments, with two and three bedrooms. But since most of these families could not afford the higher rent, they continued to stuff themselves into small spaces. Indeed, one of the problems with slum clearance was that, when families were displaced so that HBM could be built, those families seldom returned, because the new *logements*, even though they were subsidized, came with higher rents than the slummy apartments they had replaced. Of the 10,000 units built for *expropriés* by Paris authorities between 1930 and 1934, according to the National Institute for Hygiene, only several hundred were ever occupied by those people. The rest were rented *librement*.[41]

Consequently, many of the plans for new housing hatched between the wars bear the marks of an underfunded program trying to stretch its meager resources. What this often meant, in effect, was an explicit policy of giving the lower classes worse housing than middle-class tenants. Even before the war the Paris city council had proposed two new types of housing. The *type Henri Becque* offered a "confort minimum" for low rent to poor families. The *type Émile Zola* provided a fuller array of amenities at higher rents to middle-class families. The idea was to use the market rents fetched by the latter to help subsidize the former.

This strategy was revived after the war. Speaking to the municipal council in March 1927, Alphonse Loyau proposed precisely this sort of two-track solution. The idea was to build two types of HBM. The first, *le type Balao*, was intended for very poor families, those rescued from the slums and cheap hotels, whose entire lives have been precarious and miserable and for whom it will take some time to adjust to living in a community with other families who have always lived a normal life.... This sort of housing will have the advantage of rents well below *normal* housing: 50 percent less ... corresponding to the means of very poor families. (My emphasis)

In other words, people who had never enjoyed modern amenities would at least get a taste of middle-class conveniences, and this would prepare them for the next step. Loyau continued:

Even if the water-closets, on the landing under the staircase, will be shared by two families, even if apartments have no entryway but give directly into the main family spaces ... this represents a veritable paradise compared to the slums these families previously inhabited, and they are perfectly happy.... Then, when they have learned how to live in these improved circumstances, these families will be able to move on to more comfortable accommodations, if they so choose.[42]

This two-track approach to public housing did not strike everyone as unfair. Indeed, when Henri Sellier, mayor of the Paris suburb of Suresnes, tried to build "cheap housing equipped with central heat, bathrooms, proper kitchens boasting proper sinks, and incinerators for the garbage," critics accused him of "trying to house workers as if they were bourgeois."[43] In the end this was all moot, since the project never got off the ground. But it does provide some idea of the diverging expectations for the lower classes, as against those for the middle classes. As an illustration, Marie-Jeanne Dumont's essay on *le logement populaire* contains an impressive photograph of a flat from the 1930s "for the middle classes." It has a lovely parlor, tile above the kitchen sink with faucet and water heater, and a modern bathroom with a gleaming sink, bidet, and bathtub. Alas, only a much richer country could decide that the poor deserved decent plumbing, too.[44]

A dossier in the Paris Archives labeled "Aménagement de l'Îlot insalubre, no. 1" (the Saint-Merri quarter, surrounding what is now the Centre Pompidou) shows one attempt to put Loyau's principles into action.[45] Compiled in the early 1930s by the Société générale de travaux urbains (SGTU), a construction firm from the western end of the city, the dossier contains detailed plans for the creation of a new neighborhood—in the area bordered by the boulevard de Sebastopol, the rue du Renard, the rue du Temple, and the rue des Lombards—along with future plans to extend the development up to what is now les Halles. The expressed aim was "the reconstruction of the Saint-Merri quarter ... so as to bring air and light to a neighborhood where 12,500 souls live literally piled on top of one another and to bring back to this same neighborhood a population of 20,000 people to live in the most hygienic conditions." Photographs in the dossier offer convincing evidence that the neighborhood well merited tearing down.

Finances for the project were complicated. The contract in the letter to the prefect of the Seine, dated November 17, 1930, mentioned a figure of 530 million francs, doubtless making it one of the biggest public–private partnerships for reconstruction of the interwar period. The SGTU was going to do all the knocking down and putting up and would earn a future profit from rent on all the commercial and residential real estate, along with a huge subterranean car park it proposed to create. Since this was, in effect, public housing, questions about rent, and how responsive it would be to the market, had to be worked out in advance between the Société and the state. Very precise guidelines were established. If the costs of construction and maintenance turned out to be lower than what was projected, rents could be lowered. If the rent-control regime were ended, rents could be raised, but the dimensions of that would be worked out by a special commission of representatives from the SGTU and the prefect.

Arguably, the most interesting aspect of the plan lay in the disparities between the different apartments that were conceived, both in their dimensions and their amenities. They were designed in three sizes and four categories of fixtures. In category 1, flats ranged in size from one room (28 square meters) to *deux pièces* (40 square meters) to three rooms (52 square meters), all with kitchen and W.C. There was also a proposed option for *chambres isolées/chambres de bonne* [single rooms/maid's rooms] (14 square meters). It cost extra to have a *salle de bains*—that is, a washroom—in the apartment and an extra 1,100 francs a month for running water in the *chambres isolées*. Flats were larger in category 2: 52 square meters for a *deux pièces*, 64 square meters for three rooms, and 84 square meters for a *quatre pièces*—all of which had baths. The single rooms were either 13 square meters or 17 square meters. At the top, in category 4, the flats were larger still and were all furnished with bathrooms, *cabinets de toilette*, and W.C. The single rooms in category 2 were a third larger than those in category 1 and came with sinks (*lavabos*). Apartments in category 3 were even bigger. The *chambres isolées* were 20 square meters and had *lavabos*. Rents rose steeply between categories. A *deux pièces* in category 1 cost 2,150 francs per month. In category 2, rent was 6,400 francs per month. Rents for the most luxurious quarters in category 4 were not set by the commission but were subject to the laws of the market. Thus, a four-room flat of 100 square meters in category 2 was projected to cost almost 10,000 francs a month.

In sum, the poor were to be rehoused but without the *conforts* available to many of their middle-class neighbors. This would have amounted to a comparative fillip to middle-class households, many of which even on the eve of the Second World War still lacked basic amenities. In provincial cities in 1939, only 10 percent of *logements* had a bathroom; 5 percent had *tous conforts* (water, gas, electricity, sewer, central heating). A fifth of buildings were connected to a sewer system, and a third did not have both electricity *and* water. Four percent had no *conforts* whatsoever. Across the country only one *logement* in ten had a bathroom, a proportion that rose to a third of dwellings only in the tourist cities of Cannes and Nice; fewer than one in five in Paris, where half the population in the capital were still using collective toilets and outhouses.[46]

Of course, disadvantaged Parisians were unevenly distributed across the city. By 1940, for example, virtually every building in the city had running water—recalling that often this signaled water into the courtyard or the staircase and not into individual apartments—but in the working-class 20th arrondissement 10 percent did not. This was true for other modern amenities. Almost all Parisian buildings were hooked up to the gas and sewer systems, except in the popular neighborhoods of eastern Paris, where one building in ten still awaited connection. As for central heating, 26 percent of *immeubles* had it, which average translated to 75 percent in the upscale *seizième* (16th) and only 8 percent in the very unfashionable *onzième* (11th) arrondissement. Fewer than one household in five had a bathroom.

Historian André Rauch offers a positive view of the "courant hygiéniste" that inspired state support for low-cost housing and the rest of the modernizing agenda. Gradually, he concludes,

> Promoting the hygiene of the French people became state policy. The support given to constructing workers' housing demonstrates this well, when the law of 30 November 1894 gave official priority to the construction of affordable and clean public housing, with subsidized loans, tax breaks, financial preferences, etc.[47]

But Rauch gets it exactly wrong. Insufficient building; poor construction standards; old, tiny flats without amenities; rents too high for the neediest families; and an enduring gap between the living conditions of the middle class and those near the bottom of the socioeconomic ladder—looking back, not at virtuous intentions but at the cold facts of real achievement, it is hard to see French housing policy as anything but a failure. It is possible that a more market-sensitive set of policies, even combined with substantial subsidies for those who needed them, would have served the public better. Alternatively, a wealthier France could have done what a country strapped for cash could not; that is, to have the state pay for an upgrade in the housing sector. That is essentially what happened between the 1950s and the 1970s. But interwar France simply did not have the money.

Notes

1 André Tournade, *La pratique de l'hygiène en campagne* (Paris: Imprimerie Librairie Militaire Universelle, 1918), 35–9, 150–1.
2 Patricia Tilburg, *Working Girls: Sex, Taste, and Reform in the Parisian Garment Trades, 1880–1919* (New York: Oxford University Press, 2019), especially chapter 6, "Mimi Pinson Goes to War," 197–235; Maude Bass-Krueger, Hayley Edwards-Dujardin, and Sophie Kurkdjian, eds., *Fashion, Society, and the First World War: International Perspectives* (London: Bloomsbury, 2021), especially Jéremie Brucker, "The French Home Front in 1914–1918: An Investigation into Female Workwear," 182–96; Steven Zdatny, *Fashion Work and Politics in Modern France* (London: Palgrave Macmillan, 2006), 11. On hygiene and the New Woman, see Mary Louise Roberts, *Civilization Without Sexes: Reconstruction and Gender in Postwar France* (Chicago: University of Chicago Press, 1994), 82.
3 Émile Malespine, *L'urbanisme nouveau: l'hygiène et l'habitation* (Paris: Les Éditions de l'Effort, 1930), 7.
4 Fénélon Gibon, *Le fléau du taudis. Le premier remède: les habitations ouvrières* (Paris: Fénélon Gibon, 1918), 8–14. Also see M. A. Raynaud, *Les sciences physiques et naturelles, avec application à l'hygiène, l'agriculture et l'enseignement ménager. Cours moyen. Préparation au C.E.P.—Leçons de choses* (Chambéry: Maison d'Édition des Primaires, 1931), 59–60. Physician and social reformer Georges Cahen-Salvador

wrote that, in order to combat TB among children, it was necessary to get them out of the tenements and into the fresh air and sunshine of the country: "Rôle d'initiative privée en matière d'hygiène sociale," in Louis Martin and Georges Brouardel, *Hygiène sociale,* vol. XXIII (Paris: J.-B. Ballière et Fils, 1929), 527.

5 This dire judgment comes from the *exposé des motifs* for a proposal (1920)—which eventually became the Loucheur Law of 1928—to build half a million new homes, cited in Cahen-Salvador, "Rôle d'initiave privée," 529. Also see Pierre Guinchat, Marie-Paule Chaulet, and Lisette Gaillardot, *Il était une fois l'habitat: chronique du logement social en France* (Paris: Éditions du Moniteur, 1981), 53 and F. Roussel, des services municipaux d'hygiène et d'assistance sociale de Vitry-sur-Seine, "La crise du logement et l'hygiène. Le nouveau programme législative" (loi du 13 juillet 1928, dit Loi Loucheur), 3–4.

6 Yves Salaün, *Se loger: construire 20,000 logements par mois et, pour la France, une question de vie ou de mort* (Paris: Imprimerie de Montsouris, 1949), 25.

7 Jean-Claude Daumas, *La révolution matérielle. Une histoire de la consummation: France: XIXe-XXe siècle* (Paris: Flammarion, 2018), 236–7. Also see Fabienne Chevallier, "Sortie de guerre et enjeux urbains: histoire de deux projets parisiens (1919–1939)," *Histoire@politique* 3 (November–December 2007): 4; Malespine, *L'urbanisme nouveau*, 8; and Hélène Frouard, "À l'ombre des familles nombreuses: les politiques françaises du logement au XXe siècle," *Revue d'histoire moderne et contemporaine* 57, no. 2 (April–June 2010): 121, quoting the mayor of Ivry in 1925, Georges Marrane. Also see the frequent discussions about the water supply in Ministère de l'Hygiène, de l'Assistance et de la Prévoyance sociales. Direction de l'Assistance et de l'Hygiène Publiques. *Recueil des actes officiels et documents intéressant l'hygiène publique de France* (Melun: Imprimerie Administrative, published annually).

8 On conditions in Bordeaux, see Joseph Lajugie, dir., *Bordeaux au XXe siècle* (Bordeaux: Imprimeries Delmas, 1972), 66. For Lyon, see Fernand Bassé-Parton, *Le problème des taudis* (Paris: Maloine, 1938), 80. For the Yvelines, AD Yvelines, 4 U 2 25: Police Générale, dossiers "Haut commissariat au logement 1925. Crise de logement: enquête sur les bâtiments publics instructions," and "1925: Enquête auprès des administrations sur les bâtiments vacants."

9 Susanna Magri, "Les propriétaires, les locataires, la loi. Jalons pour une analyse sociologique des rapports de locations, Paris 1850–1920," *Revue française de la sociologie* 37, no. 3 (July–September 1996): 397–418.

10 AD Seine-et-Oise, 1161 W: rapport de l'assistance sociale, janvier 1939. Also see *La Population Française. La documentation française illustrée* 26 (February 1949): 3; also see Ministère de l'Économie Nationale, *Documents sur le problème du logement à Paris* (Paris: Imprimerie Nationale, 1946), 71.

11 Michel Lescure, *Histoire d'une filière: Immobilier et bâtiment en France (1820–1980)* (Paris: Hatier, 1983), 33 et suite.

12 Anaïs Albert, *La vie à credit. La consommation des classes populaires à Paris (années 1880–1920)* (Paris: Éditions de la Sorbonne, 2021), 117.

13 Ministère de l'Économie Nationale, *Documents sur le problème de logements*, 7–8, 15–16, 24–7. Also see Jean-Paul Lacaze, *Les Français et leur logement: éléments de socio-économie de l'habitat* (Paris: Presses de l'École Nationale des Ponts et Chaussées, 1989), 15–16.

14 "La question du taudis dans les différents pays moyens mis en oeuvre pour y remédier," in Ministère de la Santé Publique, *Recueil des travaux de l'Institut National*

d'Hygiène: travaux des sections et mémoires originaux, tome IV, vol. 1 (Paris: Masson et Cie., 1950), 298.
15 Ministère de l'Économie Nationale, *Documents sur le problème du logement*, 160.
16 Alain Faure and Claire Lévy-Vroelant, *Une chambre en ville: Hôtels meublés et garnis de Paris, 1860–1990* (Saint-Etienne: Créaphis, 2007), 180; also "Se loger," in *La technique sanitaire et municipal: Organe de l'Association Générale des Hygiénists et techniciens municipaux* 42, no. 3–4 (March 1947): 13.
17 On the Nozière affair, see Anne-Emmanuelle Demartini, *Violette Nozière, la fleur du mal. Une histoire des années trente* (Ceyzérieu: Champ Vallon, 2017), 208. The description comes from Yves Lequin, *Histoire des Français, XIXe-XXe siècles*, tome 2: *La société* (Paris: Armand Colin, 1983), 173.
18 Yvonne Knibiehler, *Nous, les assistantes sociales. Naissance d'une profession, témoignages présentés par Y. Knibiehler* (Paris: Aubier, 1980), 131.
19 Gaston Chevereau, *De l'étable au tableau* (Le Mans: Éditions Cénomane, 1989), 6–7.
20 Anne-Marie Sohn, *Chrysalides. Femmes dans la vie privée (XIXe-XXe siècles)*, vol. 1 (Paris: Publications de la Sorbonne, 1996), 111 and Audrey Jean-Marie, "Le logement à Paris: évolutions récentes, enjeux actuels," in Jacques Lucan (ed.), *Eau et gaz à tous les étages. Paris: 100 ans de logement* (Paris: Édition du Pavillon de l'Arsenal, 1992), 265–6.
21 George Orwell, *Down and Out in London and Paris* (London: Victor Gollanz, 1933), 2.
22 La Ligue Contre le Taudis, *Le Taudis* (Mamers [Sarthe]: Gabriel Enault, n.d.), 6–7; Badini-Jourdin is cited in Yankel Fijalkow, *Mesurer l'hygiène urbaine: logements et îlots insalubres, Paris, 1850–1945* (Villeneuve d'Ascq: Presses Universitaires de Septentrion, 1994), 203. This is a published imprint of the author's doctoral dissertation at the Écoles des Hautes Études en Sciences Sociales.
23 Céline Lhotte, *Ma mère Riquet, croquis sociaux* (Paris: Valois, 1928), 126–7.
24 Isabelle Backouche, *Paris transformé: Le Marais, 1900–1980* (Paris: Créaphis Éditions, 2016), 7.
25 Frédéric Zarch, "Le caméra sanitaire," in Didier Nourrisson (dir.), *Éducation à la santé, XIXe-XXe siècles* (Rennes: Éditions ENSP, 2002), 85.
26 On Lyon in particular, see Philippe Dufieux, "À propos de l'hygiène de Lyon (1800–1960)," in Conseil d'architecture, d'urbanisme et de l'environnement du Rhône, *Le confort moderne dans l'habitat* (Lyon: CAUE, 2007), 16–17.
27 On Toulouse, see Rosemary Wakeman, *Modernizing the Provincial City: Toulouse, 1945–1975* (Cambridge, MA: Harvard University Press, 1997), 95.
28 AD Loire-Atlantique, 5 M 28, Conseil d'hygiène meetings from 1937.
29 Colin Jones, *Paris: Biography of a City* (New York: Viking, 2004), 362 and Conseil Municipal de Paris, 1937, *Rapport au nom de la 6e Commission sur la question des îlots insalubres*, présenté par M. Louis Sellier, conseiller municipal [at the Bibliothèque de l'Hôtel de Ville de Paris], 4.
30 Quoted in Fijalkow, *Mesurer l'hgiène urbaine*, 199.
31 AP, 5 VD 2: Salubrité Publique, "Rapport au nom de la 6e Commission sur les résultats de l'expropriation de l'îlot insalubre no. 2 (première tranche), présenté par M. C. Roéland," Conseil Municipal de Paris, 1931, 2–26.
32 Conseil Municipal, reports from the 6e commission: 1931, 26 and 1937, 31.
33 Alfred Sauvy, *Histoire économique de la France entre les deux guerres*, vol. 3 (Paris: Fayard, 1972), 313; Lacaze, *Les français et leur logement*, 14.
34 Daumas, *La révolution matérielle*, 288; also Marie-Jeanne Dumont, "L'invention d'un programme: le logement populaire," in Lucan (ed.), *Eau et gaz*, 71.

35 Salaün, *Se loger*, 69; also see Roger-Henri Guerrand, "Aux origines du confort moderne," in Lucan (ed.), *Eau et gaz*, 27.
36 Ministère de la Santé Publique, "La question des taudis dans les différents pays moyen mis en oeuvre pour y remédier," in *Recueil des travaux de l'Institut National d'Hygiène: travaux des sections et mémoires originaux*, Tome IV. Vol. 1 (Paris: Masson et Cie., 1950), 309, 368.
37 For a comparison with Britain and Germany, see Nicole Rudolph, *At Home in Postwar France: Modern Mass Housing and the Right to Comfort* (Oxford and New York: Berghahn Books, 2015), 40.
38 Édouard Bonnefous, *Avant l'oubli: La vie de 1900 à 1940* (Paris: Laffont/Nathan, 1985), 453.
39 The Société Anonyme d'Habitations à Bon Marché [SAHBM], one of several private organizations that built housing for people of limited income, complained about how hard it was to evict families who had initially qualified, with at least three children under the age of thirteen, but no longer do, since those children had grown up and left home: SAHBM, *L'habitation familiale. Compte-rendu de l'Assemblée générale ordinaire du 25 mai 1928* (Paris: Imprimerie d'Ouvriers Sourds-Muets, 1928), 5.
40 Jones, *Paris*, 405.
41 Ministère de la Santé Publique, *Recueil des travaux*, 309; on the problem of rents, also see Frouard, "À l'ombre des familles nombreuses," 123 and Roussell, "La crise du logement," 13.
42 Cited in Fijalkow, *Mesurer l'hygiène urbaine*, 285–7.
43 Eugen Weber, *The Hollow Years: France in the 1930s* (New York: Norton, 1994), 68.
44 Dumont, "L'invention d'un programme," 47.
45 AP, V D5 1: Salubrité publique, "Aménagement de l'Îlot insalubre no. 1."
46 Lucienne Cahen, "Évolution des conditions de logement en France depuis cent ans," *Études et Conjonctures* 10–11 (1957): 1194, 1207.
47 André Rauch, *Histoire de la santé. Que sais-je?* (Paris: Presses Universitaires de France, 1995), 87–8.

10

Hygiene between the Wars

Rural Hygiene between the Wars

Ernst Jünger was an uninvited guest, billeting in the home of a French family behind the Somme front in 1916, when he complained about the dirtiness and the "very low moral development" of the local inhabitants. "The vain search for a water-closet," he wrote,

> is the outstanding memory one has of the villages of Lorraine. Baths appear to be unknown. I have some strange experiences of this description in France. One has to pass with a smile over certain shady sides of even the most magnificent mansions. Much as I esteem the French, I cannot help thinking that this is a characteristic side of their life. I know indeed that hostile races always call each other dirty, and that we were ourselves called 'sales Boches' by the French. Nevertheless, I feel we are fully justified in returning this compliment to the Latin races.[1]

It was not only *les boches*, however, who disparaged the standards of hygiene found in the French countryside; the French also complained about one another. Refugees from the northeast, fleeing their homes in front of the German invasion of 1940, writes historian Richard Vinen, "were contemptuous of the low, dark, dirty houses they found in the southwest." For their part, according to the Swiss-French artist Annie Vallotton, traveling around France with her sister Gitou during the German Occupation, Alsatians considered their hosts in the Limousin "dirty.... [They] use very little water, rarely speak of washing, but say to [us], 'These Alsatians are dirty! Imagine that they have their toilets in the house! That is disgusting!'"[2] *À chacun son dégoût.*

As in the case of Jünger, just because an observation is unkind, though, does not mean that it is untrue, and while German officers and French refugees might have been uncharitable in judging *les paysans*, they were not necessarily wrong about the state of things in many parts of the French countryside. As hard as it was to bring twentieth-century standards of *salubrité* to French cities, it was harder still for that half of the population who continued to live in small villages and ancient houses, where the progress of rural hygiene did not run into problems of crowding but of dispersion and poverty, and of a culture where dirt and dung were not unpleasant externalities but the essence of peasant ecology.

The Third Republic had never hesitated in its quest to civilize the peasantry, and following the end of the Great War it renewed its interest in the quality of life in the vast countryside. That interest was driven more than ever by two seemingly existential concerns. The first was the continuing "exodus" from the farm to the city. The migratory flow from the countryside to the towns between the wars was not yet the flood it became after 1945, but it worried those who saw in the emptying out of villages and hamlets a diminution of essential Frenchness and a dangerous new world of unrooted city-dwellers who would make easy prey for Jacobins and Communists. The prospect concerned the agriculture minister sufficiently for him, in 1922, to sign a decree establishing back-to-the-land committees in every department, chaired by the prefect and bringing together local administrators, engineers, and landowners. Their job was to improve life in the countryside so that "rural folk will no longer abandon their farms, and a number of those who have left will return to the peasantry on the day they find the villages attractive, modernized . . . provided with electricity, with abundant water and accessible health care." There was plenty of work to be done on this score. Of the 37,965 communes in France, observed the president of the agriculture office in the Var, 22,695 had neither a post office nor a telephone booth.[3]

Second, it was feared that the lack of hygiene in rural France was contributing to comparatively high mortality rates and national demographic torpor—more than ever after the carnage of the Great War, when the birth rate appeared to pose a sharp question about "the survival of the race."[4] Indeed, a 1947 report on the birth rate to the minister of public health cited a decline in live births from 749,000 in 1913 to 600,000 in 1944, which it pegged, rightly or wrongly, to the housing shortage that made parents reluctant to add more children to already-crowded homes.[5]

On the other side of the ledger, everyone recognized that mortality rates, especially for infants, had dropped sharply since the middle of the nineteenth century (Table 10.1). The exact numbers differ somewhat from source to source but fall within the same range, from approximately 180 per 100,000 live births in 1860 to 142 in 1901, down to 70 in 1935—although France continued to lag behind the Protestant societies: the Netherlands, England and Scotland, and the Scandinavian countries. The incidence of *mortinatalité*—that is, the death of babies in their first thirty days—followed a similar downward trajectory. Much of this success was owed to the Roussel Law of 1874 that required expectant mothers to register their pregnancies at the *mairie* and instituted monthly visits to the new mother by medical inspectors. Where the authorities were

Table 10.1 Infant Mortality Rates (p. 1000) in Various Industrial Countries, 1937–9

New Zealand	31	USA	50	Belgium	73		
Netherlands	36	England	54	Austria	82		
Australia	42	Germany	61	Italy	107		
Norway	42	Denmark	61	Spain	125		
Sweden	42	**France**	**64**	Hungary	130		
Switzerland	44	Finland	69	Poland	138		

Source: Michel Huber, Henri Bunlé, et Fernand Boverat, *La population de France: son évolution et ses perspectives* (Paris: Hachette, 1950), 355.

active in enforcing the Roussel Law, infant mortality was half the national average.⁶ The news was less encouraging on the fertility side.

The Roussel Law was only one part of a general assault on the practices depressing the size and vigor of the French population. Hygiene was another part. Instruction in housekeeping and motherhood had become a keystone of the school curriculum for girls, and shelves of new books advised mothers on the rules of *puériculture* that stressed the importance of physical activity for young children and especially the value of breastfeeding, which was "virtually incompatible in the cities with poverty and working mothers." Cow's milk is no substitute, the authorities told women, pointing out that infant mortality among breastfed babies was only about 10 percent of what it was among those fed through bottles. Taking an old message and using the latest technology, in the 1920s the government began funding a rural cinema campaign, designed to educate farmers on better agricultural techniques but also on better hygiene. Film historian Allison Murray Levine found one film, *La future maman* (1925), that focused on the proper care of newborns and framed the choice for peasant mothers as between traditional practices and modern science, using "expert" advice and didactic stories to promote the latter.⁷

These values and practices found their way into rural lives only imperfectly, even in the schools themselves. Jeanne Charrier-Lecomte grew up in the Vendée after the Great War. At her boarding school in the early 1930s, she remembered the hasty splash of water in the morning, along with a quick bit of tooth- and hair-brushing. She rinsed anything beyond her neck and hands only once a week—on Sunday, when she also changed her clothes. There were no showers at her school and a powerful culture of modesty, which meant that "between chest and feet there was never any sort of washing."⁸

As Charrier-Lecomte's memoir suggests, the old culture of partial and irregular washing in rural France was proving hard to change. Islands of resistance to the "new ways" of hygiene held fast, both in individual attitudes and institutional practices. Emilie Carles, for example, grew up poor and remote in the Haute-Savoie at the turn of the century, although she later went on to a successful teaching career and enjoyed a moment of national acclaim as a resistor to modernity and a chronicler of the recent French past. In her published recollection, *A Life of Her Own*, Carles illustrates the excessive modesty and inattention to washing of that time and place with an anecdote about her peasant father, Joseph Alais, who once looked after his toddler granddaughter for three weeks without ever changing her scratchy wool clothes because he could not bear the idea of seeing a female body, even a three-year-old's.⁹

Peasant *pudeur* was not the only barrier to more comprehensive washing. In his study of France in the "hollow years" of the 1930s, Eugen Weber recounts the experience of Magdeleine Peyronnec, the young novice who, describing her Carmelite convent in the 1930s, painted a dreadful picture of neglect, rooted in religious morality rather than rustic decorum:

> No washstand, soap, or toothbrush. Ablutions, carried out with a rag already used by others and dipped in a little water, touched only hands and face. On the first Thursday of every month, a special basin was brought round the cells for nuns to

wash their feet—no higher than the ankles. All other parts were out of bounds; cleaning or touching them would be a mortal sin.[10]

At the same time as church authorities worried about setting young girls on the road to perdition, they also joined the crusade to foster among mothers and future mothers more informed and sanitary modes of childcare since, as the Jesuit reformer Henri de Farcy observed, overworked peasant mothers "[were] certainly a cause of infant mortality." Hence, Catholic publications promoted, among other things, the need to assure the *salubrité* of wet-nurses and nannies, and they emphasized the need to sterilize whatever a baby might put in her mouth. Therefore, in contrast with their hesitation to prescribe full-body washing for young girls at boarding school or in religious training, they touted the value of daily baths for infants: having waited ten days following delivery for the umbilical cord to come off, babies should then be patted dry, sprinkled with talc, nose coated with Vaseline, and covered with blankets to keep warm. Whereas popular habits in the early nineteenth century had approved of swaddling newborns and leaving them to stew in dirty "diapers," twentieth-century doctors and nurses demanded that nappies be changed before every breastfeeding. To be sure, practice often lagged behind expert advice; one housewife in the Seine-et-Oise in 1939 told authorities that she *never* changed her son's swaddling because it was "pointless," for example. To judge by infant mortality statistics, however, this sort of advice was not without its effect.[11]

Overall, puericulture seemed to be moving in the right direction. Anne-Marie Sohn, in her survey of women and households, writes that by the late 1930s, the principle of regular washing had been established in the public mind, even if it had not become an indelible part of popular practice. And *Marie-Claire*, the new women's magazine that prided itself on its modern attitude, told readers to bathe their infants every day, carefully and in a room without drafts. Its editors were concerned about the general health of the baby rather than with cleanliness for its own sake—they worried, in particular about "toxins" that might gather on the baby's skin and thought that a warm bath would "allow him to wiggle freely and relax his nervous system"—but the effect was the same.[12]

Whatever the motivation, better hygiene for babies helped to drive down their mortality rates. This decline was steady but not constant, and it varied considerably from north to south and east to west. Both hot weather and cold weather could kill the youngest and oldest in the population. An eruption of typhoid or diphtheria—or an outbreak of diarrhea like the one that killed scores of young children in Toulon in May 1921—could push the trend in the wrong direction for a year or two. Alternatively, an economic crisis, like the one that gripped France in the early 1930s, could depress the birth rate—Dr. Adolf-August Lesage and Marcel Moine wrote, for example, that live births in France dropped from 17.9 per 1,000 inhabitants in 1930 to 13.0 in 1936: a decline of 16.2 percent—and have an adverse effect on national demography even as the infant mortality rate continued to creep down.

There seems surprisingly little pattern to the distribution of infant mortality in France. The seven departments with the worst rates were scattered across the country: Haute-Loire, Cantal, Ardèche, Oise, Côtes-du-Nord, and Meuse. The seven departments with the best rates were likewise distributed: Alpes-Maritimes, Vendée, Belfort, Aude, Loire-Inférieure, Vienne, and Pyrénées-Orientales. As for natality, the department of the Bouches-du-Rhône (essentially, Marseille) had the lowest birth rate, with 10.2 live births per 1,000 inhabitants; the Manche, in Normandy, and the Pas-de-Calais, on the Channel coast, had the highest, with 21.3 births/1,000. The ambiguous and complex details, however, could not obscure the simple realities everyone could see. Even if fewer infants were dying, fewer were being born, and population growth was flat.[13]

Those who worried about the demographic fate of the country connected it back to the ongoing exodus from the villages to the cities. The point was that, insofar as strapping young peasants were leaving their fields for city slums, the crisis in the countryside was bringing the rest of the nation down with it. It was understood, moreover, that rural emigration was driven principally by the enduring backwardness of rural France. Poor health was endemic, and it was in large part attributable to the lag between the progress of hygiene in the towns, even among the working classes, and the conditions that pertained among the peasantry. The worrying fact of poor rural hygiene and its implications for the future of France were clear enough. French males died on average three years sooner than their British, and fully seven years sooner than their Dutch, counterparts. And what chance did the French army of 1938 stand against the Wehrmacht, when the German army rejected 17 percent of young men as unfit, whereas the *armée française* was still rejecting a third of a smaller pool of potential recruits?

Apart from the congenital dirtiness of life on the farm, it was commonly agreed that rampant alcoholism was playing a critical role in the decay of French masculinity. Between 1930 and 1936, while the general mortality rate for men rose by 4 percent, deaths from cirrhosis climbed by 30 percent.[14] School textbooks had begun to address the scourge of alcohol at the end of the nineteenth century and continued to do so. The 1931 edition of M. A. Raymond's *Les sciences physiques et naturelles*, a mid-level text, told young readers that water was best to drink; coffee, tea, and chocolate were fine, when imbibed sensibly. On the contrary, "fermented beverages" (wine, cider, and beer) had no nutritive value and were best avoided by children, or at least consumed in moderation. "Distilled drinks," it added ominously, "are poison" and should be shunned, at the risk of alcoholism and early death.[15]

Of course, the advice prescribed in school texts, even when reinforced by finger-wagging teachers, consistently ran up against traditional customs, one of which was the practice of giving children alcohol to drink, that remained a live issue well into the post-1945 period. Jeanne Charrier-Lecomte, the retired teacher writing in the early 1980s, still remembered young students whose parents had sent wine for them to have with their lunch. In the same vein, an article in *Elle* in May 1959 told stories of grandparents, who had themselves been taught about the health benefits of wine, pouring a small glass for their three-year-old grandson or giving him sugar cubes dipped in cognac for a treat. The magazine reported with some horror that wine remained an "ordinary drink" in school canteens and alluded to a survey of 400 rural doctors that found that one in five of them had seen cases of parents putting wine or other alcohol in baby bottles. Of course, alcoholism was not an exclusively rural disease. *Elle* referred to an issue of the American magazine *Look*, which had published an article by an author who had spent three weeks living with a French working-class family, and which included a photograph "of a little boy who had been sent to fetch his father from the local bistrot ... and, having been offered an *apéritif*, now lay sleeping on the bar." The misuse of alcohol was an ongoing national disaster.[16]

The *Enquête*

Apprehension about a crisis of living conditions in the countryside and its implications for the rest of society were not limited to France, and it was in response to a League of Nations initiative that an inquiry into "the economic, social, and sanitary conditions" in the French hinterlands was organized under the auspices of the minister of public health, Henri Queuille, in order "to protect and to reinforce the physical and moral 'potential' [of rural France]" by improving hygiene and comfort. The plan was to have researchers from across the country investigate the material quality of life in the villages and hamlets of *la France profonde*. The results were published in two volumes: the first contained an overview of the national situation, and the second department-by-department accounts. These accounts produced a lot of raw information about circumstances across rural France, although they did not contain any reliable statistical assessments and comparisons. It appears that individual reporters for each department worked off the same list of questions and concerns, but there was no consistency in approach or assessment. Even so, the *Enquête* provides about as full a picture of peasant life in the 1930s as we are likely to find.[17]

In his survey of the results, director Maurice Vignerot states the obvious: the future quality of life in the countryside will depend chiefly on two things: electrification and the supply of potable water—both of which will in turn depend on government subsidies to rural communes. Summarizing the situation, Vignerot writes that in March 1937, of the 38,014 communes in metropolitan France, only about a third of them had running water systems. The distribution of this essential amenity varied substantially between departments and communes. In only 6 percent of departments did at least three-quarters of communes have *adduction d'eau*; in 20 percent a half to three-quarters had it; 26 percent of departments provided running water to between a quarter and a half of their communes; and in 38 percent, less than a quarter had it. This was, he remarked, a very mediocre result. And the situation was even worse when it came to the *evacuation des eaux usées*; that is, the existence of a sewer system or at least functioning cesspits.[18]

The dozens of reports that came to the editors of the *Enquête* from the departments offer little in the way of hard numbers but lots of broad observations and are informative, nonetheless.[19] Reporters focused consistently not only on the availability of electricity and running water—both *adduction* and *evacuation*—but also on the quality of latrines, individual hygienic practices, and the state of houses: Were they well built? Did they have dirt floors? Furniture? Were they crowded? Did they separate beasts and people? In the composite, the picture of *logements* drawn by the *Enquête* is either dire or encouraging, depending on perspective. Looking backward, peasant life in the 1930s appears filthy, hard, and primitive. On the other hand, judging the state of rural hygiene in the 1930s against the practices and material circumstances that had prevailed a century earlier, the improvement of life on the land had been substantial.

Electricity is perhaps the best example of this. Historian Jean-Claude Daumas writes that the proportion of communes on the electric grid climbed from 19.7 percent in 1919 to 64.4 percent in 1929 to 96.2 percent in 1937. These numbers are deceptive, insofar as a commune could have electricity without every house having it; and, in fact, Daumas adds that in 1946 only 82.5 percent of rural French *households* had electricity. Per capita usage in 1937 remained well behind that in Britain, Belgium, and Germany and a mere 40 percent of what the typical American was using at the time. The expansion of this basic amenity in France was held back by its comparatively high price and the fact that, since builders were not required to put electrical outlets in every room, they did not. In a feedback loop of stagnation, there was little popular pressure on public authorities to speed up the process of bringing electric power to the villages.[20]

Generalizations about the national state of rural electrification are confirmed, but also complicated, by the individual descriptions collected by the *Enquête*, which found that in the years leading up to the Second World War access to electricity in the countryside was highly uneven from region to region and within each department. In the relatively well-off Basses-Pyrénées, for example, the rich areas of the countryside mostly had it, and the poor areas did not. Next door, in the Hautes-Pyrénées, because of the proximity of hydroelectric power, the department was almost entirely on the grid. In the Drôme in 1937, 12 percent of the communes had no electricity, but this represented only 2.3 percent of the population; that is, the most dispersed households. In the Charente, the electrification of the countryside began only in 1924, amid what the regional office for agriculture called "a general state of filth and discomfort" and had not advanced very far before the correspondent for the *Enquête* arrived on the scene a decade later.[21]

Striking a happier note, the reporter for the Nord wrote that "the problem of electrical service to farms and houses is more or less complete." But it is hard to know exactly what this entailed. Just because peasants *had* access to electricity does not mean that they *used* it. Thus, in the Saône-et-Loire, although out of 589 communes only three were still without current, the reporter wrote that "few homes had electric light." Even so, in historical perspective this was progress. Despite its patchiness in the 1930s, a century earlier electricity had still belonged to the world of magic.

It was harder to be optimistic about any aspect of country life that involved water—water in, water out, water for drinking, or water for washing. This makes perfect sense, given the much higher cost of laying pipe and installing pumps than of stringing wire. In any event, the lack of water left a deeper impression on the peasantry than the relative availability of electricity—and was in many ways more concerning since, while the absence of electricity meant inconvenience, the absence of good, drinkable water often meant disease. From report to report, the water situation in the countryside ranged from poor to catastrophic. In the comparatively advanced Haut-Rhin, under half the 387 communes had it. Whereas the poorer Charente department was "very badly provisioned with drinkable water and most individuals used wells." In the Pas-de-Calais, the majority of villages that had been rebuilt since the war had piped water. Otherwise, peasants met their needs from often contaminated sources. In the Puy-de-Dôme, out of a rural population of 350,000, "250,000 inhabitants had no access to running water." In the Ariège, "151 communes out of 341 enjoyed piped water [that is] defective or insufficient." The reporter in the Gers warned of a water "crisis" in an area *en pleine dépeuplement*. And so on. "Into the 1940s," writes Eugen Weber, "only about one child in five [in the countryside] had access to running water."[22]

Notwithstanding the general sluggishness, some places saw palpable progress. In the town of Roziers (Lozère) just after the First World War, the municipal council set out to bring in electricity and to upgrade an "unhealthy and feeble" water supply, which had a tendency in summer to dry up almost entirely. A decade later, the citizens of Roziers enjoyed clean water running into a number of public fountains.[23] Elsewhere, efforts to improve the water supply were not always crowned with success. Sometimes, as Dr. Fernand Barbary, inspector for the hygiene service in the Alpes-Maritimes, noted, the ambitions of communal authorities ran into "the apathy, the indifference, the habits, and the sensibilities of the residents."[24] On other occasions, local initiatives ran aground, and it is hard to say why. The departmental hygiene council of the Loire-Inférieure, for example, seems to have appreciated the need to "procure healthy and abundant water" for the population around Nantes. It met regularly and considered local requests for the installation of running water systems. In November 1934, the council discussed the poor quality and feeble supply of drinkable water to the villages around La Baule. In July 1937, it heard from the commune of Varades and considered a request from the commune of Cellier, which complained that its existing water sources—old wells, mostly—"are dry in summer and offer no guarantee from a bacteriological point of view." Acting in apparent good faith, the council proposed a new system, fed by water from the Loire River. But its records do not indicate that any of these systems ever functioned before the war.[25]

In a more general sense, when the council had surveyed the communes in the Angevin countryside in 1936 on behalf of the *Enquête*, it found some modestly encouraging signs—for instance, in the small town of Mouzillon, whose 1,125 inhabitants and 342 *habitations* enjoyed an "elementary" water system made up of individual wells and a collective standpipe, as well as four "decent" *lavoirs* (washhouses), although there was not a single bathtub in the town. Ninety-five percent of its homes had electricity. The houses were made of crushed rock, the roofs of tile—with a slight pitch, since the region had lots of rain but no snow. Most had one floor. Several had two. Almost all had a loft. The walls were hard and whitewashed. There was plenty of furniture "in a good state" and spacious kitchens that functioned for eating, as well as cooking and in about 20 percent of cases, also sleeping. Two-thirds had outbuildings for the animals. All had a wine cellar. Some had manure piles, most of which were well kept. Conversely, the latrine situation was highly unsatisfactory—a matter of shallow holes generally dug at the bottom of the garden, of a "doubtful *propreté*" and without any sort of septic system.[26]

Mouzillon was comparatively fortunate. Neighboring communes displayed many of the same unsatisfactory conditions, without the compensating satisfactory ones. There was no piped water; men and beasts were provisioned out of "shallow wells." The houses were solidly built and most separated the livestock from the humans, but courtyards were a dog's breakfast, with standing water, trash, and ill-kept *fumiers*. In general, when it came to hygiene and amenities, "the situation is simply lamentable," the council told the *Enquête*, yet it finished on a modestly optimistic note: high commodity prices after the war had given peasants the means to improve the state of their farms and farmhouses, even if, in the mid-1930s, "much remained to do."

South of the Anjou, in the Haute-Vienne, virtually every meeting of the departmental hygiene and sanitation commission in the 1930s considered some local project for *adduction* in this habitually thirsty part of the country. The commission dispatched experts, who reported back to it, confirming the water problem and endorsing some sort of action to solve it—without ever managing to build a twentieth-century delivery system. Sometimes, it did not even try. At its February 1930 meeting, for example, the council heard a report on a proposal to build a small housing project along a wide country road in Panazol, just to the east of Limoges. The scheme envisioned no sidewalks, to save money, but a system of gutters was designed for better drainage. Rules were set in place to make sure that houses were properly built and the grounds maintained. There were no plans for any water pipes. Rather, "the future property owners will have to provide for drinking water on their own, according to rules laid down by [the authorities] for the establishment of wells, cisterns, cesspits, and garbage dumps." This language appeared in all the projects that came forward for the council's approval. To be sure, these housing projects and the accompanying infrastructure were an improvement on existing conditions. Consistently, however, efforts to give the locals an ample supply of clean water came up short of expectations. Limoges and its environs had to wait until after the war for a modern system of *adduction*.[27]

Not surprisingly, the snapshots gathered by reporters for the Loire-Inférieure and the Limousin fit neatly into the album assembled for the *Enquête*, not just in the case of water and electricity but for the whole scope of elements that defined rural hygiene. Some departments reported comparatively decent conditions. In the Basses-Pyrénées, ethnologist Henri Cavailles saw houses "low and long and capped with [thatch]." But the interiors were roomy and the spaces neatly divided between living and sleeping. Frequently, there was a second floor. The animals were close by, but not in the human space.[28] Next door, in the Hautes-Pyrénées, the *Enquête* found homes typically without running water or indoor privies—amenities that were, of course, extremely rare in farmhouses all across France. But they almost all had wood or stone floors; the few dirt floors were found in the kitchen. And the beds were rarely occupied by more than two people. More typically around the country, interiors continued to be dirty, chaotic, and largely without furniture or light or privacy. Courtyards were strewn with garbage and piled with leaky *fumiers*. The departmental committees often reported "progress," but they almost never reported a satisfactory state of hygiene. Overall, the anecdotal evidence collected in the *Enquête* confirms the statistical evidence from the census: the French peasantry continued to live almost entirely without modern *conforts*.

Cleaner Villages, Cleaner Villagers?

The effect of these conditions on habits of individual *salubrité* was predictable. Absent the infrastructure for keeping clean, the rural population mostly stuck to traditional practices. Customs in the Vaucluse, to take one example, remained pretty summary:

> Ideas about cleanliness have reached only the better-off households. The typical peasant performs his toilette over the kitchen sink, rather than a basin in his room. It consists of a perfunctory rinse of the hands before a meal [and] a quick splash of cold water in the morning before the animals have a drink of it. That's all.

The correspondent for Belfort noted that peasants were clean, but the facilities for washing "typically amounted to nothing more than a simple basin. . . . There were no sinks, no showers, no bathtubs, only a hand-pump by the front door feeding well water into a stone trough." Likewise, in the Finistère, conditions and practices "leave much to be desired." In the summer "young people bathe in the streams and in the sea." Otherwise, there were no washrooms, and people cared little for "the virtues of hygiene." When they washed at all it was in a small basin, which they then emptied into the courtyard, where it added fluidity to the runoff from the manure piles. At the other end of the Breton peninsula, in the Ille-et-Vilaine, the *Enquête* noted that "there were neither baths nor showers," with predictable consequences for personal hygiene.

If conditions and practices in most of France resembled those in the Vaucluse and Brittany, the *Enquête* found exceptions, especially in parts of the north and the east. In the Ardennes, *la propreté individuelle* was pretty good. Bathtubs could be found on the big farms, sinks and running water even on the smaller *exploitations*. Every home had some system of *évaculation*, and personal hygiene, especially for children, had "made great progress since the war." Similar good news in the Nord, where "plans for reconstruction of the devastated regions reserved for questions of hygiene a too-long neglected importance." Inhabitants of the department, compared to the situation elsewhere, enjoyed excellent personal hygiene, thanks in large part to the "remarkable cleanliness" of their homes, particularly in Flanders, where "the homemaker is proud of the perfect state of her house, her floors, her furniture, and the rest of her dwelling." Inevitably, though, on farms that had not been destroyed in the war and rebuilt afterward, "Hygienic facilities remain rudimentary. Leaking *fumiers* still sit right next to houses and wells, and one still runs up against an inveterate indifference to hygiene that neither persuasion nor sanctions can overcome."

Daniel Desbois spent his childhood in the region around Dijon, in a house that contained "not the least amenity." The outhouse consisted of a few planks of wood sitting over a shallow hole far from the house—which was good, since it attracted hordes of flies. There was no water in the house for a proper toilette. Animals and people drank out of the same cistern. "Comfort and hygiene hardly existed," wrote Desbois. This was true, he added, even among the local "bourgeois," whose homes were hardly better equipped.[29] Raymonde Anna Rey similarly remembered her home in the Cévennes, almost devoid of furniture: a cooker; a table and a few chairs; a cot for her baby daughter and for her son, who slept in the room with his parents; a mattress laid on some crates and covered by a bedspread. Max Chaleil grew up in the village of Brignon, Languedoc, in a 200-year-old house. The interior was hung with spices and contained a bed, an armoire, a chamber pot, and rooms with chimneys that were "never" lit. In the Haute-Loire, Joseph Cressot recalled his boyhood home, where pigs still shared the house with people.[30]

For his *thèse* at the faculty of medicine in Montpellier, Émile Guigou went off to study the state of hygiene in a nearby (but unidentified) village in the Bas-Languedoc.[31] In this commune of 3,851 inhabitants, 930 had electric lighting, but only 70 had any sort of electric appliance beyond that. With one automobile for every sixteen people, however, the village had more motor transport than the French average (one in twenty). Peasant culture in this small Protestant community, wrote Guigou, maintained the old "rigide et classique austerité." A prosperous viticulture had begun to modernize the population, especially the middle classes, still, hygiene remained substandard. People counted on the elements—sun and wind—as "purifying agents," which Guigou considered a pretext for ignoring even the most elementary hygienic practices. The village had installed a public *bains-douches* in 1933, and it was used by "an important fraction of the population." Usage nevertheless added up to an average of about one-half bath per year for each inhabitant—and even this, after some initial enthusiasm, declined.

The public water system, on the contrary, was very satisfactory, both in quality and quantity. Running water had first been piped into the village in 1898. It had not reached all the homes by the mid-1930s, but it did serve the sixty-four public fountains scattered through the village. Daily consumption was 200 liters per person, compared to 430 in Paris (not all of it for personal use), 200 in Bordeaux and Nice, and 100 in Lille. Some of the locals still used a couple of pumps that drew from wells. They swore to the water's superior quality. But Guigou's lab discovered "massive contamination" that was the source of waterborne disease, notably typhoid fever.

The houses in the village, most of them built between 1840 and 1870, were typical of peasant homes generally: crowded, dark, neither running water nor W.C. Outside, Guigou found leaky dung heaps, leaving the streets full of yellowish, nauseating puddles when it rained. The village made some efforts to keep gutters and streets clean. But without a sewer system, that proved impossible. Several proposals to build one were rejected by local voters for "weighing too heavily on the commune's budget."

Guigou paid special attention to what he called "the burning question of public toilets." In an example of good intentions gone awry, the authorities decided in 1926 to build a facility close to the slums where the working class lived without any sort of amenities, particularly functioning W.C. Under the guidance of the departmental hygiene council, the *cabinet* was connected to a septic pit, where the effluvia was rendered "absolutely odorless and colorless" before being released into the gutters. "Alas," Guigou observed, the public W.C. functioned so well, and was so popular, that the housewives from the surrounding neighborhoods came there to spill out *all* their dirty water, causing the *fosse* to overflow and to fill the streets with poisonous-smelling liquid. This forced the authorities to close the facility, since the village could not organize its expansion or regular evacuation, and it never reopened. "That is why," Guigou writes, "this village of nearly 4,000 inhabitants does not have a public toilet." On the other hand, there were two public urinals at the *bains-douches* and two public washhouses just outside the village. In the end, he concluded, "hygiene among the rural population in Mediterranean France is terribly backward."

Other sources point to improvements in rural conditions. Anthropologist Marie-Pascale Mallé writes that almost everywhere, by the 1920s, slate roofs had displaced thatch and that furniture, even if it fell short of urban standards, had become more varied and hygienic—especially the beds.[32] In the village of Carros, 25 kilometers from Nice, Dr. Barbary, the inspector of hygiene for the Alpes-Maritimes, worked with the mayor to transform the place into "a small rural center and a model village." They did it by involving the community in the changes they envisioned. At local meetings and in individual conversations, they explained to the inhabitants their ideas. They encouraged farmers to keep their manure out of the streets, to dry up their puddles, to regularly muck out their stables, and to take their garbage to the dump, instead of leaving it strewn around the property. To their satisfaction, the peasants accepted these ideas and applied them. Meanwhile, village buildings were cleaned up and classroom walls were freshly painted with frescoes of local significance. The schools were provided with running water and flush toilets. A sort of community center was built at the entrance to the village, including a dispensary and rooms for neo- and postnatal consultations, where parents could get their babies vaccinated against diphtheria. The building also contained *bains-douches*, with days reserved specifically for women and children. There was even an outdoor cinema for showing educational films about hygiene, agriculture, and natural history. All of this was entirely free to the inhabitants. In effect, Barbary wrote proudly, he and the mayor showed that "it is possible, given will and perseverance, to bring to even the smallest commune the essential elements of public and social hygiene," while it created among the citizens "the taste for a cleaner existence." Presumably, it also kept them from heading off to the city.[33]

Far from the Côte d'Azur, teacher Paul-Edouard Glath performed a similar miracle of hygiene in the Lorraine village of Bousseviller: 250 inhabitants (249 Catholics and 1 Protestant) in fifty-one houses and fifty-eight households.[34] Glath had arrived in Bousseviller in 1924 to take up his new duties as the village schoolmaster and found that "the tenue of the children left much to be desired. . . . It required some courage to get close to some of them." He compared their dirtiness to the clean and happy Alsatian villages he knew.

Glath understood that "no hygiene is possible without water," so that is where he put his initial efforts. The pump in the school courtyard did not work, and it was 200 meters from the school to the communal fountain—itself in a "lamentable state"— where most of the village got its water. The commune had no money for repairs for the pump or the schoolhouse, but Glath convinced the local blacksmith to fix the pump for free and had the children collect snails that they sold to get the money to put a spigot into the classroom, as well as to buy twenty-five individual basins for the pupils, one big basin, a jug, soap, a soap dish, thirty water glasses, and hooks for towels. He built shelves in the classroom to hold everything and provided twenty-five toothbrushes for the children, not a single one of whom had a toothbrush at home or who, in fact, had ever used one. From his residence attached to the school, which did have running water, Glath fit pipes to connect to the *postes de propreté* that he set up for the children. He conducted several inspections a day, and those students who failed had to spend 10 minutes washing. After a while, he later wrote, it became less necessary to have the children brush their teeth at school, since they had all acquired toothbrushes at home and had learned how to care for their teeth.

Figure 10.1 *Privies at the Boussevillers school before Paul-Edouard Glath.* Courtesy of Colette Sichel and Jean-David Sichel.

This was an exceptional accomplishment in the mid-1930s, when 87.5 percent of the French population reported never having seen a dentist, 12 percent claimed to have seen one in an emergency, and less than 1 percent went regularly. In response to the questionnaire from the Service Dentaire Scolaire, cited by Glath, "How often do people brush their teeth?" 45.5 percent of respondents said they never brushed, while 16.5 percent "washed [their teeth] only occasionally," and 38 percent did so "regularly." He then compared French practices to those found contemporaneously among German pupils, of whom 42.4 percent had their own toothbrush and 18 percent used "la brosse familiale." Even in Germany, however, 40 percent of schoolchildren did not brush at all, and of the 60 percent who did, "a considerable number" did so only on Sunday.

Not content with clean hands and oral hygiene among his students, Glath also attacked the disgusting privies that served their excretory needs (Figure 10.1). He replaced the wooden seats over the *trous* with glazed terracotta and installed in each stall a sink, hand-wipes, and toilet paper. He put a Dutch door in front of the urinal, which allowed the teacher to keep an eye on things, while giving the students a certain amount of privacy. And this was all scrupulously maintained (39). Obviously a man on a mission, in the evening he taught the principles of good hygiene to the adults of Boussevillers.

Barbary and Glath performed minor marvels in cleaning up their communities. As the *Enquête* makes clear, however, Carros and Boussevillers remained the exceptions.

When it came to hygiene, most of rural France was still waiting for the twentieth century.

The Smell of the Past

It is easier to measure the miles of water pipe or count the number of bathtubs than to look into people's private lives and see them in their most intimate moments. Likewise, the quality of housing and the advice being served up by schoolteachers and urban reformers provide only circumstantial evidence bearing on the main questions pertaining to the history of hygiene: How did the French think about being clean, and what were they doing about it? Were practices and sensibilities in interwar France closer to 1870 or to 1970?

We cannot smell the past to compare it to the present, but it is not hard to believe that author Henry Miller was being frank when he said of his French colleagues in the Paris office of the *Chicago Herald Tribune* that "they stank."[35] Still, other elements of native hygiene intrigued him. Miller was "won over," for example, by "the so-called Turkish toilets—'a hole in the floor and two platforms for the feet'—that provoked such feelings of dread and disgust in foreigners." And he was fascinated by the public urinals—Paris had 1,300 of them in the 1930s—which he spoke of "frequently, with tears in his eyes," according to the photographic chronicler of underground Paris, Brassaï. Hygiene was not Miller's principal interest in the *pissotières*; he was more interested in their social function. "At nightfall," he wrote, "the urinal lamps lit up with the streetlamps. These tiny chapels served an odd religion. They were public conveniences, but also meeting grounds and cruising areas for . . . the devotees of Greek love." The Paris Municipal Council could ignore the public stink of the *Vespasiennes*, as they were commonly known. But it was disturbed in a way Miller was not by their contribution to "public immorality," and the council embarked on a campaign to remove these "tearooms," whose numbers shrank dramatically. The council largely succeeded in chasing "Greek love" elsewhere, but doubtless at the cost of more open public urination.[36]

Miller was hardly a man of delicate sensibilities. But he was an American and was repeatedly struck by "the extreme poverty and lack of hygiene" that he encountered in Paris: the plumbing in the cheap hotels he frequented, where turning on a faucet set off "a gurgling that shook the whole floor"—a chaos similarly "unleashed every time your neighbor . . . took a bath or flushed the toilet."[37] American plumbing, however, was the wrong yardstick by which to measure progress in the structures and practices of *propreté* in France. Even if the water supply in Paris fell short of standards in Chicago and Kansas—or even London—it was undeniably cleaner, more ample and convenient, and less tainted with *Salmonella paratyphi* (typhoid bacteria) than it had been at the turn of the century.[38]

The same standard of limited but significant improvement can be applied to people's homes more generally. *Îlots insalubres* remained, of course. Then again, a century earlier, squalor would not have been limited to "îlots"; it would have been ubiquitous. Similarly, water might be available only out of collective courtyard spigots in many city buildings, and *cabinets d'aisance* sited on stairwells rather than in individual flats. But the stairwell was less inconvenient than the courtyard, and the spigot in the *cour* was closer than the public fountain—to say nothing of the fact that the water that came out of it was no longer drawn from the sewage-filled Seine.

Vidangeurs (cesspool cleaners) still haunted the Paris nights, slopping excrement from the cesspits that continued to lie beneath so many buildings (Figure 10.2). It remained hard, noxious labor—a nocturnal activity that Brassaï documented with his camera. But in the 1930s *vidangeurs* used pumps and not pails. This was not, after all, the eighteenth century. In other words, if the Paris of Henry Miller still stank, imagine

Figure 10.2 *Sewer worker with his security mask, Lyon* (~1935). Bibliothèque Municipal, Lyon, Fonds Sylvestre SA 19/38.

the smells in the Paris of Balzac and Hugo. Or Flaubert. Or even Proust. Of course, not all towns had modern water systems or functioning sewers by the 1930s, but some of them did. Progress mostly happens a little at a time.

Slowly, partially, and imperfectly is also a good benchmark by which to assess the success of schools in fostering cleaner pupils and cleaner families. By the 1930s, textbooks and teachers had been preaching the importance of hygiene for fifty years. Students who had been in the *écoles primaires* when the Ferry Laws were passed were now grandparents, and their grandchildren continued to hear the same lessons: washing and fresh air are good, filth and disorder are bad. Boys learned to avoid alcohol and not to spit; girls learned how to keep a neat household, to cook, and to change baby's diapers regularly.[39]

It is easy enough in the literature to find complaints that the schools had not done their job very well. "Without denying the effort the schools have made," read a report to the back-to-the-land committee in the Var, "we have often noted the failure of those efforts." Sometimes the problem lay in tradition and culture. For example, in the Catholic *pensionnat* of Georgette Florent-Decosse in the 1930s material impediments to cleanliness were fortified by religious strictures. Students were awakened at 5:30 a.m. and quickly made for the single W.C. at the end of the corridor, having assiduously avoided the "night pail" available in the dormitory. They dressed in a hurry, said a prayer, then had a quick and virtuous sprinkle of cold water on their faces. "Hands? Nails? We never cleaned them, as there was no time." In the dour atmosphere of the convent school, "one did not banter, and one did not sin."[40]

In other cases, students simply did not have the wherewithal to do as the textbooks instructed. Reflecting on her own career, Elise Palophy recalled how poorly the hygiene regimen at her boarding school mirrored the ideal promoted in the textbooks she would soon be assigning to her own students. "In winter as in summer," she wrote,

> At precisely 6 a.m. we were ripped out of sleep and out of the silence of the dormitory night. Jumping out of bed, we all joined the line for the W.C. and had quick splash of the cold water that had filled our washbowls the night before. At our minuscule tables, in front of tiny mirrors, each girl cleaned her face and washed her hands and arms, rinsing off and then dumping the water into the shared sink. Then she got dressed, made her bed, and straightened up her little *compartment*. Once a week I took a shower in one of the three stalls the school had.

As a counterpoint, however, Palophy noted that even these simple morning ablutions were unthinkable under the conditions she encountered at her first posting, at a village school in the Haute-Garonne in the 1930s, in a building that enjoyed "neither running water, nor gas, nor electricity." The dissonance led Palophy to reflect on what the director of her normal school had told the trainees: "Adopt good habits. . . . Take a bath every day." But it was useless to preach the virtues of careful cleanliness when the means to follow that advice were completely missing," she wrote in frustration. "A bath?!?" she asked rhetorically. "With what water and in what [tub]?"[41]

Jeanne Deneboude-Soulet recounted a similar experience. Having grown up in a "rather bourgeois" household at the end of the nineteenth century, her first teaching assignment led her to a one-room Catholic school in the Aveyron, where the latrine was at the far end of a long courtyard, next to a hen house. This was not unlike the encounter of Jean and Josette Cornec, upon arriving at the teachers' lodgings in the village of Daoulas, near Brest. The Cornecs expected a "comfortable and tidy dwelling." What they found waiting for them was a "shack" without any *conforts*, lit by an oil lamp, where the cellar flooded regularly, the water was 100 meters from the house, and the latrine sat at the bottom of a small garden. This appears to have been typical for rural schoolteachers.[42]

Moreover, as Ernest Monnot tragically discovered, even where amenities existed, they could be faulty and dangerous. In 1928, Monnot, who had been teaching in the village of LaBosse, in the Haut-Doubs, since 1887, had retired and gone off to live with his brother Julien in the village of Morvillars, not far from Belfort. They had central heating. Five years later, Ernest was asphyxiated while asleep by a defective furnace. Julien survived only because "he slept with his head raised."[43]

Certainly, teachers in the towns had access to better quarters, since they had salaries that made it unlikely they would have to live in slum housing. Moreover, even bad housing in the city typically had better access to *conforts* than the average country cottage, whose residents would find it more or less hopeless to follow to the letter the hygiene rules laid down in their textbooks. Perhaps the collective and unflushed courtyard privies of slum buildings would outdo all those garden latrines in sheer disgustingness. But slum-dwellers would still have a connection, imperfect as it might be, to the infrastructure of modern hygiene.

Selling Hygiene

They would also have easier access to the expanding commerce in products serving *propreté*. Indeed, if the nineteenth-century advances in hygiene are best conceived as an industrial and engineering enterprise, in the twentieth century, the history of cleanliness became part of a different historical process: the development of consumer society. Increasingly, hygiene was not the downstream effect of industrial progress, something that the state provided on a collective basis, funded by tax money and bond offerings. It was something that people purchased individually and directly.

The first thing they purchased was soap, arguably the product that more than any other brought these two histories, the industrial and the commercial, together. Through most of the nineteenth century, even when it was not taxed, soap was expensive and often hard to come by. On top of the expense, in a world that had not yet discovered germs, there was not much reason to bother using it. So, the market was limited. In 1860, Ernest Solvay revolutionized the manufacture of soap—and, it might be said, made modern hygiene possible—when he industrialized the production of soda ash.[44]

The most popular artifact of this new process in France became "Marseille soap," colorless and odorless, often cooked with olive oil. Producers had turned out 50,000 tons of it in 1842. By the turn of the century, eighty-one companies were making almost 125,000 tons, and by 1913, 180,000 tons of Marseille soap were being sold. Up until the First World War, French *savonniers* (soapmakers), most of whom were located in that Mediterranean port city, continued to make large cakes of soap, which retailers then cut and wrapped for customers. In Paris, perfumers fabricated small bars of expensive scented soap for elite consumers. The soap business changed dramatically, however, with the introduction of Cadum in 1912—"a fine and luxurious, but mass-produced product," a small bar wrapped in a package famously marketed with the iconic image of le Bébé Cadum.[45] The appearance of Bébé Cadum was a significant but not dispositive moment. Individually wrapped cakes of soap would not have made much difference to the millions of Français who lived in villages and hamlets without anywhere to buy them. In general, between the wars, even with the option for Cadum soap, old standards and a chronic lack of hot water and heated spaces meant that, in the end, the triumph of soap and water depended on the broader revolution in plumbing and standards of cleanliness that arrived only after 1945.

National habits of dental care were even more resistant to change. Plainly put, as Paul-Edouard Glath discovered in Bousseviller, oral hygiene in most of the country between the wars remained not so much negligent as nonexistent—a disturbing fact that came to light as soon as rural surveys first began to pose the question in the late 1920s. The broad answer was that, despite half a century of school lessons, peasant teeth "were *never* brushed."[46] The military's heroic efforts to promote regular toothbrushing among its forces continued to run up against the same ignorance and insouciance of peasant recruits. Commanders continued to believe, as the army dentist M. Sapet put it, a well-functioning military required that "*dental care be not voluntary but obligatory*" (emphasis in the original), and he lauded the progress that had been made among soldiers since the war, as they came to understand that "it is better to take care of your teeth than to have them extracted." Yet he also cautioned that modern practice could be slow to catch on, and illustrated his point despairingly with the story of one soldier,

> [who] came for a consultation with his mouth in a detestable state. The dentist examined him and advised him first of all go to the army coop to buy a toothbrush and toothpaste and to start using them. The next day, the soldier returned with an admirably clean mouth. The dentist complimented him, and the soldier replied: "I did not have time yesterday to go buy a toothbrush. I'll go tomorrow. In the meantime, my pal lent me his!!"[47]

All the same, inertia in some areas should not obscure progress in others, and the first order of business in getting people to change their habits was to make those changes more convenient. By the 1930s, toothbrushes, like packaged soap, were widely available for purchase, even if they were not yet widely purchased. In addition, the commodification of cleanliness brought new voices to the cause of salubrité—especially the expansion of advertising and the growing number of magazines for "modern" young women that became the vehicles both for advice on better hygiene and for marketing the products that could help them follow that advice.

Marie-Claire was a pioneer of this updated genre, which swelled in the 1950s. Under the direction of Marcelle Auclair, it published its first issue in September 1937, offering its readers content—articles, advice columns, and especially advertisements—that touched, among other topics, on the subject of hygiene. To take one early example, the second issue in October 1937 carried a piece on "lovely teeth, lovely smile"—in effect, an essay on modern dental care. In addition to regular toothbrushing, it recommended "a plate of raw vegetables, seasoned with oil and lemon," before every meal, because this promoted healthy teeth and gums. An article in November instructed new mothers to give their babies frequent warm baths. Later that year *Marie-Claire* endorsed a "cold-water toilette" for beauty and well-being: "Wake up early, walk, do sports, watch what you eat, stay away from warm water that softens the flesh and fails to stimulate the circulation." In November 1940, it told readers to shampoo their hair—"once every other month will suffice."

Other articles taught the virtues of a neat and clean home. The magazine paid special attention to the problem of droopy breasts, prescribing exercise, a healthy diet, and splashing with cold water as the cure for what was, to judge by the frequency of articles and ads addressing the issue, something of an epidemic among *Marie-Claire* readers. One story introduced readers to *Le Massosein*, a machine that touted itself as "the best device for firming-up breasts." For the time being, the emphasis in this content was on health and beauty, generally, rather than on hygiene explicitly. In practice, however, promoting the one meant promoting the other.

The ubiquitous advertisements were a key part of the growing synergy between content and commerce, and between beauty and *propreté*. For example, the magazine carried ads for Palmolive soap and Odorono deodorant. One ad for the deodorant asked readers: "Why was he always avoiding you?" and "How many young women, pretty, charming, spiritual nonetheless find a reticent 'Prince Charming'?" Odorono supplied the answer. It "surrounded you in a halo of freshness," and, as a bonus, it prevented sweat-stained clothes. Although this latter problem was easily solved, since a second ad informed readers that Lux detergent in cold water would remove those stains.

The adverts offered little vignettes to make their point: "You are a little angel," a suave but clueless husband tells his wife, who uses Lux. "You always seem to be wearing a new dress." In a second advertisement, Colgate toothpaste proposed to help unmarried women improve their odds of love: a mother shows her daughter Suzanne an old photograph and says to her, "Look my dear how lovely you were! Everyone was crazy about you!" "And look at me now," Suzanne responds sadly. "Everyone avoids me like the plague." "Listen, Suzanne," says Mom, "This may be difficult to hear, but someone needs to tell you. You need to go see the dentist about your . . . breath." Colgate to the rescue.

Marie-Claire signaled the beginning of a revolution in the women's magazine industry, "as a compromise between a luxury journal [like *Harper's Bazaar*] and a weekly publication for a more modest clientele." It was an immediate commercial success, printing hundreds of thousands of copies—its first run of March 3, 1937, was 800,000—and being read by millions of women who wanted to be both entertained and taught how to be modern.[48] Hygiene, implicitly or not, was part of that lesson. As with the schools and the military, it is impossible to gauge precisely the extent to which *Marie-Claire* readers had the means or the inclination to follow the advice they received. But it is plain to see that the magazine was prodding tens of thousands of French women in the direction of soap, toothbrushes, deodorant, detergent, and a broadly more modern approach to their bodies and their homes.

The effect of such messages was blunted by the fact that, for the majority of French people between the wars, keeping clean remained a labor-intensive affair. The mass marketing of home appliances was in its infancy, nudged along by print media and, since 1923, the Salon des Arts Ménagers, "the annual gathering of *confort* and household progress."[49] Their spread, however, was impeded by the cost of the appliances themselves, by the high price of electricity, and even by the lack of electrical outlets in most dwellings. For the moment it was only the upper classes, the more so since the supply of domestic labor was dwindling, who could afford the new labor-saving devices. In the mid-1930s, a new Calor washing machine cost the equivalent of three and a half months of a skilled worker's wages. Unsurprisingly, then, in 1938, while over a million washing machines were sold in the United States, only 4,200 were purchased in France. For most French households, along with water heaters, cookers, irons, refrigerators, and vacuum cleaners, *machines à laver* remained an undreamed-of luxury.[50]

Notes

1 Ernst Jünger, *The Storm of Steel: From the Diary of a German Storm-Troop Officer on the Western Front* (New York: Howard Fertig, 1996), 205.
2 Richard Vinen, *The Unfree French: Life under the Occupation* (New Haven: Yale University Press, 2006), 39; Gritou Valloton and Annie Vallotton, *C'était au jour le jour: Carnets (1939–1944)* (Paris: Éditions Payot & Rivages, 1995), 41.
3 See the remarks of Mlle. Bouer-Karre, a landowner in Claviers, "L'hygiene au village," and of president of the agriculture office of the Var, M. Jaubert, "Amélioration du village moderne," in Comite du retour a la terre et office agricole du Var, *Rapports présentés au Comité du Retour a la Terre, le 13 novembre 1923* (Draguignan: Imprimerie Olivier-Jouian, 1924), 3–5 and 26–9. Also see M. Ménabréa, secrétaire général de la ligue urbaine, *La reorganization de Paris et des grandes villes françaises. Appel de la Ligue Urbaine. 6e congrès national des travaux publics français à Paris les 12, 13, 14 décembre 1928* (Saint-Amand [Cher]: Imprimerie A. Clerc, 1928), 2 and Placide Rambaud and Monique Vincienne, *Les tranformations d'une société rurale: La Maurienne, 1561–1962* (Paris: A. Colin, 1977), 151.
4 Charles Laubry and Paul Jacquet, "But social de l'enseignement de l'hygiène," in Louis Martin and Georges Brouardel, *Hygiène sociale*, vol. XXIII (Paris: J.-B. Ballière et Fils, 1929), 1. On the long-term decline of mortality rates in France, see David Weir, "Economic Welfare and Physical Well-Being in France, 1750–1990," in Richard H. Steckel and Roderick Floud (eds.), *Health and Welfare during Industrialization* (Chicago: University of Chicago Press, 1997), figure 5.10, 177.
5 Charles Candiotti, "Un des facteurs de natalité: l'habitat," in Ministère de la Santé Publique, *Recueil des travaux de l'Institut National d'Hygiène. Travaux des sections et mémoires originaux* (Paris: Masson et Cie., 1947), 15.

6 Marie-France Morel, review of Catherine Rollet-Échalier, *La politique à l'égard de la petite enfance sous la IIIe République* and of Alain Norvez, *De la naissance à l'école: Santé, modes de garde et préscolarité dans la France contemporaine*, in *Population Studies* 47, no. 2 (July 1993): 374 and Marcel Moine, Charles Candiotti, and F. Allison, "Évolution de la mortalité infantile depuis 1900," in Secrétaire d'État à la Santé et à la Famille, *Recueil des travaux de l'Institut National d'Hygiène: Travaux des sections et mémoires originaux,* tome IV, vol. 2 (Paris: Masson et Cie., 1952), 774. On the Loi Roussel, see Alain Norvez, *De la naissance à l'école: Santé, modes de garde et préscolarité dans la France contemporaine* (Paris: Presses Universitaires de France, 1990), 14 and Sohn, *Chrysalides: Femmes dans la vie privée (XIXe-XXe siècles),* tome I (Paris: Publications de la Sorbonne, 1996), 322–4.
7 Alison Murray Levine, "Projections of Rural Life: The Agricultural Film Initiative in France, 1919–1939," *Cinema Journal* 43, no. 4 (Summer 2004): 46.
8 Jeanne Charrier-Lecomte, *Une femme de Vendée* (Le-Poiré-sur-Vie: Éditions le Cercle d'Or, 1983), 26, 39–40.
9 Emilie Carles, *A Life of her Own: The Transformation of a Countrywoman in Twentieth-Century France* (New York: Penguin, 1991), 122–3.
10 EugenWeber, *The Hollow Years: France in the 1930s* (New York: Norton, 1994), 182; from her memoir, Magdeleine Peyronnec, *J'ai été carmélite: reportage vécu dans le plus sévère des ordres cloîtrés de femmes* (Paris: Librairie populaire, 1937), 48.
11 A.D. Seine-et-Oise 1161 W, dossier familial no. 946, 1939. Francisque Gay and Louis Cousin, *Comment j'élève mon enfant: Puériculture, éducation, enseignement jusqu'à sept ans* (Paris: Bloud & Gay, 1927), 82 and *passim*. This book was published under the auspices of the Catholic Church and with the explicit support of the archbishop of Paris, Cardinal Dubois. Also see Henri de Farcy, S.J., *Paysans du Lyonnais: la vie agricole dans la Vallée de l'Yzeron* (Lyon: Audin, 1950), 106; Laubry and Jacquet, "But social," 32 and René Jouglet, *Les paysannes. Enfance et jeunesse* (Paris: Les Éditeurs Réunis, 1951), 39.
12 Sohn, *Chrysalides*, 305–6 and, for example, *Marie-Claire* (April 8, 1938), 39.
13 Adolphe-August Lesage and Marcel Moine, *Étude générale de la mortalité de l'enfant de première année, France entière* (Melun: Imprimerie Administrative, 1938), 9–35 passim and Marcel Moine, "Étude démographique et sanitaire des populations urbaines et rurales en France," in Maurice Vignerot, Léon Boutbien, and Aimé Dantier (eds.), *Enquête sur l'habitation rurale en France. Enquête entreprise à la demande de la Société des Nations sur la situation économique, sociale et sanitaire des campagnes au point de vue de logement, tome I: Considérations générales sur la situation de l'habitation dans le cadre de la vie rurale et de l'aménagement des campagnes avec plans et photographes* (Lille: Éditions H. Dannaud, 1939), 57–9. For the diarrhea outbreak in Toulon, see A.D. Var 5 M 18, directions from the Institut Municipal d'Hygiène de Toulon for disinfecting baby bottles and nipples.
14 Weber, *The Hollow Years*, 69–72.
15 M. A. Raymond, *Les sciences physiques et naturelles, avec l'application à l'hygiène, l'agricuture et l'enseignement ménager. Cours moyens. Préparation au C.E.P.—Leçons de choses* (Chambéry: Maison d'Édition des Primaires, 1931), 65.
16 Charrier-Lecomte, *Une femme de Vendée*, 51; and *Elle* (May 11, 1959), 26. Also see Brigitte Sandrin-Berthon, *Apprendre la santé à l'école* (Paris: ESF, 1997), 9.
17 Vignerot, Boutbien, and Dantier (eds.), *Enquête*, 3.

18 Maurice Vignerot, "Considérations générales sur l'aménagement de la vie rurale en France au point de vue de logement," in Vignerot, Boutbien, and Dantier (eds.), *Enquête*, vol. 1, 32–3; also see Secrétariat d'État à la Santé et à la Famille, *Recueil des travaux de l'Institut National d'Hygiène: Travaux des sections et mémoires originaux*, tome I, vol. 1 (Paris: Institut National d'Hygiène, 1944), 29.
19 Unless otherwise noted, the following examples are all drawn from part 2 of Vignerot, Boutbien, and Dantier (eds.) *Enquête*.
20 Jean-Claude Daumas, *La révolution matérielle. Une histoire de la consommation: France, XIXe-XXe siècle* (Paris: Flammarion, 2018), 265–6.
21 François Julien-Labruyère, *Paysans Charentais: Histoire des campagnes d'Aunis, Saintonge et bas Angoumois, tome 1: Économie rurale* (La Rochelle: Rupell, 1982), 242–3.
22 Weber, *The Hollow Years*, 69–70.
23 Gerard Berger, *Le pays de Saint-Bonnet-le-Chateau (Haut-Forez) de 1775 à 1975: flux et reflux d'une société* (Saint-Etienne: Presses de l'Université de Saint-Etienne, 1985), 409.
24 Dr. Fernand Barbary, *Un village modèle: essays d'organisation rurale réunissant les éléments de l'hygiène publique et de l'hygiène sociale* (Nice: Imprimerie de l'Éclaireur de Nice, 1927), 7.
25 A.D. Loire-Inférieure 5 M 28, Conseils d'hygiène, rapports et procès-verbaux; and 5 M 203 Habitat, habitations rurales.
26 These and the following descriptions come from A.D. Loire-Inférieure, 5 M 204: Comité départemental des habitations rurales, dossier "Enquête sur l'habitation rurale," from the chief engineer of le Génie Rural, February 29, 1936.
27 E. Affre, directeur des services vétérinaires de la Haute-Vienne, *Département de la Haute-Vienne. Rapport général sur les travaux du Conseil Départemental d'Hygiène et des Commissions sanitaires de la Haute-Vienne pendant les années 1930 et 1937*, vol. XXIX, tome II (Limoges: Imprimerie de la Préfecture, 1938), 21–2 and *passim*. For water problems in the Savoie, see M. Voutier, secrétaire général du conseil d'hygiène départemental, *Rapport général sur les travaux du conseil d'hygiène départemental et des commissions sanitaires de la Savoie, pendant l'année 1927* (Chambery: Imprimeries Réunies, 1927), 11–12 and 102–4; for the Limousin, see Albert Goursaud, *La société rurale traditionnelle en Limousin. Ethnographie et folklore du Haut-Limousin et de la Basse-Marche*, tome I (Paris: G.P. Maisonneuve & Larose, 1976), 74–7.
28 Henri Cavailles, *La vie pastorale et agricole dans les Pyrénées des Gaves, de l'Adour et des Nestes—étude de géographie humaine* (Paris: Armand Colin, 1931), 294–5.
29 Daniel Desbois, *Le pays des souvenirs* (Paris: Éditions Lettres du Monde, 1994), 23–4.
30 Max Chaleil, *La mémoire du village* (Paris: Presses du Languedoc, 1989), 34; Joseph Cressot, *Le pain au lièvre* (Paris: Stock, 1943), 57; and Raymonde Anna Rey, *Augustine Rouvière, Cévenole* (Paris: France Loisirs, 1977), 193, 124.
31 Émile Guigou, *L'hygiène d'un village languedocien en 1939. Ce qu'elle est—ce qu'elle pourrait être* [thèse, Université de Montpellier, faculté de médecine] (Anduz: Imprimerie du Languedoc, 1939), *passim*.
32 Marie-Pascale Mallé, "Maisons du nord des Hautes-Alpes: l'habitat rural entre histoire et tradition," *Terrain*, no. 9 (octobre 1987): 64. Also see Max Derruau, *Précis de géographie humaine* (Paris: A. Colin, 1964), 339.
33 Barbary, *Un village modèle*, 7–18.

34 Paul-Edouard Glath, *L'hygiène au village* (Niederbronn: Imprimerie A. Willm, 1946), passim. This invaluable book is filled with photographs of the village and the author's work at the school. Glath, a Jew, survived the Exodus of 1940 and the Occupation.
35 Brassaï, *Henry Miller: The Paris Years* (New York: Arcade Publishing, 1995), 61–2.
36 Brassaï, *The Secret Paris of the 1930s* (New York: Pantheon, 1976), n.p.
37 Brassaï, *Henry Miller*, 61–2.
38 See, for example, AP D1 S8 1: Affaires générales et collectives, prefectoral arrêté of March 18, 1926, on the expansion of the water system in Paris.
39 M. A. Raynaud, *Les sciences physiques et naturalles, avec application à l'hygiène, l'agriculture et l'enseignement ménager. Cours moyen. Préparation au C.E.P.—Leçons de Choses* (Chambéry: Maison d'Études des Primaires, 1931), 65–9 and Stephen L. Harp, *Learning to Be Loyal: Primary Schooling as Nation Building in Alsace and Lorraine, 1850–1940* (DeKalb: Northern Illinois University Press, 1998), 112.
40 Georgette Florent-Decosse, *D'hier à aujourd'hui. Une institutrice raconte* (Paris: Éditions Osmondes, 2002), 17–19.
41 Elise Palophy, *Institutrice d'hier* (Albi: Imprimerie Coopérative du Sud-Ouest, 1987), 24, 41.
42 Jeanne Deneboude-Soulet, *Je suis né à Mur-de-Barrez (Aveyron) le 13 mars 1908: Album de famille d'une enfant du Carladès* (La Téoulère: Imprimerie Bihet, 1987), 25; Jean Cornec, *Josette et Jean Cornec, instituteurs* (Paris: Éditions Clanciers-Guénaud, 1981), 14; and Paul Chaussebourg, *Sur mes chemins d'écoles* (Savigny-Levescault: Imprimerie Fabrègue, 1992), 57.
43 Association l'An 2000, *Quelques chapitres de la vie d'Émile, Ernest Monnot: instituteur à la Bosse de 1887 à 1928, un petit village du Haut-Doubs et son école* (Le Bizot: Association l'An 2000, 2002), n.p.
44 Geoffrey Jones, *Beauty Imagined: A History of the Global Beauty Industry* (New York: Oxford University Press, 2010), 77–8.
45 Roger Leblanc, *Le savon de la préhistoire au XXIe siècle* (Montreuil L'Argille: Éditions Pierann, 2001), 274; Marie-Emmanuelle Chessel, "Une méthode publicitaire américaine? Cadum dans la France de l'entre-deux-guerres," *Entreprises et Histoire* 11, no. 1 (1996): 61.
46 Jacques Fijalkow, Joëlle Garcia, Patrice Cayré, and Michel de la Cruz, *Histoire des dents: cycle 2* (Paris: Éditions Magnard, 1996), 8.
47 M. Sapet, *L'hygiène dentaire dans l'Armée. Conférence faite à l'École de Perfectionnement des Dentistes Militaires* (Étampes: La Presse Dentaire, 1927), 9, 12.
48 Michel Phélizon, "Du *Journal des Dames à Marie-Claire*," in "La presse feminine," *Informations Sociales* 1–2 (1973): 7.
49 Daumas, *La révolution matérielle*, 236 and Rebecca J. Pulju, *Women and Mass Consumer Society in Postwar France* (New York: Cambridge University Press, 2011), 182.
50 On the servant crisis, see "The Servant Problem," *The Economist* (December 17–30, 2011): 48. On the price of a Calor, see André Lejay, *L'utilisation domestique de l'électricité* (Paris: Éditions A. Pedone, 1933), 53, 86–9. The washing machine numbers come from Rebecca Jeanine Pulju, "The Women's Paradise: Gender and Consumer Culture in France, 1944–1965," (PhD dissertation, University of Iowa, 2005), 53. On the French market's resistance to vacuum cleaners, see Mary Lynn Stewart, *For Health and Beauty: Physical Culture for Frenchwomen, 1880s–1930s* (Baltimore and London: Johns Hopkins University Press, 2001), 63. For an international comparison, see Regina Lee Blaszczyk, *Imagining Consumers: Design and Innovation from Wedgewood to Corning* (Baltimore and London: The Johns Hopkins University Press, 2000), 1–2 and Sohn, *Chrysalides*, 123.

11

The Hygiene Revolution

Hygiene under the Occupation

Looking back from 1945, the interwar period saw neither a speeding up nor a slowing down of the century-long drift toward greater *salubrité*. Access to running water had continued to spread slowly; to electricity a bit less slowly. The housing crisis remained mostly unresolved. Living conditions, on the whole, were cleaner than they had been a century earlier, but the great majority of the French still went about their daily lives without modern amenities. At the individual level, evidence suggests that standards and practices became more punctilious, although not to any dramatic degree.

That is to say, the advance of hygiene had been long, slow, and uneven. But until the spring of 1940 it had moved in only one direction: forward. Defeat and occupation threw this process into reverse. Whatever progress France had made over the preceding century came to a dead stop with the arrival of the Wehrmacht and the plunder of the French economy. For four unhappy and impoverished years, material existence degraded in virtually all respects—hygiene not least among them.

Water was a partial exception to this rule. The police prefecture in Paris regularly discussed matters related to the water supply. This continued after the German invasion of Poland, and even following the Armistice in June 1940. Thus, it proposed measures to fight dysentery in October 1939 and issued several warnings in the summer of 1940, noting that the fighting had disrupted service by destroying aqueducts and cutting off electricity to the system.[1] For the most part, though, except when delivery and purification systems were disrupted by bombs and artillery—and these were not rare—the war and the Germans did not appreciably affect the volume or the purity of the water supply. Those who had access to running water before 1940 continued to have it; those who had not did not get it.

Where war and occupation did make a difference, however, especially as it pertained to hygiene, was in the availability of *hot* water. Electric water heaters belonged to the postwar world. For the moment, water still needed to be heated on the stove, and this meant that the dearth of wood and coal under the Occupation made hot water harder to come by than ever. The lack of fuel likewise deprived the French of heat, which was also a victory for grime, since people understandably hesitated to wash in cold water in a cold apartment or cottage.[2]

The effect of heating on personal hygiene did not depend entirely on the Occupation. The *Cahiers d'Enseignement Ménager Familial*, the voice of an organization that sent trained *monitrices* into the poorest and most uneducated households to teach domestic skills, noted in 1956 how cold was the enemy of clean among peasants in the Alpine regions, where the winters were long and frigid, adding that, "It is not only at 2,000 meters that bathrooms risk never being used. Even in more temperate climates, the most temperate in France, few people will perform their *toilette* in a freezing *salles d'eau*—whereby bathtubs become potato bins."[3]

Even if they did wash, moreover, it became harder to get rid of the dirt. Soap and shampoo effectively disappeared from the inventory of hygiene, as their basic components—glycerin and soda ash, in particular—were repurposed for the German war effort. What remained on the market was of exceptionally poor quality, which provoked "recriminations" from those who had to use it. Some people had recourse to do-it-yourself recipes, but without the necessary ingredients, the results were inevitably unsatisfactory. Francis Ponge, a refugee in Roanne with his family in April 1942, complained about the "bad *ersatz*" soap to be had, "which didn't lather at all." "Soap," GI Sidney Bowen wrote to his wife during his time in Normandy after the Allied landing, "must be the number one luxury, and they have very little."[4]

As Occupied France became dirtier and colder, it became sicker. The Institut National d'Hygiène, created in 1941, painted a dire picture of wartime health. The incidence of measles, diphtheria, scarlet fever, and typhoid all rose through 1943. A study of infant mortality in Marseille found that the rate surged by 40 percent between 1939 and 1942, as babies succumbed to gastro-enteric problems, principally caused by what H. Violle and A. Nabonne called the "constant and massive" contamination of milk in a hot climate without any refrigeration—an assumption grounded in the observation that numbers peaked dramatically through the summer and into the fall. According to the publication *La Population Française*, infant mortality almost doubled during the war, from 6.3 percent in 1939 to 11 percent in 1945, before reaching a new low in 1946 and declining sharply thereafter (Table 11.1).[5]

A second study focused on the increasing number of deaths from tuberculosis since the beginning of the war—30 percent between 1938 and 1943. This included a shift in the demography of the disease. The latter victims were more often young men—"subject to the same unfavorable conditions [as women] . . . the masculine sex appears to surrender more quickly," the study noted—and increasingly urban.[6] As the war dragged on, moreover, and even as the Germans departed, conditions in France got worse, and mortality continued to climb. The lack of food compounded the effect of cold and dirt. Official statistics from March 1945 showed that 55 percent of women and 75 percent of men had lost weight since 1940: "One third of urban children had growth problems," notes historian Rebecca Pulju, "and young people between the ages of three

Table 11.1 Infant Mortality Rate in France, 1938–46 (Annual Deaths of Babies under One Year Old per 1,000 Live Births)

Year	1938	1939	1940	1941	1942	1943	1944	1945	1946
Rate	65	63	89	70	74	77	78	110	73

Source: Alain Norvez, *De la naissance à l'école: santé, modes de garde et préscolarité dans la France contemporaine* (Paris: Presses Universitaires de France, 1990), 55.

and twenty-one were so adversely affected that they looked physically different from their cohort of the pre-war period." According to Colin Jones, young boys in 1944 were seven centimeters shorter than in 1935, while the child mortality rate had doubled. A letter from American Special Services Officer Harry Jackson described the children he met in Normandy as "skinny rag-a-muffins." Then again, he thought *everyone* in Normandy looked "underfed."[7]

The État Français was unarguably evil, but it took its natalist project seriously. It understood that wartime conditions were especially dangerous for children and looked for ways to mitigate the impact of cold, hunger, and dirt. The council of public hygiene in Paris, for example, recommended giving young children special *cartes de savon* that would entail extra soap rations and opening children's protective clinics, where they would receive "baths and showers and clean clothes." The authorities also launched various projects aimed at training better mothers, such as the 1942 law that made *enseignement ménager* obligatory for girls in order to prepare them for "their future roles as wife and mother."[8] Statistics on children's mortality and height and weight confirmed the casual observations of American troops that Vichy's efforts to protect the country's most vulnerable young citizens did not entirely succeed.[9]

Even among adults the scarcity of food between 1940 and 1945 effected a sort of reversal of fortune between the cities and the countryside, as urban hunger contrasted with the peasants' more direct access to nutrition. Ephraïm Grenadou, who spent the war as a young man in the Beauce, remembered the good times: "When everyone was starving and spoke only of food, we ate half again as much as before the war. I got fat." Besides the extra calories, speculated *La Population Française*, the curious dip in rural adult mortality during these "dark years" was also the result of "the regression of alcoholism in the face of penury."[10]

Bad Housing, Bad Hygiene

Public health was also pushed backward as housing conditions deteriorated and as "poor maintenance . . . the pauperization of landlords or the negligence of tenants made themselves felt on all fronts: water leaks and leaching, overflows, mold, pong, and vermin . . . even in the best neighborhoods."[11] Equally, the war put a halt to any new building or to the expansion of *conforts*. Vichy's 1941–2 housing survey laid out the bad news. A majority of apartments in the cities (69 percent) had some amenities, most often water and electricity. But those numbers ranged from 94 percent in Versailles to 25 percent in Montargis. At the other end of the scale, only 5 percent of buildings in urban France had "tous conforts"—water, electricity, heating, and gas—while 4 percent had none of these amenities. Cities in the south remained broadly more primitive.[12]

As to the situation in Paris, the Ministry of National Economy reproduced this table, taken from a 1944 survey by the tax authorities (Table 11.2). Several things stand out. First, by every measure of modern hygiene, Paris did better than the national average. Second, the typically bourgeois parts of the city enjoyed a significant advantage over working-class and socially mixed neighborhoods. Three, even in these privileged neighborhoods, only a minority of residents could boast central heating,

Table 11.2 Distribution of Amenities among the Population of Paris, 1944

Amenities	Altogether (%)	Sector A (%)	Sector B (%)	Sector C (%)	Sector D (%)
Collective W.C.	54	60	48	58	46
Private W.C.	46	40	52	42	54
Flush toilet	96	96	97	95	96
W.C. without flush	4	4	3	5	4
Outdoor W.C.	36	43	26	43	26
Indoor W.C.	64	57	74	57	74
Running water indoors	80	74	84	78	84
Running water outside	20	26	16	22	16
Wash tub .... Yes	2	3	4	2	2
.... No	98	97	96	98	98
Shower .... Yes	2	3	4	2	2
.... No	98	97	96	98	98
Bathtub .... Yes	16	14	32	9	15
.... No	84	86	68	91	85
Central Heating .... Yes	24	18	42	17	26
.... No	76	82	58	83	74

Sector A: 1st–6th arrondissements.
Sector B: 7th, 8th, 16th, 17th arrondissements.
Sector C: 9th, 10th, 11th, 12th, 18th, 19th, 20th arrondissements.
Sector D: 13th, 14th, 15th arrondissements.
Source: Ministère de l'Economie Nationale. Service national des statistiques. Direction de la statistique générale. Etudes économiques, no. 1, *Documents sur le problème du logement à Paris* (Paris: Imprimerie Nationale, 1946), 75.

while bathtubs were still rare and showers almost nonexistent. Add to this the material deprivation caused by German predations, and it is easy to imagine why standards of hygiene declined. Surprisingly, in the face of these adverse circumstances, the Vichy government continued to entertain ambitious plans to accelerate urban renewal and clean up *îlots insalubres*. Astonishingly enough, 100,000 buildings were reconstructed or repaired during the war. But, of course, none of these efforts was up to the scale of either inherited housing problems or wartime destruction.[13]

Out in the countryside, meanwhile, if people ate better than in the towns, the dirtiness of country living remained endemic. According to the 1941 survey, rural homes had substantially fewer amenities than even the most backward cities: 28 percent had none at all; 14 percent had water and electricity; 1.2 percent had water, electricity, and heat. Conditions were worst in Brittany: 52 percent of buildings had *aucun confort*; 1 percent had electricity *and* water (which was, on average 35 meters from the front door); and, apparently, no one had heating, past a fireplace or a stove.[14]

"You should really see some of the places these people have over here as homes," Charles Taylor wrote to his wife back in Georgia, having landed in Normandy only a few days earlier. "In places, part of the house is used as a barn, and the other part the people the people live in. Most of the houses are one story and the rooms have been added from time to time. Most of them are made of mud or cement, rock with shale roofs or straw-thatched roofs."[15]

Assistantes Sociales and the Politics of Social Reform

Paule-Marie Weyd, one of the corps of Vichy *assistantes sociales rurales*, left this distressing image of one not-atypical peasant dwelling in the village of La Ferrière, in the Loire Valley, in February 1942:

> Arriving at the Hamard residence, I was literally repulsed by the awful smell in this one room where everyone eats, sleeps, and washes (in whatever limited sense!), and where [I saw] three children, badly dressed and soiling the rags that served for their diapers. The floor was unwashed and covered in trash. The light that filtered through the window shone on filthy tiles, some broken-down furniture, and messy pallet-beds, even though my visit was expected. In short, not merely misery but a whole panoply of negligence.

It was precisely Weyd's job to teach the family better habits, and she reproved the wife about the condition of the house. The *assistante sociale* returned the next day, bringing bleach to clean the floor, and was astonished to find that the woman had followed her instructions, and the household, although still threadbare, "was no longer miserable and disgusting."[16]

Agents of a reactionary regime with a social conscience, these *assistantes sociales* were the gentle infantry for Pétain's National Revolution—analogous in some ways to those Third Republic schoolteachers who had made themselves the instruments of a very different "civilizing mission." Writing decades after the fact, Armelle Mabon-Fall, a historian and social worker, tendentiously described the *assistantes* as "servants of the ruling class," bringing "a reactionary discourse to working-class families," who despised them and their message. That may have been true for more politically conscious urban workers, for whom "social work" was merely another arm of bourgeois oppression. But it seems possible that the *assistantes* often received a warm welcome in the countryside. Of course, in the larger scheme of things, Vichy's intentions, good or bad, did not much matter. Challenged by popular apathy and discontent, and in the face of demand for which there was no supply, the regime's efforts to promote hygiene and public health could not rescue a desperate situation.[17]

The system of *assistantes sociales* survived the Pétain regime and became part of the civilizing mission that now belonged to the Fourth Republic, with a role that was benevolent or malignant, depending on circumstance and perspective. The *assistantes* surely saw themselves as trying to help marginal people navigate difficult lives. To those they reported on, they must often have seemed more like police than social workers. To left-wing social scientists like Mabon-Fall, they look like agents of political coercion.

To this point, the Paris Archives have a collection of court records relating to juvenile delinquency that throw an interesting light on the intersection of hygiene, dereliction, and the politics of social reform.[18] The story they tell pertains to the history of hygiene not so much because the *assistantes* were agents of civilization, in the way of nineteenth-century hygienists telling peasants to move their manure piles away from their wells, but because their reports contained in the files contain a fund of information about the intersection of dirt, disorder, and social dysfunction.

The archives are a recurring tale of drunkenness, violence, crime, poverty, neglect, emotional and cognitive impairment. The *assistantes sociales* found all these elements of human degradation when the court sent them into the homes where these wayward juveniles lived or from which they had fled. Over and over, the *assistantes* described the most appalling conditions. The mothers were drunk, the fathers absent. They both abused their children. The *assistantes* paid special attention to the level of hygiene in the homes of their unfortunate clients, neatness and cleanliness of both bodies and surroundings being a marker of orderliness and moral fitness. They focused particularly on beds—their size, the quality of mattresses and bed linen—on infestations of bedbugs and other vermin, on who slept where and with whom, and on the "proximity of opposite-sex children to one another or to opposite-sex parents."[19] More often than not, they discovered apartments that were crowded and slovenly, with a few pieces of threadbare furniture, sinks full of unwashed dishes, and assorted junk lying all over place. In sum, the suggestion is strong, not that the lack of hygiene caused social breakdown, but that the two seem to have reinforced one another. If that is true, cleanliness and order were not only weapons against medical pathologies, like tuberculosis and typhoid fever. They also served in the struggle against the social pathologies that deformed the lives of these young people. Critics might condemn the efforts of the *assistantes sociales* as "bourgeoisification," but that feels like just a derisory term for trying to help unfortunate people better organize their lives.

Old Ambitions but with Better Plumbing

A liberated France, on the doorstep of national renewal, understood the importance of decent living conditions to "the advent of a more productive, prosperous, and united society."[20] Above all, this meant modern housing.

The Germans had again made their familiar contribution to French renovation by destroying things. This time, the damage they inflicted, or caused to be inflicted, surpassed in size and scope anything they had done in the First World War (Table 11.3). Bombing and shellfire from the Germans and the Allies had leveled huge parts of many French cities: Le Havre, Rouen, Amiens, Mulhouse, Nantes, Toulon, Rennes, Tours, Orléans, Brest, Caen, Calais, Marseilles, Boulogne, Dunkirk, and Lorient. Inspector of Finances Yves Salaün figured that 600,000 *habitations* had been totally demolished and more than a million ruined to some significant extent. Urbanists, noted *La Population Française* in 1949, figured that France, to catch up, would need to build or renovate some 300,000 housing units per year for the next thirty years.[21]

At the same time, French housing stock continued to bear all the marks of thirty years of neglect and misconceived public policy. Facing an aggravated housing shortage, the state wrestled with its instincts and decided to double down on rent control and subsidies. The housing law of 1948 implicitly recognized that rents would have to rise but it proved reluctant to abandon rent and construction to the market. Instead, it issued new guidelines on the amount of rent that could be charged, according to the size and condition of apartments, imposed a tax on "underoccupied"

Table 11.3 Destruction of French Housing, 1939–45

	Nombre de batiments		
	Totally Ruined	Partly Ruined	
		More than 10%	Less than 10%
Urban structures	275,000	575,000	510,000
Agricultural buildings	85,000	165,000	70,000
TOTAL	360,000	740,000	580,000

Source: Yves Salaün, *Se loger: construire 20,000 logement par mois est, pour la France, une question de vie ou de mort* (Paris: Imprimerie de Montsouris, 1949), 70.

apartments, and created *allocations de logements* (housing allowances) to help poor families afford decent housing. But all the perversities of the 1914 regime remained. The new law did not allow rents to rise high enough to make it profitable to build new and upgrade existing housing or provide enough *allocations* to allow needy families to find suitable accommodations. The state remained bound by its distrust of the market and continued its search for modern housing on the cheap, with the same unhappy results—a desperate shortage of places to live. "In forty years," wrote the *Cahiers d'Enseignement Ménager Familial*, "in the absence of any sort of upkeep, housing has deteriorated more quickly than in four or five centuries. Our legislators . . . concerned exclusively with their reelection bear an immense responsibility."[22]

Public policy aside, the decrepit state of housing was largely a function of its age. A survey carried out during the war found that the average age of French housing was fifty-seven years—before the age of plumbing and electricity; one building in five had been erected before 1850. Aix-en-Provence had the oldest, a mean of eighty-six years. Lens had the youngest, an average of fifteen years, and no buildings older than ninety-five years—the legacy of war and reconstruction. In Bordeaux, one dwelling in five was over 100 years old. Parisian buildings averaged seventy-three years. Only 7 percent had been built since 1921, whereas 27 percent had gone up before the fall of the July Monarchy in 1848. The oldest buildings in the dense, crowded center of the city dated back on average more than a century; three-quarters had been constructed before Napoleon III became emperor.[23] Outlying arrondissements had newer but often more shoddily built structures. Even in the fashionable neighborhoods around the Arc de Triomphe and the Eiffel Tower, buildings were on average sixty years old, remnants of age of Haussmann, although only 6 percent dated back to the Second Republic.

Rural dwellings tended to be even older—113 years on average outside the war-scarred northeast, with 59 percent dating back more than a century. In the Creuse three-quarters of *logements* had been built before 1914, and the average age of dwellings in this rugged, mountainous department was ninety years. In Normandy, the average country house was 137 years old; 84 percent had gone up more than 100 years before. Roland Maspétiol, investigating the "disgrace" of rural housing for the General Association of hygienists and municipal engineers, wrote of coming across one peasant who was repairing his barn, which had been built during the Thirty Years War! Into the early 1960s, 62 percent of French housing had gone up before the assassination of Franz

Ferdinand, as opposed to only 46 percent in Britain. Ten years later, and even in view of the housing boom that began in the mid-1950s, two-thirds of *logements* in France predated the Second World War; in Britain, only 56 percent did. The disparity was even greater in the two capital cities: 87 percent in Paris versus 70 percent in London.[24]

Marshal Pétain's housing survey had inquired about *conforts* and discovered, unsurprisingly, that the most ancient houses in the poorest areas had the fewest. In Aix-en-Provence, with the oldest housing stock in urban France, a quarter of buildings had no amenities at all. Across the country, a comfortable majority of buildings by 1942 had at least water and electricity, although water into the courtyard or the landing did not mean spigots in every flat, while some 5 percent reported having *tous conforts* (i.e., water, electricity, gas, and a sewer connection), stretching from 1 percent in many cities to a quarter of the structures in the resort towns of the Côte d'Azur. An economics ministry report published in 1946 found that 98 percent of buildings in Paris had *at least one* tap for running water, 97 percent had a subscription with the gas company, 98 percent had electricity, and 94 percent a connection to the sewer line. But these numbers seem suspiciously high.[25]

As always, the older and more dispersed homes in agricultural areas, where 25 percent of the population still lived, enjoyed even less access to modern amenities. The Vichy survey did not even bother to ask about bathtubs and toilets—presumably because they were so rare. And, of course, this was all before the country had toted up the costs of war, occupation, and neglect.

The Fourth Republic, new to power and infused with the idealism of the resistance and big ambitions for social reform, could hardly have been blind to the housing crisis.[26] The country had been thinking about it, talking about it, and cooking up plans to do something about it for a century, even while the urban population annually outgrew the number of new *logements*. "Everyone in Paris is looking for an apartment," the journal *Votre Amie* wrote in September 1945. "Less than that. [Looking] for a bedroom and a kitchen, before settling for only a room. Even under the eaves. Or a waterless attic. . . . Folks are content with less than nothing." The article cited several examples. First, the Bottemberg family—the father was a tailor, a Polish immigrant—lived in one room: "We double-up on the beds," Mrs. Bottemberg informed *Votre Amie*. "My husband and I sleep on the box spring, while the five older children sleep willy-nilly on mattresses on the floor. It's only the baby who has a cradle all to himself." Second, *Votre Amie* found the Moreau family sitting four around "une table lilliputienne" in a 3 meter by 2 meter space that functioned as "living room-kitchen-dining room." Of the six children, the three oldest had been sent off to the country, while the younger ones stayed with their parents on the rue des Saules (18e), "without water, without gas, without a sink, with none of the conveniences that make life livable."[27]

Similarly, when social worker George-Day went up to see a client on the rue Marie-Stuart, around the corner from the old national library in the heart of the city, she found

> an old woman on a pallet, her thick gaze hidden by her skinny hands. What could I possibly do for her? A dog would not choose such a filthy corner to lie in. That there are human beings living in such misery in the middle of the twentieth century, amidst our so-called progress, makes me choke.[28]

Figure 11.1 *Working-class housing, Villette quarter, Lyon* (1964). Archives Municipales, Lyon, 1PH/718/2.

Meanwhile, photographs of the Lyon slums, even into the 1950s, depict conditions that would not look out of place in the shantytowns of Bogota or Nairobi (Figure 11.1).²⁹ The 1948 housing law exposed both the renewed desire to address the crisis and the constraints—above all the gruesome state of public finances—on these ambitions.

Curiously, the new regime faced little public pressure to improve the situation, perhaps because although housing in France was persistently substandard, it remained cheap. In August 1948, respondents to a survey conducted by the Institut Français de l'Opinion Publique (IFOP) agreed 46 percent to 22 percent that "the French are badly housed because they pay insufficient rents." A few years later, according to a study by the Institut National d'Études Démographiques (INED), people from across the social spectrum thought they should pay about 10 percent of income in rent. "The French," the INED concluded, "don't deny the advantages of *conforts* . . . they just refuse to pay for them."³⁰ Alex Moscovitch, a member of the Paris municipal council, complained that the French "consider paying an equitable rent to be a sin against God." In any case, the housing "crisis" did not make the top-ten list of "the most urgent tasks confronting the new National Assembly" in March 1947. In October 1946, only 7 percent named housing as their family's most pressing difficulty; a year later, 2 percent did.³¹

Table 11.4 Percentage of Income Devoted to Rent, 1940–8

Country	Before 1940	In 1948
England	22–27	15–20
Netherlands	20.5	12.5
Switzerland	20–25	13.5–17
Australia	15–20	—
Denmark	13.4	8.8
France	6–8	1–3
Italy	25	2

Source: Ministère de la Santé Publique, "La question du taudis": the figures on income spent on housing come from the report by M. Marrane to the Congrès International de l'Habitation et de l'Urbanisme, à Zurich, juin 1948, 249.

In fact, as we have seen, the French did spend less on their housing than other Europeans did, a mere 1–3 percent of their income in 1948 when the English were paying 15–20 percent, the Dutch 12.5 percent, and the Danes 8.8 percent (Table 11.4). Naturally, the amount renters paid depended upon resources, which in turn was steeply graded by class and profession. The August 1948 issue of *Sondage* recorded average annual rents of 7,800 francs for workers, 8,200 for farmers, 11,400 for white-collar *employés*, 16,500 for *professions liberals*, and 18,500 for businessmen (*commerçants et industriels*). Similarly, a survey of household expenditure in 1956 by socioeconomic category showed the middle classes not only paying more but paying a higher proportion of their incomes on rent, compared to workers and the rural classes. Still, income was not housing destiny, and the National Institute of Hygiene listed with some outrage some of the things the French preferred to pay for: the national outlay of 27 billion francs for housing in 1948 paled next to 107 billion for tobacco, 44 billion for newspapers, and 140 billion for *apéritifs*.[32] Poverty did not provide a full explanation for the lack of space and *conforts*. The French made choices.

The Stuff of Cleanliness

As the country recovered from the trauma of defeat and economic stagnation, however, these choices began to change. Kristin Ross, in her highly speculative book, *Fast Cars, Clean Bodies*, quotes Roland Barthes on the "great yen for cleanliness" that overtook the country in the postwar era.[33] Whether or not, as Ross asserts, this represented some psychic compensation for the loss of empire, there is no question that the 1950s witnessed a new emphasis on personal hygiene, as the French refashioned their old relationship to water and soap and developed a new sensibility about what constituted an acceptable level of salubriousness.

Practice naturally remained tethered to the expense and inconvenience of keeping clean. The hygiene revolution of the 1950s and 1960s therefore depended on the expansion of the housing stock and the provision of *conforts*. It required the better part of three decades for the supply of decent housing to catch up to demand. The

First Plan, in 1946, said nothing about the matter, and only in 1953 did it become an explicit state priority: pouring in public funds, facilitating the rationalization of the construction trades, and imposing a 1 percent "housing tax" on employers.[34] Into the early 1950s, the French continued to build only 70,000 or 80,000 new units a year, compared to, say the 435,000 in West Germany in 1951 alone. But the pace accelerated, and by the 1970s, France was building 400,000–500,000 *logements* annually.[35]

Many of these units were, in effect, social housing. A quarter of those in Paris were *logements sociaux et intermédiares*, and many more were built outside the Périphérique, in what are now the dreary *banlieues*, as investments rose from 53b francs in 1953 to 130b in 1955—the great majority public funds—with even more money poured into improving existing structures. This new version of public housing had a new name. What had been called *habitations à bon marché* (HBM: *inexpensive* housing) were now called *habitations à loyer modéré* (HLM: moderate-rent housing). Indeed, the new units were not meant exclusively for the poorest families, who could not have afforded the rent, but for the middling classes looking for better accommodations.[36] Nonetheless, what made all this building, and the higher rents that came with it, possible was the postwar economic miracle that made France and the French richer than they had ever been. The desire for more and better housing had always run up against the cost of it. In the 1950s that barrier began to come down.

What also made the housing boom of the *trentes glorieuses* different from what had gone on in the days of the Siegfried Law (1894) and the Loucheur Law (1928) was not just the price of rent or the unprecedented number of new apartments. It was that all of them now came with *tous conforts*. A 1951 UN report on the proportion of lodgings equipped with bathrooms ranked France, with 6 percent, barely above Spain (3 percent) and Italy (2 percent) and far behind the Swiss (75 percent), the Germans (42 percent), and the Belgians (14 percent). Moreover, according to the *Cahiers d'Enseignement Ménager Familial*, even those who had bathtubs often did not use them—because heating was so bad and homes so chilly—making bathing at best uncomfortable and at worst dangerous.[37]

The first two postwar censuses, taken in 1946 and 1954, describe the slow but steady advance of amenities (Table 11.5). We should note, perhaps, the striking absence of information about bidets, not only in the 1946 figures but in all the censuses. This is curious because the bidet, of all the bathroom fixtures, is surely the one most commonly associated with France and its traditional *toilettes*. In the absence of statistics, however, and despite the ongoing fascination with them, it makes sense that once bathrooms began to have tubs and showers, bidets would become more or less superfluous.[38]

The 1946 census showed that rural households continued to lack *conforts* in much greater proportion than their urban analogs. Thirty-eight percent of the 5.6 million village houses reported having no bathroom—the presence of which did not, in any case, necessarily indicate either running water or bathtub. None had a shower. Thirty-two percent had their own W.C., 7 percent shared with other families, 29 percent indicated no W.C. at all. It is important to note that in these instances "water closet" most often meant a *cabinet d'aisance*; that is, an outhouse without water. Cities fared a little better on this count. Of more than three million households (excluding the 51.1

Table 11.5 *Conforts* in French Households, 1946 and 1954

	No. of Households (Thousands)		Water		Sanitary Installations			W.C.	
	1946	1954	1946 in the Home %	1954 in the Home %	1946 % with Bath or Shower (% No Response)	1954 % with at least One Bath (% No Response)	1946 % WC for the One Family[a] (% No Response)	1954 % WC in the Home (% No Response)	
Rural communes	5,652.4	5,555.5	12.9	34.3	1.6 (57.8)	4.0 (93.9)	32.4 (31.4)	10.8 (23.5)	
Towns under 50,000 inhabitants	3,981.5	4,347.0	46.1	71.4	7.1 (54.0)	12.9 (81.6)	53.0 (10.3)	33.2 (7.7)	
Cities 50,000–100,000 (provinces)	467.3	519.7	57.2	80.4	7.8 (49.1)	15.8 (76.9)	48.7 (6.4)	38.4 (4.8)	
Cities 50,000–100,000 (suburbs)	255.7	369.0	73.4	81.6	12.8 (53.1)	15.8 (76.0)	56.9 (0.5)	45.2 (5.6)	
Cities more than 100,000	1,284.5	1,430.8	65.7	81.8	10.5 (50.0)	16.6 (77.4)	51.9 (5.3)	43.1 (5.0)	
Paris	1,030.3	1,179.5	76.5	78.1	16.6 (52.8)	19.4 (70.7)	51.7 (1.0)	45.9 (4.3)	
All cities >50,000 inhabitants	3,037.8	3,499.0	68.7	80.4	12.3 (51.1)	17.3 (74.9)	51.8 (3.6)	43.6 (4.7)	
France	12,671.7	13,401.5	36.9	58.4	5.1 (55.5)	10.4 (84.7)	43.5 (18.1)	26.6 (13.5)	

Source: *Études et Conjoncture. Revue mensuelle Évolution des conditions de logement en France depuis cent ans* (oct.–nov. 1957): 1222–23.
[a]Not necessarily in the home.

percent that did not answer the question), more than 70 percent had a bathroom of some sort, although only 1 percent had a shower. Fifty-two percent said they had their own W.C.—again, rarely a flush toilet—while 43 percent shared, and only 1.6 percent of respondents had no facilities at all.[39]

Naturally, not all cities offered the same level of hygienic convenience. Strasbourg, whose plumbing still bore its German birthmark, sat at the top of the standings.[40] In 1946, over 90 percent of its residences had water inside; more than 99 percent had electricity. A third had a bathroom and 37.6 percent had a tub or shower. Three-quarters had a private toilet.[41] No other city was even close, with the exception of Mulhouse, which also sat close to the German border. In Paris in 1946, just over three-quarters of dwellings had a spigot of their own—cold water, to be sure; a sixth had a *salle de bain*; and just over half had an indoor toilet to themselves. Although it is worth noting that "*W.C. réservés au ménage*" did not necessarily indicate a flush toilet under a permanent roof. At the other end of the table, the usual suspects: Le Mans, Limoges, Nantes, Rouen. Brest, in Brittany, and Calais, in the Nord, had the lowest percentage of *conforts*: respectively, 2.5 and 3.3 percent of *logements* had *salle de bains*, while the great majority had to share their W.C. with other families. Less than a third had spigots inside their homes. Aix-en-Provence, which we noted had the oldest buildings of any French city, did not report any numbers for the 1946 census. To be fair, many of the cities with the worst housing in 1946—Le Havre, for instance—had suffered terribly from Allied bombing. They did well out of the reconstruction that followed.

Under the circumstances, the old hygiene commissions, originally set up under the law of 1850, continued to field complaints about *logements insalubres* and the hygienic facilities connected to them.[42] One exemplary complaint came from two renters, an electrician and a mechanic, living in the 18th arrondissement in December 1946: "the water pipes have been frozen for two weeks; the W.C. are completely blocked-up and without their doors for six months, producing an unhealthy and disgusting stink for the tenants, and especially for children and pregnant women"—adding parenthetically, "the basement is infested with rats." Such conditions became more and more unbearable as those who had to live this way could see things beginning to improve around them.

The authorities continued to be responsive, as far as they could. The hygiene council sent an engineer to inspect the building. He noted that "the frequent *engorgement* of the W.C. comes from the tenants' negligence," and that, "while waiting for the drains to be reopened, the tenants can use other W.C. located on the stairwell of every floor," observing finally that the door of the latrine in question had been "blown off in a bombardment." In that same building the following year, the conseil d'hygiène traced a case of typhoid fever to a cross-connection of pipes, the one carrying potable water, the other non-potable water. A letter from December 1947 complained that potable water feeding a fountain for residents who did not have it in their apartments was being tainted by neighbors who insisted on washing out their "hygienic pails" and chamber pots in the fountain.

As much as the ghastly conditions of the latrines, unhappiness with sharing the means of *conforts* permeated the expressions of dissatisfaction that found their way into records of the hygiene commission. Collective facilities degraded because, where maintenance was *everyone*'s responsibility, it became, in effect, *no one*'s responsibility.

When drainpipes got blocked-up, they stayed blocked-up; filth and stench accumulated. One report by hygiene inspectors looked into a complaint about flies and noxious emissions in a building in the 20th arrondissement. "In the course of our investigation," they testified, "we observed in the sewage pipes debris of all sorts, including a dead cat, which someone had tried to dispose of by stuffing it down the drain!" The building had a concierge, but she seemed to believe that her obligations did not extend to certain parts of the building and to certain jobs.[43]

The Revolution Begins

The 1946 census captured the last moments of Old France. The next *recensement général*, in 1954, already gave evidence of the infrastructure changes that laid the groundwork for the hygiene revolution of the next twenty years. By 1954, just at the moment that the country was winding up its empire in Indochina, over 80 percent of the dwellings in French cities had their own running water. One in six had a bathtub or shower; 44 percent a toilet. Forty percent of households still shared facilities with other families, but now that more likely meant a toilet on the landing of the stairs and not an outhouse in the courtyard. Strasbourg, where 37.6 percent of dwellings were reported to have a bathtub or shower, remained the cleanest city in the country. In Paris, the figure was 19.4 percent—although in the ritzy 16th arrondissement, more than half the apartments had one of them, whereas in poorer neighborhoods only about one in ten did. Residents of the *quartiers populaires* were also more likely to use *W.C. collectifs*. Among the provincial cities, the old order of hygiene was reshuffled a bit as they rebuilt and modernized their infrastructure at different rates. If 95.7 percent of Strasbourg homes had a spigot of their own, only 52.5 percent of those in Amiens did. On the other hand, if 20.6 percent of Amiens dwellings had a shower or bathtub, in Bourges, fewer than 10 percent did. In Nice, a city that depended on tourism, about a third of *logements* had *bagnoire ou douche installée* (bath or shower), but almost 86 percent had private W.C. This put Nice at the head of the pack for *conforts*.

Opportunities for frequent and thorough washing were even sparser in the countryside, but signs of progress were beginning to appear there, too.[44] Seventy-two percent of France's 7,000 rural communes still had no running water in 1954. Yet the proportion of dwellings that did have it had tripled in eight years. A slim 4 percent claimed a bathtub or shower, but with almost 94 percent of rural households failing to provide an information on the subject, it is impossible to know precisely. All the same, memoirs of rural life in the period testify to the belated arrival of amenities, especially water—usually somewhere in the second half of the 1950s or the beginning of the 1960s. A Ministry of Agriculture survey of the situation in 1954 found enormous disparities across the countryside. It counted the percentage of the population enjoying water *par adduction* by department: at top were the Alpes-Maritimes (86.7), Seine-et-Oise (79.5), Hérault (77.4), Meurthe-et-Moselle (75.10), and Haute-Savoie (74.3). At the other end sat the usual suspects in the traditionally slower-developing parts of the country: Morbihan (12.2), Mayenne (12.6), Charente (12.7), Lot-et-Garonne and Landes (13.6).[45]

These numbers continued to improve over the next generation, which represented a significant victory for the Fourth and early Fifth Republics in their campaign to raise the level of their citizens' hygiene, health, and comfort. They nonetheless showed France still behind some of its neighbors. One study comparing the level of *conforts* in France to that in England and Wales identified some gaps in this development. In 1961, of *logements* in England and Wales, 96 percent had running water, 73 percent a bathtub or shower, and 72 percent an indoor toilet, whereas across the channel only 78 percent of dwellings had running water, 29 percent a tub or shower, and 55 percent an indoor W.C. By 1971, however, France had largely caught up. Ninety-eight percent of households in England and Wales now enjoyed running water, while 91 percent had a tub or shower, and 88 percent an indoor toilet. Corresponding figures on the French side were 97 percent, 65 percent, and 70 percent—still trailing, but much improved over a decade. The 1971 survey included a category of "tout le confort," which included 88 percent of Anglo-Welsh and 61 percent of French households.[46]

The French economist Jean Fourastié and the American anthropologist Laurence Wylie leave the abstract world of census numbers to look at conditions on the ground. Fourastié examined the village of Douelle (in the department of the Lot) at two moments—at the beginning and the end of the *trentes glorieuses*—which transported Douelle from the seventeenth century into the twentieth.[47] By 1975, children grew ten centimeters taller and lived ten years longer than they had in 1946. Infant mortality—250 per 1,000 in the eighteenth century and 85 per 1,000 in the aftermath of the war—fell to fourteen in 1975.

Well into the 1950s, most houses in Douelle had electricity but only one cold-water faucet. With only the most rudimentary facilities for washing, people rarely bothered. And with laundry still a backbreaking exercise in boiling and cauldrons, they did not change their clothes very often. A regime of hard work and poor hygiene aged women with a particular vengeance, as it always had.

By 1975, almost half the population of Douelle lived in houses built since 1950, and these were loaded with modern conveniences. The majority had stoves, refrigerators, washing machines, and televisions (automobiles, too). They do not seem to have made hygiene their top priority, however: of the 212 households, 210 had refrigerators, and 200 had televisions, but only 150 had indoor flush toilets. And even for 1975, Fourastié did not bother to count bathtubs and showers.

Wylie, the Harvard professor, tells a similar tale of progress in the Vaucluse. When he and his family arrived in Roussillon (which he named Peyrane in the first edition, to hide identities), they entered a world of old houses with few modern conveniences.[48] On the whole, he wrote, the Roussillonais displayed an "indifference to modern plumbing." Thanks to an ambitious mayor before the First World War, the village had access to clean running water, but this did not translate into modern habits of hygiene. Many homes had no W.C. at all. Instead, inhabitants used three public toilets—concrete outhouses periodically hosed out by the fire brigade. The Wylie family rented one of the rare houses in the village that had *tous conforts* but found that they were "not very convenient and comfortable" and had not been used by the people who owned the house and had installed them.

Both economic and cultural considerations, Wylie observed, held the villagers back. Many Roussillonais claimed to want modern *conforts* but either could not afford the renovations or feared advertising their prosperity to neighbors and to tax officials. That said, neither of the two richest farmers in the commune had running water in their houses, and one of the wealthiest mine owners lived in a house that lacked both water and electricity. On the other hand, if Roussillon, like Douelle, still had one foot planted deeply in the past, it likewise serves as a measure of how quickly that past was transformed. When Wylie returned in 1959, he found porcelain sinks, W.C., and even the occasional bathtub, all connected to a modern sewage system.

The Great Leap Forward

The forward march of *propreté* in Douelle and Roussillon, uneven as it was, suggests that most people wanted cleaner bodies and, over the long term, seized the chance to add *conforts* to their lives. At the same time, a residual discomfort with and fear of excessive practices never completely disappeared. Rebecca Pulju and Kristin Ross both relate the cautionary tale in Elsa Triolet's 1959 novel, *Roses à Crédit*. It is a lesson in moral hazard. Triolet follows young Martine, brought up in sordid circumstances, who feels a "delicious thrill" each time she takes a bath and who, moving to an apartment in Paris, becomes a slave to household appliances. By the end, Martine's unwholesome worship of modern things and modern ways leads her to an unfortunate end: she finishes back in squalor and is killed by rats.[49]

At the same time, the experiences described by Fourastié and Wylie show that the prospect of bathtubs and W.C. did not by itself produce a demand for them—witness the Douellais's preference for televisions over toilets. That demand had to be cultivated, both by explicit informational campaigns and through the natural effect of envy and imitation. None of this was unique to the 1950s. We have seen the old but consistently frustrated desire for better housing and noted the continuing efforts of school and army officials and public health professionals to promote more scrupulous cleanliness. What distinguished the hygiene revolution of the 1950s, therefore, was not its novelty but its scale and success.

A French Planning Commission survey in 1955 looked at the housing conditions of urban wage earners to see what amenities people had and how dissatisfied they were (Table 11.6). It discovered that, for most respondents the *trentes glorieuses* had gotten off to a slow start. Almost twice as many of those who replied said their living standards had not improved since 1950 as said they had, a sense of stagnation that was highest among older and badly paid workers.

Yet the commission's survey came at the moment when the country was on the cusp of a housing boom that would soon bring *conforts* to millions of families that had never had them before. Indeed, remarks historian Rosemary Wakeman, the failures of the past and the reemergence of France from the trauma of Occupation gave the "frenzied" construction of the 1950s a militant, revolutionary quality. Although, interestingly, the

Table 11.6 Housing and Satisfaction among Urban Wage Earners, 1955

Convenience	No. of Respondents Who Have It	No. of Respondents Who Don't Have It	Would You Like to Have It? Total %	Would You Like to Have It? Percent of Those Who Currently Do Not Have It
Running water in kitchen	79	21	13	62
Hot water (one spigot or more)	24	76	48	63
Shower or bathtub	16	84	50	60
Radio	87	13		
Vacuum cleaner	18	82	36	44
Washing machine (hand or motor)	10	90	43	48

Source: Commissariat Général du Plan, *Enquête sur les tendances de la consommation des salaries urbains: Vous gagnex 20% de plus. Qu'en faites-vous?* (Paris, 1955), 21, 40.

revolutionaries themselves were ambivalent about urban reform, seeing the need for better housing but concerned with the destruction of "authentic popular culture" in the city core.[50]

Many of these relocated families ended up in the HLM, often in what came to be called *grands ensembles*, where the price of modern plumbing was being packed and piled into high-rise apartments through a top-down process directed by politicians and architects "who thought they knew best how to provide their countrymen with modern housing and a rational urban environment." Repeated surveys showed that the French preferred single-family houses in the suburbs, while those with knowledge and power, guided by both ideology and financial considerations, believed they were better-off in the *immeubles collectifs* rising around the cities. As the mayor of Toulouse explained it with more than a *soupçon* of condescension, "The Socialist agenda was to provide decent housing for the city's working classes rather than succumb to suburban blight in the name of private property and petit-bourgeois self-interest."[51] The families moving into these buildings were not the least privileged elements of French society but members of the middle classes looking to trade up for more space and better amenities.

How satisfied were the French at this improvement in housing conditions? In fact, the question was posed over and over by various sources, both public and private. In April 1959, for example, *Elle* magazine published the results of one of its investigations, focused on families who had been "crammed" into tiny, furnished rooms in buildings "that hadn't seen a mason's trowel since the days of Baron Haussmann" but had relocated in newer, better circumstances.[52] It found that these families were almost all delighted with their new flats—airier, sunnier, more comfortable, and cleaner—for which they were paying considerably higher rent. "It is said," the article remarked, "that the French fill their bathtubs with potatoes," but, in fact, people "loved" their new *conforts* and only wanted more. When asked whether they preferred a tub or a shower—"a great referendum on cleanliness," the magazine proclaimed—43 percent expressed a preference of the former and only 21 percent for the latter. A respectable majority, 63 percent, wanted both bath *and* shower.

Other, more methodologically dependable, surveys suggested that by the 1960s, the French were feeling better housed than they had been but that the balance between satisfaction and dissatisfaction depended on a variety of factors. Predictably, those who lived in older buildings in smaller spaces and with fewer amenities typically paid less rent and expressed more unhappiness. A 1963 *enquête* by the National Institute for Statistics and Economic Studies (INSEE) found that, while fewer people now reported being "mal logé" than in the mid-1950s, a lower proportion wanted to move. Strangely, perhaps, 60 percent of respondents without *any* amenities did not consider themselves badly housed; and more than half of those who said they were badly housed expressed no dissatisfaction. Parisians were the most dissatisfied slice of the population. A 1967 poll from the Center for Research and Documentation on Consumerism (CRDC) drew a similar picture of variety and ambiguity. Among nonagricultural households, 30 percent considered themselves badly housed, a feeling most pronounced in the bigger cities by younger families, even given the same level of *conforts*. People in the middle of the income scale tended to be more dissatisfied than those at the top or the bottom. As for those who had relocated to social housing and HLM, according to urbanist Jean-Paul Lacaze, initial delight with the prospect of living in modern homes with modern plumbing often turned into disappointment, as they encountered the lack of public facilities and access to shopping, to say nothing of the "noise and promiscuity" of the *grands ensembles*. It seems as if improved circumstances were often overtaken by rising expectations.[53]

If *conforts* were one leg of the modern-hygiene stool, household appliances were a second, and the *trentes glorieuses* saw a flood of these labor-saving devices into French homes across the socioeconomic landscape. Here again, modernity was slow to arrive—the more so since, in the mid-1950s, 7 percent of residences still had no electricity; a number that was 13% in the countryside. Without much money to buy them, and without any outlets to plug them into, most people lived without washing machines, refrigerators, and vacuum cleaners—the foundations of the modern home economy. Understandably, most women were keen to acquire them. Anyone who read a women's magazine would have been saturated in advertisements for these appliances, and the consumer goods that came with them. The invention of soap flakes and detergent, for example, made washing machines more effective and desirable.[54] But housewives hardly needed much prodding to want these things that promised to make their houses so much cleaner and their work considerably lighter. Refrigerators were so few on the ground in the years after the war that architects designing kitchens for the HLM did not think they needed to provide space for them. Meanwhile, in the mid-1950s only about 8 percent of households owned washing machines, the appliances at the top of most women's domestic wish list. The Bendix, introduced in 1949, was the first model that could both wash and spin. The January–February 1954 issue of *Fémina Pratique* ran an article entitled, "The Washing Machine: How to Choose It, How to Use it." It included photographs of two dozen models ranging in price from 69,000ff for the baseline "Concord" to the Lincoln "Lux" at 195,000ff. Complementary ads for Omo,[55] the first synthetic detergent that hit the French market in 1952, and electric water heaters accompanied the article, a common case of commercial synergy.[56]

Predictably, as with every other element of better living, appliances were unequally distributed through the population. Wage earners in big cities were twice as likely to own vacuum cleaners as those in smaller cities and to have refrigerators, showers, and hot running water. Those in the smaller cities, living more often in houses and less in apartments, owned twice as many washing machines. In 1954, 2.4 percent of farmers had refrigerators and 7.3 percent had washing machines. Among "middle managers" the percentages were 15.5 and 16.4 percent, respectively; among "workers" they were 3.3 and 8.5 percent. At the same time, in the homes of "liberal professions and executives," 42.8 percent had refrigerators and 23.4 percent had washing machines.[57]

It remains true that, as historian Dominique Veillon reminds us in her history of postwar childhood, we should not overestimate the level of hygiene among the French middle classes, pointing to the rarity of decent washing facilities in most apartments, where well into the 1950s the kitchen sink frequently doubled as the bathroom sink. For a more thorough cleanup, the family might move a big basin into the kitchen. Otherwise, adults and children confined themselves to a daily *toilette succincte*, using but one *cuvette* (wash bowl) for washing hands, face, teeth, and legs. Even in the better-equipped apartments of the bourgeoisie, writes Veillon, "the bathroom with shower was tiny."[58]

Responsibility for fostering the habits of modern hygiene in young *Français* therefore fell once again on the schools. The education physical plant remained rather primitive. In 1954, according to the journal *Fémina Pratique*, more or less every school building, even the newer ones, had only a single tap. As for heat, sent to teach at a school in the 12th arrondissement soon after the war, Madeleine Verdier-Besançon remembered the bitter winter cold in a classroom with a single stove that she did not know how to maintain and that often ran out of stuff to burn.[59]

As to the substance of the lessons, they looked much like what teachers had been pounding into their pupils for a century: wash your hands; brush your teeth; clean your face and ears every day and your feet and hair at least once a week; wash your body every two or three days; and, finally, change your clothes ("several times a week in summer")—especially your underwear.[60] A school manual in 1950 echoed nineteenth-century imperatives:

(a) Use only your own personal *objets de toilette* (comb, toothbrush, etc.).
(b) Don't eat with other people's implements or drink from their glasses.
(c) Don't use your saliva to help turn the pages of your books.
(d) Don't suck on your pencil.
(e) Wash your hands before you eat.
(f) Don't spit on the floor.
(g) Fill your house with sunlight, a great disinfectant.[61]

Yet the postwar curriculum introduced several new elements. It deepened the emphasis on personal comportment and brought science and medicine into the conversation more explicitly. The hygiene curriculum was incorporated into the Certificat d'Aptitude Professionnelle (CAP), as was a discrete version of sex education. Above all, while nineteenth-century teachers may have had little success preaching cleanliness to students who had never seen an indoor faucet, even at school, such sermons had more impact on children who, although their personal circumstances might lag, could see *conforts* spreading all around them.[62]

The state supplemented the schools' efforts with a host of new organizations committed to explaining the rules of modern hygiene to young homemakers. Jeanne Grillet, president of the Household Organization League of Lyon, instructed "domestic managers," as she called them, to rent only lodgings with sufficient light, air, and water.[63] A journal for professors of home economics printed articles on proper housecleaning, the correct installation of bathrooms, and the operation of washing machines, along with advice on breastfeeding infants that was remarkably free of the usual moralisms.[64] The National Union of Teachers and Instructors of Family and Household Education, committed to "protecting citizens against ignorance . . . and giving them an elementary education in hygiene," trained agents to go into working-class homes and advise mothers on such matters as doing laundry and imparting appropriate personal habits to teenagers. The *Bulletin de la Société Française de Pédagogie* offered an enlightened education that would instill values of democracy and cleanliness in young Français. Its editors were particularly concerned that "what the schools accomplish should not be undone in the home."[65]

Bernadotte, a magazine for Catholic girls, taught its young readers to clean their rooms, open their windows, and brush their teeth after every meal. An article from "Sister Anne" explained why girls needed to keep their undergarments simple and clean and to wash them at least twice a week. If *Bernadotte* looks like an unlikely source of support for modern ways and "freedom of movement" for girls' bodies—compare this advice with the enforced dirtiness of Magdalene Peyronnec's 1930s novitiate—perhaps it merely illustrates the broad basis of the postwar hygiene offensive.[66]

Bernadotte was a niche part of a media with a large role in conveying the message that a strong France required clean, healthy citizens. In the pretelevision era, "media" chiefly meant print—in particular the new generation of magazines for (young) women that flourished after the war. *Marie-Claire*, maybe the strongest voice in this chorus, had been launched in 1937, and, under the editorial guidance of Marcelle Auclair, stressed the organic connection between hygiene and beauty. The magazine did not endorse cleanliness for its own sake at first or tie it expressly to modernity and national renewal. Nevertheless, its general concern with robust good health and attractiveness produced articles that encouraged women to brush their teeth, swab their gums with Mercurochrome, scrub their faces clean of makeup every evening, and take care that their breast did not sag. It may have prescribed baths as it prescribed calisthenics: to build beauty from the inside. Yet it directed readers to the tub and the bathroom sink with unparalleled enthusiasm.

Closed down by the Liberation because of its publisher's cozy relations with the Germans, *Marie-Claire* reappeared on newspaper kiosks in 1954. Literary scholar Susan Weiner regrets that the "once modern" magazine became "a voice for women's traditional place at home," which she saw as a betrayal of its feminist potential.[67] Maybe so, but the home that the magazine imagined for its readers was bright and clean and full of the latest labor-saving technology. The *Marie-Claire* woman was a domestic engineer, and *Marie-Claire* was her manual. She was the woman of the future.

The magazine's November 1954 issue, for example, featured the work of Équipe 54, its roving team of domestic experts (renamed for each year), helping the Faraut family to renovate the kitchen of their sad one-bedroom flat in an old building in the working-class suburb of Clichy. Équipe 54 tore out the old kitchen—a miserable affair with a small oven, two electric hotplates, and a bare spigot above a shallow sink—and replaced it with shelves and counter space, a washing machine, ironing board, and double sink with a big faucet, alongside a dinette with a small table. The before-and-after photographs, the former in black and white and the latter in color, illustrated the dramatic transformation.[68] Several years later Équipe 58 provided readers—most of whom belonged to the 70 percent of French people who lacked such amenities—with plans for "the smallest possible full bathroom." In just under 4 square meters (1.8 meters by 2.2 meters), it contained a bidet, sink with counter, and bathtub.[69]

Marie-Claire had no monopoly on this sort of thing, and advice for mounting *conforts* in cramped apartments was standard fare in the period's magazines. The 1952 edition of *L'Art Ménager Français* offered instructions on installing *salles d'eau* (washrooms) that required less than 2 square meters of precious floor space and included a *baignoire-sabot*—that is, a short sit-down bath that could also serve for soaking the wash. *L'Enseignement Technique* suggested putting the *salle d'eau* in the kitchen. This would both double up on space and take advantage of existing plumbing, which in the absence of a washroom in the home normally ran only into the kitchen. *Fémina Pratique* trumped *Marie-Claire* by giving readers the choice of fitting either a kitchen or a full bathroom into a mere 1.5 square meters of space. A February 1955 article in *Elle*, featuring the new appliances on view in the Arts Ménagers exposition, recommended a portable shower that could be wheeled into the kitchen and attached to the spigot there, then stored in some tight corner of the flat. And so on.[70]

The tools of *propreté* counted for little, however, if practice remained stuck in the dirty, smelly past. Just *how* dirty and smelly it *had been* was suggested by the response of American soldiers as they had arrived in France in 1944 and discovered a foreign country with foreign habits. Robert Peters' memoir, for example, describes in rather graphic terms the "regressively primitive" condition of French latrines and the unkempt dirtiness of the women he encountered. When we got to Paris, he wrote, "we were assaulted by odors I have ever since associated with that city—Gauloise cigarettes, cognac, perfume, horse sweat, and automobile exhaust." Historian Mary Louise Roberts writes that American troops were astonished to see grown-ups urinating openly in the streets.[71]

American military leadership must have noticed and worried about relations between the GIs and the French population, because in 1945 the US Army published a brochure titled *112 Gripes About the French*—which it republished in French with the more diplomatic title, *Nos amis les Français* (*Our French Friends*).[72] Set out in question-and-answer format, the booklet posed a series of well-rehearsed complaints about the natives and provided a commonsense rejoinder to each of them. Not a few of these "gripes" focused on the questionable practices around and facilities for hygiene the Americans encountered. To take only the most explicit:

- Gripe #43: "French Cities are filthy."
- Gripe #44: "The French are unsanitary."

- Gripe #45: "The French don't bathe."
- Gripe #46: "You ride on the subway and the smell almost knocks you out, Garlic, sweat—and perfume!"
- Gripe #47: "The French villages are pigsties. They pile their manure right in front of the houses or in the courtyards."

In general, the US Army acknowledged the truth of these reproaches but tried to set them in a sympathetic context. Thus, for example, its response to Gripe #44: "The French have lower living standards than we do in the United States. . . . Sanitary standards rise as the standard of living rises. France is not as prosperous as we are. It is not cheap to install modern plumbing." Or to Gripe #45: "The French *don't* bathe enough. They can't. They don't have real soap. They have had no soap worthy of the name since 1940. The Germans took all the soap for four years." This response also served as an answer to the accusation that "the French aren't as clean as the Germans." "Perhaps not," the army parried. "[But] if the Germans had had no soap for five years they wouldn't be as clean as they might like to be."[73] A second pamphlet, *Army Talks* (subtitled *What You Should know about France*), advised GIs on leave who were looking for a hotel that the promise of "confort moderne" needed to be taken "with a grain of salt."[74]

The women's magazine *La Femme* brought *112 Gripes* to its readers' attention in February 1946. It did not push back against the Americans' observations but agreed that the high price of hygiene in France explained its low quality. As for the complaint that the French were less efficient and energetic than the Germans, *La Femme* countered that perhaps Europe would have been better-off if the Germans had been "a bit less so."[75]

How quickly did the practices of cleanliness in France recover from their wartime decline? A survey conducted by *Elle* magazine, under the crusading leadership of its editor, Françoise Giroud, provides a snapshot of popular habits from 1951.[76] "Are French Women Clean?" reported respondents' answers to eleven "disagreeable questions" and painted a far-from-encouraging picture of *Françaises*' personal habits in the opening years of the *trentes glorieuses*. Sixty percent did not wash their faces every day. Just over half performed a full toilette daily, but 14 percent did so less than once a week. A quarter of the women said they shampooed at least once a fortnight; another quarter did so less than once a month (probably *much* less). Sixty-two percent claimed to change their underwear every day, and 30 percent changed it only once a week or less. Seventeen percent brushed their teeth twice a day, although another 50 percent brushed them at least once daily. At the other end of the spectrum, 18 percent of the women reported brushing their teeth "from time to time," while 15 percent confessed to *never* brushing. Revealingly, the survey did not ask about baths or showers, presumably because so few women had access to these in 1951.

These dreary numbers did not, Giroud noted, imply that French women cared little for their *tenue*. The great majority typically used makeup, even if they did not clean it off at night. Eighty percent of younger women (ages 18–35) wore lipstick, and although 39 percent washed their hair once a month, almost twice as many put *brillantine* on it every day. Sixty-four percent said they had permanent waves. French women, in sum, thought a lot about beauty. They just did not associate it with hygiene.

Giroud tartly dismissed the ready excuses: "I don't have the time. Or, I don't have the money." In fact, she remarked, there was no reason to think that women with more time and money were more fastidious in their habits. It would be reasonable to imagine that social class separated the cleaner *Françaises* from the dirtier ones, but Giroud did not think so: "If a shopgirl in a bakery living in a cold-water flat uses deodorant and brushes her hair morning and evening," she wrote,

> we find a law student living with her parents and having a full bathroom, who washes her girdle only every five months . . . a history teacher of thirty-seven who never brushes her teeth in the evening . . . or a twenty-eight-year-old employee at a dry-cleaning establishment who never shaves [under her arms] "because that's part of my charm."[77]

This seems unlikely, given that women in bourgeois neighborhoods had much greater access to hot water than women living in older, poorer, and more crowded sections of the cities did. But Giroud wanted to make a point: even the most fashionable of French women probably needed to clean up.

In the spirit of the age, the call for more meticulous hygiene, alongside advice on how to achieve it, became a consistent feature of *Elle*'s articles and how-to columns. But even less hip, less glossy publications jumped on this theme. For example, "22 New Year's Resolutions," an article in the January 1954 issue of *Fémina Pratique*, laid out a range of modern sanitary habits for women and young girls: weekly baths, twice-daily toothbrushing and face washing, shampooing every ten days, twice-weekly yoga, and biannual visits to the dentist, among others. The magazine offered proof of the need for this advice in its next issue, which pointed to the disturbing fact that, a decade after the Germans had stolen their last bar of French soap, the French still used less of it than virtually any other country in the developed world: a mere 6.38 kilograms per person per year—half of the what the average Belgian consumed (Table 11.7).[78]

It made the point once again in a 1957 article about a young couple in North London—a former model who now worked in a pharmacy, her husband (an architect), and their two little girls. The family's meager income meant that they had no television, car, or central heating. They spent a mere £100 a year on clothes and grew vegetables in their small backyard to save on grocery bills. The wife never visited the hairdresser or

Table 11.7 Soap Consumption by Country, 1954

Country	Kilograms per Person per Year	Country	Kilograms per Person per Year
Belgium	13.00	Canada	8.74
United States	12.00	Denmark	8.53
Great Britain	11.09	West Germany	8.33
Sweden	10.01	Switzerland	6.56
Netherlands	9.78	Argentina	6.52
Cuba	8.96	France	6.38

Source: "Le prix de propreté c'est le prix de santé," *Fémina Pratique* (March 1954): 106.

Table 11.8 Infant Mortality Rates in Europe, 1901–48

Pays	1901	1948	Diminution %	Indices (Base 100 in Sweden in 1948)
France	142	51	64.1	222
Allemagne	206	77 (1947)	62.7	335
Italie	166	70	57.8	305
Belgique	140	65	53.5	283
Hollande	149	29	80.7	126
Angleterre	152	34	77.7	148
Danemark	137	35	74.5	152
Suisse	134	36	73.3	157
Ecosse	129	45	65.1	196
Espagne	186	69	63.6	300
Norvège	91	35 (1946)	61.5	152
Suède	101	23	77.3	100
Tchécoslovaquie	147 (1923)	83	43.5	361
Etats-Unis[a]	100 (1915)	32	68	139
Canada	98 (1921–1925)	45	54	196
Irlande	99	49	54.5	213
Finlande	146	52	64.3	226

Source: Secrétariat d'État à la Santé et à la Famille, *Recueil des Travaux de l'Institut National d'Hygiène. Travaux des sections et mémoires originaux*, tome IV, vol. 2 (Paris: Masson et Cie., 1952), 774.
[a]White and nonwhite population average in 1947.

bought beauty products. But they did have a bathtub and used it. Although, to be fair, one contemporary statistician noted that one in five Londoners *never* bathes.[79]

It might have come as no surprise to readers of *Fémina Pratique* that *les anglo-saxons*, who the French considered fanatics on the subject, paid so much attention to keeping clean.[80] The editors had a larger point to make, however: that dirtiness helped explain France's high mortality rate, which was up to four times that of soapier nations (Table 11.8)—among which it counted the United States, Holland, Denmark, and Canada. Cleanliness therefore served not only aesthetic ends and individual health; it was also essential to population growth and national strength. If France wanted more babies, *Fémina Pratique* implied, it needed to wash them regularly. And, in fact, looking back, the progress of hygiene and decline in infant mortality rates in the postwar years proceeded in tandem.[81]

Women's magazines also reminded readers routinely that clean bodies were of a piece with clean homes. *Elle*'s March 1955 issue, for example, instructed homemakers on "how to aerate, sanitize, and deodorize" their kitchens and featured household items available at the Arts Ménagers exposition that made reaching this lofty standard possible. Its April 1959 number continued its series on proper "spring cleaning," adding tips for sprucing up the kitchen and bathroom to previous advice on curtains and carpets. Dozens of similar articles across the universe of women's magazines hammered home the point that a modern household required a good scouring.

The multiplying advertisements for health and beauty aids, along with those touting household products and appliances, indicate the moment when France discovered the range of offensive odors that Americans had been battling for thirty years.[82] Colgate toothpaste cleans teeth and eliminates bad breath, Odorono deodorant kills BO while protecting clothes, Charmis soap destroys odor-causing bacteria and leaves you "fresh and seductive." Advertisements warned women of the perils of hairy, sweaty underarms (Mum deodorant and Tacky Eau depilatory) and receding gums (Gibbs dentifrice). Blouses and shirts made from new fabrics such as Cotlon and Ban-Lon were peddled as being "easy to wash." Ads for Sopalin kitchen paper towels assumed that homes would have running water in the kitchen and plenty of counter space to wipe. Images proliferated of happy homemakers with bright boxes of Omo detergent or with washing machines—in electric or gas models—offering both immaculate clothes and release from the hard labor of hand laundering. Vacuum cleaners, electric floor polishers, plastic tablecloths; Lux soap for a clean face, Johnson's Wax for a clean floor, Diad makeup remover for nonacidic skin, Boldoflorine herbal tea for the health of liver and intestines, Contrexéville water to get rid of cellulite, Protecta absorbant diapers, Remington electric razors for women, cheap, washable *polychinene* underwear, Spontex sponges ("supple, light, fits in your hand")—altogether a breathtaking variety of items for keeping homes and bodies in impeccable form.

By the early 1960s, women's magazines seem to have carried fewer and fewer articles on hygiene—suggesting, if not outright victory in the war against dirt, at least an unstoppable advance all along the line. For one thing, after a century of disappointed ambitions, an extraordinary building boom had substantially expanded and improved the housing stock by the mid-1970s—much of it social housing—as the portion of family income devoted to housing rose from 3.4 percent to nearly 25 percent.[83] The implications for hygiene were enormous. From the 1962 census, which had itself marked a huge step forward, to that of 1975 the proportion of French people enjoying the amenities of hot running water, indoor toilets, and bath or shower more than doubled (Table 11.9). Inevitably, the geography and sociology of *conforts* remained more complicated. Big-city apartments were still more likely to have them than were small-town or rural households, and they were more common in more expensive and modern buildings than in older ones. A 1963 study counted the number of rural households with running water and *installations sanitaires* by housing situation,

Table 11.9 *Conforts* in French Homes, 1962–75

Census Year	Households	Toilet Connected to Sewer[a]	Hot Water Inside Home	Indoor Flush Toilet	Bath or Shower Installed
1962	14,565,169	1,983,283 19.0%	—	5,343,287 36.7%	4,211,544 28.9%
1968	15,778,100	2,846,869 25.3%	7,902,360 50.1%	8.174,040 51.8%	7,500,900 47.5%
1975	17,743,760	5,319,468 41.5%	13,429,540 75.7%	12,760,720 71.9%	12,460,180 64.3%

Source: Institut National de la Statistique et des Études Économiques, *Recensement général de la population de 1975. Résultats des sondages au 1/20 et au 15: Logements – Immeubles* (Paris, 1977), 65, 75–77.
[a]This measures buildings, not individual dwellings.

finding that owners were more likely to enjoy these *conforts* than renters, but that was still fewer than 30 percent of homes.[84]

New housing—and higher wages, which rose 4.6 percent per year between 1946 and 1976—bred new habits.[85] *Elle* found in a 1959 survey that families who had recently moved into new accommodations put more effort into keeping themselves and their homes clean.[86] The spread of labor-saving devices, accelerated by a new willingness to buy on credit and fueled by images from America, made this easier than ever.[87]

The result was a steady stream of appliances into French homes. The order in which they arrived was dictated by price and household income, naturally, but also by women's calculations of about what would most make their lives easier. Above all, this meant refrigerators and washing machines. In yet another *Elle* survey, from 1952, "100 percent [of respondents] *dreamed* of a *machine à laver.*" Between 1950 and 1960, households increased their spending on these foundational appliances tenfold.[88] They penetrated even into working-class households, a process broadly described as "democratization." Even farmhouses began to experience the tools of modern convenience.[89] According to statistics reproduced by Jean-Pierre Rioux, in 1954 only 7.5 percent of French households had a refrigerator and only 8.4 percent had a washing machine, figures which varied substantially by profession (Table 11.10). By the end of the Fourth Republic, two-thirds of upper-middle-class kitchens contained a refrigerator; the percentage of workers' kitchens that had them rose fivefold in the same half-decade. Washing machines followed the same trajectory. In 1954, fewer than a quarter of the best-equipped households had them, although, interestingly, they were more common in working- and lower-middle-class households than refrigerators—a likely indicator of what women without enough money to afford both a fridge and a washing machine wanted more. Once again, their numbers, across the social spectrum, had doubled or tripled by the end of that consequent decade, when a full fifth of French households were washing their clothes at home in a machine. By the close of the *trentes glorieuses*, nine homes in ten could boast a refrigerator and seven in ten a washing machine (although less than half had yet to install a shower or bathtub).[90]

As incomes rose and *conforts* spread, and as the share of a family budget devoted to food shrank—from 42 percent in 1949 to 28 percent in 1985—the French spent more and more money on the stuff of hygiene and health. The price of water continued to decline exponentially. In 1973, according to Jean and Françoise Fourastié, the cubic meter of water that would have cost 20 wage-hours for a common laborer in 1840 would now cost him a mere 0.3 wage-hours, a sixty-five-fold decline. Usage expanded accordingly, and the growing convenience of hot water, as households added electric hot-water heaters, made washing more agreeable (Figure 11.2).[91] By 1960, France had become the largest continental market for Lever Brothers detergent. At the same time, spending on children's clothes, perfume, soap, toothbrushes, mops, brooms, and the other bric-a-brac of cleaner living continued to climb (Table 11.11).[92]

By the end of the postwar economic miracle, France had become a much easier place in which to keep clean. Infrastructure is not destiny, however, and hygienic assets were sometimes easier to find than any daily routines for their use. Meanwhile, millions of *Français* continued to live without *conforts* well past the mid-1970s, either because they could not afford them or because they clung to lingering folk notions

Table 11.10 Level of *Équipement* of Household (as a Percentage of Households in the Category)

	motor car			television set			refrigerator			washing machine		
	1954	1959	rank[a]	1954	1959	rank	1954	1959	rank	1954	1959	rank
farmers	29	35.5	7	0.2	3.3	8	2.4	9.6	3	7.3	15.4	6
agricultural workers	3	12.1	1	–	2.1	7	0.5	3.2	1	1.8	13.4	1
industrial and commercial employers	52	50.1	8	2	15.6	4	18	34.7	7	13.2	32.8	5
liberal professions and executives	56	74.3	6	4.7	24.8	6	42.8	66.7	8	23.4	45	8
middle managers	32	57.8	3	2.5	16.1	5	15.5	39.7	6	16.4	33.1	7
employees	18	30.1	4	1.3	13.1	2	9.9	31	5	6.7	25.3	2
workers	8	21.5	2	0.9	9.7	2	3.3	16.8	2	8.5	23.2	4
non-active	6	9.8	5	0.4	5.8	1	3.7	12.1	4	3.8	11.2	3
	21	28.4		1	9.5		7.5	20.5		8.4	21.4	

[a] By the rate of increase in equipment between 1954 and 1959.
Source: Jean-Pierre Rioux, *The Fourth Republic, 1944–1958* (Cambridge: Cambridge University Press, 1987), 372.

Figure 11.2 *"75% of Parisians can have hot running water tomorrow!"* Advertisement in *Fémina Pratique* (March 1954).

about the dangers of washing or the conviction that "men should smell like men." In any case, what does the evidence say about evolving practices?

Most of it is indirect, by implication from the expanding national appetite for soap, shampoo, deodorant, after shave, and the rest. More explicitly, a well-known survey from 1975—*The French as They Are*—asked people to share their washing routines.[93]

Table 11.11 Index of Household Consumption for Hygiene and Health, 1950–9 (in 1956 francs; 1949=100)

1950	1951	1952	1953	1954	1955	1956	1957	1958	1959
104.3	104.0	115.8	122.5	129.9	139.9	152.8	163.5	164.5	170.1

Source: Ministère de l'Économie et des Finances, INSEE, *Annuaire statistique de la France, 1966: Résumé rétrospectif* (Paris, 1966), 461.

Unsurprisingly, many who were asked declined to confess their most intimate habits. Those who did usually described perfunctory morning efforts: "une toilette d'un chat" (a cat's *toilette*). For one 22-year-old rugby player, it was a "simple rinse in cold water." For young Aline Tarka: "No bath . . . [because it] takes too long to fill up. No shower. You have to wash everywhere, and I always forget to do half and end up getting dressed still half soaking." No one mentioned taking a morning shower.

Evening ablutions tended to be less rushed, and those with dirty jobs, like the auto mechanic J.-C. Vincent, often showered when they returned home from work: "a good ten minutes under very hot water." Yet they were the exceptions. A survey in *Elle* found that only 38 percent of women and 22 percent of men washed "à fond" (from head to toe) every day. More numerous were those who offered themselves a bath "as a treat," spending half an hour two or three times a week in a hot tub with "bubble bath, transistor radio, and cigarette." The most "incorrigible lazybones" saved their weekly *grande toilette* for Sunday. Even so, considering that, a century earlier, the French averaged perhaps one bath per person per year, this represented a revolution in national behavior.

Gender, geography, generation, and class bred different practices. Seventy-nine percent of women but only 56 percent of men washed before going to bed; and if seven women out of ten brushed their teeth at night, only one man in ten did so. Men shaved in the morning. (And a man who followed it with a splash of aftershave and a swipe of deodorant was probably using an item that a woman in his life had bought for him. We could speak of the "colonization" of men's bodies!). Women applied their makeup. What people care about, wrote the editors, is "appearance."

As for the old standards of modesty, twice as many men as women (28 percent of men, as compared to 13 percent of women) said they slept in the nude—with the young much more likely to do so than the old, and executives three times more likely than farmers (30 percent versus 9 percent). Only 5 percent of urban professionals still slept with a chamber pot in their bedroom in 1975, as against 40 percent of farmers. There is no surprise in these numbers: people in the countryside had less access to modern amenities and generally stuck longer to the old ways—for example, the extended Guillou family from Brittany, who preferred the kitchen sink for washing. The farm had a nice bathroom with a shower, but only the granddaughter Thérèse bothered to use it.[94]

Notes

1 Préfecture de Police, Paris, *Compte rendu des séances du Conseil d'Hygiène publique, années 1939–1940*, October 27, 1939, 304–5; June 28, 1940, 226 and July 12, 1940,

250–1. "[In June 1940]," writes Sandrine Lallam, "the Germans took pains to present their soldiers in the best possible light: the first units of the Wehrmacht to reach Paris paused to wash themselves in the Canal d'Ourq before entering the capital," in "La population de la Seine et les forces d'occupation allemandes, 14 juin 1940–25 août 1944" (mémoire de maîtrise, Paris IV-Sorbonne, 2000), 36.

2 What exactly this meant can be seen in the famous resistance memoir by Lucie Aubrac. Lucie and her husband Raymond were educated, middle-class professionals who spent most of the war in Lyon. In one scene, Raymond returns home, having been released from a Gestapo prison. "I really need to wash up," he says. The narrator continues: "Some dry wood goes into the stove, a shovelful of coal is added, a large pan of water goes on top." The apartment had no water heater. Sometime later, as the couple try to evade the Germans, they find themselves, first, at a pension on the south coast and then at a farmhouse in the Bresse. The former had neither bathtub nor shower and a collective toilet. The second had no running water at all and barely enough in the washstand to brush their teeth: Lucie Aubrac, *Outwitting the Gestapo* (Lincoln and London: University of Nebraska Press, 1993), 13, 37, 199. On the general shortage of heat under the Occupation, see Henri Amouroux, *La vie des Français sous l'Occupation* (Paris: Fayard, 1961), 145.

3 *Cahiers d'Enseignement Ménager Familial* (January–February 1956): n.p.

4 Francis Ponge, *Le savon* (Paris: Gallimard, 1967), 15 and Sidney Bowen, *Dearest Isabel: Letters from an Enlisted Man in World War II* (Manhattan: Sunflower University Press, 1992), 90. On the soap shortage generally, see Pierre Berruer, ed., *Les années 40: du pain noir à la renaissance. "Le Journal de l'Ouest": la vie quotidienne de 1940 à 1949* (Rennes: Ouest Plus, 1991), part I, 32–3 and part II, 28. For a sample of the "recipes" for making ersatz soap, see Pierre Chouard, *Alimentation et hygiène en période de restrictions, pour les collectivités de jeunesse: lycées, collèges, internats* (Paris: Les Belles Éditions, 1943), 22–3. Ironically, observed François Giroud, editor of *Elle* magazine, after the war, the shortage of soap in the short run might have popularized the use of it in the long run, as rationing and the sticker price of the ration tickets made people recognize its value: *Elle* (October 22, 1951): 15.

5 H. Violle et A. Nabonne, "À propos de la mortalité infantile par gastro-entérite à Marseille," in Secrétariat d'État à la Santé et à la Famille, *Recueil des travaux de l'Institut National d'Hygiène: travaux des sections et mémoires généraux*, tome I, vol. 1 (Paris: Institut National d'Hygiène, 1944), 316–24.

6 Pierre Boulanger et Marcel Moine, "Considérations sur la mortalité par tuberculose en France, au cours du premier trimestre 1943," in Secrétaire d'État à la Santé, *Recueil des travaux*, 193–209.

7 Rebecca Jeanine Pulju, "The Women's Paradise: Gender and Consumer Culture in France, 1944–1965" (PhD dissertation, University of Iowa, 2005), 75–6. Also see Colin Jones, *Paris: Biography of a City* (New York: Viking, 2004), 418 and Nancy D. Baird, "'To Lend Me Your Eyes . . .': The WWII Letters of Special Services Officer Harry Jackson," *The Register for the Kentucky Historical Society* 88, no. 3 (1990): 309.

8 Bibliothèque de la Préfecture de Police, Comte-Rendu des séances du Conseil d'Hygiène Publique, séance du décembre 20, 1940, 374–5 and Marguerite Reynier, *L'hygiène de l'enfant à la maison et à l'école: Hygiène corporelle. Hygiène intellectuelle. Hygiène morale* (Paris: Presses Universitaires de France, 1941), ix, 3. On the system of clothing rations, generally, see Farid Chamoune, *Des mode et des hommes: deux siècles d'élégance masculine* (Paris: Flammarion, 1993), 203. The regime also embarked on a much-needed reorganization of the French hospital system, which became the basis of

postwar reforms: see Timothy B. Smith, "The Social Transformation of Hospitals and the Rise of Medical Insurance in France, 1914–1943," *The Historical Journal* 41, no. 4 (1998): 1086.

9 In 1950, the education ministry carried out a survey of some 300,000 students, ages 6–14, recording their height and weight according to sex and location. The measurements of height and weight are difficult to interpret since they are not compared to similar cadres from before the war. The department-by-department figures, however, lay out striking differences between different parts of the country. They trace the familiar pattern of economic and social advantage and backwardness, finding that children in the Seine, the Ain, the Isère, and the Haut-Rhin, for example, are considerably taller and heavier than their peers in Normandy, Brittany, the Vendée, and the Lot. See Ministère de l'Éducation Nationale. Hygiène scolaire et universitaire et l'Institut National de la Statistique et des Études Économiques (hereafter cited as INSEE), *Tables d'étalonnage stature-pondéral des écoliers français, d'après une enquête biométrique de mai 1950* (Paris: Centre National de Documention Pédagogique, 1950).

10 *La Population Française. La Documentation Française Illustrée* 13 (January 1948): 18–19; Ephraïm Grenadou et Alain Prévost, *Grenadou, paysan français* (Paris: Éditions du Seuil, 1966), 172–3 and Richard Vinen, *The Unfree French: Life under the Occupation* (New Haven: Yale University Press, 2006), 227.

11 Elsbeth Kalff et Lucie Lemaître, *Le logement insalubre et l'hygiénisation de la vie quotidienne: Paris (1830–1990)* (Paris: Harmattan, 2008), 218.

12 Lucienne Cahen, "Évolution des conditions de logement en France depuis cent ans," *Études et conjonctures* 10–11 (1957): 1194.

13 Yves Salaün, *Se loger: construire 20,000 logement par mois est, pour la France, une question de vie ou de mort* (Paris: Imprimerie de Montsouris, 1949), 76. Also see the monthly discussions of these matters in *Compte Rendu des séances du Conseil d'Hygiène Publique et de la Salubrité du département de la Seine*, année 1942 (Imprimerie Chaix, 1943).

14 Cahen, "Évolution des conditions de logement," 1185–7.

15 Judy Barrett Litoff, David C. Taylor, Barbara Woodall, and Charles E. Taylor, *Miss You: The World War II Letters of Barbara Woodall Taylor and Charles E. Taylor* (Athens: University of Georgia Press, 1990), 212.

16 Paule-Marie Weyd, *Journal d'une aide-assistante rurale* (Paris: Les Éditions des Loisirs, 1943), 42–4.

17 À propos of the *assistantes sociales*, see Association Nationale des Assistantes Sociales, diplômées d'état, *Le 'secret' professionnel* (Limoges: Labourer & Cie., 1947), 23 and Armelle Mabon-Fall, *Les assistantes sociales au temps de Vichy: du silence à l'oubli* (Paris: Harmattan, 1995), 25–7.

18 AP 1418 W 210.

19 Sarah Fishman, *From Vichy to the Sexual Revolution: Gender and Family Life in Postwar France* (New York: Oxford University Press, 2017), 24–6.

20 Susanna Magri, "L'émergence du logement social: Objectifs et moyens d'une réforme," in Marion Segaud, Catherine Bonvalet, and Jacques Brun, *Logement et habitat: L'état des savoirs* (Paris: Éditions la Découverte, 1998), 37.

21 On wartime destruction, see Salaün, *Se loger*, 79. Also see "La question des taudis dans les .différents pays moyens mise en oeuvre pour y remédier," in Ministère de la Santé Publique. *Recueil des travaux de l'Institut National d'Hygiène: travaux des sections et mémoires originaux,* tome IV, vol. 1 (Paris: Masson et Cie., 1950), 310–13;

Catherine Dupuy, "Un logement pour vivre mieux: Enjeux communists du logement social dans une ville de banlieue parisienne: Gennevilliers (années 50–années 70)," *Cahiers d'histoire. Revue d'histoire critique* 98 (2006): 27; Danièle Voldman, *La reconstruction des villes françaises de 1940 à 1954* (Paris: Harmattan, 1997), 25; and *Population Française* 26 (February 1949): 20.

22 *Cahiers d'Enseignement Ménager Familial* [Union Nationale des Professeurs et Monitrices d'Enseignement Ménager Familial] (January–February 1956), n.p. On the 1948 law, see Kalff and Lemaître, *Le logement*, 217; Jean-Paul Lacaze, *Les français et leur logement: éléments de socio-économie de l'habitat* (Paris: Presses de l'École Nationale des Ponts et Chaussées, 1989), 15–16; Ministère de la Santé Publique, "Questions du taudis," 297; Salaün, *Se loger*, 94; and René Souriac and Patrick Cabanal, *Histoire de la France, 1750–1995. Tome 2: Société, Culture* (Toulouse: Presses Universitaires, du Mirail, 1996), 227. On the tax "sur les logements insuffisamment occupés," see the article "Se Loger ('Hygie')," *La technique sanitaire et municipal: Organe de l'Association générale des hygiénists et techniciens municipaux, fondée 1905* 42, no. 3–4 (March–April 1947): 13.

23 Audrey Jean-Marie, "Le logement à Paris: évolutions récentes, enjeux actuels," in Jacques Lucan (dir.), *Eau et gaz à tous les étages. Paris: 100 ans de logement* (Paris: Édition du Pavillon de l'Arsenal, 1992 [From the exposition opened at the Pavillon de l'Arsenal in September 1992]), 255–6. For Bordeaux, see Joseph Lajugie, *Bordeaux au XXe siècle* (Bordeaux: Imprimeries Delmas, 1972), 527.

24 On the comparison of Britain and France, see France. Groupe d'études démographiques appliquées, *Programme socio-économique de l'habitat* (Paris: Plan Construction et Architecture, 1955), n.p. Also see Roland Maspétiol, "Les caractères généraux de la vie rurale française," *La technique sanitaire* (mai–juin 1949): 61. For rural housing in general, see Cahen, "Évolution des conditions de logement," 1183–6. For the Creuse, see Maurice Robert, *Mémoire et identité: traverses ethnohistoriques en Limousin* (Limoges: Maison Limousine des Sciences de l'Homme, 1991), 147.

25 Ministère de l'Économie Nationale. Service Nationale des Statistiques. Direction de la Statistique Générale. Études Économiques, *Documents sur le problème du logement à Paris* (Paris: Imprimerie Nationale, 1946), 73–4.

26 On the theory and practice of postwar urban reform, see Rosemary Wakeman, *Heroic City: Paris, 1945–1958* (Chicago: Chicago University Press, 2009), especially chapter 7, "Planning Paris," 290–340 *passim*.

27 *Votre Amie. Le magazine de l'actualité féminine* (September 1946): 4.

28 George-Day, *Carnets d'une assistante sociale 1944–1945)* (Rodez: Éditions Subervie, 1966), 17–18.

29 Philippe Dufieux, "À propos de l'hygiène de Lyon (1800–1960)," in Conseil d'architecture, d'urbanisme et de l'environnement du Rhône, *Le confort moderne dans l'habitat* (Lyon: CAUE, 2007), 8, 26.

30 The INED study is cited in Maître Berrurier, "Le foyer et l'habitation familiale. L'homme et son foyer," from the 52e congrès des notaires de France, Biarritz, mai 31–juin 3, 1953.

31 Institut Français de l'Opinion Publique (hereafter cited as IFOP), *Sondages* (March 10–16, 1947): 52. Also Alex Moscovitch, *Renovation, Aménagement, Urbanisme: les taudis de Paris, sont-ils sacrés?* (Paris: Imprimerie Moderne de la Press, 1965), 4.

32 See the report by Eugène Claudius-Petit, the minister of Reconstruction and Urbanism, in Ministère de la Santé Publique, "La question des taudis," 249; Rebecca Pulju, *Women and Mass Consumer Society in Postwar France* (Cambridge: Cambridge

University Press, 2011), 85 and *Consommation. Annales du CREDOC* (April–June 1960): 106–9.
33 Kristin Ross, *Fast Cars, Clean Bodies: Decolonization and the Reordering of French Culture* (Cambridge, MA: MIT Press, 1995), 73. For a comment on Ross's analysis, see Herrick Chapman, "Review: Modernity and National Identity in Postwar France," *French Historical Studies* 2, no. 22 (Spring 1999): 302–3.
34 Renaud Epstein, *Un est bien arrivés: Un tour de France des grands ensembles* (Paris: Le Nouvel Atila, 2022), 11; Anne-Marie Fribourg, "Évolution des politiques du logement depuis 1950," in Segaud et al., *Logement et habitat*, 223–4; Souriac and Cabanal, *Histoire de France*, 227; and Philip Nord, *France's New Deal: From the Thirties to the Postwar Era* (Princeton: Princeton University Press, 2010), 121 and 242.
35 Nicholas Herpin and Daniel Verger, *La consommation des Français, vol. 1, Alimentation, habillement, logement* (Paris: Éditions la Découverte, 2000), 89. On the overall increase in housing, see John Ardaugh, *France in the 1980s: The Definitive Book* (New York: Penguin, 1982), 290. For Paris, see Lucan (dir.), *Eau et gaz*, 270; and Jones, *Paris*, 447. For building in Lyon, see Dufieux, "À propos de l'hygiène de Lyon (1800–1960)," 27.
36 Hélène Frouard, "À l'ombre des familles nombreuses: les politiques françaises du logement au XXe siècle," *Revue d'Histoire Moderne et Contemporaine* 57, no. 2 (avril-juin 2010): 122; Olivier Le Goff, *L'invention du confort: naissance d'une forme sociale* (Lyon: Presses Universitaires de Lyon, 1994), 74; and Jean-Pierre Rioux, *The Fourth Republic, 1944–1958* (Cambridge: Cambridge University Press, 1987), 378. On the example of Toulouse, see Rosemary Wakeman, *Modernizing the Provincial City: Toulouse, 1945–1975* (Cambridge, MA: Harvard University Press, 1997), 84.
37 Albert Laprade [architect en chef des bâtiments civils et palais nationaux], "Logements, chauffage, et hygiène," *Cahiers d'Enseignement Ménager Familial* (January–February 1956), n.p.
38 Fanny Beaupré and Roger-Henri Guerrand, *Le confidant des dames: Le bidet du XVIIIe au XXe siècle; Histoire d'une intimité* (Paris: La Découverte, 1997), 151–3.
39 INSEE, *Résultats statistiques du recensement général de la population effectué le 10 mars 1946* (Paris: Imprimerie Nationale, 1948–53) and INSEE, *Recensement général de la population de mai 1954: Résultats du sondage: Population-Ménages-Logement* (Paris: Imprimerie Nationale, 1955). Figures are not exactly comparable between the two censuses. For example, the 1946 census asked about "bathrooms" (*salles de bain*), whereas the 1954 census asked about "bathtubs" and "showers." Also, when the 1946 census asked about running water, it did not distinguish clearly between running water into buildings and running water into individual *logements*. These censuses are analyzed in Lucienne Cahen, "Évolution des conditions de logement," 1222–31 and Ministère de l'Économie Nationale. Service National des Statistiques. Direction de la Statistique Générale. Études Économiques, *Documents sur le problème du logement à Paris*, 73–4. On the rural–urban gap, see Gordon Wright, *Rural Revolution in France: The Peasantry in the Twentieth Century* (Stanford: Stanford University Press, 1964), 120.
40 *Études et conjuncture. Revue mensuelle. Évolution des conditions de logement en France depuis cent ans*, 10–11 (October–November 1957): 1243–1369, *passim*.
41 The 1946 census indicated either "reserved to the household" or "shared with others." It did not say whether these were indoors or connected to a water and sewer system. But one can speculate that this fact would be closely correlated with "water into the dwelling."

42 The following examples come from Kalff and Lemaître, *Le logement*, 207–19.
43 Ibid., 217–18.
44 Henri de Farci, *Paysans du Lyonnais: la vie Agricole dans la Vallé de l'Yzeron* (Lyon: Audin, 1950), 106; Bernard Stéphan, *Paysans, mémoires vives: récits d'un monde disparu, 1900–2000* (Paris: Autrement, 2006), 9–10.
45 See, for example, Association pour l'hygiène et le progrès social dans l'habitation, *Brée: un village français en 1963* (Paris: Édition Artistique, 1963), n.p.; Tina Jolas, Marie-Claude Pignaud, Yvonne Verdier et Françoise Zonabend, *Une campagne voisine: Minot, un village bourguignon* (Paris: Éditions de la Maison des Sciences de l'Homme, 1990), 16; Marcel Jollivet et Henri Mendras, dirs., *Les collectivités rurales françaises: étude comparative de changement social* (Paris: Armand Colin, 1971), 72; François Julien-Labruyère, *Paysans charantais: Histoire des campagnes d'Aunis, Saintonge et Bas-Angoumois, tome 1: Économie rurale* (La Rochelle: Rupell, 1982), 245; Alfred Mayer, *Un instituteur de campagne en Alsace de 1934 à 1972* (Paris: l'Harmattan, 2004), 128. For the comparative numbers, see France. Ministère de l'Agriculture. Direction générale du génie rurale et de l'hydraulique Agricole, *Trois enquêtes sur les services publics ruraux en France* (Paris: Imprimerie Nationale, 1959), 9.
46 France. Programme socio-économique de l'habitat. Groupe d'études démographiques appliquées, *L'accès au logement: filières et blocages*, chapter 4: "Le logement en France et en Grande-Bretagne: histoire et politiques" (Paris: Plan Construction et Architecture, 1995), no page numbers. The original figures came from Charles Madge and Peter Willmott, *Inner City Poverty in Paris and London* (London: Routledge Kegan & Paul, 1982), 62.
47 Jean Fourastié, *Les trentes glorieuses: ou, La révolution invisible de 1946 à 1975* (Paris: Fayard, 1979), *passim*.
48 Laurence Wylie, *Village in the Vaucluse* (Cambridge, MA: Harvard University Press, 1957), *passim*, but esp. 25, 47, 51, 139–45, 169–72, 340–1, and 380.
49 Elsa Triolet, *Roses à crédit* (Paris: Gallimard, 1959), 37–8: cited in Pulju, "The Women's Paradise," 147; and Ross, *Fast Cars*, 93–4.
50 Wakeman, *Heroic City: Paris, 1945–1958*, 292.
51 Wakeman, *Modernizing the Provincial City*, 86. On the battles between renters and planners, also see Brian Newsome, "The Apartment Referendum of 1959: Toward Participatory Architectural and Urban Planning in Postwar France," *French Historical Studies* 28, no. 2 (Spring 2005): 330 and idem, *French Urban Planning: The Construction and Deconstruction of an Authoritarian System* (New York: Peter Lang, 2009), 43, 84; also the discussion in Nicole C. Rudolph, *At Home in Postwar France: Modern Mass Housing and the Right to Comfort* (Oxford and New York: Berghahn Books, 2015), especially chapter 1, "Building Homes, Building a Nation: State Experiments in Modern Living, 1945–1952," 17–52 *passim* and idem, "Who Should Be the Author of a Dwelling? Architects versus Housewives in 1950s France," *Gender and History* (2009): 541–59. On the process by which public housing was conceived and executed, also see *La Population Française* 26 (February 1949): 18–20 and Pascal Mory, "Architecture et hygiénisme à Paris au début du XXe siècle. L'architecte entre savoir medical et pouvoir politique," in Patrice Bourdelais (dir.), *Les hygiénists: enjeux, modèles et pratiques (XVIIIe-XXe siècles)* (Paris: Belin, 2001), 159.
52 *Elle* (April 27, 1959): 98–123.
53 Epstein, *Un est bien arrivés*, 11; INSEE, *Aspects du logement en France en 1963. Éléments tirés de l'enquiête nationale sur le logement réalisée en octobre-novembre*

1963 par l'INSEE et le CREDOC à la demande du Ministère de la Construction et du Commissariat Général du Plan d'Équipement de de la Productivité. Extrait du bulletin statistique du Ministère de la Construction (Paris: Imprimerie Nationale, 1964), 21 and 43; Lacaze, *Les français et leur logement,* 19; and Pierre Ranchon. Centre de Recherches et de Documentation sur la Consommation, "Aspects du logement en France en 1967: les opinions des ménages vis-à-vis leur logement," ms. 1er avril 1969, *passim.*

54 On the invention of detergent, see D. K. Fieldhouse, *Unilever Overseas: The Anatomy of a Multinational, 1895–1965* (Stanford: Hoover Institution, 1978), 79; Abby Klaasen and Judann Pollack, eds., *Procter and Gamble: The House that Ivory Built* (Lincolnwood: NTC Business, 1988), 123–40; Oscar Schisgall, *Eyes on Tomorrow: The Evolution of Procter and Gamble* (Chicago: J.G. Ferguson Co., 1981), 134–67; and Charles Wilson, *The History of Unilever: A Study in Economic Growth and Social Change. Challenge and Response in the Post-War Industrial Revolution,* vol. 3 (New York: Frederick A. Praeger, 1968), 278–84.

55 "*Omo est là, la saleté s'en va*" ("When Omo arrives, dirt takes off.")

56 Rémy Pawin, *Histoire du bonheur en France depuis 1945* (Paris: Robert Laffont, 2013), 72–3; Jacques Rounaud, "Les trentes glorieuses de l'équipement ménager," in Conseil d'Architecture, *Le confort moderne,* 55–9. On the matter of "what women wanted," see France. Commissariat du Plan, *Enquête sur les tendances de la consommation des salaires urbains: Vous gagnez 20% de plus, qu'en faites-vous?* (Paris: Commissariat du Plan, 1955), 21; Pulju, "The Women's Paradise," 151–2; and Veillon, *Nous les enfants (1950–1970)* (Paris: Hachette, 2003), 246–7fn.

57 Rioux, *The Fourth Republic,* 372.

58 Veillon, *Nous les enfants,* 9. 94, 101–2.

59 *Fémina Pratique* 32 (March 1954): 107; Madeleine Verdier-Besançon, *Petite madame . . . ne veut plus aller à l'école* (Brive: Écritures Auto Mémoires, 2002), 31.

60 Catherine Rollet, "History of the Health Notebook in France: A Stake for Mothers, Doctors and the State," *Dynamis* 23 (2003): 163; Frédéric Zarch, "Le camera sanitaire," in Didier Nourrisson (dir.), *Éducation à la Santé, XIX-XX siècle* (Rennes: Éditions ENSP, 2002), 87. Also see *Bulletin de la Société Française de Pédagogie* 68 (March–April 1945): 59 (Although every number of this journal addresses the question, "Quel doit être le rôle de l'école dans la Nation?"); Jacques Fijalkow, Joëlle Garcia, Patrice Cayré et Michel de la Cruz, *Histoire des dents* (Paris: Éditions Magnard, 1996), 8; Louise Foulon-Lefranc, *La femme au foyer: économie domestique. Enseignement ménager et hygiène puériculture* (Paris: Librairie "l'École," 1954), 1112; and *Lettres à l'assistante. Réalités du travail social.* (Nevers: Bloud & Gay, 1947), 60.

61 Quoted in Marie-Françoise Perrier, "Lire la santé dans les manuels de sciences," in Didier Nourrisson (dir.), *À votre santé! Éducation et la santé sous la IVe République* (Saint-Étienne: Publications de l'Université de Saint-Étienne, 2002), 115.

62 *Cahiers d'Hygiène Scolaire* [La Commission Technique du Syndicat National des Médecins Départementaux d'Hygiène Scolaire et Universitaire] (December 1, 1950): 30–1.

63 Jeanne Grillet, *Hygiène ménagère* (Paris: J.-B. Ballière, 1946), 10–14 and 29–32.

64 *L'Enseignement Technique: Le Cours Féminin Professionnel et Ménager. Journal des Professeurs;* for a typical issue, see (April 1952): 152.

65 *Cahiers d'Enseignement Ménager Familial* (April–June 1956), n.p.; *Bulletin de la Société Française de Pédagogie* (March 1950): 37.

66 *Bernadotte: Illustré Catholique des Fillettes* (May 30, 1948): 334.

67 Susan Weiner, *Youth and Femininity in the Mass Media in France, 1945–1986* (Baltimore: Johns Hopkins University Press, 2001), 30, and see esp. chapter 1, "From *Elle* to *Mademoiselle*," 21–66.
68 They did not include a refrigerator, however—a comment on lagging French expectations: see *Marie-Claire* (November 1954): 126–33.
69 *Marie Claire* (February 1958): 96–103.
70 Paul Breton, dir., *L'Art Ménager Français* (Paris: Flammarion, 1952), 538, 543–8; *L'Enseignement Technique* (March 1952): 129; *Fémina Pratique* (November 1953): 73–9 and (December 1953): 84; and *Elle* (February 21, 1955): 52–3.
71 Robert Peters, *For You, Lili Marlene: A Memoir of World War II* (Madison: The University of Wisconsin Press, 1995), 57. Peters describes all this in very coarse language, which I will spare the reader. Mary Louise Roberts, *What Soldiers Do: Sex and the American GI in World War II France* (Chicago: University of Chicago Press, 2013), 52.
72 United States Army, *112 Gripes about the French* (Oxford: Bodleian Library, 2013 reprint [1945]), *passim*. The *New York Times* published a long article on the pamphlet, "The French They Have: Some Customs Rare" (February 24, 1946): 31.
73 Mary Lou Roberts writes: "Ironically, by the end of the war some Americans eventually came to prefer the Germans because, even though they were enemies, at least they were clean," *What Soldiers Do*, 51.
74 U.S. Army, *Army Talks: What You Should Know about France*, Army Talks series, vol. 11, no. 32 (August 9, 1944), 6.
75 *La Femme* 36 (February 20, 1946): 8–9.
76 *Elle* (October 22, 1951): 14–16. There was no indication as to the method of the survey, how many women responded, or how they were chosen.
77 Ibid., 15.
78 "22 New Year's Resolutions," *Fémina Pratique* (January 1954): 83.
79 *Fémina Pratique* (January 1957): 19–20. On London bathing habits, see Lawrence Wright, *Clean and Decent: The Fascinating History of the Bathroom and the Water Closet and of Sundry Habits, Fashions & Accessories of the Toilet Principally in Great Britain, France & America* (New York: Viking, 1960), 264.
80 "Americans," wrote *Marie-Claire*, "are much more concerned with the hygiene of their bodies and their hair than with aesthetics. They practice a meticulous *propreté* and are exceptionally proud of their frequent washing and bathing, without being concerned about the subsequent effects of toxic cleaning products on their skin and their faces," *Marie-Claire* (May 1955): 95.
81 Statistics on infant mortality rates appear to vary a bit from source to source. According to Alain Norvez, they declined from 110/1,000 in 1942 to 20/1,000 in 1968 and 8/1,000 in 1985: *De la naissance à l'école: santé, modes de garde et préscolarité dans la France contemporaine* (Paris: Presses Universitaires de France, 1990), 65. According to Statista, they went down from approximately 62/1,000 in 1950 to less than 25/1,000 in 1970 to under 5/1,000 by the end of the twentieth century.
82 Listerine was first marketed as a cure for halitosis in 1914, and a copywriter for the J. Walter Thompson advertising agency invented "BO" (body odor) in 1919 as the condition for which his client Odorono deodorant was the remedy—at least according to Katherine Ashenburg, *The Dirt on Clean: An Unsanitized History* (New York: North Point Press, 2007), 244–52. Geoffrey Jones offers a different story: see his *Renewing Unilever: Transformation and Tradition* (London: Oxford University Press, 2005), 12; also Marc Martin, "Le marché publicitaire français et les grands medias, 1918–1970," *Vingtième Siècle* (1988): 75–90.

83 Epstein, *Un est bien arrivés*, 11. Also see Pierre-René Lemas, "Avant-propos," in Segaud et al., *Logement et habitat*, 1.
84 See, for example, INSEE, *Recensement général de la population de 1962. Résultats du sondage au 1//20: Population-Ménages-Logements-Immeubles-Récapitulation pour la France entière* (Paris: Imprimerie Nationale, 1964), 30–1. Also see INSEE, *Aspects du logement en France en 1963*, 57.
85 Jean-Claude Daumas, *La révolution matérielle. Une histoire de la consommation: France, XIXe-XXe siècle* (Paris: Flammarion, 2018), 307.
86 *Elle* (April 27, 1959): 103, 122–3.
87 Pulju, *Women and Mass Consumer Society*, 88–9. For the effect of credit in the countryside, see Leo Loubère, Jean Sagnes, Laura Frader, and René Pech, *The Vine Remembers: French Vignerons Recall Their Past* (Albany: SUNY Press, 1985), 25–6. Also see Jacques Rounaud, "Les trentes glorieuses de l'équipement ménager," 64 and Barnett Singer, *The Americanization of France: Searching for Happiness after the Algerian War* (Boulder and New York: Rowman & Littlefield, 2013), 159.
88 Cited in Veillon, *Nous les enfants*, 246–7fn. My emphasis.
89 For example, Regina Lee Blaszczyk, *Imagining Consumers: Design and Innovation From Wedgewood to Corning* (Baltimore and London: The Johns Hopkins University Press, 2000), 2. On the appearance of appliances in rural households, see Stéphan, *Paysans, mémoires vives*, 175 and Gérard Berger, *Le pays de Saint-Bonnet-Le-Château (Haut-Forez) de 1775 à 1975: flux et reflux d'une société* (Saint-Etienne: Presses de l'Université de Saint-Etienne, 1985), 412–14.
90 Daumas, *La révolution matérielle*, 402–3. On the spread of household appliances, also see Pulju, *Women and Mass Consumer Society*, 174–6. Her figures are drawn from *Consommation: Annales du CREDOC* 4 (1959): 68 and from UNIMAREL [Union pour l'Étude du Marché de l'Électricité], *La démocratisation de l'équipement ménager* (Paris: Union pour l'Étude du Marché de l'Électricité, 1959), 2; also Jones, *Paris*, 448.
91 For decreasing expenditure on food, see Souriac and Cabanal, *Histoire de France*, 226. On new ways of spending, see CREDOC, *Études et travaux. Enquête "Conditions de vie et aspirations des Français (Vague de fin 1994). Opinion des Français sur l'environnement et appréciations sur l'eau de robinet," par Ariane Dufour. Collection Études et Travaux*, no. 6; Collection des Rapports no. 162 (October 1995): 51–5. Also see Jean Fourastié and Françoise Fourastié, *Histoire du confort* (Paris: Presses Universitaires de France, 1973), 72 and Jacqueline Niaudet, "L'évolution de la consommation des menages de 1959 a 1968," *Consommation: Annales du Centre de recherches et de documentation sur la consommation* 16 (1970): 28. Pulju, *Women and Mass Consumer Society*, refers to washing-machine coops in the mid-1950s, before households could afford their own, 170.
92 In his study of the Monts de Lyonnais, for example, ethnographer Pierre-Claude Collin found that spending on "hygiène et santé" more than doubled as a proportion of household budgets between 1950 and 1971, from 6.1 percent to 13.8 percent: *L'essor collectif des monts de lyonnais* (Paris: Insitut d'Ethnologie, 1984), 273.
93 Patrick Miler, Patrick Mahé, and Richard Cannavo, *Les français tells qu'ils sont: La fameuse enquête I.F.O.P. France-Soir, le dossier complet* (Paris: Fayard, 1975), 37.
94 Ibid., 38.

Conclusion

With one generation at the washbasin and another in the shower, the Guillou family personified the changes in the culture and practice of hygiene in postwar France. If dirt is, as anthropologist Mary Douglas put it, "matter out of place," that place clearly shifted in the 1950s and continued to shift through the rest of the century. Depending as it did on a broad reconstruction of French society, from a housing boom to a sharp rise in disposable income to a widespread sense of the need to rehabilitate the nation after two generations of calamities, France's "rising threshold of disgust" was no isolated event. It was, rather, part of a fundamental transformation of French society that had people dressing better, eating more protein, drinking less alcohol, spending more time in school, moving to the cities, and living three times as long as their great, great grandparents—the details of a process that we might call modernization.

One of the criticisms often leveled at the notion of modernization is that it takes the Western model as the One True Way. Once upon a time that way was British. As the twentieth century advanced, and especially after World War II, the term could stand as a synonym for "Americanization": richer, bigger, more bumptious, and cleaner than everyone else. Françoise Giroud, the crusading editor of *Elle*, was only the most prominent among those journalists who had done their professional apprenticeship in the United States and returned to France after the war determined to make the Old World more like the New one. Modernization also looked like Americanization in the sense that a more sanitary France fit squarely into the universe of multinational production dominated, if not completely controlled, by such American corporations as Procter & Gamble and Colgate-Palmolive.

Yet while the international culture of hygiene was becoming in many ways more homogenous, substantial national differences remained in both infrastructure and sensibilities. Census figures, along with the rituals revealed in the 1975 survey of the French "as they are," make this abundantly clear. Lynn Payer's penetrating study of differences between medical cultures further illustrates the distance that continued to separate American notions of propriety from French ones. The French, she observes, have a greater appreciation of dirt's shielding qualities. Their focus on "shoring up the *terrain*"—that is, strengthening the body overall as a barrier to disease—means that "the French see a little bit of dirt not as the enemy, but as being good for the *terrain* and worth cultivating." Sensibilities in France also remained more tolerant of natural body odors. Thus, for example, "when feminine deodorants came out, certain French consumer groups not only repeated the American argument that they could be dangerous to one's health but added that the deodorants eliminated smells necessary for sexual attraction."[1]

All the same, while practices never became identical across European borders, there was a measure of convergence, and by the end of the century the French had more or less closed the hygiene gap with their neighbors. Surveys in the 1980s indicated that the French still trailed other Europeans in the consumption of health and beauty aids. Payer writes in 1988 that the French used an average of four bars of soap a year, while the English were lathering their way through eight. Unilever estimated in the same year that the French consumed half as much toothpaste as the Swiss and half as much deodorant as the British.[2] Nevertheless, by 1989, the French were the world's third largest producer of beauty products and fourth in total sales, trailing the United States and Japan (with their much larger populations and economies) by a lot and only marginally behind Germany. And by 1998, the Scripps Howard News Service was reporting ("Study: French Smell Better Than Brits") that the French were buying just as much soap as their cross-channel rivals and showering 20 percent more often, while spending more on perfume; makeup; deodorants; and face, hand, and sun creams than any other Europeans.[3] A 2004 housing survey showed that 98 percent of French homes had a bath or shower, more or less even with Europe's tidiest households in Sweden and the Netherlands.[4]

Clearly, the revolution in manners that swept over France after World War II calls for a multifaceted explanation. The state, concerned with epidemic disease, public order, and demographic vitality, had been working for a century to clean up urban spaces and sanitize personal habits, principally through the army and the schools. The impact of these efforts had been constrained by the available technology and the limits of public finance. They also came up against a long history of practice and sensibility that set the cultural boundaries of personal and public hygiene, as well as the simple inability of most people to shoulder the costs of cleaner lives. If this history, after sputtering along since the time of Louis Philippe, began to turn decisively in the 1950s, we cannot disentangle the knot of cause and effect with any confidence. Did the availability of apartments with *conforts* and shops selling affordable soap push people into new habits? Conversely, did a surging desire to be clean pull Procter & Gamble and the Arts Ménagers behind it? Or did newfound wealth simply make possible what had always been impossible? We can say only that practice and sensibility advanced alongside plumbing and in step with the rise of disposable income.

Those who doubt the virtues of modernization have sometimes argued, not unreasonably, that change does not equal progress and that modern standards of hygiene represent above all a dubious process of waste, commodification, and bourgeois cultural hegemony.[5] But I would draw a very conclusion from this story of human betterment. For one thing, to the extent that it was a product of America envy or media influence, the hygiene revolution was not principally about superficial matters of personal bouquet and marginal luxuries. It was part of an epic change in the human condition. For another, far from being a function of manipulation and coercion, the history of hygiene is all about agency. It was a process driven forward by the desire for more comfortable, convenient, and healthier lives. Individual practices differ, of course, and it may be that humanity is not fated to an ever more well-scrubbed future. Nonetheless, whatever criticisms might be made of mass consumerism and "unnatural" standards of cleanliness, the fact remains that, once the French got used to a world of indoor flush toilets, flea-less clothes, beds without bedbugs, and lungs without tuberculosis, they never went back.

Notes

1. Lynn Payer, *Medicine and Culture: Varieties of Treatment in the United States, England, West Germany, and France* (New York: Henry Holt, 1988), 62, 67.
2. Cited in Geoffrey Jones, *Renewing Unilever: Transformation and Tradition* (London: Oxford University Press, 2005), 141.
3. "Study: French Smell Better than Brits," *Corpus Christi Caller Times*, October 23, 1998, http:/web.caller.com/autoconv/newsworld98/newsworld53.html.
4. Cited in Geoffrey Jones, *Beauty Reimagined: A History of the Global Beauty Industry* (Oxford and New York: Oxford University Press, 2010), 366–7. Also National Board of Housing, Building and Planning, Sweden, and Ministry for Regional Development of the Czech Republic, eds., *Housing Statistics in the European Union* (Falun: Intellecta Strålins, 2004), 40.
5. Science journalist Sarah Everts cast the history of deodorant as a tale of conspiracy and manipulation, coordinated principally by the J. Walter Thompson advertising firm, finishing in a sort of "false consciousness" that sold millions of dollars' worth of product to fight a nonexistent problem: body odor: see Sarah Everts, "How Advertisers Convinced Americans They Smelled Bad: A Schoolgirl and a Former Traveling Bible Salesman Helped Turn Deodorants and Antiperspirants from Niche Toiletries into an $18 Billion Industry," Smithsonian.com, August 3, 2012, n.p. www.smithsonianmag.com/history-archaeology/How-Advertisers-Convinced-Americans-They-Smelled-Bad-164779646.html?c=y&page=2. For the narrative of hygiene as a political strategy, see Patrice Bourdelais, *Les hygienists: enjeux, modèles et pratiques (XVIII-XXe siècles)* (Paris: Belin, 2001), 433–4; Jean Taricat and Martine Villars, *Le logement à bon marché. Chronique. Paris, 1850–1930* (Boulogne: Éditions Apogée, 1982), 15; and Olivier Le Goff, *L'invention du confort: naissance d'une forme sociale* (Lyon: Presses Universitaires de Lyon, 1994), 31–6.

Index

112 Gripes About the French 277–8

Abbatoirs 135
Académie Chevalier du Mérite Agricole 131
Académie Française 33
Academy of Medicine 92
Administration Générale de l'Assistance Publique 173
Agen 103
Aix-en-Provence 263, 264, 269
Albert, Anaïs 167, 198, 201, 217
Albert, Prince (United Kingdom) 71
alcohol 21, 117, 120, 295
    alcoholism 124, 167, 194, 204, 212, 237, 259
    and children 237–8
    cirrhosis 237
    dangers of 114–15, 120
Aline, Tarka 285
Allais, Joseph 235
Allier department 199
Alpes-Maritimes department 237, 240, 270
Alphand, Charles-Louis 65, 174
Alsace 113, 196–7, 213
Amélie (Princess) 17
Amélioration du logement ouvrier 163
amenities (*conforts*)
    in census 268–9, 281
    in Douelle 271
    international comparisons 267, 271, 296
    lack of 203, 257, 259, 264
    middle-class homes 168, 226–8, 259, 273
    in Paris 217–18, 228–9, 259–60, 264
    peasant homes 34, 199, 200, 241, 260, 264, 267–70, 282
    progress 266–7, 270, 277
    in Roussillon 271–2
    social geography of 270, 281–2
    in various cities 269
    working-class homes 167, 217–18, 226–8, 259, 272
Amiens 262, 270
Angot, Léon 118
Angoulême 103
Anjou 25, 113
Annales (school of history) 1
Annales des Ponts et Chaussées 63, 135
"Apaches" 163
Ardèche department 236
Ardennes department 39, 40, 187, 242
Ariège department 240
army
    barracks 96–9, 103, 104
    bathing and washing 96, 98–100, 133
    civilizing mission 94–5, 102–3, 296
    clothing 104
    dental hygiene 95, 102, 187, 250
    diet 103–4
    hygiene in 94, 97, 106
    illiteracy 112
    Lachaud commission 103–4
    latrines 97–8, 103, 133
    poor recruits 23, 86–9, 203, 237
        deformities 87, 194
        dirtiness 87–8, 95
        effect of "race" 90, 92
        geography of exemptions 89–93, 203
        height 88–9, 93–4, 132, 203
        mortality rates among recruits 88, 93
    recruitment statistics 87–91, 203
    typhoid fever 104–5, 139
    uniforms 94
    water systems 139
    World War I 211
Army Talks: What You Should know about France 278

Arnould, Jules 13
Artois 194, 212
Arts Ménagers 280, 296
Aschenburg, Katherine 59
Asnières 72, 74
Assistantes sociales (social workers) 258, 260–2
Association for the Improvement of Workers' Housing 162
Aubert, Pierre 121
Auclair, Marcelle 250, 276
Aude department 126, 237
Augé-Laribé, Michel 34–5, 200
Automobiles 271
Auvergne 39, 43, 187, 199
Auzat (Ariège)
Aveyron department 33, 39, 126, 249
Avignon 112, 134

Babeau, Albert 40, 43, 45
Badini-Jourdin, Charles 218
Bagnères (Hautes-Pyrénées) 39
Ballet, Gilbert 134–5
Balzac, Honoré de 56–7, 248
Barbary, Fernand 240, 244, 245
Barnes, David S. 60, 85, 117, 120, 144
Barthes, Roland 266
Bas-Languedoc 243
Bassé-Parton, Fernand 214
Basses-Alpes department 39
Basses-Pyrénées department 239, 241
Batallie, Charles 118
bathrooms (*cabinets de toilette*)
    in bourgeois homes 15, 168, 188–90, 228, 275
    in England 188
    and the hygiene revolution 277
    international comparisons 267
    in Paris 229
    at Versailles 12
    in working-class homes 167, 188–9, 228
baths
    in the Age of Enlightenment 14–17
    in the army 94, 99–100, 191
    for babies 185–6, 236, 251
    bathtubs 4, 16, 168, 173, 189, 228, 240, 242, 258, 260, 273, 277, 282
    danger 14, 34, 101–2, 116, 267
    frequency 16, 17, 58, 116, 119, 120, 190–2, 285
    for general health 276
    international comparisons 59–60, 188, 192, 296
    Marie Antoinette 17
    municipal pools 191
    in Muslim cities 14
    Napoleon 17
    in 1946 census 267
    public baths (*bains-douches*) 13–14, 16, 58–9, 100, 116–17, 125, 190–2, 234, 243, 244
    in the river 59
    in schools 121–2, 124, 126, 191, 248, 259
Baudrillart, Henri 37, 113, 198, 199
Bayonne 119
Béarn 187
Beauce 23, 87, 194, 259
Beaugrand, Dr. 14
Bechmann, Georges 136–7, 143
beds
    country inn 31
    in peasant homes 41, 199, 202
    in working-class homes 201, 262
Belfort 237, 242, 249
Belgrand, Eugène 72–4, 76, 135, 144
Belle Époque 163, 164
Belleville 139, 149
Belmondo, Jean-Paul 5
Bendix (washing machine) 274
Benoiston de Chateauneuf, Louis-François 16
Berlin 137, 162
Berlioz, Hector 168
Bernadotte magazine 276
Bertillon, Jacques 139, 149, 160–1
Bertrand, Dr. 92
Besançon 41, 126, 176
Bésème-Pia, Lisa 187
Bessèges (Gard) 167
bidets 2, 16, 168, 189, 192–3, 267
birth rates 132, 234, 236–7
Bismarck, Otto von 69, 76
Blanc, Henri 21
Blandford, George Fielding 59
Blanqui, Adolphe 54, 60
Bled, Edouard 140

Boell (de Baugé), E.   23, 131–2
Bogota   265
Bogros (Puy-de-Dôme)   131
Boldeflorine herbal tea   281
Bonnefous, Édouard   225
Bonnevay Law   171
Bordeaux   53, 214, 243, 263
Bordeu, Théophile de   34
Bornes fontaines (standpipes)   135
Boucher de Perthes, Jacques   32
Bouches-du-Rhône department   237
Bouchet-Saint-Nicolas (Haute-Loire)   40
Boudin, Jean-Christian-Marc   88–90, 92, 93
Bougeâtre, Eugène   42, 197
Bouiller, Robert   196
Boulogne   262
Bourbon Restoration   87, 92, 113
Bourgeoisification of the working classes   68, 167–8, 188, 212, 262, 296
Bourges   270
Boussevillers (Moselle)   244, 250
Bouvier, Jeanne   124
Bowen, Sidney   258
Brassaï   247
Braudel, Fernand   14
breasts   251
Breathless (film)   5
Brenne (Indre)   20, 35
Bresse   35
Brest   162, 262, 269
Brie region   43, 160
Brignon (Gard)   242
Brillaud, Maurice   96
Brittany   20, 22–3, 25, 42, 43, 75, 187, 194, 199, 242, 260
Broca, Paul   90, 92, 93
Broglie, Louise Comtesse de   190, 192
Brouardel, Paul   137, 139
Brubach, Holly   13
Brunet, Jean-Paul   166
Bryson, Bill   190
Bubonic plague   222
Bulletin de la Société Française de Pédagogie   276
Bureau de la Correspondance Générale et des Opérations Militaires   94
Burgundy   36

Buttes aux Cailles (municipal pool)   191
Buttes-Chaumont, Parc des   65, 74, 174

Cabanès, Auguste   12, 18, 59, 63, 188, 191, 192
Cadum soap   4, 250
Caen   262
Cahen-Salvador, Georges   213, 222
Cahiers de doléances   53
Cahiers d'Enseignement Ménager Familial   257, 263, 267
Calais   262, 269
Caleçons (underpants)   46, 189, 198, 207
Calmette, Albert   144
Calor washing machine   252
Cambry, Jacques de   22, 45
Camp, Maxime du   54
cancer   138
Cannes   228
Cantal department   236
capitalism   226
Carcassonne   112
Carles, Emilie   235
Carros (Alpes-Maritimes)   244, 245
Cavailles, Henri   241
Cellier (Loire-Atlantique)   240
Censier Juillerat   147, 149, 160–1, 185
Center for Research and Documentation on Consumerism (CRDC)   273
Centre Pompidou   227
Cerisier-Millet, Geneviève   13, 58–60
Cévennes   40, 200, 242
Chadwick, Edwin   61
Chaline, Jean-Pierre   134, 190
Challet, Louis   196
Chalmel, Théodore   31, 35, 119, 124, 194, 197
Chalonnais   35
Chambres de bonne (servants' rooms)   5, 150, 169, 228
Champagne region   187, 212
Chapelle, Antoine   61
Chaptal, Jean-Antoine   62
Charente department   41, 187, 200, 239, 270
Charles X   93
Charleville (Ardennes)   188
Charmis soap   281
Charrier-Lecomte, Jeanne   235, 237

Chateaubriand, François-René de 16
Châtellerault (Vienne) 58, 134
Chauvet, Pierre 18–19
Chavigny, Paul 32, 48
Chevallier, Fabienne 2, 72, 123, 132, 174, 214
Chevereau, Gaston 217
Cheysson, Émile 133, 162–3
Chicago Herald Tribune 247
Choisy, avenue de 148
cholera 53–5, 61, 63, 73, 74, 135–7, 150, 204
Cité des Kroumirs 165–6
Cité Doré 165–6
Cité Jeanne d'Arc 144, 161, 165–6, 172, 217
Cité Napoléon 71
Clement, Will 171
Clermont-Ferrand 23, 125, 203
Clichy 72, 145, 277
clothing
    children 198–9
    cotton 2, 3, 36, 197
    military 104
    peasants 5, 32, 35–7, 196–8
    washing 197
    working class 5
Codvelle, Félix-Paul 86, 95
Cognac (Charente) 139
Colas, Charles 34
Colgate toothpaste 251, 281
Colgate-Palmolive 295
Colin, Léon 138
Combat-Villette quarter (Paris) 161
Comité consultative d'hygiène 141
Commission on the Sanitary Condition of the Labouring Population of Great Britain 59
Commissions d'hygiène publique 70, 125, 138, 170, 259
Commissions des logements insalubres (housing commissions) 55, 57, 70, 115, 159, 160, 269
    law of April 1850 66–8, 170
    Lille 69
    number of cases 69
    Paris 269
    Rennes 69
    and water 72

Commission d'hygiène des écoles 121
Compagnie des Eaux 62
Compagnie d'Orléans 217
Compiègne 103
Concarneau (Finistère) 163
Concierges 169
Concord (washing machine) 274
Congress of International Hygiene and Demography 139, 170
Conseil de Santé (health council) 88, 172
Considérant, Victor 53
Contrexéville water 281
Corbin, Alain 2, 32, 41, 64, 76, 125, 167
Cornec, Jean 198, 249
Cornec, Josette 249
Corrèze department 134, 196
Corsica 134
Cortigis, General 99
Corvée féminine (fetching water) 140
Côte d'Azur 264
Côte d'Or department 201
Côtes-du-Nord department 236
cotton clothes 2, 3, 36
    price of 4, 197
Counter-Reformation 14
Courgey, Dr. 134
Courmont, Jules 93, 132, 143, 192
Crapper, Thomas 16
Crèches (nursery schools) 114, 118–19, 122
Crédit Agricole 196
Cressot, Joseph 43, 242
Creteil 191
Creuse department 43
Creusot company 172
Csergo, Julia 2, 14–15, 33, 62, 93, 100, 133, 135, 167, 168, 188, 189
Cuneo, Battle of 92
Cyril-Berger, Victor 163

Daoulas (Finistère) 249
Dard, Philippe 167
Daumas, Jean-Claude 136, 188, 189, 214, 224, 239
Debove, Maurice 101
Decle, Lionel 87, 95–7, 100–1
Dejean, Joan 16
Delabost, François Merry 100

Deneboude-Soulet, Jeanne   39, 248
dental hygiene   186–8, 245, 250–1, 278, 285
   in the army   94, 95, 102–3, 187
   in the countryside   45, 187
   dentists   187
   in primary school   119, 244
   toothbrushes   1, 22, 45, 59, 94, 102, 106, 119, 126, 131, 187, 235, 244, 245, 250
deodorant   4, 281, 296
Depouilly, Louis   118, 125, 133
Derode, Victor   55
Des Vaulx, Jean-Pierre   24, 34, 36
Desbois, Daniel   200, 242
Descieux, Louis Cyprien   119
Desforges, Antoine   198
Dhyus river   73
Diad makeup remover   281
diarrhea/dysentery   74, 236, 257
Dijon   200, 242
diphtheria   54, 134, 166, 194, 204, 236, 244, 258
dirt as prophylactic   34, 124
disgust
   changing sensibilities   11, 67–8, 76, 150–1
   grammar of   60, 167
   threshold of   4, 5, 12, 295
Dombes   42, 139
domestic servants   168–9
Dopter, Charles   97–8, 104
Dordogne department   32, 111, 199
Douai   101
Doubs department   92
Doudeauville, Duc de   190
Douelle (Lot)   271–2
Douglas, Mary   1, 76, 295
Dreyfus, Colonel Alfred   15
Drôme department   239
Drouinaud, Gustave   31, 194, 195, 199
Du Mesnil, Octave   144, 148, 150, 161, 165
Duclaux, Émile   63
Dufestel, Louis   121, 125, 126
Dujardin, Louis   42
Dumont, André-Alfred   161
Dumont, Marie-Jeanne   172, 227
Dunkirk   262

Durand-Claye, Alfred Augustin   145
Duruy Laws   113
Duruy, Victor   33, 113–14, 117

Echo de Paris   142
École communale de Paris   170
École d'architecture   173–4
École Normale Supérieure   126
École professionnelle for women   111
Édile de Paris   55
Eiffel Tower   148
Elbeuf (Seine-Maritime)   160
Eleb, Monique   167
electricity   217, 228, 238–9, 243, 252, 257, 274
Elias, Norbert   2, 12
Elle magazine   237–8, 273, 277–80, 282, 285, 295
Encyclopedia   16
England   59, 63, 188, 224
Erckmann-Chatrian, Emile   33
Ermaux, Annie   143
Eure-et-Loir department   23
Evans, Richard   137
exercise   251
Eymoutiers (Haute-Vienne)   36

Falloux, Frédéric Alfred, Comte de   113, 117
Falloux Law   1850   113
Faraut family   277
Farcy, Henri   236
Farcy, Jean-Claude   87
Fémina Pratique   274, 275, 277, 279, 280
Féret, A.   86, 118, 124, 132
Ferry, Jules   117, 122
Ferry Laws   85, 111, 113, 117, 118
Fichaud, E.   170
Fifth Republic   271
Fijalkow, Yankel   149, 220
Finistère department   21, 125–6, 204, 242
Flanders   187, 212, 242
Flanders, Judith   63
Flaubert, Gustave   248
Florent-Decosse, Georgette   248
Fonssagrives, Jean-Baptiste   45
Forez region   196
Fortoul, Louis   114–15
Fougère (Ille-et-Vilaine)   167

Fourastié, Françoise 4, 42
Fourastié, Jean 2, 4, 42, 62, 271, 272
Fournel, Victor 69
Fourth Republic 194, 197, 225, 261, 264, 271, 282
Foville, Alfred de 41, 42, 46, 171, 199
Foville Report 134, 160
Franco-Prussian War 86, 93, 105
Franks 90
The French as They Are 284
French navy 106
French Revolution 9, 15–16, 18, 19, 53, 65, 88, 113
Freud, Sigmund 76
Freycinet, Charles Louis de 105
Frioux, Stéphane 2, 141, 143, 147
furniture 160, 200, 202, 242

Gabalda, Joseph 145
Gaillard, Romuald 115–17
Gandy, Matthew 75–6
Garnier-Léteurrie, Théodore 45, 87, 94, 96
Garnis 56, 160, 163–5, 228
Garrier, Gilbert 43
Gascony 25, 187
Gauls 90
Gay, Frederick P. 105
Geloux (Landes) 202
Gencé, Comtesse de 190, 193
General Association of hygienists and municipal engineers 263
Geneva 113
Georges-Day 264
Germ theory 140, 174, 203
Germany 63, 93, 224
Gers department 192, 240
Gibbs dentifrice 281
Gibon, Fénelon 161, 212
Girard, Louis-Narcisse 10, 175–6
Giroud, Françoise 278–9, 295
Glath, Paul-Edouard 244, 250
Gorse, Abbé 197
Goubert, Jean-Pierre 2, 18, 133
Goubert, Pierre 20–1
Gourichon, Henri 121
Gourseau, Albert 40, 42, 202
Graud, Lucien 169
Gravelotte, Battle of 106

Great Britain 264
Grellois, Dr. 99
Grenadou, Ephraïm 259
Grenoble 56
Gretelly, Lucien 33
Grew, Raymond 113
Grignon (Côte d'Or) 119
Grillet, Jeanne 276
Guerrand, Roger-Henri 147
Guichard, Monsier 150
Guigou, Émile 243
Guilhaud Commission 141
Guillaumin, Émile 199
Guillou, Thérèse 285
Guise (Aisne) 189
Guizot, François 57, 113, 117
Guyenne 24, 187

hair
  brushed 97, 111, 116, 196, 235
  cut 85, 94, 102, 112, 121, 195
  dirty 22, 25, 32, 121
  washed 4, 33, 120, 193, 251, 258
Hall, Edith 193
Hamburg 63, 137
handkerchiefs 94
Harper's Bazaar magazine 251
Harrigan, Patrick 113
Harrington, Sir John 16
Hatton, E. 173
Haussmann, Baron George 71–6, 135, 144, 160, 175, 177, 263
Haut-Doubs region 249
Haute-Garonne department 248
Haute-Loire department 43, 236, 242
Haute-Marne department 41, 43
Haute-Savoie department 235, 270
Hautes-Pyrénées department 239, 241
Haute-Vienne department 92, 241
Haut-Forez region 203
Haut-Languedoc region 195
Haut-Rhin department 239
Havard, Louis 145
health and beauty aids 4, 296
Hébert (*bains-douches*) 191
Hélias, Pierre-Jakez 2, 42, 197
Henri IV 60
Henrot, Henri 194
Hérault department 270

Herriot, Edouard   171, 214
Heulard d'Arcy, M.   23–4
Histoire populaire de Lille   55
household appliances   252, 274–5, 282–4
Household Organization League of Lyon   276
housing
   age of   213–14, 263–4
   allowances   263
   animals in   161, 242
   company-provided   59, 172
   cost of   163, 168, 189, 214–24, 226, 229, 265–7
   courtyards   68
   deterioration of   259, 262–3
   discomfort of   43
   discontent with   272–4
   18th-century Paris   10, 11
   and *familles nombreuses*   163, 223–4, 226
   Foville Report   134, 160
   garnis   56, 163–5, 218
   Habitations à Bon Marché (HBM)   170–4, 213, 223, 224, 226–8, 267
   habitations à loyer modéré (HLM)   267, 273, 274
   housing commissions (law of April 1850)   66–9
   hygiene in   159, 277
   îlots insalubres   161, 165, 218–24, 247, 260, 269
   and immigrants   218
   international comparisons   189, 224–5
   lack of air and light   40–1, 161, 165, 167, 217
   lack of investment   216–17
   lack of privacy   45
   law of 1948   262, 265
   logements insalubres   61, 67–8, 160, 166–7, 170, 217–18, 269
   middle-class housing   167–8, 226–8
   moderately priced housing (*immeubles à loyer moyen*: ILM)   224
   and mortality   160–1, 204, 217, 220
   and national renewal   262
   overcrowding   55, 68, 161–3, 217–18, 226
   peasant housing   5, 39–46, 114–15, 199–202, 213, 240–2
   postwar expansion of   266, 281–2
   public investment in   267
   rent control   214–22, 225–6, 262–3
   shortage   212, 224–5, 234, 257, 262–4
   sleeping conditions   41
   and social dysfunction   66, 166–7, 261–2
   social housing   169–73, 226–9, 267, 281
   and tuberculosis   160–1, 212
   urban geography of   71, 161–2, 259
   Vichy survey   259, 264
   and water system   72
   World War I destruction   212, 213
   World War II destruction   262–3
Hubscher, Ronald   20, 201
Hugo, Abel   58
Hugo, Victor   22, 248
   Les Misérables   64
Hume, Sarah   196–7
hygiene
   advertising   250–1, 281
   advice   203, 275–6, 280
   American views of   277–8
   and beauty   251, 278, 285
   and the bourgeoisie   17, 76, 167–8, 186, 188, 190, 242, 275, 279
   commerce in   249–51, 266, 274, 282
   in a convent   235–6
   cost of   3, 188, 226, 229
   "courant hygiéniste"   229
   cultural resistance   195
   democratization of   282
   and demography   280
   and economic growth   159, 188
   among elites   4
   and the French Revolution   9
   and genital diseases   125, 192
   and German Occupation   257
   health and beauty aids   4, 251–2, 280, 284–5
   historiography of   2
   history of   1
   and immigrants   166

international comparisons 279–80, 296
and life expectancy 2, 5
local councils and commissions 125, 134, 135, 145, 170, 221, 240, 241
material culture of 189
men *versus* women 193, 285
in the Middle Ages 9, 13
and the military 5, 86
as modernization 1, 3, 174–5, 234, 252
and municipal government 5, 159, 175
national deficit of 63, 87, 111, 203
in the Navy 106
"old regime of" 9, 12, 131
and the peasantry 5, 194–7, 233, 238
progress 185–6, 203, 247, 248, 257, 270
religion and 22
and the Republic 85–6, 131
and schools 5, 113, 235, 248–9
and science/technology 76, 159
sensibilities 5, 12, 68, 295
in slums 166
as a strategy of power 55, 167–8
and water 132–9
and wealth 159
and women 186, 277–9
working-class habits 173, 188

Île-de-Ré 39
Ille-et-Vilaine department 22, 42, 45, 242
illiteracy 112–13
Îlots insalubres 161, 204, 218–25, 260
Indre-et-Loire department 135
Industrie à domicile 56
influenza 138
Institut d'études politiques de Paris (Sciences Po) 163
Institut Français de l'Opinion Publique (IFOP) 265
Institut National d'Études Démographiques (INED) 265
Institut Pasteur 145
International Congress of Hygiène 165
International Exposition 1867 73
Ivry-sur-Seine 134

Jackson, Harry 259
Jaeger, Hans Gustav Jaeger 199
Jayle, Dr. 125
Jeanselme, Charles 168
Jenner, Mark 11
Johnson, Steven 136
Johnson's wax 281
Jones, Colin 139, 222, 226, 259
Jones, Geoffrey 2
Jordan, David P. 73, 74
Juillerat, Paul 139, 147, 160–1
Julien-Labruyère, François 200
July Monarchy 57, 64–6, 89, 113, 174, 213
June Days 1848 54, 66
Jünger, Ernst 233
Jura department 39, 199

Kalff, Elsbeth 65, 67, 150
Kammerer, Eugène 39
Knibiehler, Yvonne 217
Koch, Robert 174
Krakow 163

La Baule (Loire-Atlantique) 240
La Bosse (Sarthe) 123, 249
La Femme 278
La Ferrière (Vendée) 261
La Ferté-Bernard 88
La Martinèche (Creuse) 20
La Population Française 258, 259, 262
La Technologie Sanitaire 140
Lacaud, Monsieur 170
Lacaze, Jean-Paul 274
Lachaud Commission 103–4
Lafont, Dr. 166
La Fontenelle (Ille-et-Vilaine) 124
Lagneau, Gustave 92, 187
"Lagraulet" 202
Lahore, Jean 169
Landais region 202
Landes department 270
landlords 67, 69
Languedoc 242
Laon 41
Laroche, Dr. 172
L'Art ménager français 277
Latin Quarter 220

latrines (*cabinets/lieux d'aisances,*
        W.C.)   57, 67, 71, 74, 103, 114,
        118–19, 125, 126, 131, 138, 143,
        145, 147–50, 159, 165, 172, 228,
        233, 238, 249, 267, 271
    census   268–9
    and cholera   150
    18th century   10, 11
    and the free-rider dilemma   150,
        269–70
    meuble odorant/chaises percées   12
    public toilets   243, 244, 247
    in schools   116–17, 125, 245, 249
    social geography of   147–9, 270
    Turkish toilets   247
    waterless   148, 150
    in working-class homes   167, 217, 221
Launay, Félix   139
laundry   25, 39, 59, 60, 104, 118, 171,
        202, 271
Layet, Alexandre   32, 33, 41
Le Couppay de la Forest, Max   38, 194
Le Goff, Olivier   55, 168
Le Havre   137, 160, 218, 262, 269
Le Mans   220, 269
Le Matin   176
Le Puy   163
Le Roy Ladurie, Emmanuel   133
Le Vigen (Limousin)   44
League of Nations   238
Lécard, Major   99
Ledru-Rollin (municipal pool)   191
Lemaître, Lucie   67, 150
Lemonnier, Elisa   111
Lens   263
L'Enseignement Technique   277
Léonard, Jacques   9, 40, 58, 133–4, 139,
        186
L'Ère nouvelle   55
Les Andelys (Eure)   37
Les Halles   227
Lesage, Adolf-August   236
Leshauris, Pierre   202
Levainville, Capitaine J.   45, 131, 201
Lévêque, Pierre   36
Lever Brothers (Unilever)   2, 282, 296
Levine, Allison Murray   235
Levraud, Léonce   145
Levroux (Indre)   92

Lhotte, Céline   218
Life expectancy   6, 203, 295
Lignières, Marcel   123
Lille   58, 63, 65, 69, 75, 134, 150, 160,
        162, 171, 222, 243
Limoges   41, 59, 63, 64, 75, 177, 241, 269
Limousin   24, 34, 40, 42, 43, 54, 95, 176,
        189, 196, 197, 202, 233, 241
Lincoln "Lux" (washing machine)   274
Loire river   148, 240
Loire-Inférieure department   237, 240,
        241
London   63, 136, 264
Look magazine   238
Lorient   262
Lorraine   113, 187, 213, 233
Lot-et-Garonne department   270
Loucheur Law   171, 224, 267
Loucheur, Louis   223
Louis XIV   12, 14, 15, 92
Louis XV   15
Louis-Philippe   55–7, 62, 296
Loux, Françoise   2, 35, 85, 101, 187, 192
Loyau, Alphonse   226, 227
Lozère department   23, 134, 240
Lux detergent   251
Lux soap   281
Lycée Janson-de-Sailly   125
Lycée Lakanal   123
Lyon   53, 54, 75, 169–71, 176, 192, 203,
        214, 217, 220, 265

Mabilleau, Léopold   38
Mabon-Fall, Armelle   261
Madrid   137
Magitot, Émile   187
Magri, Susanna   214
Malapert, François   94
Malespine, Émile   212, 214
Mallé, Marie-Pascale   243
Manche department   112, 237
Manse, Pierre   38, 121
Mantes (Seine-et-Oise)   139, 145
Marais   218
Maraise, Madame de   17
Marchix quarter (Nantes)   220–1
Maréschal, Louis-Auguste   20–2, 24, 44,
        48, 131
Marie Antoinette   17

Marie-Claire 236, 250–2, 276–7
Marne, battle of 106
Marseille 137, 204, 237, 258, 262
Martay, Jeannine 120, 187
Martial, René 166, 172
Martin, André-Justin 100, 123, 168
Marx, Karl 76
Maspétiol, Roland 263
Maurienne 112
Mayaud, Jean-Luc 194, 200
Mayenne department 270
Mazon, Albin (Docteur Francus) 43
measles 134, 138, 166, 204, 258
Melun, Anatole de 66
Menilmuche 161
Mercier, Louis-Sebastien 11–12, 18, 19, 53
Merilheu (Hautes-Pyrénées) 38, 121
Merlin, Roger 39, 163, 166
Merriman, John 59, 63
Metz 111
Meunier, Hyppolyte 46
Meurthe-et-Moselle department 113, 176, 270
Meuse department 236
Mezières 92
miasmas/miasmatic theories of disease 3, 10, 14, 40, 55, 61, 68, 98, 117, 119, 144, 160, 174
Michaud, René 148–9
Michelet, Jules 197
Midi 40
Miller, Henry 247
Ministry of National Economics 217
Ministry of Public Health 226
Ministry of Urbanism and Reconstruction 224
Minot (Côte d'Or) 21
Mirabeau, Octave 169
Moheau, Jean-Baptiste 35
Moine, Marcel 236
Moltke, General Helmuth von 69
Monfalcon, Jean-Baptiste 55, 57
Monin, Ernest 25, 32, 121
Monnot, Ernest 123, 126, 249
Monnot, Julien 249
Montagu, Lady Mary 60
Montargis 259
Montceau-les-Mines 172

Montfaucon 65, 174
Montmartre 67
Montpellier 243
Montsouris reservoir 138
Morache, Georges 89, 92, 93, 97
Morbihan department 270
mortality 195, 234
  in childhood 118
  in cities 54, 204
  geography of 236
  and German Occupation 258–9
  immigrants 56
  infant mortality 3, 20–3, 132, 194, 203–4, 234–6, 258–9, 271, 280
  international comparisons 204, 234, 237, 280
  and lack of light and air 41
  and *logements insalubres* 61, 167, 220
  in Montceau-les-Mines 172
  in Mulhouse 56
  and polluted water 38
  in Rennes 56
Morvan 131
Morvillars (Territoire de Belfort) 249
Mory, Pascal 172
Moscovitch, Alex 265
Moselle river 134
Mouzillon (Loire-Atlantique) 240
Mulhouse 59, 171, 262, 269
Mum deodorant 281
Munaret, Jean-Marie-Placide 32, 48
Municipal pools 190
Munitionettes 212
Musée Social 163, 166

Nabonne, A. 258
Nadar, Félix 75
Nadaud Law 135, 170, 175
Nadaud, Martin 20, 31, 43, 56, 180
Nairobi 265
Nancy 125, 134, 135, 185
Nantes 134, 148, 150, 162, 220–1, 240, 262, 269
Napias, Henri 41, 100, 118–19, 122, 135, 139, 168, 185
Napoleon I (Bonaparte) 17, 54, 62, 72, 92, 111
Napoleon III (Louis-Napoleon) 60, 64, 69, 71, 76, 93, 113, 263

National Assembly 217
National Convention 113
National Institute for Hygiene (*Institut National d'Hygiène*) 204, 217, 224–6, 258, 266
National Institute for Statistics and Economic Studies (INSEE) 273
National League to Combat Slums 217
National Revolution 261
National Union of Teachers and Instructors of Family and Household Education 276
Nevers 63, 124, 134, 186, 187
Nice 228, 243, 270
Nicholas I (Tsar) 73
Nièvre department 112, 125, 194, 201
Nîmes 41
Nine Years' War (1688–97) 92
Nivernais 23, 24, 39, 142
Nord department 134, 239, 242
Normandy 187, 198, 237, 258–60, 263
Nos amis les Français 277
Noyal-sous-Bazouges (Ille-et-Vilaine) 31
Nozière, Violette 217–18

Objets de toilette (toiletries) 22, 45, 114, 118, 131, 188, 196
Odorono deodorant 251, 281
Oise department 236
Old Goriot 56–7
Omo detergent 274, 281
Orléans 193, 262
Orléans, Duchess of 12
Orwell, George 218
Othe, pays d' (Aube) 42
Ouche river 200
Ourcq river/canal 16, 62, 72, 73, 113–15, 138

Pagnol, Marcel 39
Palophy, Elise 248
Panazol (Haute-Vienne) 241
Pange, Pauline de 190
Parent-Duchâtelet, Alexandre Jean-Baptiste 54, 60
Paris
    age of housing stock 213–14, 222, 263–4
    army barracks 104
    Beaubourg, rue 222
    conforts 259–60, 270
    epidemics 138
    garnis 218
    habitations à bon marché (HBM) 224, 226–7
    haussmannization 71–5
    housing commission 55, 57, 67, 70, 111, 133
    housing shortage 54, 171, 214, 224–5, 264
    hygiene commission 147–8, 150
    îlots insalubres 161, 165, 218–24, 260
    immeubles à loyer moyen (ILM) 224
    lack of space for new building 226
    Lombards, rue des 227
    Madagascar, rue de 217
    mortality 54, 138
    Mare, rue de la 217
    Marie Stuart, rue de 264
    municipal council 222, 224, 247
    municipal pools 190–1
    Pontièvre, rue de 139, 149
    population growth 53–4
    public baths 13, 16, 58, 190–1
    rag pickers 174–5
    Renard, rue de 227
    Rigoles, rue de 139, 147, 149
    Rochechouart, rue 71, 139, 147, 149
    Saules rue des 264
    schools 115
    Sébastopol, boulevard de 227
    sewers 64, 72, 143–6, 228–9
    social housing 171–3
    spitting problem 176–7
    street cleaning 175–6
    Temple, rue du 227
    and water 62, 72–3, 135–43, 228
        consumption of 135–7, 143
        fountains 147
        international comparison 136
        politics of 142–3
    Vespasiennes (*pissoitières*) 75, 177, 247
Paris archives 227, 261–2
Paris filth
    geography of 71
    lack of plumbing 10, 203, 247

noxious trades 19
Old Regime 10–11, 18
stench 18, 247
Pas-de-Calais department 237, 239
Pasteur, Louis 174
Payer, Lynn 4, 295–6
peasant hygiene 19–25, 237–8, 241–3, 261
   advice 203, 235
   and the army 94
   culture of 35, 46, 240
   problem of sources 19
   progress 193–201, 239, 241–2, 244, 271, 285
   and reformers 19–20, 46–8
peasants
   automobiles 243
   bathing 34, 242, 243
   birthing practices 20, 23–4, 195, 236
   body odors 33
   children 32, 197
   clothing 5, 32, 35–7, 196–7
   contact with towns 196–7, 201
   dental care 250
   electrification 238–40, 243
   Enquête 238–42, 245
   "exodus" 234, 237
   fumiers (manure piles) 31, 37–8, 114, 201, 240–3, 278
   furniture 41, 200, 202, 238, 240, 242, 244
   general dirtiness 22, 31, 32, 35, 37, 233, 278
   hair 33
   higher incomes 196, 201, 240
   housing 5, 39–46, 114–15, 199–202, 213, 240–2, 260, 263–4
   illiteracy 22
   lack of amenities 234, 241–3, 260, 267–9
   living with animals 5, 21, 42–3, 199–201, 242
   moral qualities 32
   outhouses 42, 200, 202, 238, 240, 242
   Peasants into Frenchmen 85
   physical deformities 22–3
   post-partem care 21, 195
   proverbs 24–5, 33, 44
   sleeping conditions 41, 43–5, 199, 201
   social distinctions 200–2, 243
   underwear 35–6, 198
   villages 37, 194
   viticulture 243
   washing habits 32–3, 42, 45, 195–6, 200, 235, 241–2
   water supply 5, 38–9, 41, 139, 195, 196, 200, 238–41, 243, 270
   women 32, 36–7, 202
Pécaut, Élie 117
Père Lachaise cemetery 10
Perdiguier, Agricole 37, 112
perfume/perfumers 13, 180, 193, 240, 277, 278, 282, 296
Périer brothers 62
Périgord 43
Périgueux 111
Perrot, Michelle 162
Perrot, Philippe 198
Peters, Robert 277
Peyronnec, Magdeleine 235–6, 276
Philippe Auguste (King) 10
Philosophes 11
Picardy 187
Picot, Georges 166
Pierrard, Pierre 58, 75
Piketty, Thomas 188
Plaisance quarter (Paris) 161
Plicque, Albert-Faron 100
plumbing
   cost of 123, 229, 278
   lack of 203, 247, 250
   in Old Regime Paris 10, 15
Poitevin bathhouse 16
Poitou region 187
Polinière, Auguste-Pierre de 57
Pompadour, Madame de 16
Ponge, Francis 258
Porte Dauphine (Paris) 223
Porte de Clignancourt (Paris) 222
Porter, Roy 11
Poubelle, Eugène 147, 160, 176
Pougy, Liane de 192
Prague 163
Procter & Gamble 295
Prompt, Pierre-Inès de 143
Propreté de Paris 175

Protecta diapers 281
Proust, Marcel 248
Provensal, Henry 173
Public *crachoirs* (cuspidors) 177
public housing
    financing problems 172–3, 227–8
    Habitations à Bon Marché
        (HBM) 170–4, 223, 226–7
public urination 10, 18, 53, 54, 64, 75, 175–7, 277
    in the army 98, 100
    Vespasiennes/pissotières 75, 247
puériculture
    and the Church 236
    among peasants 22–4, 46–7, 131, 236
    in school curricula 235, 248, 259
Puisson, Dr. 103
Pulju, Rebecca 2, 258, 272
Puy-de-Dôme department 240
Pyrénées 39
Pyrénées-Orientales department 237

Quartararo, Anne 111–12
Queuille, Henri 238

railroads 196
Rambuteau, Claude-Philibert Comte de 55, 62, 75
Rauch, André 195, 229
Raymond, M. A. 237
refrigerators 252, 271, 274, 282
Reid, Donald 76
Remington electric razors 281
Renard, Jules 22, 36, 41, 186, 194
Renaudot, Théophraste 14
Rennes 53, 56, 64, 69, 134, 142, 262
rent control 214–22, 225–6, 262–3
rent paid 215, 273–4, 281
Restif de la Bretonne, Nicolas 14
revolution of 1848 66
Revue d'Hygiène et de Police Sanitaire 177
Revue Scientifique 103
Rey, Ramonde Anna 23, 242
Reynolds, Stephen 188
rheumatism 55
Riant, Aimé 98, 115–18, 126, 144
Ribot, Alexandre 171
Ribot Law 171

Richepin, Jean 166
rickets 212
Riolacci, Major D. 99
Rioux, Jean-Pierre 2, 282
Rival, Ned 10, 18
Rivaud (public baths) 191
Roanne (Loire) 258
Robert, Maurice 23, 189
Roberts, Mary Louise 277
Rochard, Jules 65, 75, 97, 165, 175, 187, 199
Roche, Daniel 11
Roéland, C. 223
Rogers, Rebecca 85
Rome 137
Ross, Kristin 266, 272
Rouen 63, 100, 118, 134, 139, 150, 171, 176, 185, 190, 204, 217, 262, 269
Rouget, Joseph 97–8, 104, 177
Rouleau, Charles 193
Rousseau, Jean-Jacques 10, 11, 15, 35
Roussel Law 234–5
Roussillon (Provence-Alpes-Côte d'Azur) 43, 200, 271–2
Rouvière, Augustine 200
Roynette, Odile 91, 100–2
Roziers (Lozère) 23, 87, 240
Rudolph, Nicole 168
Ruffat, Michèle 2
Russey (Doubs) 123
Rybczynski, Witold 10

Sablé (Sarthe) 217
Saint-Beuve, Charles-Augustin 33
Saint-Chinian (Hérault) 123
Saint-Denis 74, 166, 176
Sainte-Agnès 13
Sainte-Appoline 187
Sainte-Marguerite quarter (Paris) 161
Saint-Etienne 62, 150, 162
Saint-Georges district (Toulouse) 220
Saint-Germain-en-Laye 145, 215
Saint-Gervais quarter (Paris) 161, 218
Saint-Jean quarter (Toulon) 162
Saint-Mâlo 113
Saint-Marcel quarter (Paris) 11, 57
Saint-Maur 140
Saint-Merri quarter (Paris) 161, 222, 223, 227

Saint-Moutier (Var) 140
Saint-Omer (Pas-de-Calais) 162
Saint-Père Marc-en-Poulet (Ille-et-Vilaine) 37
Saint-Petersburg 162
Saint-Sulpicedes-Landes (Landes) 37
Saint-Victor quarter (Paris) 161, 220
Salaün, Yves 213, 224, 262
Salon des Arts Ménagers 252
Sambre-et-Marne department 185
Saône-et-Loire department 239
Sapet, M. 95, 102, 187, 250
Sauvy, Alfred 223
Savoie 54, 131, 199
Scarlet fever 204, 258
Sceaux 191
school inspectors 118, 120–6, 132
schools
    buildings 115, 124, 275
    and dangers of alcohol 120, 237
    Falloux Law 113
    Ferry laws 111, 248
    in the First Empire 111
    for girls 111–13, 124
    hygiene in 111–12, 114–16, 124–5, 133, 244, 248, 275–6, 296
    impact on students 124, 196, 295
    and lice 120–1
    limits of education 123, 248
    and literacy/illiteracy 112–13
    normal schools 111–12, 125–6
    and the peasantry 114
    primary schools 119
    religious control of 113
    secondary schools 120
    teachers' circumstances 123, 124, 248–9
    textbooks 5, 114–15, 117, 119, 120, 237, 248
    and toothbrushing 119, 187
Scripps Howard News Service 296
Scrofula 55, 166
Seberg, Jean 5
Second Empire 67, 70, 72, 75, 76, 86, 87, 89, 92, 112, 113, 115, 118, 159, 174, 175, 185, 198, 213
Second Republic 69, 263
Seignette, Adrien 120
Seine river 16, 72–4, 139, 145

Seine-et-Oise department 197, 236, 270
Seine-Inférieure department 185
Sellier, Henri 227
Sellier, Louis 223
Séruliac (Sambre-et-Loire) 119
Service Dentaire Scolaire 245
Sewage treatment 144–5
sewers 2, 64–5, 72, 143–9, 159, 228
    cesspits, (*fosses d'aisances*) 10, 64–5, 74, 97, 117, 135, 137–8, 143–4, 146, 238, 247
    cost of 146
    in the countryside 238
    discharge into the Seine 74
    and *eaux* vannes 64
    and epidemics 64, 74, 146
    and Haussmann 73–5
    as metaphor 75–6, 144
    social geography of 147–9
    tout à l'égout 144–6
shampoo 4, 258, 278
shoes 198
showers 4, 282
    in the army 100–1
    for children 259
    in Paris 260
    in schools 248
    in social housing 173
Siegfried, Jules 160, 170
Siegfried Law 170–1, 212–14, 223, 229, 267
Simms, Frederick 69–70, 73–4
smallpox 166
soap 2, 3, 58, 106, 194, 279, 296
    Cadum 4, 250
    Charmis 280
    and German Occupation 258, 259, 278
    industrialized production of 249
    Marseilles soap 249–50
    Palmolive 251
    soap tax 188
social Darwinism 86
Société de Médecine Publique 143
Société des Crèches 118
Société d'hygiène publique de Bordeaux 41
Société Française d'Hygiène 121, 132, 133

Société générale de travaux urbains 227-8
Société mulhousienne des cités ouvrières 171
Society for Education and Association for the Sanctification of Sunday 212
Society for Improving the Conditions of the Labouring Classes (London) 71
Society for Popular Art and Hygiene 150
Sohn, Anne-Marie 122, 131, 160, 185, 195-7, 217, 236
Solvay, Ernest 249
Sondage 266
Sopalin paper towels 281
Sorbonne 115, 118
spitting 119, 176-7
Spontex sponges 281
Staffe, Baronne 186, 189-90
Stevenson, Robert Louis 40
Stewart, Mary Lynn 168, 193
Strasbourg 269, 270
Strauss Commission 176
Strauss Law 170-1, 174, 175, 196, 222
Strauss, Paul 170
street cleaning 10, 174-6
Suippes (Marne) 162
Suresnes (Hauts-de-Seine) 227
swaddling 21, 24, 195, 197, 236
Synthélabo 2

Tacky Eau depilatory 281
Taine, Hippolyte 59
Tardivon, Jacqueline 20
Tarlé, Gustave 42, 191
Taylor, Charles 260
televisions 271
Temple washhouse 59
Théron de Montaugé, Louis 122
Thierry, Henry 169
Thiers, Adolphe 57
Third Republic 85, 112, 131, 134, 174, 176, 213, 224, 261
  and hygiene 4, 68, 76, 117, 122-3, 143, 159, 185, 199, 203, 234
Thoinot, Léon-Henri 137
Thuillier, Guy 42, 62, 112, 125, 134, 142, 168

Tindall, Gillian 32
toilet paper 148
toilets 16, 116, 138, 243
toothpaste 187, 296
Toulon 135, 140, 236
Toulouse 220, 262, 273
Touraine 38, 39, 194
Tournade, André 211
tours 262
Tramways Électriques 217
Trente glorieuses 4, 267, 271, 272, 274, 278, 282
Triolet, Elsa 272
Troyes (Aube) 134, 145-6, 196
Trollope, Frances 63, 69
tuberculosis (consumption) 203, 204, 212, 262, 297
  in the army 98
  in the cities 53-5
  in the countryside 44
  among domestic servants 169
  under German Occupation 258
  in Nantes 221
  in Paris 138, 160-1, 220
  and spitting 119, 176
typhoid fever 53, 54, 74, 98, 103-5, 134, 135, 137, 138, 146, 166, 194, 204, 236, 247, 258, 262, 269

underwear 189
  in the army 97
  corsets 36-7, 198
  in the countryside 36
  culottes 199
  in history 1
  polychine 281
  price of 4
  spread of 197-8
  women's 198
Union de la Paix Social, Nantes 150
United States 224
Universal Exposition 1889 148, 171
urban filth 174, 175, 222
  from animals 54, 139
  descriptions of slums 55, 57, 265
  in early modern Paris 10, 17
  industrial pollution 54
  Moulins-Lille 55-6
  municipal garbage dumps 175-6

private squalor   175
  in the suburbs   214
urban reform   58, 75, 141–2, 174–5
  failure   57, 214, 222, 226, 228, 229
  financing   141–3, 222–5
  following World War I   212
  îlots insalubres   161, 165, 218–24, 260
  politics of   223, 273
  street cleaning   175–6
urban reformers   54, 60–1, 173, 217–18, 229

vacuum cleaners   252, 274, 281
Val-de-Grâce military hospital   86, 97–8
Valdour, Jacques   161
Valence   103
Vallin, Émile   100, 136, 143
Vallonton, Gitou   233
Vallotton, Annie   233
Valmy, battle of   86
Vanne river   73, 138
Var department   135, 234, 248
Varades (Loire-Atlantique)   240
Vauban, Sébastien Le Prestre   96
Vaucluse   200, 241–2
Veillon, Dominique   2, 275
Velay   39
Vendée region   187, 233, 237
Verdier, Yvonne   33, 198
Verdier-Besançon, Madeleine   275
vermin   31, 46
Vernois, Maxine   115
Véron de Bellecourt, General Barthélémy Alexandre   96
Versailles (city)   135
Versailles (Palace of)   1, 3–4
  amenities   259
  baths   12, 15
  lack of water   62
  toilets   12
Vesoul   115
Vialhe, Pierre-Edouard   43
vidangeurs   65, 74, 138, 143, 247
Vienna   163
Vienne department   237
Vigarello, Georges   2, 12, 15, 17, 63, 133, 168
  the "aesthetic of surfaces"   13
  dangers of water   14

Vignerot, Maurice   238
Villedary, Léon   95, 98–100
Villejuif   166
Villermé, Louis-René   22, 37, 54, 56, 60
Vincenot, Henri   124
Vincent, J.-C.   285
Vinen, Richard   233
Violle, H.   258
Virey, Joseph   33
Viry, Charles   97–9
Voiart, Elise   17
Voltaire   11
Vosges department   25, 41
Votre Amie   264

wages   282
Wakeman, Rosemary   272
Wallace, Richard
Ward, Peter   13, 17, 60, 168, 197, 198
War Ministry   88
washing   188
  babies   197, 251
  clothes   197, 271
  culture of   4, 63–4
  and demography   280
  18th-century   12, 17
  international comparisons   279–80
  lavoirs (washhouses)   240
  linen   197
  in medieval culture   13
  men *versus* women   193, 196, 285
  modesty and shame   33, 60, 101, 190, 192, 196, 235–6, 285
  partial   16, 33, 59, 192, 235, 275
  peasantry   32–3, 42, 45, 195–6, 235, 241–2, 271
  in schools   116, 119, 186, 248
  urban *toilettes*   58, 285
  women's practices   278–9
washing machines   3, 4, 252, 274, 275, 277, 281–2
water   61–4, 133, 159, 228, 247, 257, 269
  in bourgeois homes   134
  carriers   18, 62, 72, 135
  contaminated rivers   139
  costs for landlords   137
  in the countryside   194, 196, 238–42
  dangers of   14–15

economy of   76
and epidemics   133, 137, 138, 140, 194, 203
fountains   11, 18, 62, 134, 135, 147, 243, 269
and German Occupation   257
and Haussmannization   73, 76
hot water heaters   3, 168, 189, 252, 257, 274, 282–4
and hygiene   132–40, 244
international comparisons   63, 136–7, 141
lack of   11, 18, 58, 62–3, 72, 219
as metaphor   76
polluted wells   38–9, 140, 194
price of   4, 11, 62, 133, 282
public works   141
purification   141–2
Seine water   12, 62, 72, 135, 247
technology   141
unequal access   72, 74, 138–9
urban demand   53
Waterloo, Battle of   4, 92
Weber, Eugen   2, 23, 38, 85, 87, 95, 96, 133, 193, 235, 240
Weiner, Susan   276
Wellington's Foot Guards   89
wells
  in Paris   62
  polluted   63, 134
Weyd, Paule-Marie   261
Wirth, Ernestine   34
women's magazines   3, 250–1, 274, 276–81
Woods, Robert   57
Woodward, John   57
working-class
  clothing   189
  diet   188–9
  housing   226, 243, 277
  ignorance   55
  immorality   54, 60
  incomes   188
  material culture of hygiene   190
World War I   185, 211, 234, 240
  destruction of housing   212, 213
  impact on hygiene   212
  and rent control   217
World War II   217
  destruction of housing   262–3
  German Occupation   211–12, 233, 257–61
Wright, Lawrence   12, 13, 15
Wylie, Laurence   2, 200, 271–2

Yonne department   72, 111
Young, Arthur   39
Yvelines   135, 214

www.ingramcontent.com/pod-product-compliance
Lightning Source LLC
Chambersburg PA
CBHW071802300426
44116CB00009B/1175